EFFECTIVELY MANAGING HUMAN SERVICE ORGANIZATIONS

Second Edition

SAGE SOURCEBOOKS FOR THE HUMAN SERVICES SERIES

Series Editors: ARMAND LAUFFER and CHARLES GARVIN

Recent Volumes in This Series

HEALTH PROMOTION AT THE COMMUNITY LEVEL edited by NEIL BRACHT

FAMILY POLICIES AND FAMILY WELL-BEING: The Role of Political Culture
by SHIRLEY L. ZIMMERMAN

FAMILY THERAPY WITH THE ELDERLY
by ELIZABETH R. NEIDHARDT & JO ANN ALLEN

EFFECTIVELY MANAGING HUMAN SERVICE ORGANIZATIONS
by RALPH BRODY

SINGLE-PARENT FAMILIES by KRIS KISSMAN & JO ANN ALLEN

SUBSTANCE ABUSE TREATMENT: A Family Systems Perspective
edited by EDITH M. FREEMAN

SOCIAL COGNITION AND INDIVIDUAL CHANGE: Current Theory and Counseling Guidelines
by AARON M. BROWER & PAULA S. NURIUS

UNDERSTANDING AND TREATING ADOLESCENT SUBSTANCE ABUSE
by PHILIP P. MUISENER

EFFECTIVE EMPLOYEE ASSISTANCE PROGRAMS: A Guide for EAP Counselors and Managers
by GLORIA CUNNINGHAM

COUNSELING THE ADOLESCENT SUBSTANCE ABUSER: School-Based Intervention and Prevention
by MARLENE MIZIKER GONET

TASK GROUPS IN THE SOCIAL SERVICES by MARIAN FATOUT & STEVEN R. ROSE

NEW APPROACHES TO FAMILY PRACTICE: Confronting Economic Stress
by NANCY R. VOSLER

WHAT ABOUT AMERICA'S HOMELESS CHILDREN? Hide and Seek
by PAUL G. SHANE

SOCIAL WORK IN HEALTH CARE IN THE 21st CENTURY
by SURJIT SINGH DHOOPER

SELF-HELP AND SUPPORT GROUPS: A Handbook for Practitioners
by LINDA FARRIS KURTZ

UNDERSTANDING DISABILITY: A Lifespan Approach by PEGGY QUINN

QUALITATIVE METHODS IN SOCIAL WORK RESEARCH: Challenges and Rewards by DEBORAH K. PADGETT

LEGAL ISSUES IN SOCIAL WORK, COUNSELING, AND MENTAL HEALTH: Guidelines for Clinical Practice in Psychotherapy by ROBERT G. MADDEN

GROUP WORK WITH CHILDREN AND ADOLESCENTS: Prevention and Intervention in School and Community Systems by STEVEN R. ROSE

SOCIAL WORK PRACTICE WITH AFRICAN AMERICAN MEN: The Invisible Presence
by JANICE M. RASHEED & MIKAL N. RASHEED

DESIGNING AND MANAGING PROGRAMS: An Effectiveness-Based Approach (2nd edition)
by PETER M. KETTNER, ROBERT M. MORONEY, & LAWRENCE L. MARTIN

PROMOTING SUCCESSFUL ADOPTIONS: Practice With Troubled Families
by SUSAN LIVINGSTON SMITH & JEANNE A. HOWARD

STRATEGIC ALLIANCES AMONG HEALTH AND HUMAN SERVICES ORGANIZATIONS: From Affiliations to Consolidations
by DARLYNE BAILEY & KELLY McNALLY KONEY

EFFECTIVELY MANAGING HUMAN SERVICE ORGANIZATIONS (2nd edition)
by RALPH BRODY

STOPPING CHILD MALTREATMENT BEFORE IT STARTS: Emerging Horizons in Early Home Visitation Services
by Neil B. Guterman

EFFECTIVELY MANAGING HUMAN SERVICE ORGANIZATIONS

Second Edition

Ralph Brody

Sage Publications, Inc.
International Educational and Professional Publisher
Thousand Oaks ▪ London ▪ New Delhi

For information:

Sage Publications, Inc.
2455 Teller Road
Thousand Oaks, California 91320
E-mail: order@sagepub.com

Sage Publications Ltd.
6 Bonhill Street
London EC2A 4PU
United Kingdom

Sage Publications India Pvt. Ltd.
M-32 Market
Greater Kailash I
New Delhi 110 048 India

Printed in the United States of America

Library of Congress Cataloging-in-Publication Data

Brody, Ralph.
Effectively managing human service organizations / by Ralph Brody — 2nd ed.
p. cm. — (Sage sourcebooks for the human services series)
Includes bibliographical references and index.
ISBN 0-7619-2143-5 (pbk.: acid-free paper)
1. Human services—Management. I. Title. II. Series.
HV41 B689 2000
361′.0068—dc21 00-008041

This book is printed on acid-free paper.

00 01 02 03 04 05 06 7 6 5 4 3 2 1

Acquiring Editor: Nancy Hale
Editorial Assistant: Heidi Van Middlesworth
Production Editor: Sanford Robinson
Editorial Assistant: Cindy Bear
Typesetter: Janelle LeMaster
Indexer: Molly Hall
Cover Designer: Candice Harman

Dedicated to
Leona Bevis
A very special mentor
and
Phyllis Brody
My wife and best friend

CONTENTS

PREFACE

I believe that any new edition of a book should build on, update, and add value to the original. At the same time, it should preserve those aspects that are central to the character, style, and message of the first book. I have endeavored to do this with the second edition of *Effectively Managing Human Service Organizations.*

In the first edition, my goal was to synthesize a vast amount of material and condense it into an easily readable format. I intended that the book be used as a resource for busy managers (and prospective managers) and provide workable ideas. I wanted the book to be highly pragmatic and useful, not relying on any one theoretical framework but rather drawing from a variety of sources relevant for managerial decision making. I tried to find the right balance of avoiding simplistic formulas while providing guidance and concrete steps that managers can take, recognizing that dilemmas and trade-offs are associated with most managerial decisions. The primary focus of the first edition was on managing the staff of human service organizations. All these elements I have retained in this second edition.

Since the first edition was written more than 7 years ago, I have been able to obtain feedback that has caused me to want to make revisions, expand on some of the ideas, and add whole new sections. After having spent most of my professional career as a manager and executive director, I became a full-time university faculty member. This move provided me with an opportunity to teach several courses in administration. On the basis of the reactions of graduate students, I have added many segments to the book, including working with community coalitions and participating on and building teams. The students' input and that of several faculty members at other universities made me realize that a whole segment of management needed to be addressed in the second edition: fund management (including managerial decisions on an agency's budget) and fund raising. Accordingly, I have added an entire new section on these subjects to this edition.

In addition, in the period since writing the first edition, I have provided consultation to many nonprofit and public agencies. As a consultant, I could well understand and empathize with the daily demands and challenges managers face. I was asked by several organizations to assist in improving the relationship between their governing bodies and management, along with conducting strategic planning retreats, helping them with fund-raising ideas, and providing guidance in reviewing their budgets. This edition contains specific suggestions that grew out of these experiences.

Since the previous edition, I have continued to conduct workshops internationally for nongovernmental organizations. A universal interest of managers is the quest for funding. In preparing for workshops on planning fund-raising events, soliciting for planned giving, preparing proposals, and searching for funding, I developed materials that are presented in this edition.

Because this edition is broader in scope than the earlier version, I have integrated various segments by showing the reader how one segment connects with another. For example, the budget preparation process in the fund management chapter relates to the chapter on preparing effective proposals. The information on strategic planning is connected to the chapter on working with boards because this is a very important aspect of board work. Throughout the book, references are made to other segments that are relevant to the topic under discussion.

Almost every chapter contains new information that has become available since the last edition. In particular, I have added ideas to the chapters on leadership, decision making, and supervision. New legal precedents have been established on sexual harassment and terminating employees; therefore, I updated chapters related to these topics. I have also provided information on computer technology, including references to using the Internet in the search for funding.

I had two specific audiences in mind when I prepared this edition. First, I wrote it for the human service practitioner who is either in a managerial role or aspires to be in one. I believe that even experienced administrators will find value in thinking about these ideas, many of which are derived from the most current writings in the management literature. Second, I wrote for graduate students in social work, nonprofit management, or public administration who intend to become supervisors or administrators at some point in their careers. I hope that students will see value in keeping this book as a resource to consult from time to time when they are confronted with specific issues and challenges as professional managers. Having been in management roles for most of my professional career, I wrote this book to capture many ideas I wish I had been aware of as a professional manager.

This edition contains six parts. Part I sets the overall tone by focusing on aspects that are fundamental to the effective management of staff: leadership style and organizational culture. Part II focuses on how to make things happen and includes information on developing strategic plans, following through to obtain results, and solving operational problems. Part III identifies ways to enhance productivity by discussing ways to manage time better, helping employees be productive, dealing with unproductive employees, and working on such issues as diversity and sexual harassment. Part IV deals with ways to improve performance through supervision, staff appraisals, and rewards. Part V relates to effective internal and external interactions and includes improving meetings, handling conflicts, team building, participating on coalitions, and working with a board of trustees. Part VI concentrates on fund management and fund development.

Being a manager requires a comprehensive knowledge about a wide variety of issues. Although no one book can cover all possible contingencies, I hope you will gain insights that better prepare you for the wonderful and exciting managerial adventures that are before you.

I have learned much in preparing this second edition of *Effectively Managing Human Service Organizations,* and I hope you will too.

—Ralph Brody
Cleveland, Ohio

ACKNOWLEDGMENTS

In the first edition, I acknowledged more than 50 professionals who contributed suggestions, and this edition continues to build on their ideas. In addition, I have benefited from the contributions of Carl Prince, Pramod Jain, Chris Allen, James Clements, Bernadette Washington, Patty Sadallah, Thomas Woll, Mary Murray, and Phyllis Brody. Valuable insights were provided by Pat Cascarelli on human relations, William Mengerink on fund raising, and Marcella Stahm on fund management.

I am especially indebted to Ramona Albanese-Allen, who spent many months working with me researching materials for the new edition, suggesting ideas from her own experiences with several agencies, and word processing numerous drafts. I could not have completed this edition without her assistance.

For this edition, I have updated some of my previous writings, portions of which are reprinted in this edition with the permission of the publishers:

Brody, R. (1991). Preparing effective proposals. In R. L. Edwards & J. A. Yankey (Eds.), *Skills for effective human service management*. Washington, DC: NASW Press.

Brody, R., & Goodman, M. (1998). *Fund raising events: Strategies and programs for success*. New York: Human Sciences Press. The material in this book is modified from an excerpted version published in 1993 by the Federation for Community Planning.

Brody, R., & Nair, M. D. (1998). Searching for funding. *Macro practice: A generalist approach* (4th ed.). Wheaton, IL: Gregory.

Dolan, C., & Brody, R. (1991). *Planned giving.* Cleveland, OH: Federation for Community Planning.

Part I

SETTING THE TONE OF THE ORGANIZATION

Chapter 1. Leading the Organization

Chapter 2. The Culture of a Productive Organization

In this part, you will learn how to

- Identify leadership styles
- Discern how personal flaws can interfere with good leadership
- Value competencies that effective managers must have
- Understand the impact different organizational cultures have on staff behavior
- Affect staff work performance through cultural values
- Transmit major values such as job ownership, consumer satisfaction, work quality, and effectiveness and efficiency

Chapter 1

LEADING THE ORGANIZATION

All organizations require effective managers who can inspire staff, set general directions, and be accountable for the organizations' achievements. Because good management of staff is crucial, it is important to identify those special qualities that characterize an effective leader. Be aware, however, that no simple formula exists for the "perfect" manager in either profit or nonprofit organizations.

A managing partner of a leading management consulting firm, McKinsey and Company, observes that, in his work with more than 50 chief executive officers (CEOs), he has not found a perfect or "ideal" manager. The visionary leader may be poor at implementing plans; the superb implementor may have difficulty in setting directions for the organization; and the stickler for getting results may have poor interpersonal relationships.[1] Indeed, effective managers come in all sizes and shapes: extroverted or shy, personable or aloof and cold, colorless or charismatic, self-centered or altruistic, and highly logical or intuitive. The only thing they have in common is the ability to get things done.[2]

Furthermore, some argue[3] that a distinction should be made between a leader and a manager. In this view, a leader is an innovator, has a long-range perspective, challenges the status quo, and "does the right thing." By contrast, a manager "does things right," maintains the status quo, has a short-range perspective, and focuses on structures and systems. The thesis of this chapter is that effective managers must be able to provide both visionary leadership and day-to-day administrative direction.

To gain a better understanding of the manager's role, this chapter probes the following issues: (a) What is the dynamic interaction between managers, staff, and situtation? (b) What flaws can limit management effectiveness? (c) What special competencies should effective managers have to make their organizations more productive? (d) What attributes contribute to leadership? and (e) How can you diagnose your own leadership style?

DYNAMIC INTERACTION: MANAGER, STAFF, AND SITUATION

In any organization, a dynamic interplay exists between management orientation, staff behaviors and attitudes, and situational factors.[4]

Leadership Factors

Depending on their personal predisposition, each manager will reflect a different leadership orientation. Some managers prefer a *directive leadership style,* believing that they must assume personal responsibility for making major decisions and then act as a taskmaster to get things done. Although they may occasionally ask questions or allow limited dialogue, there is no doubt that the decision is essentially and primarily theirs. They prefer to "take charge." They see themselves functioning as an orchestra conductor, calling on staff to harmoniously achieve a desired result.

Other managers choose a *participative leadership orientation* in which they present ideas and invite feedback from staff. They want to retain final decision-making authority, but they also want their employees to consider alternative solutions.

Still others prefer a *delegative style.* These managers derive considerable satisfaction from giving decision-making responsibilities to their staff. If they participate in the decision process, they are comfortable in assuming no more authority than other members in the group.

Managers have their own predisposition toward one of these three orientations. Which is best for effective management? It depends on the nature of the staff and the external and internal situations.

Factors Operating Within Staff

Managerial leadership style (directive, participative, or delegative) can be greatly influenced by the way staff respond to organizational tasks and decision making. For example, if employees manifest intelligence, education, and experience, if they are motivated to be involved in decision making, if they identify with the goals of the organization, if they can manage unstructured work situations, if they have the self-confidence and self-reliance to work independently, and if they are truly invested in their work, then a manager would more likely delegate responsibilities and decision making to them.

If, however, staff are inexperienced, feel reluctant to take on additional responsibilities, require structured and unambiguous assignments, or resist making decisions, then a more directive management style may be required.[5] This kind of staff presents a challenge to those managers who value staff participation in decision making.

Situational Factors

Certain forces operating outside of the manager and employees will affect managerial style. The organization may perpetuate certain values, work habits, traditions, and expectations regarding managerial behavior. Some organizations, for example, operate under a high degree of pressure and crisis, thereby requiring a more directive management style. Moreover, an organization's size and structure will influence the nature of leadership styles. An organization with offices in different locations, for example, will tend to manifest autonomous decision making because of the decentralized nature of its operations.

The problems an organization has to deal with may affect leadership style. If a problem is complex and compels the involvement of staff with different types of knowledge and experiences, then a participative leadership style would be appropriate. If a problem requires the expertise of only the leader, however, then staff may be involved in more supportive functions.

The pressure of time is another key ingredient affecting leadership style. The more immediately a decision must be made, the more difficult it is to involve other employees. Agencies operating under emergency conditions (e.g., handling housing needs in the aftermath of a flood) require expeditious decision making. Many decisions that might ordinarily and appropriately involve staff are made unilaterally because of limited time.

Managers must be flexible in their leadership styles. Sometimes, a directive approach may be more appropriate than a delegative or participative one because of the organizational context or the nature of the situation. Where a crisis exists or where difficult budget or personnel decisions must be made, a "take charge" (directive) leadership style is appropriate. Managers need to combine approaches based on circumstances and skills of the staff. For example, in setting up a phone system, a manager might ask a staff committee to recommend a system even though their role will be only advisory. By alerting them in advance to the constraints on their participation in decision making, the manager conveys respect for their thinking and alerts them to their boundaries—reflecting both a delegative and a directive approach. Unless the manager is clear about the staff role, confusion and dissatisfaction might occur.

Leadership styles do not necessarily remain constant and can change as staff change. For example, in the beginning of a new project the manager may need to be more direct, but as staff become more familiar with their tasks and more competent in performing them the manager can take a less active role in providing guidance. Hence, there is a certain ebb and flow in the management style, as managers become more active or less directive, based on the needs of the staff.[6]

Although flexibility in leadership approaches is desirable, certain leadership styles are realistically more responsive to the needs of a highly trained professional staff and more conducive to productivity in human service organizations. Today's professional staff expect to be consulted and to exert influence, especially on those areas that have a direct impact on their own work. Most want the manager to hear and consider their ideas. They will tend to become resentful if their manager treats them as if they were easily manipulated machine parts in a factory. Indeed, leadership and a sense of accountability and empowerment in most human service organizations, as in most corporations, is being pushed down and distributed throughout the organization. In effect, everyone in the organization will have opportunities for exerting leadership.[7]

FLAWED LEADERSHIP STYLES

Every leader has flaws—some more than others. Do any of the following managerial profiles seem familiar?

The Oblivious Manager

Oblivious managers reflect a style that the best leadership is no leadership. They assume people always know what they should be doing, and these leaders are passive with regard to giving directions or creating a vision for the organization. Follow-through and monitoring are not part of their management frameworks. Although well intentioned, their lack of urgency and follow-through results in plans that either drift or become unraveled altogether. They feel so self-defeated through years of bureaucratic frustration that they define success merely as the avoidance of failure. As a consequence of their lackadaisical attitudes, they seldom encourage staff to excel, and their low expectations result in limited staff performance. These managers think that ignoring problems will somehow make them go away. They are usually oblivious to pending crises until, regrettably, the world crashes down on them. Their passivity is reflected in the often-used expression, "Whatever you want to do is fine with me." They typically abdicate responsibility for making tough decisions.

The Misleader

The problem with these managers is that they convey mixed or even incorrect messages. For example, they may ask employees to make a decision about how to make the most effective budget cuts and, on hearing their opinion, announce that the final decision will be made by the board of trustees. What they meant to ask for were suggestions that would be subject to review. They use a participative style, although being directive is more appropriate for the situation.[8] Situations calling for more participation from staff, however, are responded to with "the boss knows best." Staff never know what to expect from them or how they will react. After making many of these misleading requests, these managers can expect little investment from their employees.

The Put-Downer

Managers who humiliate employees by telling them that they are no good or that they cannot do the job, or who frequently put them down in front of others, can expect little or no investment from staff. This style creates a backlash of resentment and antagonism that is unlikely to lead to a turnaround in attitude or performance. Recently, a real-life manager called his social service staff "brain-dead" because he thought they were not working as hard as they should; the response was not a commitment to work harder but a protest in the form of T-shirts that read "Staff of the Living Dead." Typically, these managers are not as obvious; their pervasive deprecation is more subtle, conveying in many small ways that they believe staff are incompetent.

The Micromanager

Managers who reflect this profile become so invested in the work of staff that they commit the error of overinvolvement. They fail to allow people who are responsible for a job the freedom and autonomy to do it. As a consequence, staff do not have the opportunity to grow, to develop skills and experience, or to learn from their own mistakes. These managers do not believe that their staff have potential. They gain great satisfaction from getting into details that are better left for others.

The Arrogant Manager

These managers display the hubris of exaggerated pride, super self-confidence, and consummate self-importance.[9] Disregarding the contributions of the staff, they think that positive results are due only to their own special performances. When they proclaim a position or an idea for a project, they believe staff will automatically understand it and assent.[10] These managers do not take the time to clarify, discuss, and work through concerns. They think their ideas are so good that they should be self-evident and immediately accepted. They later wonder why their requests, regulations, and policies are not carried out with their same enthusiasm. Hubristic and overbearing, they never admit mistakes, even to themselves; consequently, they easily become victims of their own fallibilities. Because of a blinding sense of self-importance, they make miscalculations that may be catastrophic to the organization.

The Narcissist

Managers who fit this profile manipulate people to achieve personal ambitions; staff become instruments for their self-gratification. The work they do and the projects they carry out are not primarily for the good of the organization but for their own self-aggrandizement. They constantly connive to advance their own power positions in the organization, and they excessively control the organization's process to achieve predetermined personal goals. Narcissists are also egocentric, believing that employees are pawns they can use to fulfill personal goals.[11] Even when they use a participative leadership approach, they are still able to control the outcome. Staff go through the motions of making a decision but know that their own security in the organization depends on bending to the will of their manager. Narcissists hog the limelight so that little is left to shine on those who have actually done the real work. They may even substitute staff ideas for their own to curry favors from superiors.

The Loner

By keeping their office doors closed most of the day and seldom having contact with employees, these managers are usually seen as aloof and unapproachable. They limit contacts with colleagues and see their immediate subordinates as infrequently as possible. Loners rarely consult with staff because they do not want to be bothered with delays or objections that may lead to modifications of their original ideas. They feel like supplicants when asking for colleagues' support.[12] Through this self-imposed isolation, they contribute to the low morale in the organization because staff eventually feel ignored and abandoned.

The Charmer

The primary purpose of these managers is gaining personal acceptance from staff. To them, popularity is far more important than task accomplishment, and their charm is a cover-up for not getting things done. Their likability and good image have become substitutes for substantive achievement. Although well liked by staff because of the limited demands these managers make, they ultimately are seen as ineffectual.

The Mistruster

Managers who fit this profile constantly check on staff performance and attitudes because of their own insecurities. They take the role of monitor to its extreme by constantly checking on staff's whereabouts, reading all correspondence that emanates from their departments, and obsessively checking on what staff think about them. Their excessively suspicious nature engenders tremendous anxiety and immobilizes staff from taking initiatives.

The previously mentioned leadership flaws are obvious exaggerations, and few managers manifest these caricatures in their pure form. Any one of us, however, may lapse into some of these behaviors. Being mindful of these possibilities can, perhaps, minimize their destructive impact on an organization's productivity.

LEADERSHIP COMPETENCIES

It is not enough for managers to be constantly aware of possible flaws in their personal behavior that could affect their leadership effectiveness. They must also discern how their strengths can be used to heighten the organization's performance. Previously, it was noted that leadership style should be matched to the needs of the organization and the situation. Assuming that this match exists, there are certain traits and competencies that are of great value in managing human service organizations.

In every community, certain managers evidence outstanding abilities to get things done. The following are some thumbnail sketches based on the lives of exemplary leaders:

Waulina T. heads a suburban children's residential treatment center. Several years ago, she decided that her agency must aggressively confront the problems of the inner city even though the agency is located 12 miles away from the downtown area. She has worked hard to establish drug treatment programs in the city's school system. Her successful efforts to make her organization more relevant have earned her both great respect and an infusion of funds for her agency.

Tom L. has expanded a program of health care for homeless people to include a variety of services: drug treatment, a winter housing program, and a facility for mentally disabled women. In addition, he has organized the business and political leadership of the community to develop long-term solutions for the lack of adequate low-income housing.

Ambler M. directs a special organization designed to combat crime in the community. He had the vision to see that gangs were an increasing concern and the personal drive to provide leadership to school officials, police, and parents to help them address their concerns more appropriately.

Rothina D. infused a moribund organization with a new spirit when she became its director. Established to obtain jobs for public assistance recipients, the organization had not been able to induce the corporate community to accept its trainees until she developed an outstanding training and orientation program. She conveys tremendously high expectations to her staff and imbues them with great sensitivity to the needs of the trainees.

Smitty C. heads the local YMCA. He considers his most important managerial function to be helping staff to develop their fullest abilities. He has initiated many staff training programs, encourages staff to follow through on their ideas, and emphasizes the importance of all the staff sharing ownership and success of their programs.

Jeraldine H. is the head of a large staff unit within a mammoth bureaucracy. Her paramount concern is to help staff feel invested in their work. She has established a series of discussion meetings with her supervisory personnel, and they in turn meet with their staffs to develop a greater sense of unity and dedication toward their work. As a consequence of these meetings and a series of staff appreciation sessions, staff are beginning to rededicate themselves. Many of them are staying after 5:00 p.m. or working weekends to complete assignments. Work teams are developing innovative ideas for dealing with emergencies. Staff enthusiasm about their work has increased because Jeraldine conveys daily how important their contributions are to the community.

What do these effective managers have in common? The following sections discuss the competencies that they share that enable their organizations to perform at a highly productive level.

Articulating a Future Orientation

Effective managers are constantly seeking out trends—possible changes in demographics, funding, or political alignments—and how these trends might influence their organization. They work at formulating a vision of the future either within their own mind or by mobilizing the organization to think strategically (see Chapter 3, this volume). They have the ability to get everyone who should be involved—staff, boards of trustees, or even public officials—to focus their attention on issues leaders consider significant.[13] Sometimes, their view of the future is influenced by a profound desire to move to a higher level of performance.

Competent leaders are never fully satisfied. Even when staff are performing well and their units or the organization as a whole are accomplishing their goals, effective managers continually ask, "How can we improve, how can we do things better?" Of course, they enjoy and appreciate achievements, but they have a need to improve the status quo. They are intolerant of complacency that comes from previous successes and, as they meet one objective, they press on to another. In short, effective managers are continuously working to help their organizations grow and change to meet new situations and to focus all the members of their organization on those issues considered most significant.[14] Ambler M. had the foresight and the understanding that gangs were using the school building walls, mailboxes, and even school artwork to communicate gang messages. He convinced his organization to make reducing gang activity a priority long before other community youth organizations realized the need for it. As a result of his vision, his organization now has a unique niche and is considered the expert source on gangs by juvenile court judges, school administrators, and political leaders.

Waulina T. is continually thinking about the future of the organization. She says,

> My ultimate purpose is to leave the organization in better shape than when I became its director. That is what my predecessor did, and that is the position I hope my successor takes as well. I am always dreaming up projects for the following year. Right now I'm planning for a new building on our campus that will house adolescents referred by juvenile court. It may take 4 years to build, but we've got to begin to plan now.

Being a Social Entrepreneur

Effective managers persist in accomplishing goals even in the face of setbacks and failures. They take risks, knowing that failures may occur, and they learn from their mistakes.[15] They assume that if something does not work, they will try something else until they ultimately succeed. This perseverance and tenacity in the face of obstacles and adversity is what sets effective managers apart from their less intrepid counterparts. The leader who can articulate a vision, however inspiring and relevant, but who cannot implement it is only a prophet.[16] Effective managers proclaim, "Dammit! We're going to make this thing work one way or another!" As high achievers, human service entrepreneurs obtain satisfaction from successfully completing challenging tasks, obtaining standards of excellence, and developing better ways of doing things.[17] Unlike the business entrepreneur, the social entrepreneur does not seek mainly the reward of financial gain but rather the joy of achieving significant results.

Rothina D. can be considered a human service entrepreneur. Her quest was to create an organization that would help unemployed persons and public assistance recipients become self-reliant through employment. To do this, she obtained commitments from more than 350 companies by assuring them that they would be able to hire reliable, competent, and highly motivated employees. She built a program that accomplished this goal by convincing state and local officials that their investment in her program would produce excellent dividends for the community.

Rothina does not operate by the book: If state regulations are not supportive, then she works to change them. If her trainees need a place for their children in the summer, she establishes a summer camp program in a downtown office building. If her participants have legal problems that impede their ability to stay on the job, she establishes a legal assistance program customized to their needs. All these programs entail risks and the possibility of failure, but her commitment and entrepreneurial drive make them succeed.

As another example, Tom L.'s work requires him to bounce back time and time again. Homeless people have profound problems and needs that cannot be met through usual channels. When the welfare department was unable to give homeless people temporary shelter in the winter months because of security problems, he aggressively pursued another building and obtained help from the sheriff's department. When the state mental health department denied funding for a program to house mentally ill homeless women, he obtained a federal grant. The word "no" is not in his vocabulary. He has the drive to achieve what others might consider impossible.

Effective managers, then, are passionate entrepreneurs who continually seek ways to make a contribution. They thrive on the challenge of making things happen.

Treating Staff With Dignity

Effective managers minimize the use of command language and maximize the language of persuasion and request. They understand that they cannot coerce staff to excel; true motivation must come from within.[18] They create a climate in which staff feel so positive about how they are being treated that they willingly perform at their best. These managers show caring concern and treat staff with respect, not as "service delivery units." Jeraldine H. remarks,

> I care about my staff. We are like one big family and I encourage them to work together whenever possible. I show respect for them and they reciprocate.

> When I can manage to do so, I attend weddings and funerals of the families of my staff. But even as I strive to promote positive relationships, I maintain a degree of objectivity because ours must be a professional, not a personal, relationship.

Thus, effective managers truly care about their employees; they convey empathy and compassion to help foster a supportive work environment.

Communicating Significant Messages

Effective managers are able to articulate concepts, ideas, and philosophies in such a way that staff understand both intellectually and emotionally how they are involved. These messages are clear and uncomplicated; they speak to the heart and to the mind. Managers help staff see the relationship between what they are doing and the mission of the organization—how they are a part of the whole.[19] These managers work to shape ambiguous ideas into operational programs with clear guidelines, thereby giving structure and clarity to them. Without patronizing their staff, effective managers clarify what the work is for, why it needs to be done in a particular manner, and what constitutes successful performance. One of their major messages is that everyone must work together to achieve the organization's goals.[20] Effective managers allocate significant time and effort to developing a network of cooperative relationships among the people they believe are needed to satisfy their agendas.[21]

Moreover, effective managers communicate with—not just to—staff by listening to and incorporating their ideas and concerns. Listening is an essential but undervalued managerial skill. Given that many managers have achieved their positions because of their ability to express their ideas, they often do not realize that communication is a two-way process. The difference between mediocre managers and outstanding ones is the ability to tune in to what staff are thinking and feeling. This includes the manager's ability to listen to criticism without becoming unduly defensive when mistakes are brought to his or her attention. Jeraldine H. reflects this attitude in the following statement: "Like everyone else, I'm fallible and can make mistakes. But with staff input, I am confident we can get our efforts back on course." She knows that she plays a vital role in linking the organization's communications. Good communicators therefore have the ability to receive and to give messages effectively.

Engendering Trust

Effective managers have a deep sense of integrity. They are honest with themselves and are aware of both their strengths and their limitations. Staff respect and trust effective managers who take steps either to address their own limitations or to find ways to compensate for them.[22] Staff know what values their leaders are committed to and what positions they stand for, and they know they can count on these managers. Competent managers are careful to promise only what they can deliver, and they expect others to do the same.[23]

The trust that effective managers earn is not based on blind faith. It is built on a give-and-take interaction, which might sometimes include some degree of doubt.[24] The manager and staff feel committed to each other, but they both can also raise questions and challenge issues within a relationship of mutual respect. Maintaining this balance of respect and willingness to challenge is the essence of the implicit compact between the manager and staff.

Whether as a result of staff interaction or through their own introspective tendencies, effective managers are continuously conducting self-appraisals: "Could I have handled the situation differently?" They want to learn from their mistakes and can candidly admit they have made an error in judgment, thereby earning the respect of staff.

Effective managers with a strong sense of integrity lead by example. They know that, as role models, they set the pace for the rest of the organization. Their actions are far more significant than words. Effective managers honor requests that discussions be held confidential, give credit to employees for their good ideas, and use professional discretion in communicating employee mistakes.[25] Because managers are very visible, their commitment to the tasks of the organization and their degree of investment in the staff are continually under scrutiny. Staff view effective managers as genuine and sincerely dedicated. They are the ultimate exemplars of their organizations.

Jeraldine H. exemplifies a leader who has earned the trust of her staff. She says of them,

> They know I would not ask them to do any task that wasn't in the best interest of the clients. When I meet with staff I try to be open-minded when they raise questions concerning programs I propose because their constructive criticisms improve the original idea. What's great is that we feel a genuine respect for each other.

Effective managers are well aware, therefore, that trust is not given automatically but must be earned over time and in many ways.

Inspiring Top-Level Performance

By establishing high, but achievable, expectations, successful managers infuse in their staff a standard of excellence.[26] They create a positive and productive working atmosphere within which staff are stimulated to perform at their best.

Even as they expect high performance, at the same time they are realistic. They attempt to stretch people, not overwhelm them.[27] The words that best describe this kind of leadership are "elevating," "uplifting," and "cheerleading." Their optimism, confidence, and "can-do" demeanor mobilize staff to take on the toughest of challenges. They lead best by their personal example.

Effective managers convey a mind-set that staff members are "winners" by creating continuous opportunities for successful experiences, thereby instilling in them the confidence to seek even higher levels of achievement.[28] They allow their staff to make their own decisions whenever possible and strive to get things done through cooperation.[29] Staff respond positively to managers who delegate their authority, make their subordinates feel powerful and capable, and foster their creative abilities to do their job.[30] Encouraging people to assume greater responsibility is challenging, but the effective manager instills confidence in his or her staff by providing them with successful experiences in which they can take risks and even make mistakes.[31] As facilitators, these managers work to remove obstacles that interfere with the staff's success. They continually ask, "What can we do to help you do your job better?" and "What can we accomplish as a team?"[32]

Waulina T. expresses this idea of empowering staff when she states,

> I am a servant-leader, for I try to be responsive to what staff want me to do to help them do their jobs better. I am at my best when I can take the time to be involved with my staff, to hear them out, to figure out ways to give them the resources to do their job better. They are closer to their situation and problems than I am, and so a good part of my job is to help them fulfill their professional responsibilities.

Smitty C. inspires his staff with the following comments: "We have a tough assignment to complete in 7 days, and I know that you are up to the task. If we all pitch in, we can produce a document that we can all be proud of." Also, when the quality product is completed he says, "I am proud of the fantastic job all of you have done. I am glad that you are the kind of group I can count on."

Waulina T. places the same emphasis on facilitating staff investment and growth with the following observation:

> It is important that, as a manager, I not become too possessive of the organization. The staff must feel a deep sense of pride in their work and a sense of ownership in the organization. Whatever credit comes to me is based on the commitment and performance of my staff. If I help them grow, we all benefit.

More than 2,500 years ago, Lao Tzu, a Chinese Taoist philosopher, observed,

> A leader is best
> When people barely know that he exists,
> Not so good when people obey and acclaim him,
> Worst when they despise him.
> "Fail to honor people, they fail to honor you";
> But of a good leader, who talks little,
> When his work is done, his aim fulfilled,
> They will say, "We did this ourselves."[33]

Thus, organizational administrators continually seek to harmonize their various strengths. As managers, they work to bring order and consistency to complex organizations. As leaders, they challenge the status quo and work to meet new demands.[34] They strive to achieve their visions and simultaneously facilitate the staff's input in the direction-setting process. They are oriented to accomplishing tasks and are sensitive to the needs of their staff. They set their sights on the future while making certain to give proper attention to everyday details. They are both conveyers of messages and consummate listeners. They engender trust by respecting their staff and treating them with dignity. This blend of vision, sensitivity, and high moral purpose results in inspiring leadership.

ATTRIBUTES CONTRIBUTING TO LEADERSHIP

Research is beginning to emerge that effective leaders have certain attributes that enhance their ability to lead people. These attributes, referred to as "emotional intelligence," are (a) self-awareness, (b) self-regulation, (c) motivation, (d) empathy, and (e) social skills:[35]

Self-awareness: Emotionally intelligent people are keenly aware of their strengths, weaknesses, and desires. Those with a strong self-awareness are able to be honest with both themselves and others. They are aware of how their feelings affect them, other people, and their job performance. Self-aware people know when to ask for help, are willing to admit their mistakes, and at the same time are confident about what they can do.

Self-regulation: Operating in the midst of ambiguity and change, a self-regulated person is able to control impulses, suspend judgment, and seek out information before making decisions. These people are comfortable with ambiguity and open to change. They tend to be reflective and thoughtful.

Motivation: Highly motivated people want to achieve results because it is exciting and fun for its own sake. They desire to challenge the status quo rather than opt for power or money alone. They are energetic and persistent and generally optimistic even though they may fail sometimes. Even those who have a high degree of self-awareness about their limitations will work to stretch themselves. People who are high achievers are committed to the organization. They set high goals for both themselves and their employees.

Empathy: Considering the staff's feelings is part of an effective manager's decision process. If staff are feeling anxious or angry, an empathetic manager can acknowledge these feelings. As a leader of a team, the effective manager recognizes that various members will have different emotional reactions, alliances, and even clashes of opinions. A leader must recognize and understand these different perspectives.

Social skill: This involves the ability to manage relationships with others. Being friendly with a purpose allows managers to persuade people to move in the direction they want. By developing a positive rapport, being positive, being interested in employees as people, and building bonds, they help people deal with day-to-day frustrations. No leader can truly hope to function in isolation. The leader's job is to get work done through other people; social skills are the grease that makes this possible.

Thus, effective managers have a high level of emotional intelligence, which is required to carry out their jobs.

DIAGNOSING YOUR LEADERSHIP STYLE

Awareness of how you function as a leader within your organization is critical to being effective.[36] The more insight you have into how you react in various situations, the more you can ensure a proper match between behavior and organizational contingencies. This chapter has described several key elements that can be used to diagnose your leadership behavior: (a) leadership styles, (b) influences over staff, (c) flaws and limitations, (d) competencies and strengths, and (e) emotional intelligence. To heighten your understanding of your own leadership role, consider the following questions:

1. What is my predominant style (delegative, directive, or participative) of leadership? Are there clear benefits from using this style? Are there negative side effects? Thinking back to particular instances, have I matched the right style with the situation at hand? In the future, should I consider testing other styles?
2. In regard to types of influence, which ones do I tend to use with my staff? On reflection, should I consider modifying my influence approach either because my current one is not effective or because situations may require a different response than usual?
3. Of the possible managerial limitations or flaws, do I see myself manifesting any of them in my own leadership behavior? If so, should I make efforts to modify my attitudes or behavior to increase my effectiveness? Are there times when some of these limitations may actually be useful and necessary?
4. In the review of competencies and strengths, which ones do I exhibit? Is it within my capacity to strive for others? If so, can I find some safe ways to test an underdeveloped competency? If not, can I find others who can complement my strengths?

The exploration of these questions, either by thinking about them on your own or by obtaining feedback from others whom you trust, can be useful in considering ways to develop further as an effective manager.

NOTES

1. J. E. Bennett, Reflections on successful CEOs: The match is everything, *Cleveland Enterprise,* Winter 1991-1992, pp. 18-20.

2. P. Drucker, *The effective executive* (New York: Harper & Row, 1985), pp. 22-23.

3. W. Bennis, *On becoming a leader* (Reading, MA: Addison-Wesley, 1989), p. 45; L. H. Garner, Jr., *Leadership in human services: How to articulate a vision to achieve results* (San Francisco: Jossey-Bass, 1989), pp. 9-12; R. R. Middleman & G. B. Rhodes, *Competent supervision: Making imaginative judgments* (Englewood Cliffs, NJ: Prentice Hall, 1985), pp. 78-81.

4. R. Tannenbaum & W. Schmidt, How to choose a leadership pattern, *Harvard Business Review, 3* (1973), pp. 162-180.

5. E. S. Stanton, A critical reevaluation of motivation, management, and productivity, *Personnel Journal, 3* (1983), pp. 5-6.

6. K. Blanchard, J. P. Carlos, & A. Randolph, *The 3 keys to empowerment* (San Francisco: Berrett-Koehler, 1999), pp. 25-43.

7. L. J. McFarland, L. E. Senn, & J. R. Childress, Refining leadership in the next century, in *The leader's companion* (J. T. Wren, Ed.) (New York: Free Press, 1995), pp. 459-460.

8. M. Wadia, Parrticipative management: Three common problems, *Personnel Journal, 11* (1980), pp. 27-28.

9. R. Townsend, *Further up the organization* (New York: Knopf, 1984), p. 94.

10. P. Drucker, *Effective,* p. 25.

11. R. Hogan, R. Raskin, & D. Fazzini, How charisma cloaks incompetence, *Personnel Journal, 5* (1990), p. 76.

12. T. Caplow, *How to run any organization* (Hinsdale, IL: Dryden, 1976), p. 55.

13. National Assembly of National Voluntary Health and Social Welfare Organizations, *A study in excellence: Management in the nonprofit human services* (Washington, DC: Author, 1985), pp. 36-44.

14. R. M. Cyert, Defining leadership and explicating the process, *Nonprofit Management and Leadership, 1* (1990), pp. 29-37.

15. W. Bennis, pp. 95-96.

16. L. H. Garner, Jr., p. 9.

17. S. A. Kirkpatrick & E. A. Locke, Do traits matter? in *The leader's companion* (J. T. Wren, Ed.) (New York: Free Press, 1995), p. 135.

18. R. Townsend, p. 170.

19. National Assembly of National Voluntary Health and Social Welfare Organizations, pp. 36-44.

20. R. M. Cyert, p. 33.

21. J. Kotter, What leaders really do, *Harvard Business Review, 3* (1990), pp. 103-111.

22. W. Bennis, pp. 40-41.

23. M. H. McCormack, *Mark H. McCormack on managing* (West Hollywood, CA: Dove, 1996), p. 9; S. A. Kirkpatrick & E. A. Locke, p. 138.

24. W. Bennis, p. 140.

25. Bureau of Business Practice, Building loyalty, *Front Line Supervisor's Bulletin, 146* (1990), pp. 1-3.

26. W. N. Schultz, What makes a good nonprofit manager? *Nonprofit World* (1984), p. 32; L. H. Garner, Jr., pp. 151-152.

27. W. Bennis, p. 198.

28. T. J. Peters & R. H. Waterman, *In search of excellence: Lessons from America's best run companies* (New York: Harper & Row, 1982), pp. 83-84.

29. P. Slater & W. Bennis, Democracy is inevitable, *Harvard Business Review, 5* (1990), p. 175.

30. T. Teal, The human side of management, *Harvard Business Review, 74* (1996, November/December), p. 39.

31. R. A. Heifetz & D. L Laurie, The work of leadership, *Harvard Business Review* (1997, January/February), p. 129.

32. P. Drucker, *Managing the nonprofit organization* (New York: HarperCollins, 1990), p. 44.

33. L. Tzu, *The way of life according to Lao Tzu* (W. Bynner, Trans.) (New York: Capricorn, 1944), p. 34.

34. W. Bennis, pp. 46-47; J. Kotter, pp. 103-111.

35. D. Goleman, What makes a leader? *Harvard Business Review* (1998, November/December), pp. 93-102.

36. J. Seltzer, pp. 46-49.

Chapter 2

THE CULTURE OF A PRODUCTIVE ORGANIZATION

Effective managers are mindful that the productivity of their organizations is greatly influenced by culture. In the business world, the term *corporate culture* has come into vogue, reflecting an increasing interest in how organizational values can influence an enterprise and employee productivity.[1] In the nonprofit world, *organizational culture* indicates this same awareness that operating style, traditions, rituals, and beliefs—the fundamental values of the organization—influence the way staff think and behave.[2] It is the system of values that a given group has invented, discovered, or developed in learning to cope with its problems of external adaptation and internal integration.[3] *Culture* is "the right way to do things around here."[4]

Usually, cultural values develop over a long period of time, serve to stabilize the group, and are highly resistant to change. Frequently, these values are taken for granted and may not even be part of staff's conscious thought process. As will be shown later, effective managers can work with staff to crystallize a formal values statement to help guide the work of the organization.

Shared values give the organization a sense of direction so that individual staff see how to fulfill their professional goals in relation to the organization's goals. Above all, organizational values provide a profound sense of meaning to staff work. When influenced by a strong organizational culture, staff truly care about their work; they significantly invest themselves in what the organization represents. In some organizations in which values are weak or unenforced, those staff who do not subscribe to them (often known as "rebels" or "uncommitted drones") can contaminate the organization's culture. Where a strong culture exists, however, either people buy into organizational norms or they are encouraged to leave. Those who remain identify deeply with the organization's value system. They adopt the organization's values as their own, and their professional lives have greater significance because of this affiliation.

Although managers in most organizations will strive to develop a strong culture as a way of influencing staff performance, cultural strength may or may not be associated with effectiveness.[5] Sometimes, an older organization with a strong culture benefits from having units with diverse perspectives that question the usual way of doing things, thereby allowing the organization to be more adaptive to environmental changes. The challenge for effective managers is to harness the culture's benefits while remaining alert to the dangers of perpetuating a culture that is out of sync with the needs of the organization. Enlightened managers can avoid cultural blind spots by accommodating selective nonconformity in their organizations and by deviating from it when the situation calls for it.[6]

Effective managers serve as the primary shapers and communicators of organizational values. They influence the organizational culture by what they pay attention to, measure, and control; how they handle crises and critical episodes; how their own behavior serves as a model; how they allocate rewards and status; and how they recruit, select, promote, and fire staff.[7] Do they tolerate or challenge criticism? Do they limit or make information available to staff? Do they control or empower staff to make decisions? Are they focused more on the budget or on the people of their organization? Managers are frequently faced with these kinds of value choices.

Effective managers will always play a key role during those times when the organization faces problems, external or internal. Indeed, one of the crucial functions of leadership is to provide guidance at precisely those times when habitual ways of thinking or doing things no longer work or when drastic environmental changes require fresh responses. It is also during these transitional times that effective managers must provide staff with security to help them tolerate their anxieties of giving up old responses while new ones are being tried.[8]

Clearly, effective managers play a significant role in influencing the culture by the messages they communicate and, more important, through their own behavior. They convey expectations, stress performance, and establish a reward and recognition system that embodies what the organization deems important.

CULTURAL FRAMEWORKS

The cultural framework of an organization can affect how staff are expected to function. The frameworks can be classified as bureaucratic, entrepreneurial, achievement oriented, and socially oriented.[9]

A *bureaucratic* framework is conservative, traditional, and hierarchical. It requires its staff members to follow the rules and go through designated channels. Employees tend to avoid risks and treat rules as more important than ideas. Managers place strong emphasis on monitoring performance. For some staff, the bureaucratic organization provides stability, predictability, structure, and orderliness. Clients may find comfort in knowing they will be treated consistently. Carried to the extreme, the bureaucratic organization is driven by rules and paperwork. Its rigidity interferes with its effectiveness by suppressing innovation and by preventing adaptation to environmental changes. The safety of saying "no" is stronger than the risk taking involved in saying "yes" to innovative ideas.

An *entrepreneurial* framework is characterized by creativity and risk taking. Staff members are committed to experimentation and innovation. They like to act as brokers and "deal makers." If carried too far, however, the organization becomes poorly focused, and its excessive experimentation leads to confusion, even anarchy, and unprincipled opportunism.

An *achievement-oriented* framework stimulates staff to set challenging objectives, establish plans to reach them, and pursue them enthusiastically. People have a strong sense of accomplishment in achieving what they set out to do. In excess, however, members may be pushed to set unrealistic and unachievable objectives that could lead to subsequent frustration and disillusionment. In such an extreme situation, staff may begin to feel that they are operating in an overly demanding, "sweatshop" environment.

A *socially oriented* framework is characterized by an emphasis on relationships. Staff feel a strong sense of support and caring among themselves. The work culture has a commitment to both staff and clients. If the organization is poorly focused or irresponsible, however, excessive involvement can lead to rambling decision making and lack of direction.

Awareness of these predominant styles can be useful in determining when modifications are necessary to enhance an organization's effectiveness. Achieving the proper balance so that an organization does not become any one "type" to an excessive degree frees it to encompass other organizational frameworks that can help accomplish organizational goals. A public organization, such as a human services department, out of necessity must be oriented to rules and regulations, and its members must accept these values. To achieve maximum effectiveness, however, a bureaucratic organization must allow entrepreneurial or social influences. A governmental agency that adheres to the most rigid procedures can still tolerate and even encourage innovative problem-solving approaches that meet its clients' needs and give staff a sense of satisfaction. County human service department managers, for instance, might aggressively initiate, with the local mental health board, a joint diagnostic assessment program based on the conviction that, with better diagnoses, fewer youth would need to be placed in institutions. Imbued with a new entrepreneurial spirit, staff could then secure local start-up funding from a foundation. Similarly, even an innovative and risk-taking organization, such as one developed to creatively address race relations in an ethnic neighborhood, will at times require policies, procedures, and a hierarchical decision-making process.

Sometimes, an organization's value emphasis shifts because of changing circumstances. An organization that is suddenly faced with reduced funding from its primary source may have to become more entrepreneurial and sales conscious. Those members who were accustomed to a less pressured, congenial atmosphere may have to adjust to the new, more competitive value emphasis. For example, staff whose only responsibility is to focus on the needs of clients may be pressed into soliciting funds—a new role and new value emphasis dictated by external realities.

Thus, values constitute the sum total of an organization's culture. The organization's productivity is affected by the employees' attitudes and behavior, which in turn are affected by the values they hold. Among those positive values that characterize salutary aspects of a productive service organization are staff's profound commitment to their jobs (job ownership), the primacy of the consumer, and the critical importance of work quality.

JOB OWNERSHIP AS A CENTRAL VALUE

One of the highest values an organization can engender in its staff is that of job ownership. Employees must care so much about their work and be so invested in it that they do whatever it takes to get the job done. When they are this committed and dedicated, they work as if they were in business for themselves. This could mean working extra hours, responding in special ways to the needs of the people they serve, or advocating changes in organizational procedures for the benefit of their clientele.

How does this profound commitment to the job come about? The organizational culture can promote a climate that furthers job ownership by instilling in staff a sense of higher purpose, emotional bonding, trust, stakeholder involvement, and pride in their work. The result is that staff feel good about their work and want to invest themselves more fully in it.[10]

A Sense of Higher Purpose

Fortunately, most staff who work in the human service field prefer an organizational culture that emphasizes making a contribution, serving others, and individuals feeling that they are a part of something larger than themselves. They typify the third worker in the following story: A traveler encounters three men at work. Each is asked what he is doing. The first says, "I am laying bricks." The second says, "I am making a wall." The third replies, "I am building a cathedral." Staff who share a genuine vision, who want to excel and learn, not because they are told to do so but because they want to, experience a common destiny.[11] If staff believe the work of the organization can make a difference in the lives of the people it serves, they will be inspired to invest themselves more fully.

In religious settings, the imperative to achieve a sense of higher purpose is referred to as a "calling." One need not have a religious incentive to feel a profound sense of dedication, however. As one manager noted, "We are absolutely committed to taking our clients out of poverty forever." She conveys to her staff zeal to accomplish this overriding cultural value. Everyone—office staff, counselors, teachers, job finders, and research analysts—feels this deep commitment. The greater the belief in the significance of their work, the more likely it is that staff will be productive.

A Sense of Emotional Bonding

An organization in which people deeply care about each other fosters strong allegiances and a powerful sense of togetherness. Their sense of bonding produces feelings of comfort and security. Feeling wanted and cared about, they like to come to work because they find their relationships emotionally and intellectually fulfilling.

This feeling of common fellowship is particularly important in organizations in which clients make high demands and work pressures are tremendous. Staff are required to be so giving and so responsive to others' needs that care and support fostered by positive work relationships is especially important. Effective managers therefore encourage a congenial work atmosphere and positive interpersonal relationships among staff.

A Sense of Trust

This value is not easily defined, but employees know it when they have it and they also sense when it does not exist. Perhaps when trust exists, we tend to take it for granted, but its absence can cause tremendous problems for an organization. If the organization's leadership conveys the expectation that everyone should work hard but managers are seen taking long lunch breaks and not investing time in their own work, they will be mistrusted. In contrast, a sense of fairness is conveyed throughout the organization if, for example, everyone experiences a salary cut because of funding reductions.

Trust is built on honest interpersonal relationships. It is based on the assumption that staff are all trying to work for the common good. Certainly, they may evidence self-interest at times, but they must also be willing to put aside their individual agendas for a greater benefit. This value encourages and promotes mutual commitment.

A Sense of Stakeholder Involvement

An organization that espouses this value fosters stakeholders at every level. All staff believe they must invest themselves for the common goals to be achieved. Throughout the organization, there is a sense of empowerment to make decisions, to be invested, and to care about what is happening. At the same time, they understand and appreciate that various stakeholders—management, supervisors, service staff, clients, support staff, and board members—all participate in the overall purpose of the organization. They all believe that they are partners in a common venture.

The following is an example of fostering stakeholder involvement: The manager of a YMCA proudly announces to his staff that the receptionist's idea to encourage current members to invite their friends to an open house resulted in a 20% increase in memberships. He says, "I am so proud that she and everyone else in the organization is thinking about ways to increase our membership." A sense of involvement permeates the entire organization.

A Sense of Pride in One's Work

Effective managers instill the idea that staff should be the very best they can be. Because of a collective sense of pride, each organizational member gains a reputation for providing a superior quality of service. In business, slogans, such as "Quality is our most important product" or "Quality is job #1," are created to promote this value. These could just as easily be the maxims of human service organizations. Periodically, effective managers ask staff, "What makes you most proud of the organization? What gives you the most satisfaction?"

Professional growth contributes to pride. Effective managers present staff with high work standards that are attainable if they expend reasonable effort and if they are given the proper training and supervision. When staff feel proud of what they do, they become upset if something goes wrong. They ask to be trained so they can improve their performance. They want their organization to invest in them so they can produce high-quality work.

THE PRIMACY OF THE CONSUMER AS A CENTRAL VALUE

In business transactions, customers pay for goods or services, and their satisfaction is based on the extent to which their expectations are met. Those receiving services from human service organizations are called clients or service consumers. For them, consumer satisfaction is also determined by the extent to which their expectations are met.

In the business world, customer satisfaction is constantly being emphasized. Employees are urged to listen to their customers and be more responsive to them. The popularized term *total quality management* emphasizes a customer-focused service.[12] Employees are reminded that a dissatisfied customer will tell 8 to 10 people about the problem.[13] Meeting and, if possible, exceeding customer expectations is a strong value in the business world.

Comparing the business customer with the human service consumer has its limitations. The business customer typically pays for services rendered. If enough customers are dissatisfied, the bottom line of the business will be affected. In the human service field, many different kinds of "customer" needs must be met. In addition to the persons receiving the service (consumers), there are trustees, volunteers, fund donors, service advocates, referral sources, elected officials, and community leaders who must all be satisfied with the effectiveness and efficiency of services delivered. Each has different expectations about the organization, and some of these may not even be compatible. Political officials, for example, may emphasize cost reductions, whereas human service advocates may emphasize reaching out to more clients. Although the concept of customer is not entirely analogous, there is enough similarity to make the point that human service organizations are in business primarily to meet their clients' needs—and this fundamental idea must always be kept in the forefront if the organization is to stay in business.

Because human service consumers rarely pay the full cost of service, some organizations may not feel the same obligation to respond to their needs as if they were full-paying customers. Human service organizations, however, must emphasize the primacy of the client. The following sign was hung in the administrative offices of a public housing authority:

> We believe that our clients are not an interruption of our work; they are the very purpose of it. We are not doing them a favor by serving them; they are doing us a favor by giving us an opportunity to do so.

Even when human service organizations espouse the belief that their clients are their reason for being, many factors can prohibit this from being their core purpose. If program funding is received from a third party, consumers may not have a direct way to express their concerns because they are not paying for the service. If consumers are considered fungible—that is, if there are so many people waiting to be served that dissatisfied ones can easily be replaced by others—then there may be little or no impetus to deal with the discontent. If too great an emphasis is placed on administrative or staff convenience, then meeting the needs of consumers becomes secondary. For example, staff may prefer to work a 9-to-5 day, but working parents can only attend marital counseling sessions before or after work. If the delivery of services involves more than one organization, or more than one unit within an organization, their competitive feelings can result in consumers becoming highly fragmented and overly burdened with bureaucratic procedures.

The antidote for these inhibitive factors is a value commitment to—even an obsession with—meeting consumer needs. Effective managers must clarify to employees that this is fundamental. Organizations must develop a good feedback system and a method for reminding staff of the primacy of consumers. One major way of obtaining feedback is through periodic formal surveys. Just as hotels, restaurants, and car repair shops ask their customers regularly for suggestions on how to improve their services, so too human service organizations no doubt could benefit from such formal surveys of their constituents. Some organizations use a feedback device titled "Give Us a Grade," in which the service consumer is asked to answer a variety of questions regarding expectations, to provide a description of care provided, and to provide a rating of services. Encouraging comment cards and letters—both positive and negative—will help staff understand how their services are perceived.

Some organizations even assign management staff to pretend they are consumers. They may call or visit an office where they are unrecognized to determine firsthand how their concerns are handled.[14] This is a common practice in retail stores that arrange for management, staff, or outside "professional shoppers" to experience what it is like to be treated as a customer. The purpose is not to evaluate specific individuals as much as it is to determine how responsive the system is to consumer needs. Experiencing the organization as a consumer can reveal discrepancies between how things should work and what actually occurs.

In addition to feedback, organizational management should provide orientation and training to improve staff proficiency and performance and to help them better tune in to consumer needs. Applauding staff who have gone out of their way to be responsive to consumer needs and to obtain results furthers this fundamental organizational value. Role-playing exercises and problem-solving simulations provide concrete, clearly understandable examples of how the organization can work to add value to the lives of the consumers they serve.

The message being promoted throughout the organization is that everyone serves "clients" directly or indirectly. Hence, if employees are not involved in direct service, then they should be facilitating the work of those who are. This means that everyone in the organization has a client to serve: supervisors facilitate the work of their staff, accountants provide needed information to management, and computer operators create essential documents for management.[15] Consistency between rhetoric and actions is vital if employees are to believe and accept that the organization sincerely cares about its consumers.

Many obvious clues indicate whether an organization is "consumer friendly." Telephone calls are answered promptly. The reception room is inviting, and the receptionist conveys a warm welcome to visitors. Staff genuinely convey positive acceptance and go the extra distance to be helpful to clients. Appointments are promptly kept; apologies are given if clients have to wait. Clients are treated as genuine partners by engaging them in activities that assist the agency. For example, they may be asked to serve on advisory committees to make suggestions to improve agency services.[16]

These are small efforts, perhaps, but they project the organization's fundamental emphasis on the dignity and importance of the client or customer. Also, they do not occur by happenstance. The culture of caring permeates the entire organization as it continually reinforces this primary value in staff meetings, annual reports, training programs, and documents describing particular programs. Effective managers do not tolerate denigrating comments about clients or coworkers. Through special training and supervision, staff learn how to treat clients with respect and dignity, even when they have to cope with hostility and complaints. By frequently stressing its commitment to caring and proving that commitment repeatedly, the organization develops a reputation for being responsive to the needs of the people it serves.[17]

WORK QUALITY AS A CENTRAL VALUE

The productivity of any human service organization is affected by the quality of its work. Quality is one of the major factors in determining whether an oranization has achieved it goals and should continue to receive community support. Hence, effective managers emphasize the value of delivering a quality service.

Two critical dimensions constitute the productive delivery of quality service in human service organizations: service outcome and process. These dimensions are difficult to separate and may even blur in the minds of the clients. *Service outcome* refers to the results of the service. Clients wanting to obtain employment would be satisfied if, as a result of the service, they got the jobs they wanted. Clients seeking advice want substantive ideas that can aid them in improving their relationships with spouses. Well-delivered services require that staff have a thorough understanding of the services they are providing and an ability to analyze their consumers' situations. Quality service outcomes in large part require staff to be effective in meeting the needs of their consumers.

The process dimension of quality service is determined by how staff interact with their clients. Attitudes and behaviors related to service delivery are reflected in the following kinds of questions:

- Are consumers made to feel important by the way in which staff respond to them?
- Are their negative feelings responded to by staff?
- Do they feel that there is a high level of concern for their welfare?
- Do they feel appreciated for who they are, despite their problems?

In other words, does the staff establish the kind of relationships that help consumers feel good about coming to them for services?

Effective managers stress both service results and process because these values interrelate. One without the other would likely result in the perception of inadequate service. The technically competent staff that displays little evidence of caring and commitment could produce consumer dissatisfaction, as would a personable but technically incompetent staff.

Ensuring quality must be a value that permeates the entire organization—from top management to service providers. Because service providers have primary contacts with clients, they must be integrally involved in all aspects of delivering quality services, including determining what they are, how they are carried out, and what corrective actions may be required.

Because the meaning of quality can be nebulous, it is not enough for an organization to espouse the importance of it. Through explicit policies and procedures, managers must devise ways to help staff become better oriented and more sensitive to work quality. Standards need to be established; if these are not met, a corrective response becomes necessary.

For example, if through quality control procedures it is determined that information errors on client eligibility have risen above a certain threshold, this discovery would trigger specific responses, such as training or improved supervision. By establishing standards and developing mechanisms to measure them, the organization conveys that it is serious about improving the quality of the work it performs. The creation of a quality assurance committee can provide a structured means of carrying forward the quality assurance value.[18]

The following are some guiding concepts that could be considered in enhancing quality control:

Timeliness: How quickly can clients be seen after a request is made?

Correctness: How error-free is the work?

Competence: How qualified are the staff?

Reliability: Does the agency deliver what it promises?

Accountability: Is the work properly reviewed? Are problems addressed?

Service demeanor: How pleasantly and courteously are clients treated?

Accessibility: How responsive is the organization to requests?

Handling of complaints: To what extent can the organization react to client concerns?

Flexibility: Can the organization modify its services to meet special needs?

COMMUNICATING THE ORGANIZATION'S VALUES

Managers can articulate their organization's values in a variety of formal and informal ways—at staff meetings, in orientation materials, or during ceremonies honoring staff for their commitment.[19] When staff behavior reflects important and positive organizational values, managers can take steps to expand it, to improve it, and to reinforce it. For example, staff who have displayed outstanding work on behalf of clients can be praised in the agency's newsletter.

Because communicating what the organization stands for is very important, consider putting values in writing in a special document called a "values statement" or in the personnel policies manual. Sometimes, value statements are prefaced with "We believe in . . ." or "We believe that . . ." By putting values in writing, members of the organization make clear what they are committed to, and where conflicts exist they can be openly dealt with. Periodically reviewing values can serve to strengthen the organization's commitments and invite initiatives.[20] Table 2.1 illustrates how the managers and staff of one organization became engaged in developing an official values statement. Note that the statements in the document contain values on how the organization will respond to clients, staff, and other organizations. Having made explicit what the agency stands for, managers are now able both to evaluate and to influence organizational practices, procedures, and performance. Of course, each organization should engage its members in creating its own unique values statement.

Table 2.1
Values of a Children's Services Center

1. We are committed to work on THE CUTTING EDGE with the most difficult cases, the children and families other programs reject.
2. We believe effective TEAMING is essential to good therapeutic services.
3. We want to offer the finest TRAINING for our staff.
4. We want to IDENTIFY and SOLVE our problems, not LIVE with them.
5. We believe that EXCELLENCE is achieved through vigorous GOAL SETTING/GOAL ATTAINMENT processes and we want to be very self-conscious about our results.
6. We are a service-driven organization, committed to being RESPONSIVE to those who come to us for help.
7. We are committed to treating one another and all we seek to serve with respect and dignity.
8. We believe we need to establish the POWER OF FAMILIES whenever possible.
9. We are a mental health MASH unit and should always be responsive to the needs of those WAITING to access our services.
10. We are committed to PROGRAM INNOVATION and will continue to introduce new concepts, new approaches, and new technologies to meet emerging needs.
11. We believe that children should be served in the LEAST RESTRICTIVE and MOST APPROPRIATE service alternative.
12. We believe in the importance of AFTER CARE.
13. We believe in the principles of EQUAL OPPORTUNITY for clients and staff.
14. We believe that services to children and families should be offered with the highest level of CULTURAL SENSITIVITY.
15. We want to PARTNER with others in the development and delivery of services.
16. We believe the QUALITY OF OUR SERVICES can always be improved.

SOURCE: Adapted from Parmadale Children's Village (1991).

In summary, managers are mindful that the organization's culture has a strong influence on staff behavior and performance. Cultural values are entrenched as traditional ways of thinking and doing and are developed over a long period of time. Effective managers can influence the shape and strength of staff values by stressing job ownership, by emphasizing the importance of meeting the needs of service consumers, and by making certain work quality encompasses both service delivery and outcome. Every organization would benefit from a periodic examination of its values to determine which need clarifying or modifying. Effective managers must periodically assess how they can help staff make the organization's values their own.

NOTES

1. R. J. Ellis, Centel Corporation: Using human resources programs to support cultural change, *Wyatt Communicator* (1992, Spring), pp. 4-9.

2. T. E. Deal & A. A. Kennedy, *Corporate cultures* (Reading, MA: Addison-Wesley, 1982), p. 78; E. H. Schein, *Organizational culture and leadership* (San Francisco: Jossey-Bass, 1986), p. 9.

3. E. H. Schein, Coming to a new awareness of organizational culture, in *The great writings in management and organizational behavior* (L. E. Boone & D. D. Bowen, Eds.) (New York: Random House, 1987), p. 445.

4. What is culture? *Commitment Plus, 3* (1985), p. 1.

5. E. H. Schein, Coming to a new awareness, p. 450.

6. V. Sathe, Implications of corporate culture: A manager's guide to action, *Organizational Dynamics* (1983, Autumn), p. 22.

7. E. H. Schein, *Organizational culture,* pp. 224-225.

8. E. H. Schein, *Organizational culture,* pp. 451-452.

9. F. Petrock, Corporate culture and productivity, *Nonprofit Management Strategies, 7* (1991), pp. 13-14.

10. M. Beer, B. Spector, P. R. Lawrence, D. Q. Mills, & R. E. Walton, *Managing human assets* (New York: Free Press, 1984), pp. 81-83; J. H. Boyett & H. P. Conn, *Maximum performance management* (Macomb, IL: Glenbridge, 1988), pp. 31-34; R. E. Herman, *Keeping good people: Strategies for solving the dilemma of the decade* (Cleveland, OH: Oakhill, 1990), pp. 74, 286; R. Howard, Values make the company: An interview with Robert Hass, *Harvard Business Review, 5* (1990), pp. 133-143; T. J. Peters & R. H. Waterman, *In search of excellence: Lessons from America's best run companies* (New York: Harper & Row, 1982), pp. 75-77, 319-325.

11. P. M. Senge, *The fifth discipline* (New York: Doubleday & Currency, 1990), p. 9.

12. Total quality management, *Commitment Plus, 4* (1990), p. 1.

13. Improving customer satisfaction, *Commitment Plus, 1* (1988), p. 1.

14. R. Townsend, *Further up the organization* (New York: Knopf, 1984), p. 25.

15. S. Marash, Blueprint for quality improvement, *Personnel Journal, 3* (1989), p. 122.

16. J. Carl & G. Stokes, Seven keys to an excellent organization: Fostering innovation and respect, *Nonprofit World, 5* (1991), pp. 18-22.

17. L. H. Garner, Jr., *Leadership in human services: How to articulate a vision to achieve results* (San Francisco: Jossey-Bass, 1989), pp. 152-154.

18. C. Coulton, *Developing quality assurance programs: Managerial considerations and strategies* (unpublished manuscript, 1990).

19. D. R. Conner & B. Gold, Hospital corporate culture and its impact on strategic change, *Dimensions in Health Care, Peat Marwick* (1993, May), p. 3; V. Sathe, p. 19.

20. D. C. Eadie, *Changing by design* (San Francisco: Jossey-Bass, 1997), pp. 146-148.

Part I Review

SETTING THE TONE OF THE ORGANIZATION

1. LEADING THE ORGANIZATION

- Leadership style is influenced by the personal orientation (directive, participative, and delegative) of a leader, by the way staff respond to their work, and by organizational and situational factors.
- Taking into consideration the various factors noted previously, the preferred leadership approach in most human service organizations is one that emphasizes staff participation.
- Be aware of major leadership flaws that can affect staff productivity.
- Effective managers enhance their leadership competencies by being future oriented and entrepreneurial, treating staff with dignity, expressing the important values of the organization, operating with the highest degree of trust, and working with staff to achieve their highest potential.
- Effective leaders have certain attributes, referred to as "emotional intelligence," that enhance their ability to lead: keen staff awareness, social control, strong motivation, sensitivity and empathy, and comfort with people (social skills).

2. THE CULTURE OF A PRODUCTIVE ORGANIZATION

- Organizational values are important because they provide meaning, direction, and inspiration to staff.
- Different organizational styles—bureaucratic, entrepreneurial, achievement oriented, and socially oriented—emphasize different values, although none is likely to be found in its purest form.

- Job ownership is enhanced when staff have a profound sense of purpose, experience emotional bonding through fellowship, function in a climate of mutual trust, are involved in all aspects of the organization, and are imbued with a sense of pride.
- Effective managers stress the primacy of the consumer through both the quality of the service and the way it is provided.

Part II

GETTING THINGS DONE

Chapter 3. Strategic Planning

Chapter 4. Implementing Action Plans

Chapter 5. Problem Solving

In this part, you will learn how to

- Gain greater mastery over the future of the organization through strategic planning
- Establish an inspiring mission statement
- Address critical issues
- Take specific steps to implement a strategic plan
- Relate changing circumstances to a strategic plan
- Set achievable objectives
- Anticipate possible unplanned consequences
- Handle resistance to change
- Initiate innovative projects that can be transferred to the entire organization
- Plan for contingencies
- Work out details of an action plan, including implementation of assignments
- Take corrective action based on feedback
- Make decisions by analyzing problems and considering alternatives
- Monitor results and take corrective actions if necessary

Chapter 3

STRATEGIC PLANNING

PLANNING STRATEGICALLY TO EMBRACE CHANGE

Human service organizations operate in a continually changing and even turbulent environment. The needs of clients change over time, funding patterns shift, staff come and go, and the attention of community leaders and the media move to different social issues. Today's focus on homelessness, substance abuse, and child welfare may be ephemeral. Social issues that momentarily capture the community's attention can be replaced by other "social fads." Because of the inevitable and constant nature of change, both internal and external, effective human service managers must be prepared not only to cope with it but also to initiate and embrace it.

Not all change is necessarily good, nor is all resistance to change necessarily inappropriate. Too much change, the wrong kind of change, or change from one activity to another without clear purpose can create special problems, be disorienting, and even threaten the organization's survival. Maintaining the status quo can be stabilizing and can keep an organization from being in constant flux.

Strategic planning is the most common term used to describe the process of addressing change. It is the development of a set of future goals accompanied by a set of actions to help achieve these goals.[1] Typically, strategic planning charts a course for a multiyear period. It helps the organization focus on fundamental issues that require ongoing, concentrated attention. Effective managers employ strategic planning to develop continuity and focus as a means of dealing with change in a more purposeful way. They are also aware that through a strategic planning process they can stimulate their organization to make innovative changes.[2]

Here are some examples of organizations that made changes without the benefit of a strategic plan. First, an organization established to be an advocate for women's issues shifts its focus over time to providing needed services—counseling, day care, and job referral. Its original reason for being, advocating on behalf of women, becomes more difficult to sustain and is eventually discontinued as the organization drifts to a service emphasis—to the dismay of the organization's founders, who think the organization's original priorities have been distorted.

As another example, a service agency shifts its attention from providing counseling in the inner city to offering employee assistance programs for those who can pay a fee. Momentarily, funds increase, but 2 years later its primary funding source drastically cuts its support because the organization has abandoned its original focus.

Finally, consider the example of a health agency coalition that has as its mission providing direct services to women with small children. In its quest to obtain additional money, it modifies its focus from direct service to developing an information database. Its new emphasis on funding moves it in a different direction—away from direct service and toward data collection and analysis—causing a serious schism among staff.

The previous examples describe organizations that altered their basic purposes—from advocacy to service, from serving inner-city residents to serving fee-paying employees, and from an emphasis on health services to data analysis. These changes are not inherently good or bad. They reflect responses to immediate situations, but they did not occur purposefully within the context of an overall plan. Only when an organization gives focused, purposeful attention to selected issues can it be said to be involved in strategic planning.

The previous examples deal with changes in direction that affect fundamental aspects of these organizations, and they are important to address because an organization can drift into carrying out activities that may not be related to its primary reason for being. As Drucker proposed,

> Only when a nonprofit's key performance areas are defined can it really set goals. Only then can the nonprofit ask: "Are we doing what we are supposed to be doing? Is it still the right activity? Does it still serve a need?" And above all, "Do we still produce results that are sufficiently outstanding, sufficiently

危机

Figure 3.1. *Crisis:* Danger and Opportunity

> different for us to justify putting our talents to use in that area?" Then you can ask, "Are we still in the right areas? Should we change? Should we abandon?"[3]

The value of asking these fundamental questions is that they help an organization assess its current status so that it can control its future. Probing these issues helps the organization to gain greater mastery over inevitable internal and external changes. Hence, an organization will be in a better position to determine where it is, where it wants to go, and how it wants to get there.

Two circumstances invite a strategic review. The first involves a threat to the organization. Funding cutbacks, legislation that is detrimental to the organization, and competition from another human service organization that could lure clients away are the kinds of crises that compel a response. Business cannot go on as usual when the organization faces major difficulties; it must react to the crisis or face serious consequences. It is interesting to note that the Chinese symbol for crisis (Figure 3.1) is a combination of two words: danger and opportunity. The sense of crisis can galvanize a reactive response, stimulating the organization to reassess its strategic directions so that the danger may be turned into an opportunity for positive change.

The second circumstance is more subtle and might not seem to prompt strategic planning. When everything is going "right"—when the organization is strong, when funding is ample, when clients are being well served, and when staff and volunteers are feeling positive about the organization—introspection might seem unwarranted. It is at just such a time, however, that effective managers must discern whether there are dark clouds on the horizon in the form of staff and volunteer leader complacency, potential competition for funds, or a possible change in community interest. There are countless examples of both profit and nonprofit organizations that have gone out of business because they were not constantly vigilant in examining their overall performance. Strategic planning disciplines managers to assess the organization and its environment even when things are going well.

If the normal pattern of the organization is to continue providing services without questioning whether they can be improved, then there will be little stimulus for making modifications. An interesting aphorism states, "If you always think what you've always thought, then you'll always get what you've always gotten." By proactively searching for new ways to improve programs or processes that develop staff, you invite the organization to reach higher levels of productivity. You want to be able to slough off yesterday's less productive and less relevant programs and procedures to make staff and other resources available to meet emerging needs and to better fulfill the organization's mission.[4]

For example, suppose your organization has been providing a teenage counseling service for many years, but you now find that attendance is waning, although not enough to discontinue the counseling program altogether. The situation is not yet at a crisis but could be in a year or two. Your analysis shows that teenagers do want the opportunity to talk with someone but in a more informal setting than is now provided by the agency. Your approach is to change your point of contact from in-office interviews to a more informal crafts and sports facility. Your willingness to improve propels you to seek other ways to reach your adolescent population.

Some organizations will even adopt the policy of organized abandonment. Every service, program, and client category is open to question. The organization asks, "If we were not already doing this, and based on the information we now have, would we be doing the same things?" Asking this question invites the organization to make changes.[5] Abandoning things that no longer work pushes the organization to constantly improve.[6] The organization develops the attitude of innovating to improve the quality of services. For example, an organization dealing with substance abuse clients will constantly be searching for successful interventions, and these organizations will be willing to abandon interventions that do not produce results.

Hence, by forecasting its future, setting goals, and considering new opportunities and threats, an organization can concentrate on its most critical problems and choices. Through strategic planning, it can engage key organizational members on every level in communicating and forming a consensus on significant decisions about their future.

Barriers, however, can impede effective strategic planning. The process may consume time and money that could be spent on more immediately compelling projects. Smoldering problems may surface that must be handled. Staff who rely on intuitive or "gut" feelings to determine how to operate may question a time-consuming, systematic planning approach. They may resist the sometimes difficult introspection of examining how their efforts contribute to—or detract from—the organization's mission. Also, organizations facing an immediate crisis (e.g., a severe decline in funding) may have to devote significant energies to the urgent current situation before taking time to think long term. If there is a potential lack of devotion to carry out the plans, then strategic planning can only lead to frustration. Finally, if major decision makers lack the conviction to follow through or tend to make poor decisions based on faulty assumptions, then strategic planning may result in more harm than good.

These limitations should serve as reminders that although strategic planning can be a powerful tool, it is not foolproof. Even so, effective managers must embark on strategic planning to improve performance, stimulate thinking about the future, encourage teamwork, handle organizational issues, and provide a sense of renewal.

DEVELOPING THE STRATEGIC PLANNING PROCESS

Every organization must develop a strategic planning process that is compatible with its own interests, strengths, and limitations. What works for one organization will not necessarily work for another. The format that follows has been used by several different planning consultants and can be used flexibly by most organizations.[7]

Getting Organized

Before embarking on the strategic planning process, consider the following important points. First, effective managers are aware that although the trustees of their organizations must be involved in strategic planning, staff must also be engaged so that each will be committed to implementing the ideas generated. Everyone must share a conviction that the hard work and time involved will be productive for the organization. Second, be realistic about the time investment that will be required. The planning process will require many hours of staff and volunteer time. Anticipate the amount of time involved in meetings and the homework required between them. It may be desirable to set aside a full day or part of a day to give concentrated time to special issues. Third, consider the broad participation of staff, board members, funders, government officials, and others involved with the organization to avoid possible schisms. At a minimum, a committee should consist of key representatives from the staff and the governing body of the organization.

In addition, other participants could include clients and respected leaders and representatives from collateral organizations. Persons from outside the organization could either participate directly in the process or be asked to react to specific ideas.

The reason for emphasizing participation is that the stategic planning process is almost as important as the resulting plan. Working together helps educate members inside and outside the organization, builds commitment, and mobilizes participants to take action.[8] A plan that is not the result of the active engagement of participants will tend to be a lifeless document, the result of ritual behavior, rather than a call to action.

The leadership of the process could either be the responsibility of the executive director, if it is a staff-focused undertaking, or it could come from a selected board member serving as chair of a board strategic planning committee. Some organizations rely on an outside professional facilitator who can provide a degree of objectivity and neutrality to the process.

A note about facilitators: One advantage is that they can assist in keeping the group focused on tasks and also be sensitive to group processes and interactions. A good facilitator will not take over the group's planning process or usurp management's role but will provide a structured process within which decisions will be developed and implemented.[9] If you cannot afford the full services of a facilitator, then consider relying on a consultant or an adviser to provide technical assistance on an as-needed basis or use as an adviser a colleague who has previously been through a strategic planning process.

As you embark on the process, determine whether the strategic plan will be applied to the total organization or to specific units. Also determine what time frame the plan should cover—typically 3 to 5 years. This time period stimulates you to think beyond your current operational planning but is not so far into the future that it could become unrealistic.

Conducting an Analysis

To get everyone thinking as a team, it is important to lay a proper foundation. Provide the group with a common understanding of the organization's past, its current operations, and the values under which it operates. Also present the services of the organization, its staffing pattern, its current and projected financial situation, and other salient facts. A good analysis requires thinking through your mission statement; focusing on fundamental questions; conducting a resource audit; examining strengths, weaknesses, opportunities, and threats; and considering the organizational life cycle.

Developing a Mission Statement

A good mission statement should be lofty and inspiring, concise, and capable of being easily understood and remembered. It should reflect the organization's fundamental purpose and should indicate what the organization wants to accomplish in relation to the beneficiaries of its work. A major emphasis is on defining what impact the organization wants to effect.[10] The following are examples of mission statements:

1. The mission of the neighborhood centers is to support the strengthening of Todo City neighborhoods through programs and activities that are designed to
   ~ provide social services to families;
   ~ increase community education;
   ~ facilitate the support of social, economic, and political participation of neighborhood people; and
   ~ advocate institutional change.
2. As an integral member of the community, our mission is to assist individuals with mental retardation and developmental disabilities in choosing and achieving a life of increasing capability such that they can live, learn, work, and play in the community and to assist and support their families in achieving this objective.
3. Our mission is to ensure that appropriate, timely, accessible, and effective mental health and substance abuse services are available to people of all ages. Highest priority is to be given to adults and children with severe mental health disabilities who live or work in our geographic area.

Most organizations take considerable time and perform many rewrites before they can arrive at a simple statement. To make their mission statements readily apparent to both staff and outsiders, many organizations place them on their stationery, calling cards, and signs at their building entrance. Most important, the mission statement should be used to guide fundamental organization decisions, such as whether to seek certain kinds of funding, whether to alter population mix, or whether to add or diminish functions or services. The mission establishes boundaries for organizational activity and guards against the tendency to thoughtlessly chase opportunities or diversify.[11]

Asking Fundamental Questions

Although each organization is unlike any other and will differ in relation to its mission, funding, and style of operating, all must grapple with four fundamental questions as part of the strategic planning process.

What Business Are We In? Most organizations perform several services and serve multiple populations. How the organization defines these services determines which services and clients it will emphasize. A child welfare agency, for example, could define its basic purpose as ensuring the well-being of children under its care, or it could define its focus as keeping families intact. The former might involve long-term foster care and the latter intensive family counseling.

What Business Should We Be in Now? As part of this analysis, one will also want to review why the organization exists now. The organization may have been formed 10 or 20 years ago with a mission to serve a particular target population but now serves different populations with different needs. Some organizational members may be operating under a myth that the organization continues to provide services for those it is no longer able to serve. One of the values of strategic planning is that it forces organization members to ask the question, "If we did not currently exist, would we be created to meet the needs we are now trying to meet?"

What Business Do We Want to Be in a Few Years Down the Road? As a strategic planning exercise, it may be useful to imagine what the organization might be in 3 to 5 years. Are there new clients to be served, or can the organization prepare itself to serve current clients better in the future? Is there new legislation in the offing that could provide needed funding? To give shape to this "crystal ball" thinking, the strategic planning group may want to capture its ideas about the future in a "vision statement." The group would go through an exercise of thinking how clients, services, staff, funding, and other aspects of the organization might be the same or different.[12]

In considering your vision, you could improve on what the organization is doing now, or you could change your directions entirely. For example, an organization providing activities for the mentally and physically disabled could shift from viewing itself as a good caretaker (offering recreational activities and limited workshop experiences) to providing programs and advocating for legislation that helps disabled persons function more adequately in the mainstream society. The vision statement might then describe how the organization would add job developers and group home staff so disabled persons might function more independently. Thus, the vision statement encourages strategic planning participants to think about what they would like their organization to be in the future.

What Will Happen if We Stay in the Same Business? Continuing in the same direction could have negative consequences in a changing world. For example, regarding your day care program you find that, because of a change in the law, teen mothers are returning to school. You may decide to keep your current location, or you may conclude that you should relocate centers in the schools.

The strategic planning process therefore requires you to intensely examine not only the organization's current relevance but also whether you need to make changes that will better position the organization to deal with its future.[13]

Conducting a Resource Audit

The resource audit provides a structured process to inventory the organization's existing and available resources needed to achieve its mission. As part of its review, the strategic planning committee would do the following:

1. Review programs and services to determine whether each one can be justified in relation to the organization's mission
2. Examine the structure at every level of the organization, including job descriptions, staff responsibilities, and formal processes
3. Determine the organization's management of staff and funding
4. Identify significant community trends and issues that might impinge on the organization's functioning
5. Carefully examine the extent to which other organizations are duplicating services or competing for funding or clients

Major organizational trends and their implications would be identified in this analysis phase. For example, it may be determined that proposed programs may require staff with different expertise and experience; the findings could have long-term implications for upgrading current staff or hiring new staff.

The SWOT Process

Included in the analysis phase should be an assessment of internal (organizational) and external (environmental) factors. The acronym SWOT is intended to convey that, for the internal analysis, you would want to review strengths and weaknesses and, for the external analysis, opportunities and threats.

In examining your organization's internal strengths, you would obviously want to continue doing the things you do well. You would ask, "What are our staff and volunteers best able to do, and how can we build on these assets?"

Examining weaknesses requires candid discussions about where things are falling short or, in the case of programs, what needs are beginning to wind down. Are staff not as prepared as they should be for doing their jobs? Is your organization encountering severe financial constraints? Are you losing clients because the program is no longer relevant or for other reasons? Focusing on weaknesses or constraints will provide imperatives for directing new energies or redirecting efforts to make needed changes.

Of course, internal weaknesses can be caused by external realities. For example, in a public agency, the lack of statutory authority and funding to carry out needed programs may limit the ability to serve some clients, even though they need the agency's services. Conversely, the legal requirement to process every client who walks into a public agency may limit the desired quality of service. These constraints suggest that focusing only on internal improvements may not be sufficient to improve services. By being aware of these external constraints, the strategic planning group can begin to consider ways to mitigate them. Instead of concentrating only on improving staff performance, for example, attention would be given to changing regulations or the law.

The term *scanning the environment* is used to describe a process of examining both opportunities and threats. Scanning involves selectively examining relevant economic, social, and political trends that now or in the future could affect your organization. A change in local public administration, reduced federal funding, expansion of women in the work force, and many other factors can have a powerful impact on the directions of the organization. Some organizations prefer to conduct the scanning process prior to preparing the mission statement because the scan may influence the organization's essential emphasis. As an alternative, the strategic planning group can develop a tentative mission position and be prepared to modify it if the scanning process reveals new insights.

Scanning the environment is no easy task. Thousands of dollars can be spent on surveys resulting in little more than a momentary snapshot of community perceptions. Most organizations have limited resources and so may have to rely on published census data and studies sponsored by local universities, the United Way, or a local planning council. In addition, the strategic planning group could compile its own list of major assumptions or "key realities" that could have an impact on the organization. An agency serving adolescents, for example, might identify the following key realities:

1. Teen pregnancy, already at a high rate, will continue.
2. AIDS among heterosexual adolescents will reach epidemic proportions.
3. Teen unemployment is likely to decline for those who graduate from high school but increase for those who do not.
4. The school drop-out rate will continue to increase unless steps can be taken at the elementary school level to keep students from failing.

These and other key realities would be based in part on data and in part on the general knowledge of professionals or community experts. They should be considered to help determine the future focus of the organization.

Opportunities can be manifested in various ways. A possible new funding source, such as the United Way announcing a special grants program for children, may provide opportunities not previously considered. A recently recognized community problem, such as a drastic reduction in welfare grants, severe overcrowding in detention home facilities, or an increase in the high drop-out rate, may offer opportunities for new services and special funding. Unfortunately, in the human service field, community crises sometimes provide opportunities.

External threats or constraints can be obvious or subtle. A reduction in funding can obviously affect the effectiveness of programs and even whether the organization will continue to exist. Subtle threats are often difficult to discern. For example, another organization beefs up its staff to replicate what your organization is doing, or a formerly successful camping program begins to lose some participants because of the increasing availability of other recreation options. Loss of funds, competition from other organizations, or change in community interest are ever-present threats that may—or may not—require special attention, depending on how events unfold. These threats could prove to be either bogeymen or genuine.

In the strategic planning process, members of the organization may find it desirable to specify anticipated opportunities and threats and then assess whether they have the capability to deal with them. Furthermore, the staff must determine whether they have the requisite resources—time, funding, expertise, and experience—to address the future. If not, are they prepared to do what is required to strengthen their capability? A candid assessment of capabilities will affect planning for the future.

Examining the Organizational Life Cycle

As part of the analysis, it may be helpful to understand whether the organization is in a growth, maintenance, or declining stage of its life cycle. As is true of all living organisms, an organization experiences growth and decline that should be factored into the strategic planning process.

The growth stage is characterized by newness, high energy on the part of staff, and considerable creative activity. The strategic requirements involve developing good communications, establishing credibility, ensuring long-term funding stability, and clarifying internal and external relationships.

In its maintenance stage, an organization experiences slow, measured growth, has long-term stability, and may evidence a decline in some elements of commitment and productivity among staff. Strategic requirements might involve redesigning programs and services, improving operational efficiencies, maintaining ongoing funding, and sustaining staff commitment.

An organization in its declining stage encounters serious reductions in resources, clients, and staff investment. Organizations with a single source of funding are particularly vulnerable if there is a danger of funding being discontinued. The strategic requirements involve a high sense of urgency, a radical alteration in securing resources, and drastic modifications in programs. The sense of urgency necessitates major refocusing or repackaging. Redefining the organization's mission, activities, and allocation of resources can infuse the staff with a new sense of energy and purpose.

In large part, whether an organization is experiencing growth, maintenance, or decline will be influenced by the "industry" in which it participates. An organization providing counseling to adolescents may experience growth (or decline) in drug, AIDS, or suicide prevention counseling depending on the political climate and mood of the community. Hence, phases of the organization can shift based on the environmental context.

Many organizations have elements of the growth, maintenance, and declining stages simultaneously. Prior to examining the critical issues facing the organization, it may be useful to determine the degree to which it reflects one or more of the life cycle stages.

Examining Critical Issues

To keep the strategic planning process from becoming a perfunctory ritual in which participants go through the motions of involving themselves superficially, you must focus on critical issues. You need to ponder what significant problems, what burning issues, cry out for resolution. If you are primarily concerned with how to attract clients to the organization, for example, you may need to focus your strategic planning on various ways to reach them. If your burning issue is poor staff morale, then you would concentrate on how to improve it. If future funding is a concern, this would become your focus of attention. Thus, a critical issue is an unsolved problem requiring resolution because of its potential impact on the organization. Critical issues become "strategic" when they (a) involve high stakes, such as dealing with new funding opportunities or serious decline in client attendance; (b) require intensive attention that cannot be left to routine planning, such as taking the initiative to form an association with other agencies; and (c) cut across various operating units of the organization, such as developing a new service that involves the marketing, accounting, and program staff working together. In summary, critical issues are strategic when they delineate where the organization should be heading.[14] Suppose the critical issue at hand is how well the agency's services are designed to meet client needs. The following are examples of the kinds of questions the strategic planning group would consider in planning organizational programs:[15]

1. What changing community needs are of special interest to the organization?
2. Should our program be improved by (a) penetrating our market to serve more clients with current services, (b) expanding our product offerings

(e.g., group counseling and job finding) to our existing clients, (c) marketing our current services to different clients (e.g., different geographic areas), or (d) diversifying both our services and our clients (e.g., offering a new service—vocational training—to new general assistance clients)?

3. Should we phase out certain services or programs that are declining or are incompatible with other services?
4. Should our basic funding pattern be modified, diversified, or more focused?
5. Should we make major modifications in the organization by (a) replacing some staff with others having different skills or (b) retraining staff to perform their functions differently?
6. Should we abandon programs or services or contract with others?

These are illustrative of the kinds of critical issues and questions that could be raised, depending on the organization's focus of interest. An essential part of the strategic planning process is for each organization to identify its unique critical issues. Sometimes these critical issues can be undramatic, although important, such as installing a new computer system or building a relationship with collateral organizations.[16] Identifying critical issues concentrates attention on areas that are either currently or potentially of greatest concern.

Because every organization has finite resources, it is not likely that more than a few critical issues can be addressed at any one time. Priority decisions must be based not only on the organization's ability to have an impact but also on the cost of not addressing the issue.[17] Once you have selected a few critical issues, formulate actions appropriate for each. Then pinpoint accountability for follow-up and prepare a timetable.

Suppose the strategic planning committee of a family counseling agency is concerned about meeting the needs of its clients. Table 3.1 shows how it might formulate one of its critical issues.

The strategic planning process should take place over a period of several months rather than during a 1- or 2-day retreat so that staff and governing board members have an opportunity to do the necessary homework of gathering facts and preparing action plans. On the basis of information and facts, the strategic planning committee is in a position to determine what the organization should do during the next few years to resolve critical issues.

Table 3.1
Strategic Planning Format

Critical issue

Funds are diminishing, preventing our hiring new staff at a time when client demands are increasing.

Key realities (partial listing)

Internal

- Our staff is committed but overworked.
- Management strongly believes that client needs must be met, despite fiscal constraints.

External

- Federal, state, and local business funding is not likely to expand.
- Other agencies offering similar services are limited.

Actions

1. Expand new funding sources, such as special events and Friends of the Agency Campaign.
2. Expand volunteer base from 10 to 50.
3. Hire and train three nonprofessionals.
4. Develop self-help groups.

Accountability

Four agency task groups, each headed by management staff, will develop plans for each action. The team leaders will report monthly to the executive director on progress being made.

Timetable

Each task group will establish a specific timetable for Year 1 and more general timetables for Years 2 and 3 (see Chapter 4 for work plan and timetable format). First-round plans will be prepared within 2 months.

Drafting the Strategic Plan

From your planning group, select one or two members to draft a strategic plan based on the critical issues identified. The draft plan would likely include the following elements:

- Mission statement (revised if necessary)
- Vision of the organization in 3 to 5 years

- Goals to be accomplished in 3 to 5 years
- Internal strengths and weaknesses and external opportunities and threats (or internal and external key realities)
- Critical issues
- Actions for each critical issue
- Accountability and timetable for each critical issue

By incorporating implementation actions in the strategic plan, you ensure that the planning process leads to results.

In the process of drafting the plan, certain unanswered questions may emerge that will require further deliberations. The value of calling the initial plan a "draft" is that it can be reviewed by a variety of constituents—clients, staff, funders, and community leaders—to ensure that all elements of the plan properly fit and that it is workable. Special attention should be paid to possible flaws or negative consequences so that the final result is a sound and viable plan acceptable to the major decision makers of the organization, including the executive director, the board of trustees or relevant public officials, and key administrative staff.

Transforming plans into action requires that tactics be considered and assignments be made and monitored (see Chapter 4 for implementing action plans). A good feedback system must be in place to ensure that programs are kept on track.

Some organizations may tend to become complacent after the strategic planning document is prepared because of overemphasis on preparing the plan at the expense of making needed changes and following through.[18] So much energy and effort may have gone into preparing the strategic plan that participants assume they have created a master plan that will guide them indefinitely.

Dynamic Planning

To counter what can end up as an inflexible strategic plan, a counterpoint approach is sometimes proposed. This approach may be referred to as "dynamic planning" or "emergent strategy," meaning that strategies evolve over time and are based on modest attempts to deal with changing circumstances. Because of the heightened pace of change, strategies gradually emerge to deal with new situations. The emphasis is on bottom-up learning—encouraging staff to try new approaches and then see what happens. This spontaneous decision-making process is continuously responsive to change resulting from opportunities or setbacks. When changes occur (e.g., new technologies, legislation, and funding alterations), planners may find it beneficial to review mission statements, reformulate goals and objectives, and redraft action plans in an ongoing process that has no beginning point and no end point. In contrast to a comprehensive plan that may attempt to accomplish too much in too little time, dynamic planning continually tests ideas, obtains feedback, and reshapes plans.[19]

For example, an opportunity may arise that allows the organization to implement services to a previously unserved population. In turn, this may require reorienting the mission statement to encompass new directions emerging from changing programs and target populations. Thus, dynamic planning helps the organization deal with political, social, and economic realities and also helps ensure that risks involved in embarking on new directions can be dealt with realistically.

Fundamental to dynamic strategic planning is thinking opportunistically. Managers continually ask, "What new opportunities can we take advantage of?" This is part of a never-ending search for new possibilities. Risk taking is built into a trial-and-error process in which failure is always a realistic possibility.

In Chapter 1, effective managers were described as having a vision of where they want to take their organizations. In reality, through a dynamic strategic planning process, "little visions" frequently emerge. These are small-scale ideas that, if worthwhile, develop into ambitious undertakings. Not all these emerging ideas necessarily emanate from managerial staff.[20] Consider the following example:

> A counselor expressed concern that she could not concentrate on the psychological needs of her clients because they were so deeply concerned about keeping their children fed. Moved by the plight of her clients, the counselor asked her director to allocate space for agency volunteers to bring in bags of food. From this small beginning emerged a greatly expanded food bank, which now provides supplementary food for public assistance recipients seen by the agency.

To respond to today's ever-changing environment, managers must encourage their staff to acquire adaptive solutions and take responsibility for problematic situations. No longer can agencies rely only on leaders who have a vision and require staff to mechanically follow them. Dynamic planning thus requires the work of everyone in the organization and not just those in the managerial role.[21] Effective managers are aware that staff will develop ideas that may provide exciting new opportunities for the organization. All staff must develop keen insights about the possibilities of innovative interventions to meet changing needs.[22]

Dynamic strategic planning fosters an ability to seize the moment of opportunity, take corrective action, and reformulate plans. It prevents premature commitment to a rigid solution that may not allow the organization to be responsive to unpredictable events. If one thinks of a plan as a road map to a destination, there may be detours along the way that need to be considered and to which one needs to adjust.[23] The key elements of dynamic planning are flexibility and experimentation.

Effective managers recognize the importance of the dynamic process. A meaningful strategic plan therefore combines a comprehensive strategic plan and a dynamic planning process that sensitizes the organization to changing circumstances. Strategic planning provides a general course—a direction with specific action steps focused on critical issues identified by participants at a particular point in time. As new events precipitate unforeseen changes (e.g., new competition shifts in funding and new client requests), however, adjustments are made, including if necessary adjustments to the very mission of the organization. Incorporating dynamic planning into the strategic planning process can periodically affirm your current directions and activities or convince you to embark on new directions based on contingencies. Through strategic planning, you try to anticipate the future of your organization, even when you know that future is not certain. Organizations will have to make difficult choices that commit them to particular directions, but these directions may be altered through changing circumstances.[24] Thus, if an organization has taken 2 or 3 months to formulate a 3- to 5-year strategic plan, it may wish to conduct an annual "dynamic" review to determine whether modifications are necessary.

In summary, strategic planning focuses attention on both the process and the content of ideas. The planning process by itself, however, is insufficient. Without a plan of action—strategies—well thought out ideas can easily end up as reports on a shelf.[25] By engaging significant constituencies (staff, board members, public officials, funders, clients, and representatives from other organizations) in the process, a common vision and direction emerge. Bringing various units of the organization together fosters a commitment to cooperate and coordinate in implementing the plan. The process encourages various parts of the organization to mesh their efforts.

During strategic planning, the organization takes stock to determine how best to position itself to deal with its future. The process disciplines the organization to make tough decisions about priorities because not everything it wants to do will be possible with the resources available. Strategic planning clarifies what must be pruned to take advantage of new growth opportunities.[26] It helps to establish boundaries of what the organization will do and what it will not do. Through strategic planning, the organization also determines what special needs must be addressed to develop a plan that is both comprehensive and capable of being modified in the ever-changing human service environment.

SUMMARY OF STEPS IN DEVELOPING A STRATEGIC PLANNING PROCESS

1. Determine why you want to develop a plan for your organization's future. What benefits do you envision from embarking on an intensive process? Do these clearly outweigh possible disadvantages?
2. Ensure that the organization's leadership is committed to the process.
3. Form a strategic planning group.
4. Analyze your situation, including strengths, weaknesses, opportunities, and threats.
5. Develop a vision of what the organization would be like in 3 to 5 years.
6. Prepare (or revise) a tentative mission statement, which may be altered later in the strategic planning process.
7. Identify, after considerable input, the most critical issues facing the organization.
8. Prepare action plans containing 3- to 5-year goals, implementation activities for the first year, and names of those accountable for followthrough.
9. Draft a plan that is reviewed by a planning group, staff, board, and selected persons outside the organization.
10. Implement the plan with the intent of making changes as circumstances change.
11. Update the plan annually, and at least every 5 years conduct an in-depth analysis.

NOTES

1. S. N. Espy, Planning for success: Strategic planning in nonprofits, *Nonprofit World, 5* (1988), pp. 23-24.

2. S. P. Joyaux, *Strategic fund development* (Gaithersberg, MD: Aspen, 1997), p. 31.

3. P. Drucker, *Managing the nonprofit organization* (New York: HarperCollins, 1990), p. 141.

4. P. Drucker, *The effective executive* (New York: Harper & Row, 1985), pp. 59-71.

5. P. Drucker, *Management challenges for the 21st century* (New York: Harper Business, 1999), p. 74.

6. P. Drucker, *Managing the nonprofit organization,* p. 31.

7. B. W. Barry, *Strategic planning workbook for nonprofit organizations* (St. Paul, MN: Amherst H. Wilder Foundation, 1986), pp. 1-72; R. T. Crow & C. A. Odewahn, *Management for the human services* (Englewood Cliffs, NJ: Prentice Hall, 1987), pp. 118-125; F. Moon, Decade of transition: The strategic plan as action blueprint for the 1990s, *Management Issues, KPMG Peat Marwick* (1990, August), pp. 1-2; F. Moon, Step one of strategic planning: Discover your organization, inventory your resources, and identify issues, *Management Issues, KPMG Peat Marwick* (1990, September), pp. 1-3; F. Moon, Building a strategic plan: The second step toward an action blueprint for the future, *Management Issues, KPMG Peat Marwick* (1990, October), pp. 1-3; F. Moon, The annual operating plan: Converting long-term strategies to achievable tasks, *Management Issues, KPMG Peat Marwick* (1990, November), pp. 1-4.

8. D. C. Eadie, *Changing by design* (San Francisco: Jossey-Bass, 1997), pp. 164-166.

9. A. M. Renauer, A trained facilitator can be instrumental in successful strategic planning, *Management Issues, KPMG Peat Maurwick* (1990, April), pp. 2-3.

10. P. Drucker, What business can learn from nonprofits, *Harvard Business Review, 4* (1989), pp. 89-93.

11. D. C. Eadie, *Changing by design,* p. 153.

12. P. Senge, A. Kliener, C. Roberts, R. B. Ross, & B. J. Smith, *The fifth discipline fieldbook* (New York: Currency, 1994), pp. 208, 282-284, 427.

13. S. N. Espy, Where are you, and where do you think you're going? *Nonprofit World, 6* (1988), pp. 19-20.

14. B. W. Barry, p. 40; D. C. Eadie, *Changing by design,* pp. 160-161; W. Weber, B. Laws, & S. Weber, Real world planning: Fresh approaches to old problems, *Nonprofit World, 2* (1987), p. 25.

15. S. N. Espy, Putting your plan into action, *Nonprofit World, 1* (1989), pp. 27-28; S. P. Joyaux, pp. 53-54.

16. D. C. Eadie, *Changing by design,* pp. 144-145.

17. D. C. Eadie, Planning and managing. In *Skills for effective management of nonprofit organizations* (R. L. Edwards, A. Yankey & M. Altpeter, Eds.) (Washington, DC: NASW Press), p. 294; D.C. Eadie, *Changing by design,* p. 163.

18. D. C. Eadie, Planning and managing, p. 454.

19. S. Cohen, *The effective public manager: Achieving success in government* (San Francisco: Jossey-Bass, 1988), pp. 126-127; T. M. Hout, Are managers obsolete? *Harvard Business Review, 77*(2) (1999), pp. 161-168; J. B. Quinn, Strategic change: Logical incre-

mentalism, *Sloan Management Review* (1978, Fall), pp. 3-16; T. Wolf, *The nonprofit organization: An operating manual* (Englewood Cliffs, NJ: Prentice Hall, 1984), pp. 81-83.

20. A. Campbell & M. Alexander, What's wrong with strategy? *Harvard Business Review, 75* (1997, November/December), p. 46.

21. R. A. Heifetz & D. L. Laurie, The work of leadership, *Harvard Business Review* (1997, January/February), p. 134.

22. A. Campbell & M. Alexander, What's wrong, pp. 50-51.

23. S. P. Joyaux, *Strategic fund,* p. 64.

24. T. M. Hout, *Are managers obsolete?* p. 168.

25. P. Drucker, *Managing the nonprofit organization,* p. 59.

26. T. Caplow, *How to run any organization* (Hinsdale, IL: Dryden, 1976), p. 205; P. Drucker, *Managing the nonprofit organization,* pp. 46-48, 55, 102, 142.

Chapter 4

IMPLEMENTING ACTION PLANS

This chapter provides a framework and guiding principles for getting things done. Good strategic planning can easily go nowhere unless effective managers are astute about how to carry out their plans. The best laid decisions can go astray unless managers develop a well thought out plan of action. Working with staff, effective managers establish annual objectives that contribute to the overall strategic plan. They involve staff in the decision-making process because by doing so they ensure proper implementation of plans. They anticipate that staff may be resistant to change, and they develop contingency plans to deal with possible unforeseen events.

In addition, effective managers consider small-scale pilot projects as effective means for implementing plans. To ensure that plans are carried out well, they develop mechanisms for handling details. Finally, effective managers monitor the implementation process to determine whether corrective actions must be taken to keep their plans on track.

SETTING OBJECTIVES

To properly carry out plans, effective managers work with staff to establish objectives. In some organizations, the terms *goals* and *objectives* are used interchangeably, but it is usually useful to distinguish between the two.[1] Typically, goals represent long-term endeavors, sometimes as long as 3 to 5 years, and may even be timeless. Examples of these goal statements are "improving access to health care services for low-income persons" or "improving communications between board members and staff." A goal statement containing a time horizon might be "increasing the financial resources of the organization by 30% within 4 years."

Objectives represent relevant, attainable, measurable, and time-limited goals to be achieved. They are relevant because they fit within the general mission and goals of the organization and because they relate to problems identified by the organization. They are attainable because they can be realized. They are measurable because achievement is based on tangible, concrete, and usually quantifiable results. They are time limited (usually a year); this time frame helps the organization demonstrate concrete results within a specified time period.

Kinds of Objectives

Impact objectives specify outcomes to be achieved as a result of program activities. They detail the return expected on the organization's investment of time, personnel, and resources. The following are examples:

- To place 20 children in adoptive homes in one year
- To secure jobs for 35 juvenile delinquents in 5 months
- To increase the number of foster children reunited with their natural parents from 40 to 50 by June 30

In writing impact objective statements, consider the following criteria:

1. Use an action verb that describes an observable change in a condition—to "reduce," "improve," "strengthen," or "enhance."
2. State only one specific result per objective. An objective that states two results may require two different implementations and could cause confusion regarding which of the two objectives was achieved. For instance, "to reduce the recidivism rate by 10% and obtain employment for 20 former delinquents" is an objective with two very distinct aims.
3. Make objective statements realistic. Do not decide to decrease recidivism rates by 50% if staff and financial resources would at most allow you to reduce recidivism by 25%. Do not set such unreasonably low objectives, however, that the organization's credibility is called into question.

Service objectives are the organization's tally of activities provided or services rendered. Sometimes, these are referred to as activity objectives. Examples include the following:

- To serve 300 clients in the program year
- To conduct 680 interviews
- To provide 17 neighborhood assemblies
- To interview 20 children needing foster homes

Operational objectives convey the intent to improve the general operation of the organization. Examples include the following:

- To sponsor four in-service training workshops for 40 staff members
- To obtain a pilot project grant of $10,000 within 6 months
- To increase the number of volunteers by 150
- To reduce staff turnover from 20% to 10% annually

Operational objectives are essential to enhance the way an organization functions. They are a means to the end for which the organization was established. By providing in-service training, for example, an organization improves the way it serves its target populations.

Product objectives are designed to provide a tangible outcome to benefit a target population. They are used to achieve impact or activity objectives. The following are examples of product objectives:

- To obtain passage of House Bill 41
- To develop a neighborhood family support system
- To review and critique a specific piece of legislation
- To open four schools in the evening for recreation
- To provide a media effort on teen pregnancy prevention
- To establish a weekly clinic
- To distribute the brochure throughout the community
- To sponsor a conference or a forum
- To coordinate a communitywide campaign on mental health
- To mobilize community support for Medigap legislation

Formatting Goals and Objectives

Which of the four types of objectives should an organization emphasize? The answer depends on the goals of the organization and its primary work efforts. Within the organization, different units may need to emphasize different types of objectives. For example, the unit dealing with clients will likely use process and impact objectives; an administrative unit would likely develop product or operational objectives.

Some might argue that impact objectives are the most important. It is not enough for an organization to proclaim how well its processes are working and ignore whether it is having an impact on those it was established to serve. Because impact objectives emphasize measured outcomes, they should be the focal point for most service organizations. Agencies are in business to achieve results, which means they must demonstrate the impact they are having on clients. Therefore, the focus should be on attaining the impact objectives through the other kinds of objectives previously described. The following illustrates the relationship between an impact objective and other objectives that contribute to it:

Goal: To improve foster care services

Impact objective: To decrease the number of children waiting each month for a foster home from an average of 150 to 170 to an average of 100 to 120

Service objective: To conduct a recruitment campaign that will increase the pool of prospective foster parents from 10 to 60

Operational objective: To hire two additional recruitment staff

To conduct an in-house training program on foster care

Product objective: To produce a training manual

The advantage of this format is that it makes quite clear that the achievement of an interim activity or operating objective is not an end in itself but a means to an end. In the previous example, the organization can consider itself successful only if it reduces the number of children waiting for foster homes. The interim objectives of conducting a recruitment campaign and convincing commissioners to hire additional staff, even if successful, are means to accomplishing the primary or impact objective of reducing the number of children waiting for foster homes.[2]

Figure 4.1. Risk, Target, and Impact Populations

In establishing objectives for serving clients, the organization should clarify risk, target, and impact populations. The risk population is the total group in need of help. For example, in a certain community, there may be 800 ex-offenders who could potentially benefit from an employment service. A target population is the group toward which the program is focused. For example, only 70 of 800 are employable and therefore qualify for services. The impact population is the group that actually benefits from the program. Of the 70 served, only 45 may actually find jobs (Figure 4.1).

Cautions About Objectives

Because managers in human service organizations are likely to be engaged in establishing objectives, it is important that these be developed with certain caveats in mind. Although a powerful tool, objective setting does have its limitations. Several cautions should be considered.

First, not all objectives lend themselves to quantifiable measurement. For example, counseling programs are more difficult to quantify than employment or housing programs, in which results are measurable. Be careful, however, not to select only those objectives that are measurable. Perhaps the most important things your organization does cannot be quantified.

Second, objectives should not conflict with each other. For example, the objective statement "to improve the recording of staff accomplishments" may actually reduce the effectiveness of the agency's services as staff devote more time to documenting services than to carrying them out. Achieving the objective "to reduce organizational costs" may result in serving fewer people because part of the cost reduction may limit public information about the organization. Always be mindful of possible undesirable effects.

Third, because objectives may be in conflict with each other, and because overemphasis on one objective may have a detrimental effect on the achievement of others, managers must continually seek a proper balance and a way of integrating the organization's various objectives. There is always the danger that each unit in an organization may independently set and achieve its own objectives, unmindful of its impact on the objectives of other units. For example, in striving to achieve the objective of making the organization better known in the community, the public information unit may be making such extensive demands on staff to handle speaking engagements that less time is available to achieve the objective of increasing client services.

Fourth, the setting of objectives requires everyone in the organization, including the board of trustees, management, and front-line staff, to be responsible for their work. Constituents of all parts of the organization should understand how they are contributing to the objectives and hence to achieving the organization's mission. This is risky because when objectives are not achieved there is a tendency to blame those who let the organization down. Insight that leads to further improvement in service delivery, not blame, must be the outgrowth of heightened accountability.

Finally, objectives should be designed to stretch, but not break, staff. The value of objectives is that they stimulate staff to extend themselves to reach a predetermined target. If the target is set too high and is virtually unachievable, the result will be a highly frustrated and even disgruntled staff. If set too low, objectives lose their potency to foster staff investment and productivity. Hence, effective managers devote considerable thought to the objective-setting process.

ANTICIPATING UNINTENDED CONSEQUENCES

Human service organizations inadvertently experience unintended consequences, either because members do not sufficiently do their homework or because situations occur that nobody could have predicted. Obviously, you can do little about unforeseen events, but with a little extra effort and disciplined thinking you can identify potential trouble spots.

Preparation is essential before taking action. Painters do not just start painting: They devote as much as 80% of their total time preparing a job before ever making their first brush stroke. Similarly, it is important to think through in detail ahead of time what will happen as a result of a decision before it is made. Regrettably, many efforts fail because not enough time is spent ensuring that those who will implement a decision are prepared to do so.[3]

Consider the following example: In a juvenile court, a decision is made to provide intensive probation for delinquents who evidence high-risk behavior, such as repeated felonious offenses. To carry out intensive probation, 10% of the probation officers are given a small caseload (no larger than 10 clients), and these clients are seen frequently. The decision appears to be a good one because the clients begin to manifest a low rate of recidivism. A by-product, however, is that the remaining probation officers have to take on even larger caseloads, with unintended results being lower staff morale and less time available to work with clients, who then evidence an overall increase in recidivism. Had the focus of attention not been entirely on the new program, perhaps the potential negative consequence of the decision could have been prevented.

In the medical field, the word *iatrogenic* is defined as an inadvertent, medically induced illness. No such word exists in the human service field, but there are certainly many instances in which a particular decision, although beneficial in many ways, can produce negative side effects. Just as penicillin, prescribed to cure pneumonia, may cause patients who are allergic to it to go into shock, so too specially created social programs can have negative side effects. Subjecting unemployed persons to a job training program with no possibility of employment, placing clients in jobs without providing adequate day care, releasing mentally disabled patients in the absence of proper community supports, or incarcerating juveniles with no provision for rehabilitation are among many examples of plans that can produce negative results because managers did not adequately anticipate the negative consequences of the intervention.

Indeed, it is a common occurrence that well-intentioned interventions produce responses within an agency that offset the benefits of the intervention. Organizations, like individuals, tend to produce unintended compensatory responses when new efforts are attempted.[4] A person stops smoking but then gains weight. An overprotective mother develops in her child the inability to resolve his or her own problems. At the organizational level, an agency that expands its volunteer activities may inadvertently reduce staff initiative.

An overzealous manager who works to ensure that no mistakes are made reduces the ability of staff to grow and learn from experience.

Thus, certain actions may possibly lead to a detrimental condition that is as bad as, or even worse than, the original problem. Carefully weigh whether implementing a particular course of action may be worse than the problem it is intended to solve.

HANDLING RESISTANCE TO CHANGE

Resistance to change in an organization alerts managers that a problem may exist. Even if staff are involved in the planning process, some may be reluctant to accept decisions that require them to change. In most cases, general and profound changes will create more resistance among staff. This should not be surprising because the more fundamental and extensive the change, the greater the possibility that staff will lose something of value, such as stature, power, or employment. Moreover, if they misunderstand or misperceive change, they are likely to be resistant. For example, a decision to allow staff to have flexible hours can cause them to become angry if they interpret it to mean that they may be required to work weekends. Even positive and well-intentioned decisions for change can invite negative reactions if they are not fully explained.

Resistance is also likely to emerge because of differing perspectives of work demands. What management views as a positive alteration in procedures may be considered by staff to be a disruption of their current tasks and to be an intrusion into their work style. For example, a new administrative request for additional client information may be quite useful in documenting the need for expanded services. To management, this makes sense, but to staff this request may be one more imposition on what they believe is an already overloaded schedule. If it is not possible to reprioritize their responsibilities, then management should at least acknowledge the new burden placed on staff.

Therefore, when making a major decision, anticipate possible resistance so that you will be able to respond appropriately. Staff, for example, might feel incompetent to handle new data analysis responsibilities, and they may need special training before the decision is implemented. If the decision requires the development of different relationships or reassignment to new settings, then build in special support efforts to ease the transition. If the change will cause staff to lose status, then renewed efforts at building self-esteem, such as special recognition ceremonies, may be necessary.[5]

Before implementing change, ask the following: "How are staff likely to perceive the change, and how can we communicate our understanding of their situation during the change process?" Of course, in tuning in to staff concerns, it is important to distinguish who is complaining. Certain staff typically want to ventilate their concerns, in which case a sympathetic ear is all that may be necessary. There may be real justification for staff concern, however, that requires a special response.

Staff will certainly be resistant if they do not understand the purpose for the change. They must understand the rationale for the change and have confidence that the proposal is well thought out and that problems will be addressed. Staff need to know what will happen, who will do it, when it will take place, and how it will happen.[6] Be up front with them about any difficulties they are likely to encounter. A request to modify reporting procedures, for example, will receive more acceptance if staff understand that decision makers will be able to use the information to identify aggregate needs for funders.

The degree of organizational investment of time, energy, and personal commitment in the status quo will affect the extent to which staff may resist change. A new approach to treatment may be difficult to implement because much of the organization's funding and staff training have gone into current counseling approaches. Staff have a stake in preserving their investment. Of course, if the current mode of operation is not achieving positive results or is resulting in dissatisfaction on the part of clients or funding bodies, then staff may be more amenable to proposed changes. Effective managers sense when the forces pushing for change are stronger than those resisting change. Even when resistance is strong, however, effective managers are prepared to exert their influence based on the conviction that the current way of doing things is not producing sufficient results.

Sometimes, it is wise not to implement a plan because staff strongly oppose it. Effective managers tune in to why staff are challenging the change. Certainly, timing is involved in decision making, and the wisest course when in a quandary may be to delay until a more positive climate occurs. Using a football analogy, you would "punt." If staff are currently resisting a plan, there may be good reasons to delay implementation procedures. Rather than forcing a premature decision on them, allow enough time to pass so that new information surfaces or different circumstances occur that could soften their reactions.

Perhaps when you encounter strong resistance, instead of fighting it, you need to draw on its energy source. For example, in the sport of judo, you learn to use the strength of your opponent by taking advantage of a proper leverage point. Staff complaining about new reporting procedures, for example, can be asked to make their own suggestions. Their negative energy can be turned into positive suggestions as they become partners in resolving the problem.

INITIATING AND IMPLEMENTING PILOT PROJECTS

Often, managers must maintain current programs and services and simultaneously consider making significant changes. The effective manager must determine how to generate projects without creating such great resistance and conflict that they are doomed before being tested. One way to deal with this is to create ad hoc temporary staff teams to work on pilot projects. The teams can test new ideas and work out project glitches before the projects are diffused through the rest of the organization. Often, new ideas do not work correctly the first time. Problems invariably occur that nobody even considered.[7] Through pilot projects, staff develop flexibility to experiment with new ventures. If the pilots fail, they can be aborted without serious consequence to the rest of the organization; if they succeed, they can be expanded.[8]

When staff embark on a small-scale, manageable undertaking, when they are committed to the task, and when they operate within a climate that favors innovation, pilot projects are more likely to succeed.[9] The pilot project must be conceived with a reasonable chance for success. By having a clear beginning and end, by having focus, and by achieving modest and measurable improvements, the pilot project team is spurred on to continue their efforts and, later, to spread the word about their success.

A project that focuses on achievable, short-term, and urgently needed results has the best chance of success. A task group can be quickly assembled to focus on problems requiring immediate and urgent resolution. Staff are assigned based on their expertise, experience, or other strengths. Their focus of attention should be on developing a breakthrough that can have great implications for the rest of the organization. They must strive for success in a few weeks (not months), be eager to tackle the challenge, and concentrate on achieving results with available resources.[10]

Pilot projects can involve a variety of efforts: reformulating the information flow of the organization, experimenting with new services, or developing new procedures. Whatever the project, its small-scale nature allows staff to test ideas, be creative, and determine under what conditions the project works. By approaching the project on an incremental, trial-and-error basis, the organization avoids the possibility of a large-scale failure. If something does not work, the team can make corrections before implementing the project on a larger scale.[11]

All of us have had the experience in our personal lives of establishing achievable goals and, having achieved them, then developing the confidence and the capacity to strive for more ambitious goals. This could apply to losing weight, managing finances better, or striving for a higher academic degree. Success builds on success. This is also true with organizations. As a pilot program successfully goes through several phases, the confidence of the staff to tackle more challenging tasks increases. To achieve ultimate success, the original design of the pilot program may need to be revised as staff discover new and better ways to achieve their goals.[12]

Sometimes, a crisis can lead to the creation of a pilot project that mobilizes special effort and attention. Staff are brought together with the expectation that they will be motivated to generate high energy and investment. The sense of urgency demands that the project receive the highest priority because the immediate resolution of the problem is an absolute must. Crisis projects could include (a) expanding outreach efforts to attract more clients or face the consequence of immediate reduced funding, (b) improving safety procedures after a staff member was mugged leaving work, or (c) increasing client job placements by 20% in response to political pressures. Labeling the project a "crisis" focuses needed attention and rallies everyone to find a solution to a pressing problem. There is a danger, however, that must be noted: Short-term successes from crisis management may become so intoxicating that they prevent the organization from adopting a long-range strategic approach to resolving problems. Therefore, be wary of overusing crisis management and having it become a way of life.

Unfortunately, even successful pilot projects may not spread throughout the organization. A project can be terminated because of insufficient efforts to institutionalize it or because current policies and practices are not in harmony with it.[13] For example, a specially designed support program for school dropouts conducted outside of the schools may not be absorbed into the system because of incompatible values and practices such as the inability to give special attention to at-risk students or resistance to modifying the curriculum. In addition, some pilot projects tend to attract extra resources and highly motivated staff not available on an ongoing basis.

It is one thing to initiate change by engaging a small number of staff in a pilot project and dealing with their initial resistances; it is quite another to spread the change throughout the organization and to make it a permanent part of the way the organization operates. If the groundwork has been laid well, staff will be receptive to the change. Also, if they have been involved in diagnosing what needs to be improved so that they do not believe that the change has been foisted on them, staff are much more likely to accept the change. The key is not to overmanage the change process, not to convey from on high, but to engage staff from all levels of the organization in thinking through and implementing the change.[14]

The same approach used in implementing a pilot project needs to be considered when expanding it throughout the organization. Other units need the opportunity to develop their own approaches to the change and to make suggestions that will mend possible flaws from their particular perspectives. The entire organization needs to feel the same excitement that occurred during the creation of the pilot project. Sometimes, it is better to let each unit "reinvent the wheel"—that is, to discover its own way of implementing programs.[15] Those who were involved in the pilot project can be assigned to work with other units so that they can "seed" the new ideas and infect other parts of the organization with their enthusiasm.

In addition, diffusing change throughout the organization requires continuous reinforcement and feedback. Frequent interaction needs to occur between management and staff. This ongoing interest and investment is communicated both formally and through the grapevine.[16]

Sometimes, for the change to take root the organization must establish a parallel or alternative structure to carry out the new program while preserving the original one.[17] Suppose, for example, that the organization wants to reach out to a new clientele such as an ethnic group that previously has not used the services of the organization. Instead of replacing the current outreach and intake services, the organization could establish a special unit to supplement the regular client access process. The new unit would have linkages with the organization's basic services and still develop its own special style, its own consensus on operations, and its own value system. Eventually, the experiences of the parallel unit may result in the entire organization incorporating new ideas and behaviors.

To ensure expansion of a project, effective managers identify and select an enthusiastic, committed staff member to take the assignment. The term *intrapreneur* has been coined in the business world to reflect the idea that one person should be held accountable for developing products and services of the enterprise.[18] Human service organizations can adopt this same concept of a "social intrapreneur" or champion who zealously works to diffuse a successful project throughout his or her organization.[19]

Successful pilot projects can also be expanded through just-in-time training programs for staff. The purpose of the training is not to provide general information lectures but to offer skills training through role playing or simulations for those who must learn new behavior patterns.[20] Frequently, the training is provided in a series of sessions over time so that staff can practice their new skills and share problems they are having in implementing the change.

As an effective manager, you should help staff invest in the new project by describing how services can be improved and, if appropriate, how the staff will benefit. In selling the new change, be careful not to disparage current methods because to do so may discourage those who feel positive about the current mode of operation. Finally, allow time for people to adjust to the change. People have become comfortable with the status quo; they will need time to develop new attitudes and new patterns of behavior.[21]

In summary, initiating and expanding pilot projects in an organization requires an interesting balancing act. On the one hand, top management must be committed to change because it is they who communicate the organization's values and set the implementation process in motion. On the other hand, expansion of the project must have the support of, and a sense of ownership by, those involved in implementing it. Both management and staff must be involved in the process of change in such a way that all staff feel dedicated to following through and implementing it.[22] The challenge, therefore, is to work at finding the right balance so that everyone feels a common commitment.

CONTINGENCY PLANNING

Effective managers assume that certain events can obstruct the implementation of plans as originally conceived. Contingency planning imagines the unlikely; by thinking of the range of possibilities in advance, you may be able to gain mastery over them should they occur.

Suppose, for example, that you are experiencing a large increase in the number of clients needing service. Staff are already overtaxed. To meet your obligations, you have applied for additional funding, and a decision is pending. Among your contingency plans could be the following:

Plan A: If you receive less funding than hoped for, you could consider hiring paraprofessionals working under close supervision.

Plan B: If the funding request is rejected, you could determine the reasons and be prepared to reapply.

Plan C: If expanded funding continues to be unavailable from this one source, you could consider an aggressive fund-raising campaign.

Plan D: If, after reapplying, you are again rejected, you could consider either cutting staff or reducing salaries.

Plan E: If no funding is available, you could restrict the number of clients and redirect unserved persons to other agencies.

Plan F: If new funding is not possible, you could consider an innovative way of working with clients that achieves results at lower costs, such as group counseling sessions or telephone conferences.

As can be seen from the previous illustration, contingency planning helps managers develop the discipline to think through a situation to prepare for possible events that could have an impact on the organization. In fact, a special form of contingency planning is called "fail-safe" analysis, in which one purposefully gives attention to those possibilities that could cause one's plan to fail.

Before you embark on your program, search for potential problems: What political leader or board member or staff member could torpedo the idea? What staff or resource constraints could keep the program from getting off the ground? Which organizations must cooperate if the program is to succeed?" Sometimes, a colleague outside of the organization can be asked to give an objective critique or even serve as the "devil's advocate" to ferret out potentially explosive situations.

Decisions that do not allow for the possibility of glitches are dangerous ones because they give managers the false sense of security that nothing can go wrong. The reality is that plans have a low probability of succeeding unless major problems are anticipated and addressed. Fail-safe contingency planning focuses attention on possible problem areas and forces one to think about solving them before they occur.

Contingency planning is like a game of chess. You have to anticipate your opponent's moves and consider protecting your flank, even as you take the offensive. You cannot be so concentrated on moving ahead with your plans that you lose sight of where you might be vulnerable. As in chess, contingency planning requires your constant assessment of the potential consequences of every move. Unlike a game of chess, the forces that can unravel a plan may not reside in an "opponent" but in more amorphous forces, such as the lack of adequate staff training. The point of the chess metaphor is to encourage you to be on guard for unexpected possibilities, even as you move forward.

Effective managers encourage contingency planning by stimulating "what if . . ." scenarios or questions. In a foster home recruitment drive, for example, you would ask, "What if recruitment materials don't arrive on time?" "What if it rains on the day of the promotional event?" and "What if staff are unable to answer inquiries?" Of course, these things may not happen, but if they do you will have thought about them in advance and taken the proper precautions.[23]

Thus, contingency planning helps to anticipate and thus prevent problems before they occur. Planning is proactive, in contrast to reacting to problems after they occur. Of course, not all events can be anticipated, and in some circumstances you want to have the flexibility to respond to unexpected opportunities. The advantage of proactive planning, however, is that you can minimize or neutralize the possibility of downside risks by anticipating how you will deal with them.

WORKING OUT THE DETAILS OF A PLAN

Attention to detail is a prerequisite for implementing a successful project. By anticipating specific outcomes as much as possible, you increase the likelihood that plans will be carried out properly. Even so, planning involves some degree of speculation; therefore, be prepared to revise even the most well thought out plans.[24]

To systematically structure the implementation phase, it is useful to think of major activities and specific tasks. Major activities can be completed within a specified time period and include the following elements:

- They are essential for achieving an objective.
- They should result in one identifiable product, such as a report, a meeting, or completion of a major assignment.
- They can occur either in sequence or simultaneously with other activities.

Tasks are specific jobs required to accomplish a major activity. Contributing to a major activity, tasks are usually achievable in a few days or weeks by specified individuals or units of the organization. Although specifying tasks can sometimes be time-consuming and tedious, the process more readily ensures the completion of major activities and implementation of proper actions. Moreover, effective managers use the opportunity of programming the work plan to determine whether adequate resources are available to properly complete the job or whether resources should be redeployed from low- to high-priority endeavors. Later, if there appears to be a lack of progress in achieving a major activity, managers can more readily pinpoint the specific problem that led to the breakdown.

IMPLEMENTING TASK ASSIGNMENTS

Two approaches can be considered in specifying tasks: (a) reverse-order planning and (b) forward-sequence planning.[25]

Reverse-Order Planning

In reverse-order planning, the organization begins with the final result to be achieved and identifies the tasks that contribute to activities by reviewing the question, "What must we do just before reaching our final result, and then what needs to be done before that, and before that, and so forth?" until the beginning point is reached. For example, in organizing a staff speakers' bureau, the process of reverse order might include the following tasks:

Promote speaking engagements (last task).

Train speakers (fourth task).

Prepare speakers' kits (third task).

Recruit volunteer speakers (second task).

Plan training sessions (first task).

Forward-Sequence Planning

In forward-sequence planning, the organization begins with what it considers to be the appropriate first set of tasks and then asks, "What should we do next, and what after that, and so forth?" until reaching the end result.

Whether the organization uses the reverse-order or forward-sequence planning approach, it is important to consider the preparation that will be necessary to complete each task.

In actual decision-making situations, organizations usually combine reverse-order with forward-sequence planning. That is, staff typically consider by what date they want to achieve a particular result and then review all the tasks they need to complete prior to that deadline. If the predominate approach is reverse-order planning, staff will find it useful to employ forward-sequence planning (and vice versa) to double-check that no task has been omitted.

TIMELINE CHART

The implementation process requires that controls and reporting procedures be developed to determine the rate of progress compared with the original implementation schedule. The process pinpoints responsibility and identifies reporting dates. By establishing accountability for who does what by when, you have a warning system that will indicate when you are in trouble.

A timeline chart (sometimes referred to as a Gantt chart) is useful for implementing decisions and projects because it provides a visual overview of what needs to be done, who needs to do it, and within what specific time frame it should be accomplished.[26] A timeline illustrates how various tasks should be subsumed under major activities in a comprehensible, easy to construct format. The chart clarifies the beginning and ending points projected for each task and shows at a glance what efforts must be made within a specific time period. For example, in Figure 4.2 certain major tasks in the public relations activity must be under way in July and August. The chart also pinpoints accountability by designating the person responsible and, if appropriate, members of the team. By using a timeline chart, you can determine on a continuous basis whether you are on schedule; if necessary, revisions can be made as a result of new information.

	MAY	JUNE	JULY	AUGUST	SEPTEMBER	OCTOBER	PERSON IN CHARGE	SUPPORT
Develop a plan and structure								
Appoint task force							Ahorn	Kim, Peg
Interview foster care agencies, parents, and staff							Slenk	Metz
Formulate foster care plan							Lapoor	Nalon
Prepare public relations materials								
Identify profile of children							Meyers	Mitika
Identify profile of potential foster parents							Botelli	Owitz
Prepare PR campaign strategy							McVelan	Fume, Fenn
Prepare bus posters							Madams	Jaress
Prepare radio tapes							Jacob	Hilltan
Prepare TV ads							Hender	Hampar
Prepare speakers' kit							Halligy	Queen
Contact public media							Gerdeim	Ebony
Submit materials to media							Curl	Chap
Prepare foster care manual								
Prepare outline and drafts							Callder	Rucy, Brut
Obtain foster parents' reactions							Bedford	Thom, Stom
Revise draft							Ponte	Alex
Prepare staff								
Plan processing procedures							Brrod	Clawes
Prepare phone instructions							Dunkin	Remes
Prepare follow-up materials							Serdan	Vinder
Orient staff							Bosmy	Pacian

Figure 4.2. Campaign Plan (Objective: To Recruit an Additional 100 Foster Parents by the End of the Year)

NOTES

1. M. Schaefer, *Implementing change in service programs* (Newbury Park, CA: Sage, 1987), p. 31.

2. P. M. Kettner, R. M. Moroney, & L. L. Martin, *Designing and managing programs* (Newbury Park, CA: Sage, 1990), pp. 105-110.

3. P. Drucker, *Managing the nonprofit organization* (New York: HarperCollins, 1990), p. 32.

4. P. M. Senge, *The fifth discipline* (New York: Doubleday & Currency, 1990), pp. 59-60.

5. R. T. Crow & C. A. Odewahn, *Management for the human services* (Englewood Cliffs, NJ: Prentice Hall, 1987), pp. 128-132; T. Kirby, *The can-do manager* (New York: AMACOM, 1989), pp. 55-58.

6. R. T. Crow & C. A. Odewahn, p. 132.

7. P. Drucker, *Management challenges for the 21st century* (New York: HarperBusiness, 1999), p. 87.

8. M. Schaefer, pp. 72-74.

9. Work in American Institute, *Productivity through work innovations* (New York: Pergamon, 1983), pp. 110-111.

10. R. H. Schaffer, Productivity improvement strategy: Make success the building block, *Management Review* (1981, August), pp. 46-52; R. H. Schaffer, *The breakthrough strategy* (Cambridge, MA: Ballinger, 1989), p. 5.

11. R. H. Schaffer & K. E. Michaelson, The incremental strategy for consulting success, *Journal of Management Consulting, 2* (1989), pp. 1-5.

12. A. Etzioni, *The active society: A theory of society and political processes* (New York: Free Press, 1968), pp. 296-299; Work in America Institute, pp. 141-142.

13. E. E. Lawler, *High involvement management* (San Francisco: Jossey-Bass, 1986), p. 222.

14. M. Beer, R. A. Eisenstat, & B. Spector, Why change programs don't produce change, Harvard Business Review, 6 (1990), pp. 158-166; Work in America Institute, p. 135.

15. M. Beer et al., pp. 158-166.

16. Work in America Institute, pp. 125-126.

17. Work in America Institute, pp. 120-135.

18. J. M. Newman, Compensation programs for special employee groups, in *Compensation and benefits* (L. Gomez-Mejia, Ed.) (Washington, DC: Bureau of National Affairs, 1989), p. 185.

19. P. Drucker, *Management challenges,* pp. 87-88; P. Drucker, *Managing the nonprofit,* p. 68.

20. R. H. Schaffer, Quality now! *Journal for Quality and Participation* (1989, September), pp. 22-27; Work in America Institute, p. 137.

21. Bureau of Business Practice, *Front line supervisor's standard manual* (Waterford, CT: Author, 1989).

22. E. E. Lawler, p. 219.

23. R. von Oech, *A whack on the side of the head* (New York: Warner, 1983), p. 62.
24. S. N. Espy, Putting your plan into action, *Nonprofit World, 1* (1990), p. 28.
25. R. Brody, *Problem solving* (New York: Human Sciences Press, 1982), pp. 149-151.
26. M. Schaefer, pp. 88-89.

Chapter 5

PROBLEM SOLVING

Once an organization has determined its strategic plan, which includes its mission and goals, it is able to concentrate on daily administration (tactics). Much of this day-to-day management is focused on solving problems and making decisions. Often, problems are complex, ambiguous, cumulative, and multifaceted. Sometimes their causes cannot be fully known, and their resolutions may require the involvement of many different participants. Hence, the problem-solving process requires an effective manager's keen judgment, intuition, and an understanding of the dynamics of a situation. Although there are no cookbook solutions, no simple formulas, it is useful to consider a series of steps to guide the problem-solving process, as summarized in Figure 5.1.

STEP 1: ANALYZING THE PROBLEM

The term *analysis* denotes separating a whole into its component parts. Problem analysis thus entails breaking generalized concerns into delineated segments. Good problem solving requires moving beyond such generalized statements as "staff morale is low," "absenteeism is too high," or "there is poor communication between departments" to achieve greater clarity about the nature of the problem. It involves identifying and examining discrepancies between goals and actual results, specifying the problem as clearly as possible, determining the boundaries of the problem, clarifying different perspectives, and identifying insidious problems.

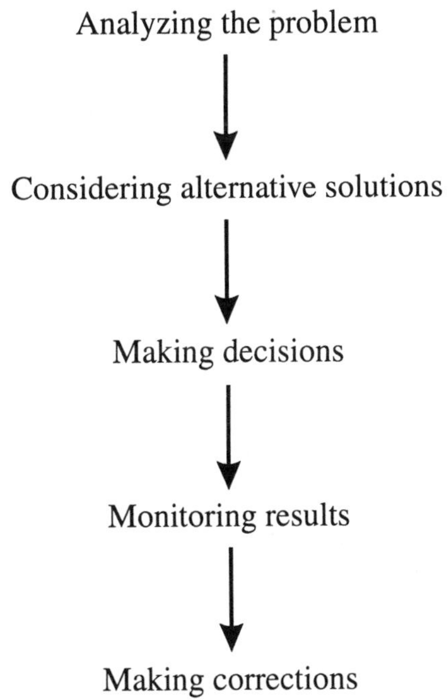

Figure 5.1. Steps to Guide the Problem-Solving Process

Identifying and Examining Discrepancies

A problem can be defined as a felt need or a discrepancy between an existing condition and one that is desired.[1]

One of the major approaches managers can use to identify organizational problems is to determine whether a situation or circumstance is preventing the organization from achieving its mission. Always focus on this first; otherwise, you may become trapped in a flurry of activities and problem-solving endeavors that may, in the long run, detract from your fundamental purpose. Effective managers give concentrated attention to those issues and problems that primarily affect the organization's mission and goals. Search for discrepancies between what the organization must achieve and what actually occurs.

Establishing measurable objectives and then determining later whether they have been achieved alerts managers as to whether a problem exists. For example, in an adult training workshop for the disabled, if your objective of having 80% function independently within 1 year is not met, you know a problem exists that must be addressed. Similarly, a problem becomes obvious, for example, when a unit of the organization does not meet its predetermined objective of contacting 125 clients in a given month. The fact that the unit is reaching only 85 clients should signal concern because of the gap between the predetermined benchmark and the actual performance.

Specifying the Problem

Even if concrete objectives have not been established, staff or management may feel a vague sense of uneasiness: Something is wrong, but, at least initially, there is a lack of clarity regarding what is the problem. Someone might ask, for example, "Why aren't we serving more clients?" A general consensus might be that more clients could be served but ambiguity exists about whether "the problem" is fewer clients in general or fewer clients from a particular geographic area or income level. Does the problem reside in the clients—something operating within them or their situation? Do they have difficulty getting to the agency because of changes in public transportation, or have their perceptions changed about their safety in going to the agency? By taking the time to obtain facts in any problem situation, you can avoid premature and impulsive solutions, or what is captured in the phrase "ready, shoot, aim."

To analyze a generalized problem more specifically, be clear about exactly when the problem occurs, who is affected by it, and where it occurs. Furthermore, strive to understand the causes and underlying conditions of the problem. If, for example, you note that absenteeism among staff has increased, determine whether the problem is pervasive, and therefore indicative of a morale issue, or limited to a few staff, requiring disciplinary considerations.

Trying to identify the cause of a problem can be exceedingly difficult. In reality, a cause-effect chain of relationships can exist for any problem. One could analyze, for example, that absenteeism is caused by low morale, which is caused by feelings of being ignored, which in turn is caused by an organization that is built on an authoritarian structure in which little communication occurs. To isolate one simple cause contributing to one single effect can be an oversimplification. You may not know until after you have attempted to diagnose a problem, formulated a response to it, and obtained feedback that your "solution" is not working. You then may need to concentrate on another possible solution.

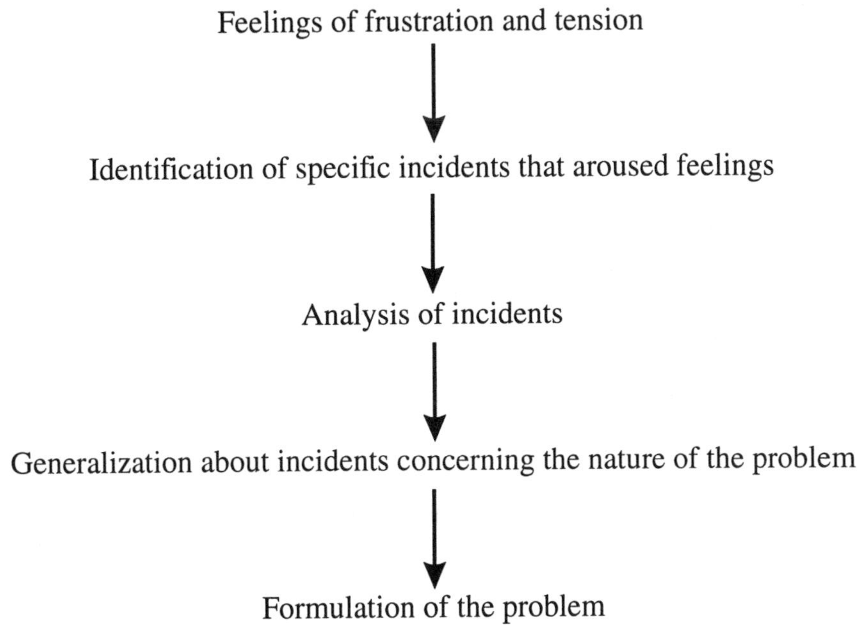

Figure 5.2. Determining the Nature of the Problem

In analyzing problems, an inductive approach of identifying concrete examples or critical incidents can be useful, especially if the nature of the problem is vague. By pinpointing the specific situations in which the problem occurs, you begin to get a handle on it. You move from specific incidents to determining the nature of the problem, as shown in Figure 5.2.

Determining the Boundaries of the Problem

By defining the problem, you set boundaries around it; you determine what it is—and what it is not. A good procedure to ensure accuracy of focus on the problem is to prepare a written problem statement. By putting your thoughts in writing, you develop more precision, and you discipline your thinking. In addition, you have a statement that you can refer to and revise if necessary. The danger of not putting your problem in writing is that your thoughts may remain vague and amorphous and hinder the problem-solving process.

In your problem statement, define key terms so that those engaged in the problem-solving process have a common frame of reference. The simple question "How can we reduce absenteeism?" requires defining precisely what is meant by the term *reduce*—from what to what—and what is meant by *absenteeism*—as it refers, for example, to sick leave, conference attendance, or unexcused absences.

Typically, problems tend to be narrowed too quickly, thereby cloaking the real problem. In conducting a problem analysis, determine whether a particular manifest problem is exceptional or whether it reflects a larger issue. Does a particular problem reflect an idiosyncratic situation or a more general pattern? If it is unique, then pragmatic, expedient approaches may be used. If it is a general problem, then more fundamental change may be required. To treat a general situation as if it were a series of unique events can be a major miscalculation.[2]

If you defined the problem, for example, as "staff are taking too many sick leave days," you limit your exploratory process and may not consider whether organizational policies may in fact be the real problem. "How can we deal with excessive absenteeism?" may be a better way to formulate the issue. In defining a problem, your goal should be to clarify what will be included in the problem's parameters and to decide, at least initially, what will not be part of your initial exploration. Determining the problem's boundaries is a way of moving from an unfocused, amorphous, and ambiguous concern to a more targeted focus of attention.

Therefore, the reason for defining the boundaries of a problem and devoting so much time to its analysis is that by doing so you determine the nature of potential solutions. If you view the problem as absenteeism among many staff, that will lead you down one path. If you have narrowed it to unexcused absences on the part of a small number of staff who are unenthused by their work, that will lead you down another. Before you take a path toward any solution, you should be quite certain that this is the path you intend based on your problem analysis. Therefore, in any process of formulating a problem, be aware that reformulation may be necessary.

Clarifying Different Perspectives

In any discussion, participants invariably come to the table with their own perspectives. There is an old fable of six blind men touching different parts of an elephant. Each one senses the elephant in a particular way based on the part he touches. So too with problem analysis, people will sense a problem based on their individual experience with it.[3] Imagine the following kind of group discussion on why the agency is not achieving its objective of reaching its predetermined quota of clients per month:

Employee A: The problem is that I schedule appointments but my clients continually cancel, and so I find that I have time on my hands.

Employee B: The problem is that clients do not find it easy to get to our agency from where they live. Public transportation has deteriorated, and, unless clients have a car, they are not able to keep their appointments.

Supervisor: The problem is that clients cannot schedule appointments when we're open. When I have followed up with people who have missed appointments, they tell me that if we were open evenings and weekends they would find it easier to leave their children with someone.

Administrator: The problem is that too many staff seem to be absent on Mondays or Fridays and this is affecting our client count. It would be higher if staff were more available on those days.

Each one has a different perspective of the problem, and therefore each will have an approach about how it should be analyzed and eventually addressed. If, for example, employee B's perspective is to be pursued, then one solution may be to design ways to deliver services to clients outside the agency building. If, however, the focus turns to the administrator's perspective, then emphasis would be placed on reducing staff absences. Because perspective is very influential in determining both problems and their solutions, it is crucial that the various perspectives be articulated as explicitly as possible. This should be done by asking participants to convey their different perspectives. As a particular perspective on the problem develops, those with different views will have to decide whether or not to "buy in" to the problem as it is eventually defined.[4]

In all organizations, various individuals and groups are likely to have vested interests—that is, issues they consider vital to their own functioning. These vested interests will certainly influence their perspectives. The management of the organization, for example, is likely to focus on efficiency problems, whereas these may be of little concern to employees. Fringe benefits are likely to be of special concern to employees, whereas meeting legal requirements will be of paramount concern to management. Because of these different perspectives, it is always desirable in formulating the problem to ask, "Who owns which part of the problem?" The ownership of the problem will greatly influence who wants to do something about it—that is, who owns the solution.

Identifying Insidious Problems

Sometimes, problems lurk beneath the surface, accumulating or growing over time until finally they explode. Several analogies can be used to describe this phenomenon: small waves forming in the distance culminating in a tidal wave that capsizes the boat, a small leak in the roof going undetected for many years and finally resulting in its collapse, or a symptomless cancer doing damage to the body. The common aspect of these insidious problems is that they seem too small to require attention, but unless detected early they can cause great damage.

Similarly, insidious problems exist in organizations. They can take the form of small annoyances that, if not addressed, can become significant and explosive problems. For example, staff who are treated like machines eventually find a way to communicate their grievances—through strikes or disinvestment in their work.

Occasionally, a manifest problem identified initially may be a symptom of a much larger latent problem. The high rate of absenteeism involving a significant segment of the staff may, on further investigation, reflect a sense that staff feel exploited because they are not receiving their desired share of vacation days compared with the staff of other organizations. They may be using sick leave as a way of compensating for their feelings of exploitation. If this is so, then the more fundamental problem is how to deal with these feelings. Sometimes, too, it is the proverbial straw that breaks the camel's back—that is, something that appears small and insignificant but inexplicably causes an outburst of negative feeling. Only on review might one be able to trace the series of earlier episodes that contributed to what appears to be an inappropriate reaction. Had the problem been identified while it was minor, the later, more damaging crisis might have been avoided. Clearly, "small" problems should be handled immediately.

STEP 2: CONSIDERING ALTERNATIVE SOLUTIONS

In any attempt to address a problem, it is important to develop and then critique alternative solutions. This approach rests on the assumption that for every decision to be considered there can be a range of alternatives. It is essential to realize that any action we take, any decision we make, is only one possibility out of a multitude of options.[5] We must consider alternatives because there are usually many paths we can take to resolve a problem. This concept is especially useful for those managers who are prone to think their way is the only way. In the event that one of the paths leads us astray, we have others on which to fall back. Considering alternatives also sharpens our thinking for the approach we finally select. Frequently, it is the second or third or tenth idea that can help solve the problem, not the first. In examining how to solve a problem, several precepts should be considered to guide the process.

Developing Criteria

Problem-solving criteria should be established as benchmarks against which to compare alternatives. They should encompass the organization's limits and expectations and will likely vary according to the problem under consideration. For example, with regard to a problem of staff going outside the building for lunch and thus taking extended lunch hours, the solution of in-house lunch arrangements might have to meet the following criteria: (a) annual cost to organization less than $1,000, (b) tasty and well-prepared food, (c) cost to staff limited to the hourly rate of the lowest paid employee, and (d) effective pest and insect control in new lunch area. The decision to use a lunch truck may be made after comparing various alternatives.

Using another example, suppose you wish to alter office space. As you consider different plans, you might establish the following criteria: (a) cost less than $7,000, (b) reduced background noise levels, (c) increased intraoffice communication, and (d) reduced movement between work areas. As you evaluate each plan, you would compare it with the preestablished criteria, realizing that some alternatives will better meet the criteria than others.[6] Although you may want to place numerical values on the criteria as a way of prioritizing them, in reality this is rarely done. Usually, you can make a decision based on a general understanding of which plan best meets the criteria.

Making Ideas Concrete

As you consider various possibilities, think in concrete, future-oriented terms by asking the question, "Suppose we were to select a particular approach, what would we expect 1 year from now?" By anticipating the future, you discipline your thinking to think through one or more of the proposed ideas to determine how they would play out in reality. Recall the in-house food service idea discussed previously. Actually visualize the flow of traffic to and from workstations, imagine staff using the lunch area in the wintertime, and consider the demands that would be made on your facility. By taking time to think through the idea, you gain an appreciation of its possibilities and limitations prior to making your final decision.

Making abstract ideas or plans concrete is especially important in considering ways of serving clients. By visualizing how clients would be served, you determine how they would be routed through your system and how the information flow should occur.

One of the best antidotes to thinking too abstractly in the decision process is to go on the firing line for a period of time. Walk in the same door that your clients use and follow their path through your system. Sit where they sit for a while to get a feel for what it is like to wait in the waiting room. Hear their conversations and observe the professionals who serve them. Call the office as if you were a client to get a sense of how the organization responds. Get out in the field and actually see how the operations are working. As a result of this kind of direct experience, you may be in a better position to judge the value of your current and proposed decisions.

Considering Trade-Offs

Every plan, however good, probably has inherent limitations. In your zeal to convince others of the efficacy of one approach compared to another, you may tend to overlook limitations or negative consequences. To combat these blind spots, build into your thinking the concept of trade-offs to acknowledge that there are disadvantages in addition to advantages inherent in any course of action. For example, your plan to reach out to clients by sending staff to their homes will greatly improve contacts with those who formerly did not go to the office for interviews but at a cost of reducing the total number of clients served in a given period. The concept of trade-offs means accepting that every benefit has a cost. Considering any one alternative idea over others is a matter of weighing whether the advantages or disadvantages of one are greater than those of other options. This probing injects a greater degree of reality into the problem-solving process and forces you to examine the downside of even a good idea before you make your final determination.

Sometimes, the word "satisficing" is used to express the thought that there may be no one best solution to a given problem. The word was coined to convey the idea of finding solutions that both satisfy and suffice. Furthermore, it suggests that the search for an ideal but perhaps unattainable solution should be discontinued if a reasonable one—perhaps having some inherent limitations—can be found.[7]

The concept of satisficing decisions can help the effective manager make imperfect decisions in an imperfect world. An old axiom, "The ideal is the enemy of the good," conveys that waiting to make a perfect solution may prevent one from considering other worthwhile ideas. We can accept the reality that even good decisions have their inherent limitations and therefore not be immobilized into thinking we have to make decisions that will have to satisfy everyone. For example, a decision to shift staffing to serve a selected group of clients means that others will be receiving less. Moreover, if we know our decisions will be satisficing, we can experiment with courses of action that, if they do not work, can be abandoned and replaced by other alternatives under consideration.[8] Agonizing over alternatives can result in indecision, which can be worse than making a less than perfect decision.[9] In short, satisficing decisions help us to overcome paralysis by analysis.

Of course, in making satisficing decisions, effective managers should not be blinded to the possibility that they may not fully or adequately solve a problem. Some decisions will provide only interim or ameliorative relief. Because of resource limitations or other constraints, they may not entirely correct or prevent problems.[10] Managers must live with this reality; by recognizing the temporary nature of the intervention, they can be prepared to seek more substantive solutions.

STEP 3: MAKING DECISIONS

If problem solving encompasses formulating a problem statement and examining potential alternatives, then decision making is the process of choosing from among alternatives and implementing an approach to deal with the problem. Perhaps this distinction between problem solving and decision making is artificial. If there is any value in the demarcation between them, it is that the former implies a probing phase and the latter an action phase. Clearly, one flows into the other.

Keep in mind that making decisions involves taking risks, and you must therefore prudently consider all possible consequences. Also be mindful that in most human service organizations good decision making usually results from involving staff in the process because their participation usually leads to a greater commitment and more integrated follow-through.

Making Risk-Taking Decisions Prudently

Most decisions involve some degree of risk because their impact cannot fully be appreciated until they are actually implemented, and because no one can predict the future with complete accuracy. Given that uncertainty is inherent in risk-taking decisions, the possibility of failure always exists. The following questions can be useful in dealing with decisions that involve risk:

1. Does your decision increase something of value? Ask whether the service you are thinking of adding is available elsewhere in the community and therefore not needed. If it already exists, can you do it better and with fewer resources? If so, then the decision may be to go forward; if not, then the idea may need to be abandoned.
2. Is the decision of such minimal consequence that it can be made quickly and at the lowest echelon possible within the organization? Lightweight decisions should be made quickly so that staff can move on to more important issues. The effective manager helps staff take on small-scale, confidence-building decisions and allows them to make small mistakes. Staff can then grow in their capacity to deal with more significant decisions.[11]
3. Can the decision be considered an experiment so that, if it works out, it can be developed and refined, but if not it can be aborted? For example, the organization makes a decision to provide services away from the main office, but even after you have conducted surveys you are not certain which locations clients are most likely to use. For a period of time, you might try using libraries, shopping malls, or religious facilities. After testing different places, staff will learn which are best—or whether none of them are suitable. The experimental approach allows staff to be open-minded before making a final decision.

4. Are the potential negative consequences of a decision so great that such a decision should not be made? Suppose productivity is being affected by interpersonal rivalry between two units in the organization. Should there be a major reorganization of staff and activities because supervisors are feuding with each other? A painful reorganization to accommodate a rivalry between two units may or may not result in a reduction in tension. Once the reorganization has occurred, even if the results are much less than desired, the decision cannot easily be undone. In summary, you must weigh the benefits of a particular decision against its costs. Indeed, the costs may outweigh advantages and may therefore serve as a deterrent to making what seems like a more appropriate decision.

Risk taking can have both minor and major consequences. Some decisions can be reversed; that is, if something goes wrong, you can shift to another course of action without the organization or the clients suffering. These are risks that you can afford to take. Some risks, however, have great significance, financially or otherwise, and the action may not be reversible; the consequences could be felt for years. These are the decisions you must weigh most heavily. Therefore, in your analysis, ask whether the downside risks are such that the organization could withstand them if things went wrong. When making high-risk decisions, effective managers seek input from trusted colleagues both inside and outside the organization to gain objectivity and differing perspectives.

Being Boldly Tentative

If this statement sounds contradictory, it is because decision makers must be both courageous and flexible with their decisions. To be bold means to go forward with plans that do not necessarily please everyone but are nevertheless viewed as proper after all the positive and negative aspects of the decision have been considered. Compromises and half measures will not do. Being tentative, however, means having an outlook that is experimental and testing ideas on a provisional or temporary basis to determine if they will truly work.

Suppose, for example, you want to mount a program that requires three full-time staff members to organize and work with the residents of the community. You determine that without these outreach staff you are not likely to fully engage the residents, which could negatively affect the overall program. You might decide that using one staff member instead of the required three will only result in frustration and a sense of failure. Your decision would therefore be based either on embarking on the program with the appropriate staff or on delaying implementation until the proper staff resources are available. Resist the temptation to make an administrative or crowd-pleasing decision that, in your estimation, is eventually bound to fail. It is better not to have started than to arouse expectations, leading to more frustration. In this instance, half a loaf is not better than no loaf.

Certainly, some decisions are inherently difficult. Eliminating unproductive programs or removing inefficient but likable staff can produce reactions that are painful, but to have them linger and drain resources may be a worse alternative. In this context, "biting the bullet" has special meaning. During the Civil War, before anesthesia, wounded soldiers either had to undergo amputation or lose their lives to the gangrene that was spreading through their limbs. During the surgical procedure, biting the bullet was a way to endure this painful experience. Hence, symbolically, biting the bullet has come to mean making a painful choice to avoid an even more catastrophic consequence. Your decision to act is based on your assessment that the benefits outweigh the costs and risks. Your decision requires both intellectual judgment and courage.

Because of the fast pace of change, managers will be forced to make decisions when complete information is not available or when there is uncertainty about the future. In these circumstances, managers and staff will need to take risks that may result in failure. The best approach is to recognize these failures, respond promptly, and move forward.

There is something to be said for making tentative or preliminary decisions that are subject to modification. Because any alternative can have negative consequences, and because it is often impossible to anticipate the negative effects of a decision, it is useful to allow time for modifications and challenges prior to making a final selection. This requires a willingness to experiment, to test ideas, and to allow staff and clients to react to an idea before fully implementing it. The aphorism "The map is not the territory" can be translated to mean that a plan, however well thought out, may not fully encompass the reality that it intends to reflect. Trying ideas on a small scale to "work out the bugs" may be necessary before embarking on a bold venture.

Involving Staff in Decision Making

An ancient Chinese proverb states, "Tell me, I forget; show me, I remember; involve me, I understand." Involving staff in organizational problems or decisions that affect them and their performance not only enhances their understanding but also engages them so that they become invested in a positive outcome.

When staff are empowered to participate in making decisions, their sense of self-esteem and competence becomes linked to accomplishments. When they are involved and have a stake in their work, they feel enthusiastic about and committed to it. Effective managers recognize that, when staff have a say in decisions that affect the work environment in general and their jobs in particular, the result is greater job involvement and satisfaction.[12] In other words, when staff have been part of the problem-solving process, the implementation process will flow quite naturally. Shared decisions work because there is authentic collaboration.[13]

Every effective manager has had the experience of turning problems over to staff and seeing positive results emerge. For example, one manager concerned with the high rate of absenteeism asked the employee committee to wrestle with the issue. The committee came up with the idea of rewarding staff who had fewer than three absences a year with an extra day's vacation. The overall agency record improved by 10%. As another example, managers in one agency who were concerned that clients were not attending scheduled appointments formed a task force of outreach staff to explore possible solutions. After many discussions, the staff concluded that the agency should borrow a vehicle to transport clients three mornings a week from a nearby agency that needed its minivan only in the afternoons. Staff also agreed to be available on a rotating basis two nights each week to meet with clients who found it difficult to make day appointments. (For more discussion on task forces, see Chapter 6.)

Genuine staff involvement does exact a price from both management and employees. Supervisors may believe that traditional prerogatives are being undermined and that staff involvement dilutes their authority. Effective managers accept the trade-off of diminished control for increased staff involvement because employee ideas are needed to improve the quality, service, productivity, and efficiency of the organization.[14] Another concern is that staff may have to invest considerable time in meetings that take them away from other assignments. In the long term, however, time invested in the process of work improvement will likely increase their ownership in the organization's work and a commitment to be more productively engaged in their jobs.[15]

Japanese business managers have long been aware that the participatory decision-making process takes more time, but once decisions are made the implementation process quickly proceeds because those who will be carrying out the decision have already been consulted.[16] In the United States, both profit and nonprofit organizations increasingly rely on task forces for engaging staff and implementing plans.

The director of a $100 million organization whose mission is to improve the lives of those with mental retardation and developmental disabilities wrote the following about the importance of staff involvement:

> Based on my years of experience, the single most important element in the success of any organization is gaining, maintaining, and enhancing the investment of the participants in the accomplishment of the mission, goals, and objectives of the organization. I have learned through often bitter experience that simply "being in charge" is no guarantee of success. What I have found to be most effective in gaining improvements in effectiveness and efficiency is placing a greater share of the burden of responsibility for success upon the individual members of the organization.
>
> The only way I know to accomplish this is to encourage people to "use their noodles" effectively by not presuming that either I or some other person in charge will have the right solution. In this way, everyone's hands are on the oars, so to speak, and our job as managers is to help guide the process by presenting enough valid information and support so that staff will raise pertinent questions and propose valid ideas. Of course, what one discovers along the way is that this requires a rather high level of knowledge and intelligence among the members, so it is necessary to be much more selective in the appointment of staff.
>
> What typically happens if the process works right is that the atmosphere created or "culture" is one of responsibility to each other, to the mission of the organization, and to the public. Malingerers typically do not last very long in such an environment.[17]

Watching Out for Decision-Making Pitfalls

Making difficult decisions is undoubtedly one of the greatest challenges that managers face. To improve their decision-making processes, managers should be aware of the following flaws that may lead them astray: (a) clinging to the familiar, (b) overly justifying past decisions, (c) only seeking confirming supporting evidence to support one's case, and (d) framing issues poorly.[18]

Clinging to the Familiar

Managers, like most people, tend to base decisions on information they have received in the past. For example, in estimating the number of clients to be served in the following year, you may be unduly influenced by the number that you served the previous year, even though circumstances might have changed. Relying on old information may not necessarily be conducive to dealing with current realities. Therefore, it is important to be open-minded in seeking information and opinions from a variety of sources to push your mind in fresh directions.

This flaw is also related to holding on to the status quo for decision making. It is safer to rely on the familiarity of the status quo than to take responsibility for trying something that is not familiar and that may be subject to criticism. In most organizations, particularly large bureaucratic ones, people are more likely to be sanctioned for doing something than for doing nothing. Omission is safer than commission. The consequence of standing still as the world is moving is failing to seize new opportunities. Maintaining the status quo may be the best choice, but you do not want to choose it just because it is comfortable. Always consider other possible options, and weigh the positives and negatives before making a decision.

Defending Past Decisions

This flaw is based on making a previous choice and justifying it even when it is no longer valid. For example, you may have hired an employee and provided extensive training only to realize belatedly that you should not have hired that person in the first place. Making an investment of time and money in the incompetent employee is irrecoverable, but rather than dismiss the individual you choose to live with your mistake. If you dismiss the poor performer, you may believe that you will be perceived as having poor judgment. It may seem better to keep the employee, even though this decision compounds your previous, faulty decision.

To deal with this flaw in decision making, it is helpful to accept that even the wisest of us make errors in judgments. Develop the kind of organizational climate that allows people to acknowledge their mistakes and then be able to move on. Identify situations that are not working out. Accept that decisions made earlier, based on the information then at hand, may now require reassessment.

Seeking Confirming Evidence

Because managers all have biases, they may tend to seek out "facts" that confirm their point of view while avoiding data that contradict it. Therefore, the tendency is to decide on a course of action and then to be convinced the position is right, based on information that supports it, while ignoring data that may challenge it. The remedy is to develop a mind-set of seeking out data from a variety of sources and to permit oneself to be genuinely exposed to counterarguments. For many managers, the idea of playing out "On the one hand . . . On the other hand . . ." may cause them to feel an uncomfortable degree of ambiguity before making a final decision. This honest exploration, however, will sharpen one's thinking. Avoid putting your subordinates in the position of being "yes people" and of only feeding back your preconceived ideas. Encourage discussions in which ideas can be offered freely and easily—and then be challenged.

Framing the Question Too Narrowly

A poorly framed issue can greatly affect decision making. If you ask the question, "How can we make transportation more available for our clients so that they can arrive for their appointments?" you invite discussions regarding transportation. If you frame the issue as "How can we make our services more accessible to our clients?" however, you open up many issues, including the hours that your agency is open, the possibility of using your van to go where your clients are, and even the idea of decentralizing services. To avoid adverse effects of improperly framing the problem, consider reframing it in different ways. Examine, especially at the end of your reframing process, whether a different solution might have been implemented if you reframed the question. When others on your staff make recommendations, explore whether the issue should be framed differently.

The previously mentioned common flaws in decision making reveal that perceptions and biases can influence choices. Being aware of these tendencies can result in your being reflective about your assumptions and disciplining your thinking so as to reduce errors in judgment.

STEP 4: MONITORING RESULTS

The decision-making process is not complete until managers and staff review the results of their efforts. In the course of carrying out activities and tasks, some actions will result in partial or even complete failures. Staff will make mistakes, errors in judgment will occur, and some things will inevitably go wrong. Monitoring results is the best way to assess whether the current reality compares with plans made earlier.

As discussed in Chapter 4, monitoring results should be based on objectives that have been written in advance. Objectives should be quantifiable or measurable in a clear way so that their success or failure can be determined during the review process. This helps the organization conduct an assessment by allowing it to compare intended results with actual outcomes.

To ensure accountability for results, organizations must determine standards for monitoring and controlling activities. For every objective, there should be a performance indicator that will clearly demonstrate the extent to which the objective is being achieved.

This is difficult for many human service organizations because the outcomes of services are quite variable and do not easily lend themselves to quantifiable and objective data analysis. It is difficult enough to determine in some quantifiable way, for example, the extent to which a couple has improved its marital relationship through counseling; trying to aggregate in some reasonable format the progress made by 220 couples seen during a year is indeed formidable. Demands for increased accountability, however, make evaluation of results one of the major challenges that human service organizations must address.

Although recognizing the tremendous challenge involved in developing performance measures, agencies nevertheless have options for monitoring services, including the following:

1. Improvement in the number of program participants
   - ~ *Example:* the number of persons who remain employed for 6 months
   - ~ *Example:* reduction in the rate of recidivism among previously convicted drug addicts
   - ~ *Example:* the number of elderly persons in a nutrition program who maintain independent living
2. Satisfaction of program participants
   - ~ *Example:* the number of consumers who rate the counseling service as satisfactory
3. Improvement in service efficiency
   - ~ *Example:* reduction in waiting time

~ *Example:* improvement in response time for emergency requests

Effective monitoring requires good input of information and proper packaging for decision makers. With the prevalence of computers, reports can be generated to reveal deviations from targets. In this way, client information audits can reveal discrepancies between predetermined objectives and actual performance in much the same way that budget analyses are conducted to reveal variances in financial projections.

For information to be useful in the monitoring process, it must be timely and relevant. The information must be significant both for reporting to external funders and policymakers and for internal decision making. It must be user-friendly and not so complicated that staff are overwhelmed by it. Such information should be useful not only for analyzing the impact of services, as discussed previously, but also in conducting analyses of the activities and work of the organization's units. A good information system should be able to answer questions such as the following:

- Are the activities of the unit contributing to the accomplishment of objectives?
- Are costs for conducting the work excessive in relation to meeting objectives?
- Are services provided in a timely manner?
- Is the level of service improving or declining?
- Are staffing levels appropriate for accomplishing objectives?

STEP 5: MAKING CORRECTIONS

The purpose of monitoring is to identify performance deviations so that corrective action can be taken.[19] The value of identifying deviations from predetermined standards is to stimulate staff to think about how they can get back on course or to revise the objectives so that they are more realistic. Self-correction is possible only if, as a result of the self-assessment process, the organization is prepared to ask difficult questions. If the organization does achieve its objectives, the following questions could be asked:

- Given the nature of the problem and the resources that were available, were the objectives set too low?
- Was the cost worth the accomplishment?

- Even though you achieved the objectives, does the basic problem remain essentially unchanged?
- Does solving this particular problem create other problems that must be handled?
- Has reaching these particular goals interfered with the achievement of other objectives; if so, do the balances have to be redressed?

If the organization does not achieve its objectives, the following questions should be asked:

- Were adequate resources (staff and funding) available to do the job?
- Were objectives set unreasonably high?
- Was the timetable appropriate?
- Given the time and financial constraints and other demands, should the organization redirect its energies to other broad problem areas?

The review of success, partial success, or failure of objectives provides a springboard for future decision making. Because organizations generally operate under less than ideal conditions, they may achieve some objectives partially and others not at all. Through the monitoring process, staff may become keenly aware that a discrepancy exists between their aspirations and the actual outcomes. They may not have been able to select the optimum solution for a given problem because of inadequate resources, political constraints, time pressures, or finances. When not able to provide the optimum solution, they may have to settle on a second- or third-best approach. Confronted with this reality, staff can either despair and do nothing or they can use the opportunity to determine changes that need to be made in the problem-solving process.

This dynamic quality of decision making is evident, paradoxically, even if one succeeds. Solving one problem sometimes creates or uncovers another. Suppose, for example, that to encourage staff to develop more initiative and independence you send them to special training programs. As a result, they are more prone to challenge supervisors and the organization's authority. This newly created problem may require supervisors to be trained in dealing with staff who raise provocative issues that challenge traditional ways of doing things. Thus, the resolution of one problem may create other problems that then must be dealt with, suggesting that the decision-making process is never-ending. Obviously, this does not apply in all instances, but it may help to explain why one must always be vigilant in regard to the affairs of an organization.

In summary, the problem-solving process is dynamic and subject to continuous revision. It involves analyzing problems, establishing objectives, developing alternatives through both rational and creative approaches, and designing and implementing action plans. Monitoring and assessing results promotes a review of whether to make changes at any point in the process. For example, problems may need to be redefined because the objectives established to address them are set too low and are unchallenging, because the objectives are set too high and are difficult to achieve, or because the objectives did not solve problems and new objectives need to be developed that are more on target. Perhaps you need to consider a different strategy that reflects changing circumstances. Finally, the activities and tasks you choose may require alteration if it becomes obvious that they are insufficient and will not achieve your desired objectives. It is through this continuous review and revision that an organization can take necessary corrective actions.

The willingness to base decisions on a critical review of changing circumstances is at the core of the problem-solving process. This attitude reflects a planning style that is open to constantly changing conditions, flexible in adapting to new needs, and capable of making modifications based on new situations.[20] By accompanying a built-in review with flexibility, an organization can avoid adhering to an approach that does not work. It embraces the complex and kaleidoscopic nature of the real world in which everything is in constant flux. The problem-solving process is never-ending and ever challenging.

NOTES

1. C. H. Kepner & B. B. Tregoe, *The rational manager* (New York: Berkley, 1974), pp. 20, 44-47; R. G. Murdock & J. E. Ross, *Information systems for modern management* (Englewood Cliffs, NJ: Prentice Hall, 1975), p. 471.
2. P. Drucker, *The effective executive* (New York: Harper & Row, 1985), p. 125.
3. P. M. Kettner, R. M. Moroney, & L. L. Martin, *Designing and managing programs* (Newbury Park, CA: Sage, 1990), pp. 39-40.
4. R. Brody, *Problem solving* (New York: Human Sciences Press, 1982), p. 27.
5. V. Dishy, *Inner fitness* (New York: Doubleday, 1989), p. 75.
6. M. Doyle & D. Straus, *How to make meetings work* (New York: Berkley, 1976), p. 240.
7. R. G. Murdock & J. E. Ross, p. 485.

8. T. J. Peters & R. H. Waterman, *In search of excellence: Lessons from America's best run companies* (New York: Harper & Row, 1982), pp. 134-135.

9. E. Bliss, *Getting things done* (New York: Bantam, 1976), p. 71.

10. C. H. Kepner & B. B. Tregoe, p. 132; H. Reynolds & M. E. Tramel, *Executive time management* (Englewood Cliffs, NJ: Prentice Hall, 1979), p. 164.

11. R. Townsend, *Further up the organization* (New York: Knopf, 1984), pp. 50-55.

12. R. S. Schuler, *Personnel and human resource management* (3rd ed.) (St. Paul, MN: West, 1987), p. 437.

13. M. Doyle & D. Straus, p. 243.

14. R. Stayer, How I learned to let my workers lead, *Harvard Business Review, 6* (1990), pp. 66-83.

15. Employment involvement: What it's about, *Commitment Plus, 9* (1989), pp. 1-4.

16. W. Bowen (Ed.), Japanese managers tell how their system works, *Fortune* (1977, November), pp. 127-138.

17. M. Donzelia, personal communication (1991, December).

18. J. S. Hammond, R. L. Keeney, & H. Raiffa, The hidden troups in decision making, *Harvard Business Review* (1998, September/October), pp. 47-58.

19. R. T. Crow & C. A. Odewahn, *Management for the human services* (Englewood Cliffs, NJ: Prentice Hall, 1987), p. 97.

20. R. Brody, p. 198.

Part II Review

GETTING THINGS DONE

3. STRATEGIC PLANNING

- Strategic planning helps managers anticipate change and take steps to prepare for it.
- Through the process of strategic planning, the entire organization—staff, board of trustees, funders, public officials, and management—develops a focus and a common direction.
- Use the strategic planning process to examine fundamental questions such as "What business should we be in now and also 3 to 5 years from now?"
- After examining internal strengths and weaknesses and external opportunities and threats, the organization should be able to identify critical issues. The organization should develop a mission statement that clearly and succinctly expresses an inspiring vision of what it intends to achieve.
- Strategic planning should be a dynamic process that allows the organization to respond to new developments and unforeseen changes. Be prepared to revise and update the plan as circumstances warrant.

4. IMPLEMENTING ACTION PLANS

- To heighten accountability for getting things done, set achievable and measurable objectives.
- Distinguish between impact, activity, process, product, and operational objectives. Establish objectives that challenge staff. Chart progress toward achieving objectives so that staff can see the results of their work.

- Examine possible consequences—negative and positive—for every plan.
- Expect staff, sometimes for good reason, to resist change. Consider ways either to address the resistance or to modify original plans based on it.
- Develop pilot projects to obtain achievable, short-term, and urgently needed results. Then take steps to diffuse the innovation throughout the organization.
- Develop contingency plans ("what if" scenarios) because things can go wrong.
- Concentrate on the details of a plan, such as specifying assignments and preparing a timeline.

5. PROBLEM SOLVING

- Determine if a problem exists by identifying whether there is a discrepancy between what you want to achieve and actual results.
- Sharpen the focus of a problem by defining its boundaries. Clarify different perspectives on the problem.
- Distinguish manifest from latent problems. Also clarify whether the problem is unique and isolated or pervasive.
- Watch out for insidious problems because if they are not addressed they can eventually cause much damage.
- Follow the sequential problem-solving process of analyzing the problem, considering alternatives, making decisions, monitoring results, and making corrections.
- In the decision-making process, develop criteria to be used in weighing various alternatives. Also, strive to make abstract ideas concrete and specific.
- Involvement of staff in vital issues concerning the organization heightens their investment and commitment.
- Consider that risks and trade-offs are involved in every decision.
- An assessment should always occur, if only to determine what corrective actions, if any, need to be implemented.

Part III

ENHANCING EMPLOYEE PRODUCTIVITY

In this part, you will learn how to

- Diagnose a time problem
- Make the best use of time to get things done
- Establish priorities for you and your staff
- Avoid time-wasting efforts
- Combat procrastination
- Recruit and match the right staff to the job
- Conduct a nondiscriminatory interview
- Provide proper staff training
- Relate organizational structure to functions
- Undertake a job analysis to increase employee productivity
- Restructure jobs to deal with changing circumstances
- Use job enrichment to increase staff commitment
- Conduct a workload analysis to deploy staff properly
- Set up the physical environment to foster positive work attitudes
- Deal with the special problems of substance abuse and AIDS

- Take corrective actions to deal with unproductive employees
- Terminate employees properly
- Help staff deal with stress
- Manage staff diversity
- Deal with sexual harassment in the workplace
- Address complacency and stagnation
- Be sensitive to inequities

Chapter 6

TIME MANAGEMENT

FACTORS AFFECTING TIME MANAGEMENT

Despite our best efforts to use time wisely, we tend to waste precious moments. Why are we not able to gain better control of our time? Many explanations can account for why managing time is a major problem.

First, managers' jobs are nonroutine, and their days are filled with interruptions and unexpected requests for their time: important phone calls that interrupt the flow of work, emergency conferences to deal with crises, correspondence needing immediate response, and staff complaints that require special attention. As a result of these constant interruptions, the attention span of most managers for any given task is quite limited. Most business executives can devote 30 minutes or more without interruption only once every 3 days and typically can devote less than 9 minutes to any one issue.[1] Managers in the corporate world, in fact, often do not completely plan their days. They carry on brief and personal conversations with people outside their own immediate chain of command to feel the pulse of the organization. Even successful managers "waste" time walking through the halls of their organization engaged in random conversations that offer them the opportunity to gain insight into what staff are thinking. They build strong human relationships and networks that may prove useful to them at a later time.[2] Managers in human service organizations use their time in a similar manner.

Second, managers also have ancillary responsibilities. Not only do managers have demands that are inherent in the job but also their positions require them to be on committees for other organizations, attend ceremonial functions, and communicate with colleagues outside of their organizations. They live in an interdependent world that requires them to respond to colleagues' requests and agenda items as part of the give-and-take of professional relationships.

Third, natural time wasters are built into managers' jobs. Salespersons call and ask them to think about the latest telephone or computer innovations. Colleagues ask if they can take time to talk with a friend who wants to gain information about the job market. Managers find themselves frittering away time doing nonessential work. They spend time sorting through junk mail and returning phone calls to people who do not answer.

Finally, certain tasks have limited payoffs. Some assignments are risky because their outcomes are unpredictable and can result in failure. Taking precious time to work on a proposal that may not get funded or advocating for legislation that may not be passed, however, is a necessary aspect of managers' work that, although frustrating and time-consuming, may lay the foundation for later successes.

As a result of these and other demands on time, managers are unable to give concentrated attention to important priorities that could help them achieve the organization's mission and goals. They have a greater list of things to do than can ever be accomplished and therefore tend to end each day feeling frustrated and overwhelmed. They have a gnawing and unproductive sense of frustration for having taken on too much and not accomplishing what they consider to be most important. Faced with this ongoing demand on time, effective managers should give special attention to diagnosing problems that are preventing them from using time more efficiently. In the following sections, some practical suggestions on diagnosing and planning time are discussed.

DIAGNOSING THE TIME PROBLEM

To get a better handle on how your time is spent, try a self time study. Keep a time record analysis as shown in Figure 6.1 for each day of a normal workweek to help you determine what activities are consuming your time.[3]

1. Enter on the appropriate line what you are doing every 15 minutes.
2. At the end of each day, write in the priority column A, B, C, or D.
   - Column A: Your activity was important and urgent.

Time	*Activity*	*Priority A-B-C-D*
8:30 a.m.		
8:45 a.m.		
9:00 a.m.		
9:15 a.m.		
9:30 a.m.		
4:00 p.m.		
4:15 p.m.		
4:30 p.m.		
4:45 p.m.		
5:00 p.m.		

Figure 6.1. Time Record Analysis

~ Column B: Your activity was important but could have been done at a different time.
~ Column C: Your activity was low priority but of some marginal value.
~ Column D: It was not necessary for you to be involved in the activity.

Of course, the definition of what is high or low priority is somewhat subjective but certainly should be based on expected accomplishments you have established for yourself and your unit. Identify which activities (e.g., lengthy phone conversations, drop-in visitors, and unproductive meetings) might be curtailed because they have little to contribute to your goals and objectives.

An alternative diagnosis method is to keep track of your time on a selective basis, focusing on those problem areas you believe are consuming an inordinate amount of time.[4] This kind of selective record keeping can identify your trouble spots. Of those activities taking more than 1 hour per week, ask

- Which could be eliminated?
- Which could be done in half the time or less?
- Which could be delegated to someone else in the organization?

Asking these questions can help you determine where to focus your efforts and revise your work patterns.[5]

Another approach is to do what one director of a children's institution does with his employees. When staff complain about not having enough time to complete administrative responsibilities because of the daily demands of working with the children, he helps them distinguish the urgent from the important based on previously agreed-on priority objectives. He requests that they list their typical activities at the end of a given week and the amount of time devoted to each. Reviewing time in supervisory conferences provides clues as to which activities can be given lower time investments to free up time for those of high priority based on mutually determined objectives.

To conduct an employee time study,[6] summarize how your time is spent. Those categories shown in Figure 6.2 were identified, for example, as major categories in the children's institution mentioned previously. The major categories in your own work will differ, so modify the chart to fit your particular situation.

In examining the data, determine whether you are concentrating on the correct priorities designed to achieve your objectives and whether you are leaving sufficient time for long-range projects. Use the chart to determine with your staff where time needs to be allocated. The purpose of this review is to make certain that all time is concentrated on the highest priority activities.

PLANNING THE USE OF TIME

Because employees typically believe they have too much to do in too little time, working harder or longer is not a solution. Effective staff limit the amount of unproductive time and place greater emphasis on those activities that have the greatest importance in relation to mutually agreed-on objectives. It is easy to get caught in the "activity trap" in which time is filled with busywork that is not focused on the highest priorities and is not goal directed.

The best advice is to plan your use of time. In so doing, however, you may experience a paradox: You may not have enough time to plan and yet you cannot gain more time until you do. Certainly, planning takes time, but planning saves time. In general, those who do not plan sufficiently devote too much time to correcting, controlling, and monitoring staff activities. Take time to plan!

Employee Name: ______________________________

Actvity Categories	*Hours Spent*
Direct contact with children	
Individual interviews	19
Interviews with family	4
Contacts with outside agencies	
Preparing reports	2
Phone contacts	1
Conferences	4
Contacts with colleagues	
Conferences	3
Training	2
Administrative	
Daily reports	3
Monthly reports	2
Total week	40

Figure 6.2. Employee Time Study

DETERMINING PRIORITIES

Priorities can be based on urgency or importance. Activities that are important but not urgent tend to be put aside. For instance, handling a staff complaint could take precedence over a report due next week, even though you recognize the report may take 25 hours to accomplish. When your work is unstructured and open-ended and you are able to function with considerable autonomy, you may experience little pressure to complete an assignment immediately and therefore may tend to delay working on it. Because it is possible to wait, and because other matters always press for your attention, you ignore the task until suddenly it demands your attention. Hence, to avert disaster, you must give attention to important, although not necessarily urgent, matters.

Only by anticipating what you need to accomplish over a long period of time and preparing for these tasks can you avoid the possibility of constant turmoil—that is, handling one problem after another on a crisis basis. Of course, if you enjoy the sense of panic, the thrill of staying up all night, the rush of excitement that comes with handling last-minute crises, then you can ignore these suggestions.

How does one determine priorities? First, identify those activities you judge to have the greatest return on your investment of time. An hour spent now on preparing a memo on an anticipated staff concern may save many hours of troubleshooting later. Because the effective use of staff time is typically a major responsibility, you should give staff-related issues prime consideration.

Whether you should give attention to the immediacy of a staff complaint or put that request off to concentrate on the report depends on your priorities. If your primary objective is to boost staff morale, then handling the staff complaint is imperative. If the report is essential to obtaining better services or funding for the agency's clients and this is your highest priority, however, then you would delay handling the staff complaint. The point is that, at the outset, you must be quite clear and focused on what you must accomplish to achieve your primary objectives.

Second, determine your major responsibilities—those things you must do to carry out your job competently. These include prescribed tasks—work that is required by your own supervisor or by the organization's work flow, such as attending weekly staff meetings or completing monthly reports. An effective manager continuously asks whether particular time demands help further the organization's mission and are related to agreed-on goals.

A third priority consideration is whether someone else is depending on your activities—for example, a client waiting for your services, a colleague waiting for your analysis to incorporate it into a report, or your boss waiting for a reply to an important question.

Setting priorities initially requires your making a random list of activities, some being more important than others. Now you must determine which items are most important and which are least important. To establish priorities (most important), you must have posteriorities (least important), which are activities that need not be done immediately and items that should be done by others.

Setting priorities means making an ABCD list, broken down as follows:

Priority	*Explanation*
A (highest priority)	An activity that is both important and urgent because it provides the best payoff in accomplishing the organization's mission
B (medium priority)	Important, although not urgent; it is necessary to achieve a significant objective
C (low priority)	An activity that contributes only marginally to the achievement of an important objective
D (posteriority)	Neither important nor urgent; it could be delayed, minimized, delegated, or even eliminated

To further refine your priorities, assign numbers to each lettered category, such as A-1, A-2, A-3, B-1, and B-2. By adding priority categories to your list of items, you can discipline yourself to concentrate on the A and B items and minimize time spent on C and D items. If there are items such as "call back salesperson" or "straighten out files" on your C list and on your A list is "write an introduction to a 30-page report due tomorrow," you know where you must give your time and attention.[7]

To make time for priorities, you must give special attention to eliminating D items. These are time wasters that detract from your ability to carry out major assignments. Attending meetings called by other organizations, reading junk mail, attending unproductive conferences, or accepting assignments that could easily be delegated elsewhere are examples of time wasters. If you can answer the question "What would happen if I did not undertake these activities?" with the reply "Nothing of consequence," then you should not be doing them. Weed out D items.

It is possible that what was previously on a C or B list may, as time passes, now be on your A list. The thank-you letter that should have been written 10 days ago must now be written. Therefore, be prepared to reorder priorities each day. Constantly ask the following question: "What is the best use of my time right now?"[8] By forcing yourself to ask this question, you will keep uppermost your most important priorities and you will discipline yourself to put aside less important (but perhaps more enjoyable) activities.

Writing a list of priorities can be useful in structuring time; particularly if your job is not routine, however, expect the unexpected to occur. Leave time for emergencies that may require immediate attention. Assume that it is an imperfect world, and give yourself a time cushion to deal with unforeseen events.[9] Troubleshooting may be a standard part of the position because you may have to deal with the responsibilities of your subordinates in addition to your own. Their concerns become yours and therefore must be added to your A list.[10] The list is a tool to increase productivity, but it must be used flexibly.

Prepare a priority list each day, and as you complete tasks check them off. If you do not complete the major activities scheduled for the day, determine whether the time frames you have established for them are realistic. Ideally, you should feel a sense of accomplishment in completing the priorities you set for yourself. Some managers prefer to make priority lists at night so that they can start working on them immediately each morning.

Preparing a Daily Work Plan

A daily work plan (Figure 6.3) is another helpful format in prioritizing time commitments.[11] It consists of the following categories:

1. Appointments
2. Phone calls
3. Tasks
4. Follow-up list

This one-page format tells you what you need to concentrate on during the day.

Restructuring Time: The 80/20 Principle

The 80/20 time rule is derived from the principle developed by Vilfredo Pareto, a nineteenth-century Italian economist who analyzed the distribution of wealth in his time (80% of the wealth was held by 20% of the people). The concept has been modified as applied to time management to mean that if all activities are arranged in order of their value, 80% of the value would come from only 20% of the activities, whereas the remaining 20% of the value would come from 80% of the activities.

Date: ________________

APPOINTMENTS

Time	*Person/Place*

TASKS

Task	*Priority*

PHONE CALLS

Caller	*#*	*Re:*

FOLLOW-UP

What	*When*

Figure 6.3. Daily Work Plan

The 80/20 rule suggests that, of 10 things to do, doing the most important 2 will yield most (80%) of the value to you or your organization. The key to effective time management is to focus on the right 20% instead of on low-value activities for which the payoff is small. In other words, do not become bogged down on low-value activities (priority Cs and Ds). Develop the ability to say "no" to organizational requests that are on your C and D lists. Of course, the 80/20 rule should not be taken too literally. Percentages are a way of conceptually illustrating that more time could profitably be spent on a few highly critical issues or activities.

The Exception Principle

To take advantage of precious time, managers must determine where to concentrate their energies in relation to their supervisory responsibilities. When managers establish a baseline with clear standards for staff to properly complete their activities, then any unacceptable work will be obvious. Managers do not need to review everything—only those activities with outcomes that deviate from the predetermined standards. Observing "the exception principle" allows managers to give limited attention to reviewing ordinary, acceptable performance and concentrate instead on major deviations or unacceptable work patterns requiring a remedy.

Activities could include job performance, quality of written materials, and behavior of employees. These invite special scrutiny to spot exceptional behavior. For example, you have established the expectation that phones will be answered within four rings. As long as the calls are answered promptly, attention to the phone answering system is not necessary. If staff do not answer within five or six rings, however, then the situation may require special attention. Hence, comparing actual performance with expected performance helps the manager to identify the exceptions that require attention.[12]

BLOCKING OUT TIME

Occasionally, you need to find time to undertake long-range projects that require sustained periods of concentrated attention. One hour of time will be worth more than four 15-minute time slots scattered throughout the day. You should mark the time blocks on your calendar and generally try to protect them, making exceptions only for special situations or emergencies. Reserve the time block as if it were an important scheduled meeting, canceling it only as you would cancel the meeting.

Use your time blocks for the following kinds of activities:

- Writing an outline or draft of a major report
- Thinking about a major problem
- Completing difficult assignments
- Taking the time to visit branch offices
- Developing better relationships with significant staff, inside or outside the organization
- Working on a major project, such as a fund-raising campaign or legislation

To block out time, you must prune activities; some things have to be let go to make room for other activities. Also, in scheduling time blocks, determine the rhythm of the organization. For example, if the organization annually requires a heavy investment of time to prepare the budget in November, this would not be an appropriate time to set aside a time block for a major new project.

If a project requires concentrated attention, schedule a time block in a quiet room away from the office to prevent telephone interruptions or unexpected visitors. You may have to use weekends, evenings, or early mornings to make time blocks available. You may not want to do this on a regular basis, but occasionally, to get the job done, you may have to work extra hours. An hour spent from 7:30 to 8:30 a.m. or from 5:00 to 6:00 p.m. may be far more valuable than small intervals snatched during a hectic day. You may also need to establish "availability hours" so that staff and others trying to reach you will not feel shortchanged. By making yourself available at certain times, you can more easily set aside a time block. Of course, this approach must fit your management style; some managers prefer an open-door approach, in which case they may need to block out evening or weekend time.

Set deadlines and subgoals within the period you have allocated for your time block. By setting these deadlines, you discipline yourself to complete discrete pieces of work. Subgoals provide a target and keep you on track. Thus, within each block of time, you should achieve a specific subgoal—for example, complete an outline, write four pages of a report, or finish an analysis of a staff problem.

If the task is too large to complete within a limited time period, then segment the tasks into smaller, more manageable portions and discipline yourself to complete action on one segment before stopping. This way, you will avoid leaving loose ends when you put the task aside. You will have completed one phase of the project and will be ready to begin the next. The emphasis is not on putting in time but on completing tasks. Develop a compulsion for closure.[13]

COMBATING TIME GOBBLERS

In the course of a given workday, certain endeavors tend to waste time and produce limited results. The ideas listed in the following sections are no doubt more than any one person can implement in trying to combat time gobblers. They will not work for every manager all the time. Consider the following items as a smorgasbord of suggestions from which you could select those that fit your working style.

Handling Incoming Work

- Never handle a piece of paper more than once. If it is paper that requires a reply, do so now. If a short report is required, do it now. The main objective is to get the report off the desk.
- To handle the tremendous flow of paper, discipline yourself to see that each piece of paper is handled by (a) acting on it immediately, (b) referring it to someone else, (c) filing it, (d) discarding it, or (e) in special circumstances delaying action pending other necessary events.
- Have an assistant who is aware of your priorities highlight the main points of all correspondence.
- For all reports longer than five pages, request a summary sheet.
- Arrange to have a place for every piece of paper you save.
- Critically examine correspondence, especially intraorganizational letters and memoranda, to determine whether your response should be a phone call or a handwritten note.
- Consider whether staff can handle communications through phone calls or face-to-face contact rather than though long written reports.
- Have an assistant sort your mail based on your guidelines on routine materials that can be discarded, filed, or rerouted. Give screening authority regarding fund solicitations and sales letters.
- Carry reading material with you to take advantage of "dead time," such as waiting for a meeting to begin, waiting for transportation to arrive, or sitting in a large meeting in which some of the items do not require your attention.
- Respond to incoming correspondence by writing a reply directly on the letter.
- Use computer networking to quickly exchange drafts with colleagues.
- Attach documents to e-mail for quicker review.

Organizing Paper Flow

- Clear your desk of clutter periodically so that you do not waste time trying to find materials. If necessary, arrange to work occasional evenings or weekends to clean up.
- Before designing a new form, consider whether it is truly necessary, what it will accomplish, and whether the current form can be simplified or eliminated. What effect would the new form have on other departments? How much money and

time would it cost to process the form? How much training time would be required? Use the new form for a few days to ensure that it works.

- Use stick-on note tags to indicate what needs to be done with each item, especially for giving your assistant filing instructions. Stack items in priority piles to ensure that you deal quickly with "A" items.
- Create a "next step" list that identifies the various steps required to accomplish a particular task.
- Develop a tickler file that sorts, by days or months, projects that must be accomplished in the future.
- Establish at your desk a few working files you are likely to need in the next few days. These are projects you are currently working on that require your continuous attention.
- Schedule time for you or your assistant to clean out files once or twice a year.
- Divide incoming items into four categories: dump it, delegate it, delay it, or do it.
- Divide work that arrives on your desk into four categories and color code them—for example,
    - ~ Red folder: mail/memos, primary—contains items for immediate attention
    - ~ Orange folder: mail/memos, secondary—contains items of lesser importance
    - ~ Green folder: contains items requiring signature
    - ~ Yellow folder: easy reading—contains everything that could be ignored for a week without causing problems
- Remember that there is a place for everything, and everything should be in its place. This will greatly reduce clutter in your life.
- If you have to keep track of many files, use hanging folders in which you can put several file folders. For example, a hanging folder designated as "personnel" could contain individual file folders of people in your department. Then create a master list index of all your hanging folders. When it is time to file, you will know exactly where to place paperwork. Also, you will know where you can retrieve needed information.
- Ask people to put their requests in writing. Keep them in a special place until you have answered them.
- Be choosy about what to read. Practice the art of skimming materials, looking for the most significant and relevant aspects. Concentrate on the introduction and conclusion.
- Keep uncomplicated paperwork handy so that you can work while waiting for people on the phone.

- Get your name off of unnecessary mailing and circulation lists.
- When writing, use short and simple words.
- If you wish your memos to be typed, give the typist your handwritten note and a blank memo form with your signature on it.
- Take courses in word processing, using spreadsheets, making presentations, and scheduling. All managers must become proficient in the use of these time-saving tools.
- Organize your computer files by categories so that materials can be easily found.

Managing Conversations

- Keep a small notebook in which you can write names of people you meet and a brief record of issues discussed with them.
- Organize your thoughts before beginning a conversation or a phone call. Know what you want to say, say it, and omit everything else.
- Although socializing is enjoyable, remember to limit it so you can get your tasks done.
- Drop-in visitors present a special problem. Although they are important for relationships in and outside the organization, they can detract from accomplishing certain responsibilities. Be courteous and friendly, but also maintain control. Of course, some spontaneous conversations may prove to be highly productive, so be flexible with this guideline.
- If a staff member asks to meet with you, consider meeting in his or her office instead. It will be easier for you to leave when the business is concluded.
- If possible, meet drop-in visitors outside your office so that you can easily end the conversation.
- Request a brief summary of issues that you can review before a meeting or discussion.
- Keep a clock in full view for yourself and visitors so you can be aware of the passing of time.
- Have a file card with agenda topics available for each person with whom you are likely to meet so that you are prepared to discuss specific items with them.
- Establish a time limit when a visitor arrives, and be candid about the time pressure you are feeling. If your time is limited, ask the visitor to set up another appointment.
- Encourage staff to prepare any necessary facts and figures for the discussion.
- To let the visitor know that you are ready to complete the discussion, use such phrases as "before we finish" or "before we wrap this up."
- Allow time each day for interruptions and unscheduled events.

- Learn to say "no" if someone asks if you have a minute.
- Stand up and move the visitor toward the door when you are ready to conclude the discussion.

Managing Telephone Calls

- Instead of using separate telephone memos, use an 8 ½ × 11-inch chart that provides columns for date, caller, time, and message. Place the charts in a notebook so you can track infrequent callers. This will save you time because you will not have to search for separate memos.
- Try logging your phone calls for several days. If you find that some are unnecessary or could be handled more efficiently by someone else, tell the switchboard operator to reroute them.
- Sometimes, callers tend to ramble. They go into great detail about a situation before getting to the point. Encourage them to state the "bottom-line" issue and then go back to fill in the details. This will help focus the discussion.
- If most of your interruptions are from your boss, do not assume that you must put up with them. Pick a judicious time to explain that you are trying to get better control of your time and would appreciate a mutually agreeable time to discuss routine matters.
- To make a phone message brief, (a) tell the person in one sentence why you are calling, (b) explain it briefly, and (c) say what you plan to do or what action you want the other person to take.
- When you leave the office, indicate when you will be back so callers know when to reach you.
- Indicate to the caller your time constraints: "I only have 3 minutes because of an important meeting I have to prepare for. Will our discussion take longer?" Usually it will not, and your announcement will push the caller to get to the point.
- Consider faxing your ideas in advance of a phone call to better focus the conversation.
- Keep a list of frequently called numbers by your phone. If possible, program your phone for those you call often.
- Don't play "telephone tag." Let your assistant know when you will be available again or ask about the best time to reach the other party. Make an appointment through the secretary to call back at a specific time. Use phone mail to receive and communicate messages.
- Certain times are generally better for returning calls: early morning (8:00-9:00 a.m.) and at closing (4:00-5:00 p.m.).
- If you find that you must stay on the line to prevent telephone tag, have available material that you can read while waiting.

- Establish quiet hours during which you will not accept calls except in an emergency or from special persons you designate.
- If you are in a tremendous time bind, try to limit the time you will accept calls, such as from 2:30 to 3:00 p.m.
- Outline topics to discuss before calling.
- Set aside a particular time for calling. Make as many calls as you can at one time. Inform the switchboard or your secretary that you want to be told when a caller is waiting on the line.

PROCRASTINATION

Procrastination is the avoidance of starting or following through on a task that you have defined as important and necessary. The basis for procrastination is usually fear of failure, particularly when undertaking unfamiliar or complex assignments. This fear can be heightened if managers wonder whether the outcome will be as good as their own high expectations. Perfectionism can be paralyzing. To overcome this paralysis, you may need to develop more tolerance for your own frailties, at least enough to get started on the challenging assignment you must undertake. You might even humorously tell yourself, "If a thing is worth doing, it's worth doing badly."[14]

To prepare yourself for the awesome assignment, ask, "What is the worst that could happen if I try and it does not work out as well as I hoped?" The "worst" may not be so terrible after all. Also ask, "What is the consequence of my delaying?" Because you are faced with the prospect of having to do it anyway, procrastinating only delays the inevitable.

A good rule of thumb is to do the unpleasant things first, not last. If you have many tasks to complete, you may naturally want to start with the least demanding. Perhaps this is why staff do not like to set priorities; the largest, most frightening jobs having the most risk frequently rank as the top priorities.[15] Instead of delaying, devote the first part of the day to dealing with uncomfortable issues. By concentrating on the onerous tasks first, you can be free to enjoy the more pleasant ones later. Your attitude should be one of "Let's handle the pain first and get it over with."[16] Try not to leave the office at the end of the day without resolving a vexing problem. Otherwise, the problem festers and preys on your mind during your off hours.

Give yourself deadlines for written assignments, and make them known to others with whom you work closely. Your deadlines can be divided into immediate (this week), intermediate (in the next 3 weeks), and long term (what must be achieved in the last week of the project). Then, start long before the deadline so you can pace yourself accordingly. Admit to yourself that you are resorting to escapism when you catch yourself wasting time. Think, "I am wasting my time by not working on my 'A' project."

Be aware that the inability to say "no" can cause procrastination. You may overcommit yourself and then procrastinate because there are not enough hours in the day to get all the work done. Train yourself to ask how long projects will take to complete. Provide a list of your current responsibilities to your supervisor, and then discuss which are high priority items and which might be set aside temporarily.

When faced with an overwhelming task, divide it into smaller parts. By doing one part at a time, you break the assignment into manageable pieces. For example, a large writing assignment can be divided into sections, each requiring concentrated attention. Reward yourself when you reach a milestone in a long project.

If you find that you are putting off an assignment, it is helpful to analyze your mental blocks to determine whether you can take a new approach. You may need more information to help you resolve the issue. Perhaps you lack conviction about the assignment and may need to confront your superiors with a recommendation for a different course of action.

To speed up your decision-making process, you might ask yourself, "What will I know in the future that I don't already know?" If your response is "nothing," then make the best decision you can make and move on. If you need to obtain more information or confer with other staff members, put the document in a pending folder and use your date book to remind yourself when you must make the decision.[17]

In dealing with subordinates who tend to procrastinate, avoid giving orders that will result in passive compliance and even resentment. Strive to foster commitment by asking, "When can you get started on the rough draft?" and "How much will you be able to complete by X date?" Break long-term, amorphous, or complex tasks into short-term, well-defined projects.[18] By putting boundaries around them, you can reduce the anxiety associated with open-ended, vague assignments.

The same fear of failure that may cause you to procrastinate will no doubt affect the performance of your staff. If procrastination has been a staff problem in the past, it may be helpful to identify assignments in which they can experience clear success and recognition. You can then build on these successes for more challenging work. You may need to help them establish timelines that are realistic, assist them with the quality of their work, and pinpoint what needs to be done to finish on time.

If possible, provide choices for staff with regard to how they will implement the assignment. For example, ask them when they can reasonably complete an assignment, then come to a mutual agreement. Let them give you feedback if they think they will have trouble with the assignment. Help them determine a timetable for completing an outline, for example, or the first section of a report. Clarify whether they can give up other priorities to focus on the latest assignment. Convey your positive sense that they can succeed in doing a good job. Let them know that if procrastination is likely to be a problem you are prepared to help them address it.

Effective managers are mindful of how they and their staff use their time. The guidelines on how to better use time should be considered judiciously. Be aware that both you and your staff have a life outside of work. Finding the right balance among your different priorities is an ongoing challenge. Focusing on outcomes and developing a flexible work schedule may ease the pressure.[19] Do not become so efficient in the use of time that you neglect spontaneous or urgent assignments. Allow enough slack time in your busy schedule to deal with unanticipated events, such as client emergencies, correspondence that must be handled, urgent meetings, and staff complaints. These are not isolated intrusions but rather part of the routine of the workday. Although allowances must be made for the unexpected, effective managers can still take action to be the masters of their time.

NOTES

1. Leadership at work, *The Royal Bank Letter, 7* (1980), p. 3; H. Mintzberg, The manager's job: Folklore and fact, *Harvard Business Review, 2* (1990), p. 164.

2. J. P. Kotter, What effective general managers really do, *Harvard Business Review, 77*(2) (1999, March/April), pp. 154-159.

3. H. Reynolds & M. E. Tramel, *Executive time management* (Englewood Cliffs, NJ: Prentice Hall, 1979), pp. 13-15.

4. A. Lakein, *How to get control of your time and your life* (New York: New American Library, 1973), p. 47.

5. R. N. Askenas & R. H. Schaffer, Manager can avoid wasting time, *Harvard Business Review, 3* (1982), pp. 98-104.

6. A. Uris, *101 of the greatest ideas in management* (New York: John Wiley, 1986), pp. 284-286.

7. H. Smith, Hyrum Smith's simple steps to much better time management, *Bottom Line Personal* (1999, March), pp. 11-12.

8. A. Lakein, p. 96.

9. M. H. McCormack, *Mark H. McCormack on managing* (West Hollywood, CA: Dove, 1996), pp. 45-46.

10. A. Uris, p. 292.

11. H. Reynolds & M. E. Tramel, pp. 15-17.

12. A. Uris, pp. 127-129.

13. E. Bliss, *Getting things done* (New York: Bantam, 1976), p. 180.

14. A. Lakein, p. 96.

15. T. Kirby, *The can-do manager* (New York: AMACOM, 1989), p. 145.

16. M. S. Peck, *The road less traveled* (New York: Touchstone/Simon & Schuster, 1978), p. 19.

17. B. Hemphill, Organize your increasingly complex work life, *Bottom Line Personal* (1999, June), pp. 9-10.

18. R. N. Askenas & R. H. Schaffer, p. 101.

19. S. D. Friedman, P. Christensen, & J. DeGroot, Work & life: The end of the zero sum game, *Harvard Business Review, 76* (1998, November/December), p. 121.

Chapter 7

GETTING AND KEEPING PRODUCTIVE EMPLOYEES

A skilled, committed, and caring staff is the essence of every productive human service organization. In addition to hiring the right people and working to develop them, effective managers need to ensure that the organizational structure fosters productivity and that jobs are properly analyzed. It is essential that employees are well motivated, their jobs inherently satisfying, their workload balanced properly, and their physical environment conducive to work. Your goal should be to keep the best staff, even during periods of contraction. Getting and retaining good employees require your constant attention to the work atmosphere.

FINDING THE RIGHT PEOPLE FOR THE JOB

Productive organizations require that competent staff be matched with the right jobs. When a vacancy occurs, often the immediate reaction is to contemplate filling the position. It may in fact be better to use the vacancy as an opportunity to consider whether existing staff might be deployed differently. Assessing the strengths and weaknesses of current staff in relation to the results you want to achieve is an ongoing process, but it should occur especially at the time of a vacancy. Through this assessment, you can determine what specific expertise or competency would be needed to complement other staff skills.[1]

Because hiring new staff can commit an organization financially for many years, you should examine several options. Consider redeploying existing staff, as noted previously. A second method is to hire temporary employees during critical work periods without assuming a long-term obligation.[2] A third approach is to borrow people from other organizations to take on special assignments. Temporary and borrowed employees provide the organization with flexibility, although there may be some loss of commitment.

One of the best sources for filling vacancies is your own organization. People who have demonstrated competency and growth in their skills are obvious recruits. The clear advantage of promoting from within is that you are obtaining a known entity, and staff feel positive that they can be upwardly mobile. Skills used in one role may not necessarily be suited for another, however. The human service counselor may or may not be able to function as a manager. Moreover, a policy of promoting from within invites staff to have expectations, which could lead to their being disillusioned if they are not selected. This can be of particular concern if job announcements or postings are listed to comply with the law and affirmative action policies but hiring decisions are made even before the postings have been made public, thus making interviews with current employees a sham. If internal recruitment is to be truly meaningful, sincere efforts must be made to review candidates and to take the time to explain to those rejected why they were not selected.[3]

CONDUCTING A NONDISCRIMINATORY INTERVIEW

The term *bona fide occupational qualifications* describes those qualifications that are necessary to perform the normal activities of a position. In conducting an interview, the most important thing to keep in mind is that if you have a legitimate concern about a prospective employee's ability to meet the job requirements then frame your questions accordingly. For example, if weekend and evening work is required, ask whether this presents a problem. If, however, you do not need the information for actual job-related reasons, do not ask. You would not ask a female applicant the ages of her children, what child care arrangements she has made, or whether, as a woman, she has reservations about working alone at night. Similarly, you would not ask about a candidate's religious or civic affiliations.[4] Therefore, your focus of attention is on those essential job functions that have been identified in the job description.

In interviewing potential staff for positions, special care must be taken to avoid illegal discrimination involving racial, gender, age, place of origin, and disability. If a person in one of these categories is otherwise qualified and then rejected in preference for someone else, the organization may then be subject to a discrimination lawsuit.[5] It is not enough for the organization to proclaim that it has an affirmative action policy. Specific plans must be in place that demonstrate recruitment of minority employees, such as advertising in minority newspapers and contacting minority professional associations.

In conducting the interview, be especially mindful of how you document the following:

1. If a person does not meet the bona fide job requirements, document the specific reason. Never use language such as "overqualified," which could imply age discrimination.
2. If the person lacks the experience or education required, be sure to document this.
3. Avoid documenting marital status and dependents. Also, do not note whether they own their own homes or how long they have lived in them.
4. Do not document arrest records or military discharge. These questions have been removed from employment applications because they discriminate against minorities. Check your state laws regarding whether felony convictions are permitted; some states require that references to convictions be accompanied by statements that convictions will not automatically disqualify job applicants.
5. Questions about health and disabilities must be related to the job. Do not document, for example, how a person with a disability will get to work.[6]

The following questions are designed to focus on job performance. Customize these interview questions to fit the particular position you are attempting to fill.[7]

Background relevancy

- What do you consider to be your major qualifications for this kind of work?

- What in your educational background is relevant?
- In your previous work experiences, what projects or tasks are relevant to this work?
- What assignments do you think you are best (least good) at?

Qualifications

- What are your best qualities as an employee aside from technical competence?
- What are your weakest qualities as an employee; what areas do you need to develop further?
- How do you keep informed of work-related issues in your field?

Expectations

- What are the major outcomes you expect from this job?
- What are your short- and long-range goals, if any, at this time?
- How does this job fit with your long-range plans, if any?
- What part of your work has given you the greatest satisfaction and the least satisfaction?

Work pressure

- How do you determine which activities have the highest priority on your time?
- How have you handled situations in which expenses threaten to exceed the budget for your unit?
- If you have ever had to change priorities, how did you handle the situation?
- How have you dealt with unforeseen circumstances?
- How do you determine which job assignments get top priority?
- How do you cope with pressures on the job?
- Can you describe a situation in which you sought consultation from your supervisor?
- What procedure do you use to keep track of things that require your attention?

Accomplishments

- What were your objectives for last year and how did you go about achieving them?
- What are your two greatest accomplishments? How were these planned and implemented? What was your most difficult task, and how did you deal with it?
- Can you give an example of when you did more than was required for your job?
- What performance standards do you set for yourself? What do you do if you find yourself not meeting these standards?
- Have you had an experience where initially you failed to gain acceptance of an idea and succeeded later? What made the difference?
- Can you give an example of surmounting an obstacle to reach an objective?

Analysis and decision making

- Describe a project or idea that you originated in the past 2 years.
- What do you do to keep informed about possible work-related problems?
- What was the best decision you ever made? What were the alternatives? How did you go about making it?
- What was the toughest decision you had to make last year?
- How have you gone about dealing with a work-related problem?

Supervision

- How do you normally assign work to employees?
- How did you handle a situation in which you had to help a staff member solve a problem or meet an objective?
- How have you handled (or would you have handled) supervising former peers?
- How would you handle a situation in which you had delegated responsibility and the work was not done as expected?
- How would you handle poor performance or work attitude?

- As a supervisor, describe how you help to make your subordinates' work easier and more fulfilling.

Cooperation and independence

- How have you worked with staff in your unit, members of other units in your organization, or staff from other organizations?
- Can you describe a situation in which you expressed concern or disagreement with your agency's policies?
- Can you give an example of when you consulted with your boss before proceeding and an example of acting independently?
- Have you ever undertaken a project that was not popular with some people? How did it work out?
- With what other departments did you normally work on your previous position?
- What are examples of how you solved or failed to solve problems?

Staffing decisions should be based on the competency and talents of staff matched to job requirements. A strong accountant may be reticent and shy in interpersonal relationships, but this may matter little as long as the books are in order. An outreach worker may use poor grammar but have the ability to establish excellent relationships with residents of the community. Although writing skills are occasionally desirable, this talent is not a major factor in an outreach job. People with strong talents may also have weaknesses; only if these weaknesses could seriously affect job performance would an otherwise strong candidate be disqualified. Although you are seeking to understand weaknesses and flaws that may have an impact on the performance of recruits, your primary interest is on the strengths that recruits bring to the job.[8] A fundamental approach in hiring staff is to concentrate on strengths and not be unduly concerned about those weaknesses that are likely to be inconsequential.

A major reason newly hired staff quit is that they have unmet expectations based on misinformation about the responsibilities and opportunities of their positions. Sometimes during recruitment interviews, employers tend to discuss only positive elements of the job while ignoring less attractive realities. This emphasis may depend on how eager they are to hire those staff who are in short supply in the marketplace. If prospective employees have other options, they may tend to overemphasize the job's positive aspects. In general, however, a preferred approach is to discuss candidly all elements of the organizational reality. Effective recruiting requires managers to communicate clearly such job qualifications as the education, skill, and experience needed for the job and the salary range for the position. The more definitive the organization can be about the expectations and demands of a job, the more likely it will identify a suitable candidate who will remain with the organization.[9]

The recruitment process should be taken seriously because if it is not done well the result can be a "revolving door" involving continuous processing of applicants. Employee turnover can be both disruptive and costly. To reduce turnover, take the time to invest in the recruitment process so that a selection can be made from among qualified candidates. Do not make the mistake of hiring someone without thoroughly checking references. If possible, identify employers or colleagues who were not given as references. Be alert to the possibility that a glowing report can be a way for another employer to pawn off undesirable employees on your organization.[10]

A telephone discussion is much more informative than a letter of reference because you can ask more specific questions. In the telephone interview, determine how the applicant performed on prior assignments because this, more than anything else, offers clues about how he or she will perform in the future.[11]

Sometimes, former employers are reluctant to give information about a job applicant because they fear possible litigation. The following are questions that can prompt former employers to give information without their risking a lawsuit:

- Can you provide factual information, such as dates of employment, final salary, and titles?
- What responsibilities did the applicant have?
- Can you pinpoint professional strengths and weaknesses that your former employee showed that might apply to this new position?
- How would you compare this former employee with peers on work-related assignments?
- Were there any major problems that affected your former employee's performance?
- Would you rehire this person for this or another position in your organization?[12]

Investing in the recruitment process helps ensure a proper match between applicant and job. There is an old saying that you should never try to teach a chicken to give milk; it wastes your time and annoys the chicken. Taking the time to hire the best person for the job will save considerable grief in the long run.

DEVELOPING STAFF

As interest in improving productivity increases, organizations will naturally want to improve staff capabilities. Training alone, however, has its limitations. Training programs to develop staff must build on the staff's internal desire to improve. Programs must also provide sufficient reinforcement and feedback to ensure significant positive impact.[13]

Good staff development must be built on both a "job-needs" analysis and a "person-needs" analysis. The tasks, information, and skills necessary to do the job can be determined from current employees and their supervisors. The person-needs analysis can be determined by comparing actual employee performance with predetermined performance standards. Those staff performing below proficiency level will be candidates for staff development.[14] In addition, staff should be encouraged to take responsibility for performing their jobs properly. Do not guess what they need—ask them.[15]

In considering how staff development can be used to enhance productivity, keep several points in mind. First, training should fit within the overall strategy of the organization. Staff development should assist the organization in dealing with its future requirements. For example, if the organization intends to emphasize advocacy efforts, then staff should develop skills along these lines. If the organization needs better marketing, then this should be stressed in staff development.

Second, because what staff learn in training sessions can sometimes elicit negative reactions from colleagues and supervisors when they return to their jobs, take certain steps to ensure a receptive climate. Trainers need to be mindful of the environment in which new skills are to be applied. Managers can often benefit from an orientation session that helps them prepare for staff returning from training.[16] Managers should not be caught off guard; in fact, they should be encouraged to create opportunities to implement new ideas and skills on the job. For example, after being in a training session, some staff may want to challenge the way communications are handled within the unit. By anticipating this in advance, the manager will be in a better position to handle these new job demands constructively and positively.

Third, probably the best training occurs on the job. Although one can gain knowledge in a formal training process, the development of long-term skills and behavioral changes are more likely to occur as part of a job experience. The advantage of on-the-job training (OJT) is that it provides relevance and reinforcement for the actual work to be done. Small organizations with limited budgets for formal training capability will primarily need to rely on OJT and one-on-one monitoring. The disadvantages of OJT are that it may require a sustained trial-and-error period, and staff may need assistance in identifying patterns and general concepts that can be applied to other situations.

Fourth, in addition to OJT, training that is anchored in reality provides good opportunities for growth. Special assignments can help develop skills. For example, staff may be asked to provide leadership to a team assignment, thus gaining leadership skills as part of the experience. Also, staff may be rotated to jobs in another unit for a 3-month period as a means of developing new skills. This attempt at cross-functional mobility helps staff to understand the views of various functional specialists and become more adaptive to changing job requirements. The organization thus becomes more responsive and flexible in meeting new demands.

Fifth, a useful off-the-job development technique is the case method of training, which draws on actual problems and situations experienced by staff. If done well, the case method does not engender "correct" answers from experts but fosters considerable staff participation and encourages a high level of independent thinking. The value of the case method approach is that it pushes participants to explore possibilities and to question assumptions.

Finally, all training should contain opportunities for feedback using multiple criteria that include the trainees' reactions to the sessions and materials and responses from their supervisors on how well they are applying training to the job. In this way, the training is subject to continuous examination and revision.

STRUCTURING THE ORGANIZATION TO BE PRODUCTIVE

The quality of staff work and interactions can be influenced by the organization's structure because structure helps to determine who will work with whom on what tasks. The following sections discuss questions about structure that pertain to increasing staff productivity.

How Can Structure Relate to Functions? The purpose of structure is to allow the organization to divide its work into various units and then provide ways to integrate this work. No one structural format is appropriate for all organizations because structure should fit unique needs and should emerge from an organization's goals and objectives.

In his analysis of major corporations, Alfred Chandler showed how the form of the organization follows its function.[17] This same concept can be applied to human service organizations. For example, if the organization provides services over a large geographic area, it will likely decentralize its delivery of services. If agency services need to be coordinated with other integrating programs, then staff teams could be established. Form should always follow function.

Structure can also be affected by the composition of the staff. In some instances, the structure emerges out of special strengths or weaknesses that staff possess. For example, a manager with strong interpersonal skills may be weak in handling administrative details. Elaborate structures are sometimes built based on special qualities of the staff, and when certain staff leave restructuring may be necessary. Hence, structure takes into consideration both the organizational tasks and the attributes of staff available to fulfill them.[18]

What Is the Best Way to Structure Staffing Patterns? An organization can have a variety of staffing patterns on which to develop a structural framework. Jobs can be organized by (a) *specialization,* in which all similar jobs are placed in one department (e.g., financial activities); (b) *service programs,* with all positions clustering around a particular service (e.g., counseling); or (c) *site location,* with different positions coordinated at the site (e.g., outreach offices).[19] These different formats can be combined depending on what an organization must accomplish. Sometimes, only through a process of trial and error will the proper structure emerge. Even in these cases, there may be trade-offs because no structure is likely to work optimally under all conditions.

What Structural Formats Can Be Used to Coordinate the Work of the Organization? Every organization develops one or more structures to help carry out their functions. Usually, one structure is predominant, but it is possible that several coexist. Moreover, a structure suitable at one time may be altered to meet a special situation at another time. Effective managers continually assess their organization's structural emphasis to maximize its use of scarce resources and the productivity of staff.

The *bureaucratic* or *hierarchical format* is commonly used in large human service organizations. Staff have specialized jobs, are accountable to a higher authority, and are promoted on the basis of competence. Despite the negative connotation attributed to the term *bureaucracy,* the bureaucratic format persists because it helps coordinate the work of any people. In some organizations, standardizing procedures through a bureaucratic format helps reduce friction and ensures predictability of response.[20]

The *market format* allows staff to change assignments based on changing needs. High turnover is normal. Staff are attracted by either compensation or a particular assignment. Considerable negotiating and bargaining occur between the organization and employees. In human service organizations, an example of this approach is staff hired to fulfill the requirements of a 2-year proposal with no commitment for permanent employment.

The *matrix* or *cross-functional format* provides an opportunity within a hierarchical structure for staff to work on a goal-oriented project on an ad hoc basis. Once the project is complete, participants return to their functional units. For example, staff from the departments of counseling, fiscal management, public information, research, and childcare might cooperate to carry out new methods of reaching potential clients.

The advantage of this approach is that it fosters coordination and stimulates staff to focus on problems from different perspectives. Of course, the fact that members of the team continue to have ongoing responsibilities within their own units and have dual lines of accountability can cause problems. By anticipating problems and yet making the expectations of a temporary or focus assignment clear, the matrix approach can be an effective way to deal with issues that cut across functional areas of responsibility.[21] Increasingly, organizations are relying on the matrix or cross-functional approach to heighten commitment, encourage collaboration, and engender creative thinking.[22]

Structural emphasis may need to be modified with changing circumstances. During times of fiscal contractions or periods of innovation, the market approach may be suitable. If implementation of routine tasks is needed, then a hierarchical emphasis makes sense. Certain structures can interfere with an organization's goals, however. For instance, a task force designed under the matrix plan for a particular purpose may strive to exist beyond its original intent because staff enjoy working together, and what was once an asset to the organization becomes an impediment to the usual flow of work and should be abandoned. Obviously, the issue of structure should periodically be revisited to ensure that organizational needs are being met.

Restructuring Jobs

To meet changing needs, organizations have to reorganize periodically. Occasionally, management should consolidate the work of units to increase efficiencies, reduce duplication, improve the flow of work or communications, take advantage of new technologies, and respond to changing consumer patterns. Some of the special circumstances that would warrant organizational restructuring are discussed in this section.

Funding reductions may require combining some tasks. Work formerly done by managers may either be discontinued or transferred to line staff during this downsizing.[23]

Office automation—word processing, electronic mail, audiovisual conferences, and information retrieval systems—allows organizations to redesign jobs so that more time can be spent providing direct service.

Alternative work schedules, including flextime, job sharing of part-time jobs, permanent part-time employment, work sharing (involving staff willing to accept reduced hours and pay to preserve their jobs), work-at-home schedules, and compressed workweeks, are trends that require the organization to revise jobs.[24] Adjustments must be made in the need for colleague interaction, accountability to supervisors, and group decision making.

Competition for good staff may force an organization to restructure its jobs so that the best people are not lured away. If high-quality staff see little opportunity for promotion, or if they find their jobs inherently limiting, then the job structure may need to be refashioned to retain them. Perhaps paraprofessionals can be hired to perform less complex tasks while high-level staff are given more challenging assignments, with accompanying increases in salary. Of course, there is a limit to how much restructuring an organization can do to keep good people. Staff do outgrow their jobs at times, and the preferred option may be to accept their moving on.

The need to reduce errors and achieve better results may require reengineering.[25] If an organization's multiple layers cause delays in decisions or improperly completed work, a radical restructuring of jobs may be necessary. For example, when a high degree of specialization requires clients to shift from one staff member to another, delays are inevitable and accountability becomes blurred. Jobs may need to be redesigned for greater emphasis on achieving results and less emphasis on processing clients or paper.

Of course, reorganization can produce negative side effects. It can disrupt informal patterns of communication, which are very important for organizational functioning. It can be used by some managers to avoid dealing with problems that could be solved in less traumatic ways. It can create tremendous anxiety, suspicion, and insecurity for staff who become disoriented by the change of relationships.[26] One organization experienced so many alterations during the course of a year that staff coined the phrase "Etch-a-Sketch agency" to reflect the capricious nature of the structural changes. Although reorganization should be considered an option in changing circumstances, an organization should not undertake it without considerable forethought and attention to possible repercussions.

CONDUCTING JOB AND WORKLOAD ANALYSES

The design of jobs has a critical impact on organizational goals and employee performance. The way tasks and responsibilities are clustered can affect productivity. Unsatisfying or highly demanding jobs are difficult to fill and contribute to high turnover. Hence, thoughtful job design benefits both the organization and the staff.[27]

All organizations should undertake a task analysis of their major jobs. This analysis provides clear job expectations, facilitates performance reviews, connects staff with the goals of the organization, provides continuity during staff turnover, ensures an evenhanded approach to salaries, helps in identifying training needs, and assists in determining staff support required to perform certain activities.[28]

A job analysis can either be similar to a job description or it can contain an even more detailed list of tasks to be carried out by staff. For example, if one of the major activities in a job description is to use a "client information system," a task analysis would indicate to staff the kind of files they should keep, the information they must provide to other organizations, and the information they must collect. Similarly, if another major activity is "participating as a member of a team," the detailed job analysis would specify expectations in relation to cooperative relationships outside the organization and responsibilities as a team member within it.

A good job analysis should be conducted by various people in the organization, and it should include discussions between supervisors and staff, an inventory of tasks, conferences with job analysts and experts, structured and unstructured questionnaires completed by job incumbents or by supervisors, and documentation of critical incidents that reflect major aspects of the job. Through a negotiating process between staff and administration, an organization clusters its inventory of tasks under major activities and scales them down to a manageable number.[29] The resulting job specifications would include the skills, knowledge, training, and experience required to perform each job.

The result should be a sufficiently detailed job description so that employees understand their assignments, to whom they report, what results they should generate from their work, and the level of quality and the quantity of work expected of them. You might consider detailing specific behaviors that are expected of them; for example, in a placement facility, children are not to be left unattended. A good job analysis can provide, where appropriate, a high degree of staff autonomy and flexibility because staff know precisely what is expected of them.

An important purpose of job analysis is to ensure that staff have proper support. Staff will be more productive when they have the proper tools, information, clerical backup, and support of colleagues whose jobs complement theirs. For example, in a counseling agency counselors must believe that the intake staff are conducting thorough initial diagnoses and making proper referrals. Jobs should be designed so that all staff can fulfill their proper roles, and the various organizational units are properly integrated.

Moreover, a good job analysis ensures a balanced workload. Employees who are inundated with tasks or who have an inordinate number of clients are likely to feel overburdened and perhaps even exploited. They may make critical decisions that have tremendous impact on their clients based on inadequate information. A solution would be to base caseloads on reasonable expectations of the time that it takes to complete various tasks. The next step would be to establish standards that reflect the staff's ability to deliver quality and timely services.[30]

Organizations are beginning to analyze caseloads on the basis of the number of problems presented, their intensity, and the nature of the intervention that will be required.[31] A systematic weighting process categorizes needed services by degree of severity: (a) slight (requiring little or no time investment), (b) moderate (requiring biweekly contact), (c) high (requiring considerable involvement, at least weekly), or (d) critical (requiring several hours each week and perhaps even daily contacts). One staff member might have 35 moderate cases, and another might have 10 critical cases. Therefore, the value is in the organization's ability to shift service emphasis from less critical to higher-risk subpopulations, thereby permitting a differential and more purposeful deployment of staff.[32]

ENRICHING JOBS

If possible, staff should experience inherent satisfaction in what they do. They must believe that their work is worthwhile if they are to feel truly committed to it. Peters and Waterman's observation that excellent companies tap the inherent worth of the task as a source of intrinsic motivation can certainly be applied to human service organizations.[33] In fact, human service organizations have an advantage over profit-making organizations in that many of the staff are attracted by the opportunity to contribute to and enhance people's lives.

To increase job satisfaction, organizations can try a variety of approaches, of which job enrichment is the most appealing. Other approaches include work simplification, job rotation, and job enlargement.

Work simplification creates very specialized jobs, each consisting of a few operations. This allows staff with limited training and experience to perform the work. An example is the creation of a staff aide's position to conduct a limited form of interviewing. Job rotation permits staff to take turns performing several work-simplified jobs. It provides more flexible work assignments and reduces monotony. Job enlargement results in adding more components to a job so as to reduce boredom, add meaning and variety, and make the work more challenging. If this is accompanied by an increase in pay so that staff do not feel exploited, enlarging the job can be a positive step toward reducing stagnation. Although work simplification, rotation, and enlargement play important roles in fulfilling organizational needs, it is through job enrichment that staff are most likely to experience an increase in their work motivation.

Job enrichment provides staff with an opportunity to experience an entirely new job requiring new skills and talents. Typically, job enrichment allows staff to discern outcomes of their work; they know they are having an impact. Also, staff experience a new level of independence, autonomy, and discretion in performing the work.[34]

For example, suppose that a veteran secretary has been performing her work competently but expresses concern about the routine nature of her work. She has been attending school at night and has less than 1 year left before she completes her undergraduate degree. There is less need for her to perform typing because of the advent of word processors in the organization. The solution may be to enrich her job by making her a paraprofessional with new responsibilities such as interviewing clients and making referrals to other agencies.

Certainly, for job enrichment to succeed, individuals must be capable of expanding their skills. Job enrichment should be influenced by a sense of individual accomplishment, achievement, and competence. Without proper skills, enriching jobs could overwhelm staff. When upgrading job responsibilities, do so initially on a trial basis before committing to a permanent assignment. This will permit a careful review of the staff and the new job requirements.

Successful job enrichment may be affected by other aspects of the organization. Supervisors must be especially responsive to the new needs of staff. Staff may feel that they deserve higher pay, which must be taken into account. Special training may be required.[35] Staff whose jobs are not enriched may express resentment and jealousy. Despite these constraints, the requirements of an increasingly sophisticated workforce and the quest for continuous job stimulation will propel human service organizations to concentrate on job enrichment programs.

PHYSICAL ENVIRONMENT AND STAFF PRODUCTIVITY

Certain aspects of office design can contribute to staff being unproductive. These concerns may be obvious, but because they occur frequently management in all organizations must be prepared to address them.

Staff who are squeezed into close quarters have no sense of privacy and may spend an inordinate amount of time socializing. If space is at a premium, one method of dealing with this problem is to install wall dividers designed to reduce the "bull pen" atmosphere.

Give immediate attention to uncomfortable staff environments created by conditions such as poor heating in the winter and poor air-conditioning in the summer. Expect staff to be distracted from their tasks if they are forced to work under poor environmental conditions. Money spent on refurbishing formerly gloomy surroundings is a good investment. People should feel good about coming to work.

The traffic pattern can also have an impact on productivity. For example, as staff walk to and from the fax machine, the copier, and the water fountain, they can too easily socialize or disturb other staff whose offices are en route. Be mindful of how staff physically move through the organization.

The location of the manager of a unit can have an impact on productivity. It is sometimes tempting to put managers together, removed from their respective staffs. Although communication between managers is certainly desirable, this should not be done at the expense of losing close contact with their staffs.

DILEMMAS ABOUT KEEPING GOOD PEOPLE

Effective managers must continuously work to keep good staff. Funding reductions and the natural desire of good staff to seek better opportunities elsewhere, however, can present tremendous challenges to managers who work to keep the organization functioning at an optimal level.

When Funding Reductions Force Termination

Because of cutbacks at the federal, state, and local levels and increased competition for funding from foundations and localized funding drives such as the United Way, many human service organizations sooner or later must deal with funding contractions. This harsh reality requires managers to undergo considerable soul-searching about whether to freeze wages or reduce staff. The dilemma, of course, is that if you freeze wages or reduce the number of hours to avoid layoffs you run the risk of increasing the level of staff malcontent and jeopardizing the organization's overall productivity. Laying off staff, however, could mean diminishing services. In general, effective managers opt to lay off unproductive staff while striving to keep the best. They use the cutbacks as an opportunity to communicate with the remaining staff their importance to the organization and their need to continually work for increased productivity—a painful but necessary decision. One manager described her soul-searching decision as follows:

> About 2 years ago, I began to experience my budget becoming tighter. I was faced with a plateau in funding from my government source, and with inflation I had to begin figuring where I could make cutbacks without affecting

> my program. I trimmed telephone, supplies, and other costs, but the fact was that 75% of my budget was in personnel. Faced with an additional decrease last year, I had to make a difficult decision of limiting staff salary increases. Then, 6 months ago, I realized that I could not escape the difficult decision to cut back staff. To make the best possible decision under trying circumstances, I examined systematically both my functions and activities. As a result of my analysis, I determined that some of our educational activities were now being provided by another organization and that agencies that used to rely on us for training were drawing upon their own internal resources. Furthermore, I determined that some of the functions carried out by education and training staff could be handled by other members of the organization. I came to the difficult—but proper—conclusion that I should eliminate the educational director's position. Unless I did so, I would have to cut funding for other needed services. Although this decision caused me personal anguish since she was a longtime, loyal employee, I knew I made the right decision.

Clearly, what influenced the painful decision to let go of a dedicated employee was the harsh reality of the budget. Had the budget continued to expand, it is possible that the underused employee might have been retained. Additional work might have been found, or there might have been more tolerance for the "downtime" when the staff member was moderately unproductive. Budget reductions in human service organizations, no less than their counterparts in profit-making companies, impose a sometimes necessary pruning process.

When employees must be let go, they can be given a longer than usual time period to search for other employment. Agencies sometimes tolerate 1 or 2 months of inefficiency to allow the person to search for another job. Some organizations prefer not to keep the unproductive employee on the job and therefore provide severance pay. In addition, employees could be provided with outplacement counseling to assist in their job search. Recognize that there could be fallout from letting an employee go. Other employees begin to wonder, "Are we next?" There may be an undercurrent of resentment and hostility when a valued colleague has to be terminated. It is extremely important to clarify the status of the remaining employees to squelch rumors and offer assurances.

When Good Staff Are Offered Better Pay Elsewhere

Sometimes, valuable employees present a dilemma because they are offered more lucrative jobs elsewhere. The employee would prefer to remain, but the increased pay is just too enticing. As discussed earlier, one way of dealing with this problem is to restructure the employee's responsibilities to justify a competitive salary. If this is not possible and a slight increase in the current salary does not provide sufficient incentive, you are then faced with the dilemma of either increasing the salary significantly (assuming you have funding to do so) or accepting the employee's departure.

As a general rule, it is not a good idea to keep staff simply to avoid having to find a replacement. More important, however, you should avoid consenting to excessive salary increases just to retain an employee because to do so may, in the long run, do more harm than good. Other staff will learn about the increased salary sooner or later, and they will resent the fact that one of their colleagues is receiving a salary far out of line with the organization's pay scale. They might feel the need to resort to a similar tactic to boost their own salaries.[36] The internal problems caused by avoiding the departure are likely to be far greater than the benefits of keeping the staff member. Keeping good people is a desirable objective but not at all costs. It is best not to hold an employee back when better opportunities are available elsewhere. This positive attitude reflects well on you and on the organization as a place to learn and grow.

NOTES

1. S. Cohen, *The effective public manager: Achieving success in government* (San Francisco: Jossey-Bass, 1988), p. 32.

2. S. Cohen, p. 32.

3. M. Beer, B. Spector, P. R. Lawrence, D. Q. Mills, & R. E. Walton, *Managing human assets,* (New York: Free Press, 1984), p. 91.

4. Alexander Hamilton Institute, *Lawsuit-free documentation: A manger's guide to fair and legal recordkeeping* (Ramsey, NJ: Author, 1997), p. 13; Alexander Hamilton Institute, *Interviewing made easy: The right way to ask hiring questions* (Ramsey, NJ: Author, 1999), pp. 4-7.

5. R. S. Schuler, *Personnel and human resource management* (3rd ed.) (St. Paul, MN: West, 1987), p. 169.

6. Alexander Hamilton Institute, *Lawsuit-free documentation,* pp. 13-15.

7. Alexander Hamilton Institute, *Interviewing made easy,* pp. 8-23.

8. P. Drucker, *Managing the nonprofit organization* (New York: HarperCollins, 1990), p. 148.

9. R. S. Schuler, p. 127.

10. M. Beer et al., p. 75; T. Caplow, *How to run any organization* (Hinsdale, IL: Dryden, 1976), p. 134; R. E. Herman, *Keeping good people: Strategies for solving the dilemma of the decade* (Cleveland, OH: Oakhill, 1990), pp. 100-101; G. T. Milkovich &

J. W. Boudreau, *Personnel/human resource management* (5th ed.) (Plano, TX: Business Publications, 1988), pp. 376-377.

11. P. Drucker, p. 146.

12. Alexander Hamilton Institute, *Interviewing made easy,* pp. 23-24.

13. R. S. Schuler, p. 427.

14. R. S. Schuler, p. 403.

15. P. Drucker, p. 153.

16. G. T. Milkovich & J. W. Boudreau, p. 550.

17. A. Chandler, Jr., *Strategy and structure* (Garden City, NY: Doubleday, 1966).

18. S. Cohen, p. 54.

19. R. T. Crow & C. A. Odewahn, *Management for the human services* (Englewood Cliffs, NJ: Prentice Hall, 1987), p. 10.

20. M. Beer et al., pp. 178-179; R. T. Crow & C. A. Odewahn, pp. 26-28.

21. R. T. Crow & C. A. Odewahn, pp. 28-29.

22. T. J. Peters & R. H. Waterman, *In search of excellence: Lessons from America's best run companies* (New York: Harper & Row, 1982), pp. 270-277.

23. R. S. Schuler, pp. 453-455.

24. R. S. Schuler, pp. 461-464.

25. M. Hammer, Reengineering work: Don't automate, obliterate, *Harvard Business Review, 4* (1990), pp. 104-112.

26. S. Cohen, pp. 60-61.

27. G. T. Milkovich & J. W. Boudreau, p. 125.

28. R. E. Herman, pp. 178-179; P. J. Pecora & M. J. Austin, *Managing human services personnel* (Newbury Park, CA: Sage, 1987), pp. 24-25.

29. G. T. Milkovich & J. W. Boudreau, pp. 135-144; P. J. Pecora & M. J. Austin, p. 25; R. S. Schuler, p. 98.

30. Public Children Services Association of Ohio, *PCSAO caseload study* (Columbus, OH: Author, 1988).

31. C. J. Coulton, S. Keller, & C. R. Boone, Predicting social workers' expenditures of time with hospital patients, *Health and Social Work, 1* (1985), pp. 35-39.

32. C. Mills & C. Ivery, A strategy for workload management in child protective practice, *Child Welfare, 1* (1991), pp. 35-43; L. Sametz & D. Hamparian, *Innovating programs in Cuyahoga County Juvenile Court: Intensive probation supervision and probation classification* (Cleveland, OH: Federation for Community Planning, 1990), pp. 1-48; R. G. Wiebush & D. Hamparian, *Probation classification: Design and development of the Cuyahoga County Juvenile Court model* (Cleveland, OH: Federation for Community Planning, 1986), pp. 1-20.

33. T. J. Peters & R. H. Waterman, p. 72.

34. M. Beer et al., p. 160; G. T. Milkovich & J. W. Boudreau, p. 127; R. S. Schuler, pp. 448-449.

35. E. E. Lawler, *High involvement management* (San Francisco: Jossey-Bass, 1986), pp. 95-100.

36. S. Cohen, p. 42.

Chapter 8

DEALING WITH UNPRODUCTIVE EMPLOYEES

Despite efforts to hire the right person for the job and then to provide proper training, some staff may perform poorly. Effective managers must properly diagnose the problem, including understanding special situations that could affect employee behavior. Moreover, they will likely have to confront two increasingly important issues—substance abuse and AIDS. Furthermore, effective managers may need to take corrective actions when employees are unproductive and, if necessary, apply disciplinary measures. When all else fails, termination may be the only proper recourse.

DIAGNOSING THE PROBLEM

Some employees perform poorly because management has not clarified organizational policies or because supervisors have not properly defined work priorities and expectations. Other employees may take advantage of lax office procedures by arriving late or socializing excessively. Still others may require more structured work assignments or may have been mismatched with their jobs.[1] These problems are generally correctable in supervisory discussions. Policies can be enunciated, work priorities delineated, expectations clarified, office procedures tightened, assignments structured, and reassignments (if feasible) made. Following corrective action, unproductive staff will presumably improve their job performance and functioning.

By discussing the problem directly with the employee, you can determine whether extenuating circumstances should be addressed. For example, you may discover that an otherwise productive employee is frequently late to work because he or she takes his or her child to day care in the morning. You could consider altering the rules about lateness so that he or she can make up the time by working an extra 30 minutes at lunch. Of course, this is a judgment call based on your overall analysis of the situation. It is possible that providing flexible time for one employee could create problems with the rest of the staff. Hence, in making your diagnosis, consider both the circumstances particular to the employee and the likely responses from the rest of the members of the organization.

DEALING WITH SPECIAL SITUATIONS

Staff may be unproductive in a variety of ways. The following sections present some common profiles that may need to be handled.

The Dead-Ender

Staff at the top of their job classification with no place to go can feel stymied and may need special motivation. To prevent their high motivation from deteriorating, consider the following:

- Seek their advice and suggestions on how they can continue as high performers even if they are at the top of their pay scale. By doing so, you demonstrate that you value their opinion.
- If possible, give them additional decision-making responsibilities.
- Assign them trainees; they will gain satisfaction from serving as mentors.
- Provide out-of-the-ordinary assignments that offer challenge and a chance to shine. For example, put them on loan to another department in which their talents and abilities can be appreciated.

Frequently, staff who feel they are at a dead end will not communicate their concerns directly, but their below-average performance may be a clear sign of their disinvestment. Excessive absences, increased socializing, or frequent arguments may be symptoms that require corrective action. Convey your concerns and expectations before their behavior turns into complete indifference.[2] Explain what has gone wrong with the employee's performance and what steps can be taken to correct the situation. Ask the staff member to explain the reason for performance decline, and determine together how to rearrange staff priorities. As with other employees who may be performing poorly, it is important to keep proper documentation to justify any action you take now or in the future.[3]

The Passed-Over Employee

Being denied a promotion can be discouraging and frustrating and may result in staff disengaging from their work. The first step is to talk privately with the employee to explain why another person was selected. The emphasis should be on what makes the other person more qualified, not what makes the employee less qualified. If the employee has shortcomings, you might suggest how these might be eliminated. In addition, you could work out a plan for additional assignments or special studies that would enhance the employee's competitiveness for future job openings. By reinforcing employee self-esteem and providing practical assistance, you help him or her reengage in his or her work.

The Technophobe

Sometimes, an otherwise competent employee is unable to take on new assignments or deal with new technologies, especially involving the use of computers. Frequently, the employee fears failure and, moreover, experiences tremendous discomfort in having to be taught by younger staff who are more familiar with new technology. After all, this could involve role reversal in which the subordinate becomes the leader, even the criticizer. If possible, select peers instead of junior staff to be the teachers of new technology. Even if this is not possible, supervisors must be clear and unequivocal: Although accepting the resistance as an understandable temporary response, the organization is committed to having staff grow with the new technologies.

In addition to conveying clear expectations, the organization needs to show its support and recognize the anxiety of the technophobic. This supportive atmosphere can be created by feelings of camaraderie that everyone is participating in a "community of learning." Managers need to recognize that staff productivity may be lower for a time while employees learn new skills. Staff may even need to be relieved of some duties to lessen overall work pressures. The organization must provide training—not only one-time workshops but also ongoing consultation and troubleshooting.

The Mismatched Employee

Sometimes, employees are hired into jobs that subsequently prove to be wrong for them. Although mismatched, staff have other skills, talents, and commitment that warrant their being retained but perhaps not in the position for which they were hired. Rather than terminating the employees, one option is to assign them to other positions for which they are better qualified, even if the positions are lower paying. Reducing salary is a calculated risk, but if the alternative is terminating a worthwhile employee, it is important to help the staff understand and accept the situation.

The Work Climate Spoiler

Some employees poison the work atmosphere with their sour demeanor. Their grumpy mood negatively affects the rest of the staff, although they may be quite competent in their main job responsibilities. If their work requires only minimal interaction with staff or clients, then some latitude can be given them. An accountant in the back office or a secretary in the word processing center with this attitude might be more tolerable than a counselor working directly with clients. Other work spoilers are employees who constantly gossip, spread malicious rumors, or seek gratification by pitting one employee against another. You need to convey the severity of your concerns and your desire for a more constructive attitude; work spoilers cannot be tolerated.

The Work Laggard

Sometimes, new staff who may not be used to the work ethic of the organization tend to slough off work or generally be unresponsive to requests to produce. They may be dilatory in carrying out work assignments. Ordinarily, these behaviors could be grounds for dismissal, but if you believe these employees' behaviors can be changed, you need to remind them in unambiguous terms of the consequences for indolent behavior. A good practice is to provide a handbook to all new employees that provides work performance expectations. Sometimes, you may need to allow a period of time for adjustment and a considerable amount of discussion regarding tardiness, absenteeism, excessive use of sick time, personal phone calls, or reading non-work-related material on the job to allow staff to accept the work ethic of the organization.

The Poorly Trained Employee

You may find some staff to be unproductive because no one has ever taken the time to fully explain their responsibilities and walk them through their assignments. They may be thrust into situations for which they are ill prepared because of poor hiring decisions. For these employees, training and supervision are key elements. They may need to be sent to a formal training program or at least be provided with a mentor who can work with and guide them during their learning period.

All the previously mentioned "types" of employees have two things in common: They are not performing up to the standards of the organization and could potentially be fired. In fact, some managers take the understandable position that the excessive concentration required to change unproductive employees presents a serious drain of time and energy and creates resentment among productive staff. You need to discern whether straightening out an unproductive employee is worth the effort. There are few things more exciting, however, than salvaging an unproductive employee and taking pride in his or her new and sustained achievements and contributions.

POLICY POSITIONS ON SPECIAL ISSUES AFFECTING PRODUCTIVITY

In recent years, and no doubt continuing into the future, two major problems have dominated urban communities: substance abuse and AIDS. Because of the implications on the workforce, these issues must be confronted.

Substance Abuse

No matter what the reason, no human service organization can tolerate substance abuse among staff. To ensure the safety, quality, and productivity of their workforce, organizations must make their substance abuse policies clear in writing. By articulating an unequivocal policy position, organizations provide fair and ample warning to employees who are substance abusers.

How is it possible to detect a substance abuse problem among your staff? Search for the following signs: missed deadlines, sudden mood swings, erratic behavior, falling productivity, and slurred speech. These symptoms may not necessarily be indicative of a substance abuse problem but may provide clues if such a problem exists. Keep a confidential diary in which you record specific instances (date, time, and nature of incident) of inappropriate behavior. With written evidence, the staff member is less likely to deny the existence of a pattern.

Prepare and post the agency's position on substance abuse and have employees sign an acknowledgment that they have read it. Employees should understand that if they violate the organization's policy they could be suspended without compensation. Some organizations require staff violators to enroll in a rehabilitation program and to authorize disclosure of successful completion of the program. The employee would remain on probation during treatment. Those who voluntarily choose treatment should, if possible, be provided with medical insurance benefits and counseling programs.[4]

Be aware that the 1990 Americans With Disabilities Act (ADA) protects recovering drug users and alcoholics in organizations with 25 or more employees. The ADA makes it unlawful for employers to refuse employment, deny promotion, or otherwise discriminate against those with disabilities, recovering drug abusers, or alcoholics. To deny a person a position or a promotion based only on the history of alcohol or drug abuse is in violation of the ADA. Persons who have recovered or are recovering alcoholics or drug abusers are protected under the law. Of course, current alcoholics or drug abusers are not protected by the ADA.[5] An appraisal record can document declining performance that may indicate a substance abuse problem and can give the employer "reasonable suspicion" required by many states to test for substance abuse and to take disciplinary action, including discharge.

In conducting an investigation of a suspected drug or alcohol abuser, be prepared to hear denials and do not push the employee into a confession. It is not necessary to determine the personal problem or what precipitated it. Focus only on work performance. Do not moralize, and do not ask questions such as "Why do you drink?" Avoid making idle threats, but do give a timeline in which improvement must occur. If you determine that the employee is intoxicated at work, arrange for someone to drive him or her home because the organization could be held liable if there is an accident. Prepare a detailed, written report after the incident and give a copy to both management and the employee.

The key to helping rehabilitate an employee is a fair, firm, and conscientious manager. Managers can help best by focusing on job performance, by following the discipline policy explicitly, and by periodically reviewing the employee's performance.[6] Develop a recovery plan with the employee that states how he or she will obtain help for the substance abuse problem.

AIDS

Employees affected by human immunodeficiency virus (HIV) may not be unproductive, but other employees, out of their own misguided anxiety and fears, may be diverted from accomplishing their work. To counter potential rumors and myths, human service organizations should provide a written policy position clarifying that persons with HIV infection will not be denied employment or promotion because of their condition.

Most important, the policy should convey that current medical knowledge indicates that AIDS cannot be contracted from normal daily contact, and therefore disciplinary action will be taken against any employee who refuses to work with or near an HIV-infected client or coworker. Employees need to understand in no uncertain terms that, if they refuse to work in these circumstances, they are free to search for employment elsewhere. Staff should be made aware that the Federal Rehabilitation Act and the Americans With Disabilities Act of 1990 prohibit discrimination against employees with disabilities, including those with AIDS and HIV infections.[7] Meanwhile, to allay fears, the policy should make clear that the organization will also take disciplinary action against any HIV-infected person who engages in behaviors that place others at risk. Of course, confidentiality of the employee's physical condition must be protected, and information should be available only on a "need-to-know" basis.

Managing Persons With Disabilities

The ADA makes it unlawful for employers to discriminate against individuals with disabilities in regard to hiring, firing, compensation, training, advancement, and all other conditions of employment. The responsibility for enforcing the ADA is the Equal Employment Opportunity Commission (EEOC). Employees have a right to a jury trial and to punitive and compensatory damages when there is a finding of intentional discrimination.[8]

If the organization has a fair and rational appraisal system (see Chapter 11), then actions taken by the organization will stand up in court. An employee with a disability who is not performing his or her job despite being given reasonable accommodation can be subject to disciplinary action, including termination. The EEOC will expect to see a record of substandard performance appraisals. Furthermore, the ADA does not require that an employee with a disability be promoted or offered training that would make advancement possible if either action would place undue hardship on the employer.[9]

An employer can hold staff with disabilities to the same standards of production and performance to which staff without disabilities are held. A double standard should not be applied in such a way that persons with disabilities receive less discipline than any other employee. Again, it is important that the appraisal process document poor performance to avoid claims of discrimination.

Persons with disabilities can provide an organization with challenges that must be addressed. For example, a person with epilepsy whose disease is under control because of medication does not necessarily present a risk to the children under her care. A person with a stuttering problem who meets the qualifications of being a counselor must be considered for that position. A person who is somewhat obese is not covered by the ADA, but one who is severely obese—more than 100% of the norm—is under its protection. This is the purpose of the ADA.[10]

In considering a person who might qualify under the ADA for a position in the organization, all questions must be focused on the job and not on the person. For example, you would not ask

"Are you taking medications that would make you drowsy?"

"Have you ever been treated for mental health problems?"

"How did you become disabled?"

"Have you ever been treated for an inability to handle stress?"

"How often have you used illegal drugs in the past?"

These questions cannot be asked because they focus on the disability. The provisions of the ADA were designed to prevent discrimination against individuals with hidden disabilities.[11]

You could ask persons with disabilities, however, whether they could perform the functions of a particular job with or without reasonable accommodation. You could inquire about how they would perform particular job-related functions and whether they could meet the job attendance requirements. You could ask whether they currently are using illegal drugs. These questions must be aimed at determining their ability to perform essential job functions and not at discovering the existence or severity of a disability.

If a person is hired, a reasonable accommodation must be made. Be sure that this does not mean inflating performance appraisals for employees with disabilities because this might make the employees think they deserve to be promoted because they are doing a better job than is the case. To avoid a discrimination lawsuit, it is important that good documentation indicate the reasons for failing to promote. This documentation must be fair and accurate.[12]

TAKING CORRECTIVE ACTION TO CHANGE BEHAVIOR

When employees manifest attitudes or behaviors that interfere with meeting performance standards, corrective action must be taken. Usually, the supervisor takes the initiative and formulates a performance plan that clarifies acceptable performance standards, identifies actions needed to meet those standards, provides a specific timetable, and states consequences if improvement does not occur.

In preparation for the performance interview, the supervisor should document substandard performance and behaviors. The interview should be straightforward, firm, and nonthreatening. The supervisor should convey that, although the organization values the staff member, there can be no compromise on job performance.

Confronting an unproductive employee can be a profound experience for both the supervisor and the employee. It requires a consistent and direct approach to help employees face issues they might want to deny or minimize. Ultimately, it should help unproductive employees accept responsibility for their behavior and implement specific steps to improve it.

For confronting an unproductive employee, the following paragraphs provide specific guidelines that are useful in most situations.

Document specific, concrete behaviors that reflect the deteriorating work performance or unacceptable behavior and the circumstances in which they occurred. Concentrate on the results of behavior rather than on the individual's shortcomings. For example, emphasize the lateness of reports rather than the employee's tendency to procrastinate. This approach will help diminish the employee's feelings of being personally attacked.

Discuss the unacceptable behavior as soon as possible after it occurs. Do not wait for the year-end evaluation to discuss events that happened 4 months earlier. Immediacy adds potency to the discussion.

Conduct the discussion in private. Public reprimands can embarrass staff, and their "losing face" makes them more resentful and resistant to change.

To emphasize the caring and supportive concern you have for the employee, identify strengths in addition to limitations. Few people do everything wrong, and most do far more right than not. By being positive, you provide a context within which the criticism can be tolerated more easily. When the employee does make progress, acknowledge the turnaround. Applaud the new behavior as a way of reinforcing it.

Avoid making value judgments and moralizing for impaired work performance. If personal or emotional problems are offered as explanations, you can be sympathetic without abandoning your expectations of quality work performance. Employees must be seen as adults responsible for their own behavior, but you may need to encourage some to seek counseling with the understanding that doing so would not jeopardize job or promotion opportunities.[13] Because of the recognition that employees' personal lives can spill over into their work attitudes and behaviors, many organizations offer employee assistance programs that provide confidential interviews to troubled staff.

Focus on changing behavior. You should be clear about specific behaviors you want the staff to change. You should involve the employee in finding a solution, remembering that your purpose is not punishment but changing unacceptable behavior. Because the employee will feel defensive, it may be helpful to use "I" statements, which indicate your point of view—for example, "I am concerned about your attendance" or "I want you to make an effort to be more cooperative."[14]

PROGRESSIVE DISCIPLINE

Many states follow the "employment at will" doctrine, which states that unless a definite period of services is specified in an employment contract, hiring is considered to be "at will." Subject to specific legal restrictions, an employer has the right to discharge an employee at any time without notice and for any reason or for no reason at all. This has been upheld by the U.S. Supreme Court as being constitutional.[15] Progressive discipline must be viewed within the context of this employment at will doctrine.

In contrast to the employment at will provisions, human service professionals are sometimes covered by collective bargaining agreements or civil service rules, which provide for due process and "just cause" standards. Normally, agency personnel practices provide for a grievance appeal process, usually limited to an internal appeal within the agency, with no opportunity for an impartial third party. Some agencies, under their collective bargaining agreement, permit a discharged employee to have representation at the point of discipline and throughout the grievance procedure. The grievance is submitted to arbitration if the management and the union cannot resolve the discharge grievance. This third-party arbitrator is jointly selected by the parties and conducts an impartial hearing that is binding on both. Typically, selected arbitrary agreements require progressive discipline—counseling, verbal warning, written warning, and suspension—prior to discharge. The value of voluntary arbitration is that it avoids wrongful discharge lawsuits and protects against abuse of managerial authority.[16]

Whether agencies operate employment at will or just cause, they will follow a set of procedures or deliberate steps in addressing performance problems or disciplining their employees, depending on the extent to which employees have violated the rules or exhibited unprofessional behavior. These explicit progressive discipline policies provide guidelines for both management and employees regarding expected staff behaviors and consequences for noncompliance. By following the following steps, you are fair to the employees, you avoid capricious actions, and your disciplinary process will hold up in court:

1. Provide the employee with explicit expectations for behavior and performance. Generally, most problems can be solved by clarifying ambiguous expectations.
2. If the problem continues, convey a verbal warning specifying how expectations are not being met. Reach an agreement regarding how the employee can correct the problem. Depending on the problem, you may want to issue more than one verbal warning. During this phase, individual or group counseling may need to be provided to help the person correct the problem.

3. The next step is to send a written warning, including a description of the behavior that is expected of the employee and what the employee is perceived to be doing wrong. Convey how you expect the employee to correct the behavior or overcome the problem. Indicate what the consequences will be if the employee does not correct the problem within a specified time period. It is possible that an employee may request a transfer to another unit. He or she may be in the wrong job, or the chemistry between staff and supervisor may be affecting work performances. A change in position may therefore resolve the problem. Whether the employee remains or is transferred elsewhere, indicate, if appropriate, what kind of support will be given. Specify that further disciplinary action may be taken if the problem persists. If the employee refuses to sign the warning, another supervisor should immediately be brought in to sign the written document and acknowledge the employee's refusal.

4. If the problem persists, the next step is a consequence, often in the form of suspension—giving the employee time off without pay, usually 1 to 3 days, to convey how serious the problem has become. If you tell your employee that a suspension will result from repeating the problem, you have to follow through unless the staff member offers a reasonable explanation. Some organizations use a variation by providing a paid suspension, with the requirement that the employee return with a written plan on how he or she will correct the problem. To convey that employee attitudes and behavior will be closely scrutinized upon return, inform the employee that he or she is on probation. The employee must understand that termination may result if performance problems continue.

5. The final step, of course, is termination. This will be discussed in more detail later.

In some special circumstances, a direct consequence may be necessary that requires bypassing the progressive approach outlined previously. For example, in a children's residential treatment center, if staff have been irresponsible in monitoring children's behavior, several days' suspension may be necessary immediately to convey the severity of the situation.

Moving beyond the verbal warning to a more serious consequence should, if possible, be detailed in advance.[17] In all the steps prior to termination, it is important to convey that you think that the employee is capable of changing behavior. In some instances, it may be better to place staff on probation, perhaps up to 3 months, to emphasize that there will be a period of close scrutiny. Some behaviors may be sufficiently serious to warrant suspension or termination, such as misusing or stealing agency property, sleeping on the job, verbally abusing clients, and physically abusing a child. Each organization should determine its response to unprofessional behavior in its personnel practices.[18]

To protect employees from capricious, arbitrary acts, organizations should develop a grievance procedure that permits staff to appeal decisions. This procedure should be clearly outlined in the organization's personnel practices manual.

HANDLING THE INCOMPETENT EMPLOYEE

In some extraordinary situations, you may find it very difficult to fire an incompetent staff member. Requirements of civil service or union procedures may prevent this, and, in the real world, political considerations may be a factor. These barriers do not automatically mean that you should not terminate an unproductive employee. Some effective managers confront obstacles to terminating an unsatisfactory employee with credible documentation and tremendous resolve and conviction, even to the point of putting their own jobs on the line. Nevertheless, if termination is not possible, the manager must develop a strategy to ensure that the incompetent staff member does not "contaminate" productive employees with his or her bad work habits and poor attitude.

Some organizations develop an unimportant special assignment for the unproductive employee that is unlikely to result in much damage to the organization if it is not performed competently. Some go so far as to isolate the incompetent staff person in the least desirable physical space. These are "last resort," desperate actions that should not continue indefinitely. Be aware, however, that putting an employee in an undesirable situation can be construed as a "constructive discharge"; this could invite a lawsuit in which the employee charges that he or she was placed in working conditions that were so intolerable that he or she was forced to quit.[19]

Another approach is to assign the least essential function to a team of poor performers, sometimes called a "turkey farm."[20] Of course, this could backfire and create embarrassment for the organization. A variation of this idea is to loan an unproductive member who has some redeeming qualities to another unit or another organization, thereby removing the troublesome staff person and breaking up patterns of dysfunctional behavior. In some instances, this could be a positive move for both the employee and the organization. By placing the unproductive staff member in a new setting with different work relationships and job requirements, it is possible that a better performance from the employee can be induced. Again, these suggestions are made with extreme caution; some managers have a policy that they will in no circumstances retain incompetent employees.

Terminating Employees

Because human service organizations are in the business of rehabilitating people, there may be a tendency to hang on a little longer and hope the incompetent employee will improve. Recognizing that some circumstances make it exceedingly difficult to terminate employees, managers nevertheless must be willing to act with the conviction that terminating staff is a necessary and essential part of keeping an organization productive. The reality is that employees can be mismatched with their jobs, can lack motivation to work, may evidence behavior that warrants termination, may be unwilling to carry out the tasks that help the organization achieve its mission, or all these. If attempts to improve performance do not seem to work, then termination is necessary for the continued health of the organization. Grounds for firing include the following:[21]

- Physical violence
- Sexual harassment or assault
- Gross insubordination
- Alcohol or drug use during work hours
- Repeated shirking of responsibilities
- Lack of skills to perform required tasks or to meet objectives
- Chronic or excessive absences
- Dishonesty, including falsification of employment records and expense accounts
- Carelessness that causes actual or potential harm
- Continued incompetence, despite training

Staff incompetence is not always easy to spot. A person may be generally destructive but may still perform an important function. An incompetent staff member may be a nice person. Termination should occur when the organization's work becomes threatened or when retaining a poor performer significantly affects the work of others or the organization's ability to function. Keeping unproductive staff members is unfair to others in the organization who must make up for their failures and untangle their messes.[22]

Legally Sound Disciplinary and Termination Processes

In taking disciplinary action or terminating employees, effective managers must be careful to avoid the organization's becoming entangled in costly and time-consuming lawsuits. If employees believe that their employer does not adopt or enforce fair and consistent procedures, litigation alleging discrimination or violation of implied contractual obligations can occur. Watch for the types of problems discussed in the following sections.

Lack of Clear and Consistent Policies. The absence of clear, written policies can lead to the inconsistent treatment of employees. If staff believe they are treated differentially because of gender, race, ethnicity, age, or physical or mental disability, they may resort to litigation. Policies should state conditions under which termination can occur. Supervisors must be instructed on the importance of impartially enforcing regulations; otherwise, staff could claim bias. Progressive discipline policies should be circulated so that all staff clearly understand the ground rules for professional behavior.

Inconsistent Evaluation History. Terminated employees may insist that their appraisal history be reviewed; therefore, you should avoid being trapped in the inexplicable situation of having given acceptable performance appraisals or merit salary increases to marginal employees. Consistently document unsatisfactory performance by providing a "paper trail" that records disciplinary actions and performance reviews. Indicate on the record where even small problems are occurring so that a pattern of marginal performance becomes clear. The best approach for dealing with unproductive employees is to keep extensive, fully documented records so you can establish just cause for any eventual terminations. Documentation is the single most effective weapon in any type of legal action.[23]

This record should be free of any statements mentioning age, race, sex, national origin, religion, or disability. It should be free of derogatory statements and subjective descriptions. For example, instead of saying the employee has a "bad attitude," the employee's conduct should be specifically described. All previous written disciplinary warnings or performance reviews should have been signed by the employee, acknowledging awareness of supervisory concern.

Letting Subjective Biases Affect Termination Decisions. If supervisors show partiality in the enforcement of regulations by favoring one employee over others, the result could be a charge of bias. Be certain that you treat discipline and termination actions consistently by reviewing whether other employees in similar circumstances would be treated in the same way. Check potential biases with other members of the administrative staff to ensure you have followed correct procedures. By focusing on performance, supervisors reduce the risk of being accused of capricious and discriminatory behavior. Inform employees of performance criteria in advance, and clarify expectations in measurable and identifiable terms.[24]

Be aware that wrongful discharge lawsuits can be filed if discrimination can be shown regarding age, disability, race, religion, and sex. Firing or demoting someone more than 40 years old without documented proof, terminating an employee with a disability before exhausting all the accommodation efforts, discharging a minority person for an offense for which nonminority employees were not discharged, terminating an employee who has a sincerely held religious belief, and demoting a female employee because she did not get along with men in the organization are all situations that can result in challenges in the court.[25]

Failure to Inform Staff That Their Positions Are in Jeopardy. Litigation is likely to occur when employees can claim they were unaware that their performance could result in adverse consequences; they can say they were denied the opportunity to take corrective action.[26] Occasionally, some supervisors may place negative observations in an employee's files but then not share the information—a procedure that can backfire when a lawsuit is filed. Negative written reviews must include specific problem areas or mention of inadequate performance, ideas for improvement, and a stipulation that continued similar problems will result in adverse action. A good procedure provides the employee with the opportunity to comment on, or even dispute, the performance appraisal. At the very least, the employee should sign the appraisal form.

Discipline Documents

Most organizations have written policies and formal warning systems to address possible employee problems. Assuming that a progressive discipline system is in place, a supervisor should be able to provide documentation that lists both the positive and negative aspects of staff performance and behavior. If an employee's record includes previous favorable appraisals, then you would prepare a detailed description of the reasons why performance is no longer considered satisfactory. Furthermore, the reports should be prepared on a regular basis and should avoid any bias.[27]

If an employee has received a final warning notice, the language should be clear and specific: Termination will result from one more of the same infraction. It is a good idea to have all disciplinary documents signed by both you and the employee before a copy is placed in the personnel file.[28]

To avoid being legally burned in a potential lawsuit, managers should observe the following procedures:[29]

1. Initiate training or counseling to indicate that you have been fair in trying to improve performance.
2. Document verbal warnings and provide for the employee to sign off on your notes to indicate that he or she has been made aware of your concerns.
3. Make certain that the employee is aware of consequences should the situation be repeated.
4. Obtain a second opinion from upper management before you actually fire an employee to ensure your termination is based on concrete evidence and not subjective factors.
5. Provide the employee with a valid reason for termination and a copy of the rule that has been violated.
6. Consider having the employee voluntarily sign a release from future legal claims. This may require providing the employee with more than the normal severance pay. Encourage the employee to obtain legal advice before signing it.
7. To avoid a potential defamation or slander lawsuit, indicate only that the person worked for the organization during a given period of time.

In summary, check with your attorney regarding the possibility of "unjust dismissal" if you have any doubts. Effective managers realize that, although there is no absolute way to prevent lawsuits, by operating fairly, communicating frequently and candidly, and documenting thoroughly, potential litigation can be avoided.[30]

Conducting the Termination Interview

If you must terminate an employee, the following guidelines may assist you:

- Avoid poor timing of the termination: birthdays, anniversaries, holidays, or Fridays. Termination early in the week allows time to wrap up loose ends promptly instead of allowing the individual to "stew" during the weekend.
- Determine in advance the benefits to which the person is entitled, including unused vacation, pension disbursement, and severance pay.
- Arrange, if feasible, for outplacement counseling.
- Determine in advance exactly what you will say in the interview. Be specific about when the person is to leave.
- Allot no more than 30 minutes for the interview to say what you have to say and come to closure.
- Accept what the employee has to say in his or her defense, but do not become argumentative. Anticipate and respond without being defensive to the question "Why me?"
- Say something positive about the individual, but do not be excessive. Avoid transmitting "mixed messages" that may convey hope to the employee that something can be negotiated.
- Immediately following the meeting, contact all those persons who must know of your action firsthand.
- Minimize discussion of dismissed employees. Respect their dignity and the confidentiality of your decision. Discuss the situation only with those who absolutely need to know.
- Take pride in knowing that you acted constructively, honorably, courteously, and aboveboard.[31]

In some circumstances, employees could be encouraged to resign. They benefit because they preserve their dignity in the outside world, and they improve their chances for reemployment. The organization benefits because it avoids potential legal battles.[32] Some organizations resort to a generous "severance" payment in exchange for a signed waiver indicating the resignation was voluntary and no lawsuit will be forthcoming. This should be considered with utmost caution, however, because of possible repercussions from staff who may resent the special consideration given to the departing, unproductive employee.

NOTES

1. P. J. Pecora & M. J. Austin, *Managing human services personnel* (Newbury Park, CA: Sage, 1987), p. 42.
2. Bureau of Business Practice, *Front line supervisor's standard manual* (Waterford, CT: Author, 1989), pp. 14-15.
3. Alexander Hamilton Institute, *Conducting successful appraisal interviews: The right way to discuss employee performance* (Ramsey, NJ: Author, 1998), pp. 25-26.
4. National Institute of Business Management, *Fire at will: Terminating your employees legally* (New York: Author, 1991), p. 13.
5. Alexander Hamilton Institute, *What every manager should know about the Americans With Disabilities Act* (Ramsey, NJ: Author, 1997), p. 5.
6. Alexander Hamilton Institute, *A manager's guide to creating a drug-and-alcohol-free workplace* (Maywood, NJ: Author, 1991).
7. National Leadership Coalition on AIDS, *Small business and AIDS: How AIDS can affect your business* (Washington, DC: Author, 1991).
8. Alexander Hamilton Institute, *What every manager should know about the Americans With Disabilities Act,* p. 1.
9. Alexander Hamilton Institute, *Conducting successful appraisal interviews: The right way to discuss employee performance,* p. 32.
10. Alexander Hamilton Institute, *What every manager should know about the Americans With Disabilities Act,* pp. 6-9.
11. Alexander Hamilton Institute, *What every manager should know about the Americans With Disabilities Act,* pp. 28-30.
12. Alexander Hamilton Institute, *What every manager should know about Americans With Disabilities Act,* pp. 29-32; Alexander Hamilton Institute, *Interviewing made easy: The right way to ask hiring questions* (Ramsey, NJ: Author, 1999), pp. 26-34; Alexander Hamilton Institute, *Lawsuit-free documentation: A manager's guide to fair and legal recordkeeping* (Ramsey, NJ: Author, 1997), pp. 32-33.
13. T. K. Connellan, *How to grow people into self-starters* (Ann Arbor, MI: Achievement Institute, 1980), pp. 141-143.
14. Alexander Hamilton Institute, *A manager's guide to the do's and don'ts of discipline* (Ramsey, NJ: Author, 1998), pp. 24-25.
15. S. C. Kahn, B. Berish Brown, M. Lanzarone, & B. E. Zepke, *Legal guide to human resources* (3rd ed.) (Boston: Warren, Gorham, & Lamont, 1994), p. 801.

16. M. Tambor, Employment-at-will or just cause: The right choice, *Administration in Social Work, 19*(3) (1995), pp. 45-57.

17. T. K. Connellan, p. 132.

18. Alexander Hamilton Institute, *A manager's guide to the do's and don'ts,* pp. 10-11, 20-21; R. T. Crow & C. A. Odewahn, *Management for the human services* (Englewood Cliffs, NJ: Prentice Hall, 1987), pp. 612-613; R. E. Herman, *Keeping good people: Strategies for solving the dilemma of the decade* (Cleveland, OH: Oakhill, 1990), pp. 83-85; P. J. Pecora & M. J. Austin, pp. 93-97.

19. Alexander Hamilton Institute, *A manager's guide to avoiding termination lawsuits* (Ramsey, NJ: Author, 1997), p. 19; Alexander Hamilton Institute, *A manager's guide to the do's and don'ts,* pp. 28-29.

20. S. Cohen, *The effective public manager: Achieving success in government* (San Francisco: Jossey-Bass, 1988), pp. 48-50.

21. Alexander Hamilton Institute, *A manager's guide to avoiding termination lawsuits,* pp. 1-38.

22. R. Townsend, *Further up the organization* (New York: Knopf, 1984), p. 76.

23. National Institute of Business Management, p. 2; Alexander Hamilton Institute, *A manager's guide to avoiding termination lawsuits,* p. 18.

24. Alexander Hamilton Institute, *A manager's guide to avoiding termination lawsuits,* p. 18.

25. Alexander Hamilton Institute, *A manager's guide to avoiding termination lawsuits,* pp. 27-34.

26. S. D. Bruce, *Face to face: Every manager's guide to better appraisal and discipline interviewing* (Madison, CT: Business and Legal Reports, 1989), pp. 87-113; S. A. Goering, Steps can protect company from ex-employee lawsuits, *The Plain Dealer* (1990, August 21), p. F2; Alexander Hamilton Institute, *A manager's guide to avoiding termination lawsuits,* p. 19.

27. Alexander Hamilton Institute, *Lawsuit-free documentation,* p. 30.

28. Alexander Hamilton Institute, *Lawsuit-free documentation,* pp. 28-29.

29. Alexander Hamilton Institute, *A manager's guide to avoiding termination lawsuits,* pp. 19-24, 35-37.

30. Alexander Hamilton Institute, *Conducting successful appraisal interviews* (Maywood, NJ: Author, 1991); National Institute of Business Management, pp. 1-40.

31. R. L. Swain, 66 ways to avoid trouble when terminating the long-termer, *The Human Resources Professional* (1989, September/October), pp. 28-31; Alexander Hamilton Institute, *A manager's guide to avoiding termination lawsuits,* pp. 22-26.

32. T. Wolf, *The nonprofit organization: An operating manual* (Englewood Cliffs, NJ: Prentice Hall, 1984), pp. 61-62.

Chapter 9

HUMANIZING THE ORGANIZATION

Interpersonal and emotional problems affecting work performance are bound to occur in organizations. If not handled properly, they tend to fester until they cause great damage and require a tremendous investment of time and energy—efforts that could be better spent on achieving the goals of the organization. When an organization has to expend significant resources to deal with incapacitating stress, debilitating conflicts, stagnating staff, cultural and gender biases, or perceived inequities, it becomes sidetracked and much less productive. Because problems affecting interpersonal relationships are a fact of life, effective managers must confront them and work toward humanizing the work environment.

MANAGING STRESS

Imagine reading the following ad in your local newspaper:

> Job opening for a committed professional willing to work long hours for low pay. You will experience many complaints, fatigue, and irritability that will likely result in emotional and physical exhaustion. You may be required to make painful decisions for which you no doubt will be criticized. You will be working with difficult clients who are victims of neglect, abuse, and exploitation and who are living under deplorable conditions. Your supervisors will be demanding and highly critical, and you will have limited opportunities to make decisions. You will never have the resources to do the job properly. You are more likely to experience failure than success. Moreover, because it will be so difficult to measure the results of your efforts, you may not even be aware of success when you do achieve it.

Of course, no such advertisement would ever appear, but the fact that such terms as "job stress" and "job burnout" have become so prevalent is a reflection of the tremendous pressure and demands that staff involved in the delivery of services must endure. Stress can occasionally become so severe that it causes physical and emotional exhaustion.[1] Because stress has become an increasing concern, there may be a tendency to focus attention on trying to get rid of it altogether. This should not, however, be your objective. It is not only unrealistic to try to do so, but also some degree of stress actually contributes to productivity.

Many employees do work well under pressure; anxiety and tension mobilize their energies. These staff experience "positive stress."[2] In high-performance organizations, staff are expected to function under pressure. They are held accountable for obtaining results and are constantly pushed to do better. Offsetting this pressure, however, is a sense of accomplishment and of being part of a staff team whose needs are considered important. Hence, the goal of service organizations is not to be stress free but to provide a work environment in which the pressures of the job are not so demanding that they immobilize staff.

Organizational Stress Factors

Certainly, the work of many human service organizations is inherently stressful. Staff who make critical decisions regarding whether children should be removed from their homes because of neglect or abuse experience tremendous stress, as do welfare or Red Cross staff whose work entails finding emergency housing, or employment staff who are responsible for finding jobs for school dropouts. Unfortunately, frustration and tension are an integral aspect of these jobs, and learning to manage stress is essential.

Certainly, some organizationally caused stress can be controlled enough to reduce the harmful impact on staff.[3] Organizations should be aware of—and do something about—the types of stressors discussed in the following sections.

Role Ambiguity

If staff are unclear about their objectives and tasks, they will be confused about what is expected of them. Job descriptions and mutually agreed-on objectives can reduce this great sense of uncertainty.[4]

Overload (or Underload) of Work

Some organizations are addicted to work. This is a particularly insidious problem because we highly value dedication. When the demands of the job regularly require 60 or 70 hours a week to complete assignments properly, however, the workload has gotten out of control, not unlike a disease. An organization fostering this problem needs to analyze and seek ways to address its unusually heavy workload demands. Conversely, an organization may provide professional staff with too little to do; the resultant underachievement engenders feelings of uselessness and boredom among those directly affected and a sense of inequity among other staff members who resent the way in which work is distributed.

Contradictory Expectations

Some organizations state one kind of promise or expectation in their mission, but staff experience something quite different in their daily professional lives. The incongruity between the ideal and the reality leads staff to become disillusioned and deflated. For example, the organization may espouse the ideal of wanting to improve the lives of poor people but then may require staff to impose layers of regulations on clients before they qualify for services. Contradictory expectations also create stress when staff have to report to multiple lines of authority and juggle the demands of different supervisors. This occurs especially when staff are encouraged to participate on ad hoc, problem-solving teams while still maintaining home-base responsibilities. In these circumstances, staff have the awesome responsibility of reconciling the different priorities of their managers.

Poor Planning

If the management of the organization does not prepare carefully, small problems can be exacerbated, eventually causing undue stress on staff. For example, because of inadequate preparation, a computer error in a public assistance agency results in clients receiving checks in the amount of $3 instead of $300. As a result of the system foul-up, staff have the extra burden—in addition to their already demanding schedules—of handling these new complaints. The tremendous feelings of frustration could have been avoided with better planning.

Laid-Back Atmosphere

An overly permissive atmosphere can also cause undue stress. For example, consider an agency that provides outpatient counseling for teenagers. In its quest to establish a family feeling of warmth and informal relationships, the agency permits a 2-hour lunch break, unfocused supervisory sessions in the park, and "shooting the breeze" with teenagers. Because of this commitment to an informal relaxed atmosphere, however, clients are not required to notify the agency when they must miss their appointments. Moreover, staff are not held accountable for their work, nor do they set objectives. There are no guidelines for handling crises such as suicide attempts. The results are that work does not get done, and staff believe that they are overworked because they work 60 hours each week. The laissez-faire atmosphere, paradoxically, causes the staff to feel tremendously burdened and "burned out."

Poor Match Between Staff and Jobs

Stress can occur as a result of staff being assigned work that is beyond their abilities such as when an effective staff person promoted to a supervisory position finds the job too demanding. Conversely, stress can occur when employees are assigned jobs that only minimally use their skills—for example, highly motivated college graduates being assigned menial, routine work.[5]

The Supervisor's Role in Handling Stress

Staff may need assistance in understanding how their own attitudes can affect their propensity for stress. As supervisor, you should be aware of danger signals and be prepared to assist staff in dealing with the inevitable stresses of the job. For example, you can anticipate that staff who begin with a high degree of enthusiasm and seemingly inexhaustible, youthful energy are headed sooner or later for some disillusionment. You know, too, that those staff who require crises in their work to compensate for unfulfilling personal lives are bound to experience exhaustion from always giving and never receiving.[6] These staff may feel unappreciated or experience excessive, unfulfillable client demands. Simultaneously, they may be unable to distance themselves sufficiently from the situation to return refreshed the next day. They need guidance to alter their personal habits that have trapped them in the exhaustion cycle.

The following paragraphs provide suggestions for helping individuals manage their personally stressful situations.

Help them reconnect with those aspects of their work they truly enjoy. In this way, they can balance the problematic parts of the job with those that give them satisfaction. Encourage them to rediscover what attracted them to the job in the first place. Have them list their "sources of joy" and work together to help accentuate those activities.[7]

Put them in touch with a support group of staff who are having similar experiences. This could take the form of an informal communication network with colleagues who are experiencing similar kinds of stress or with others outside the organization who are good listeners.[8]

Help identify and change whatever is causing stress. For example, if time pressures are becoming extraordinary, then develop methods for helping staff to manage time better (see Chapter 11). Similarly, if clients or coworkers experience excessive feelings of anxiety, help them recognize the pattern. By identifying the causes of their stress, you help them take the first step to gain control of it.

Recognize that some staff overinvest themselves in their work to the point of exhaustion. Their passion for their work and commitment to their clients, although at first a blessing, can become a curse. For periods of time, they fly high with extraordinary energy and verve but may eventually become worn out and crash to the ground. Encourage these staff to seek outside interests so that the problems of the job are put in perspective. Normally, the personal lives of staff are not the business of a supervisor; they may become so only if the sense of exhaustion is so great that the staff are functioning poorly on the job. Staff need to come to work ready to deal with demanding challenges. The supervisor could encourage a form of active relaxation, such as sports, a hobby, or perhaps connection with a small social group. The point is that positive personal life experiences can greatly assist staff in facing on-the-job tensions.[9]

Assist staff in developing work habits that can help reduce unnecessary tension and anticipate crises. For example, help staff anticipate work assignments so that they do not experience last-minute, extraordinary pressures in addition to their already demanding schedules. If handling crises is a natural part of the workload, help them develop an "inoculation" to stress. By simulating difficult situations through role-playing and by discussing a crisis plan with staff in advance, they will be more likely to handle problems that arise with more skill and sensitivity.[10]

Develop realistic expectations with frustrated staff about themselves, results of their work, and the use of their time.[11] Some staff demand more of themselves than the situation will ever allow. For example, given the nature of the particular target population of young cocaine addicts without family supports, the recidivism rates are likely to be quite high. Staff need assistance in measuring "success" not in relation to "curing" their clientele but in helping them achieve some limited degree of progress with their clients' educational, employment, and social goals.

If all else fails, help them consider leaving the stressful situation. You could transfer them to another unit or change their assignments to better suit their abilities and interests.

In summary, manageable stress is a natural part of a productive organization. Only when staff find that they have the inability to cope with the pressures of the job does negative stress becomes an issue. The best antidote for handling stress is to convey high expectations within a supportive organizational climate. Effective managers help staff address those factors that cause them stress and simultaneously take pains to mitigate unnecessary organizational stressors.

MANAGING DIVERSITY

Approximately half of the U.S. workforce consists of minorities, immigrants, and women. White American males are becoming a statistical minority. In the human service field, workforce diversity has become an increasing reality that effective managers must be prepared to address.

Because the workforce is no longer homogeneous, situations such as the following are becoming more frequent:

A black female supervisor criticizes a white male subordinate for an error he committed on the job, and he believes she is throwing her weight around.

Two female colleagues complain about the "bitchiness" of their female supervisor (a term they would not use to describe a male supervisor).

A newly hired black professional feels excluded when two of his white colleagues do not invite him to lunch.

A white supervisor is reluctant to challenge a Hispanic employee for not completing his work on time.

> A black male is criticized for being tardy for several consecutive days and believes that he is being singled out because of his race.

These are not easy matters to resolve because they require great sensitivity and understanding. Some organizations consider complying with affirmative action requirements the end of their responsibility. Managers hire qualified minority and female applicants and then place the burden on these new staff members to make the necessary adjustments. Simply placing people of diverse backgrounds together, however, does not necessarily create a positive, culturally rich work atmosphere. Employees naturally tend to cluster with people like themselves and with whom they feel comfortable, which can produce cultural misunderstandings and feelings of prejudice in other staff members. Moreover, as a result of the changing workforce, managers will find themselves dealing not just with diversity but also with unassimilated diversity. People with different cultural backgrounds are increasingly reluctant to accept assimilation.[12] Therefore, affirmative action is a necessary, but not sufficient, means of addressing diversity.

To move beyond affirmative action, organizations need to manage diversity in a way that achieves the same level of productivity and quality from a heterogeneous workforce that was obtained from the formerly homogeneous workforce.[13] This should not require compromising standards or denying upward mobility to those who have merit, including white males. Rather, competence must count more than ever as each member of the organization is encouraged to perform at his or her fullest potential. The emphasis must be on creating an organizational climate in which all members of the staff will be stimulated to do their best work.

Managing diversity is not a single program for addressing discrimination. Rather, it is a process for developing an environment that works for all employees.[14] It involves a holistic approach of creating a cooperative environment in which all kinds of people can reach their full potential in pursuit of organizational objectives. It is not just a program for addressing discrimination.[15]

To take advantage of a heterogeneous workforce, effective managers can take proactive measures such as those discussed in the following paragraphs.[16]

Establish a baseline of data regarding the number of women and minorities in your organization. This "snapshot" is an essential first step against which future progress toward meeting affirmative action requirements can be assessed. Many government contracts stipulate that the organization must take affirmative action as a condition of receiving funds, and the baseline provides evidence that efforts are being made to hire women and minorities.

Establish guidelines and goals so that managers are responsible for promoting competent minorities and women (e.g., "increase women in upper level positions from 5% to 20% within the next 3 years"). Evaluate individual managers on the basis of their assigning high-potential minorities and women to pivotal jobs that could lead to upward mobility.

Develop policies that reflect the gender diversity of the workforce. Some organizations provide alternatives for maternity, disability, and dependent care benefits. They also provide part-time work, flexible work hours, job sharing, work-at-home arrangements, and paternity and maternity leaves.

Establish quality improvement teams or committees headed by senior staff to encourage progress for talented minorities and women. For example, they could initiate mandatory gender and racial awareness training designed to identify practices, procedures, and individual behaviors that work against minorities and women.

Sponsor frequent celebrations of racial, gender, ethnic, and religious differences. Print articles about the diverse workforce in the organization's newsletter with emphasis on successful employee experiences. Ensure equal celebration of holidays that are special for different religious and ethnic groups.

Create a new paradigm that emphasizes a learning perspective. Establish a climate that encourages people to bring fresh ideas into the organization based on their life experiences. For example, a mental health agency would hire a former mental patient to provide services and to participate in discussions of ways to reach persons with emotional problems. An organization striving to reduce substance abuse in a community would hire a former substance abuser. An employment training program would seek the advice of former clients. Taking advantage of the insights and the skills of these persons greatly enriches the effectiveness of these organizations.

Encourage management staff to examine their assumptions and expectations regarding minority groups. Avoid putting persons in a second-class status by expecting less of them compared to other people on the staff in regard to attendance, punctuality, and performance.[17] Be careful, however, not to establish unrealistically high or unattainable objectives that set up staff for failure. Selecting people for positions for which they are not qualified only to meet diversity goals can be harmful both to the people involved and the organization.[18]

Develop or expand summer intern programs with emphasis on minorities and women. Establish recruiting contacts with minority and women's organizations. Advertise in minority and cultural publications.

Conduct regular attitude surveys of the entire organization to determine how and in what ways women and minorities experience prejudicial attitudes. Include in exit interviews questions that determine whether biases played a factor in decisions to leave.

Establish "core groups" of 8 to 10 people led, if possible, by a skilled facilitator to stimulate informal discussion and self-development and to allow staff to candidly express experiences with prejudice in the organization. Those who have concerns about their supervisors' subtle, prejudicial attitudes may be more likely to communicate directly with them based on support and feedback from the group. The result is that both staff and managers will become more aware of their own biases.

Concentrate staff and managerial training on issues affecting everyone in the organization on the basis that interpersonal relationships and people-managing skills are not limited to dealing with issues of prejudice.

Assign a coach, personal advocate, or sponsor to promising minorities and women so that they have the same opportunity as other employees to move up the organizational ladder. Coaches should encourage those with whom they are working to ask for help, especially if roadblocks are encountered.

The previously mentioned measures are some of the ways in which private and nonprofit organizations are implementing their commitment to diversity. The approaches are not intended to give special advantages to minorities and women but to ensure that those with talent have an opportunity to advance. They are based on the fundamental assumption that diversity is a reality in the workplace that requires awareness, vigilance, and proactive efforts so that all staff can achieve their potential and contribute fully to the organization.

HARASSMENT IN THE WORKPLACE

Nonsexual Harassment

It is important to be aware that an illegal hostile environment involving harassment need not necessarily have anything to do with sex. If a supervisor creates a hostile environment for an employee, this may be considered harassment. If a supervisor of one gender treats an employee of another gender differently from employees of the same gender as the supervisor, then a court ruling could favor the employee. For example, if a woman supervisor treats a man differently in her department by assigning him a heavier workload or setting more unrealistic deadlines than she would for women employees, the male employee may seek redress in the courts for sexual harassment on the basis that his supervisor created a hostile environment.

On the basis of a review of lawsuits in which the employee plaintiff prevailed, the following are examples of illegal harassment:

- Mimicking someone's speech or accent
- Imposing religious views on others
- Referring to a coworker by a derogatory name
- Singling out a coworker and subjecting him or her to ridicule
- Ostracizing an employee

To keep the morale high in the organization and to avoid possible lawsuits, managers should ensure that all employees are treated fairly and without bias.[19]

Dealing With Sexual Harassment

Although harassment can take different forms, the most common episodes involve sexual harassment. In any organization, sexual harassment is grounds for disciplinary action, including dismissal. On the basis of accusations made by clients, any overt sexual advances made by staff to clients or pressuring clients into sexual acts are violations of professional ethics and compel termination hearings. Supervisors who use their position to make overt demands for sex from subordinates abuse their power and should also be subject to termination.

Sexual harassment involves unwelcome sexual advances, requests for sexual favors, and other verbal or physical conduct that involves the following:[20]

- Submission is made either explicitly or implicitly a term or condition of an individual's employment.
- Submission to or rejection of such conduct is used as the basis for employment decisions affecting an individual.

- Such a conduct has the purpose or effect of unreasonably interfering with an individual's work performance or creating an intimidating, hostile, or offensive work environment.

Certainly, there is a "gray area" involving sexual harassment. Coworkers can mutually agree to engage in intimate relationships without harassment being a factor. When mutuality is absent and when men and women have different perspectives about their relationships, however, personal and organizational turmoil will most likely follow. For example, although some employees may think that sexual references or jokes are harmless amusement, others believe these comments are offensive. When an employee puts his or her arm around another employee's shoulder, is it a sign of friendly affection or a sexual overture? Is telling a person that she looks attractive a genuine compliment or a subtle come-on? Is a request to go out for a drink after work a sign of camaraderie or a prelude to a sexual advance?

These interactions between employees in the workplace can be fraught with ambiguities. They can be reflections of friendships, or they can border on unwelcome advances. The courts have defined sexual harassment on the job as

> any unwelcome sexually oriented behavior, demand, comment, or physical contact, initiated by an individual at the workplace, that is a term or condition of employment, a basis for employment decisions, or that interferes with the employee's work or creates a hostile or offensive working environment.[21]

The pattern of harassment is dominated by, but not limited to, heterosexual overtures of men to women. Men can be harassed by female supervisors, and both men and women may experience homosexual advances.[22]

A fundamental prerequisite for preventing sexual harassment in the workplace is for the chief executive and official policies to convey that it will not be tolerated. The climate and the organizational culture must be such that employees will feel comfortable refusing overtures. They need to be able to say, "This joke, this behavior, this comment offends me, please stop." Just as racial jokes have become taboo in the workplace, so too must behavior suggestive of a sexual overture be considered out of bounds.

If offensive behavior or comments persist, women (or men) need to know that they can talk with supervisors who will not trivialize their concerns. Supervisors need to receive training so that they can be in a position to investigate it, report it to their superiors, and take disciplinary action. If the banter, sexual jokes, or flirtations move beyond an acceptable range, however staff define it, they must believe that they have recourse. In instances in which the supervisor is unresponsive or the supervisor is the cause of the problem, employees must feel free to communicate to someone else in the organization who can deal effectively with their concerns. Staff must believe that they work in a nonthreatening environment that protects their sense of self-respect and personal dignity. A person can be a victim even if he or she is not directly involved with the harasser. If an employee can prove that he or she was passed over for a promotion because the other candidate had a relationship with the supervisor, he or she could be a victim of harassment.[23]

To prevent sexual harassment from escalating to an illegal, hostile environment, effective managers can help employees use a variety of self-defensive techniques. These techniques are designed to match the intensity of the offense. Through role playing, employees can become comfortable in asserting themselves in stopping offensive behavior. For example, employees can ask politely for offenders to refrain from engaging in mild forms of harassment: "Jack, those cartoons on your wall are offensive to me, will you please remove them because I find them offensive." A second techniques is to tell the offender that the particular behavior is of concern: "Mary, your sex jokes are bothersome to me and I would appreciate you stopping them." Another approach is a warning that unless the behavior discontinues a complaint will be filed: "Bill, that gender slur is unprofessional, and if you do it again I will file a complaint against you and the agency." These various techniques are thus designed to help employees recognize when harassment crosses the line and to take action against it. Employees are encouraged to take responsibility to assert themselves when others engage in offensive behavior.[24]

Should an employee believe that he or she must communicate his or her concerns beyond communicating with the offender, then managers should consider taking the following steps:[25]

- Make it easy for an employee to register a complaint by establishing clear, written procedures describing how to file a complaint, with whom, and in what form.
- Appoint an investigator from outside the department. This is especially important when a supervisor is accused of harassment. Inform staff that complaints may be registered with the human resources professional, the supervisor's boss, or with top management.
- Ensure that the accuser and the accused understand that false statements can be grounds for discharge.

- If a supervisor is accused of harassment, ensure that he or she understands that any form of retaliation will not be tolerated.
- Give the accused fair and objective consideration when obtaining his or her side of the story.
- Have witnesses sign statements.

The previous steps are designed so that the organization can take proper action. It may also be necessary, however, to acknowledge to employees that if remedies are not forthcoming the employees have recourse to an outside party. Employees should be made aware that, if they wish to pursue a legal remedy, they can contact their state discrimination agency or the federal Equal Employment Opportunity Commission. They need not have an attorney to file a claim, but they may wish to speak with one who specializes in employment discrimination. Under the Civil Rights Act of 1991, victims of sexual harassment are entitled to punitive and compensatory damages for pain and suffering as well as any lost pay.[26]

Because accusations of sexual harassment can be highly subjective, it is important that protocols be observed so as not to recklessly impugn the reputation of staff. They may not have ulterior motives and may not be aware that their remarks or behavior are offensive. Each situation must be assessed on its own merits, with both parties having an opportunity to resolve their concerns in a confidential manner. Dialogues should occur throughout the organization on possible misuses of power, misperceptions, and insensitivities. The goal should be an atmosphere in which men and women operate on a cordial, professional basis.

No-Dating Policies

Office romances will sometimes occur, and policies dealing with them have to be carefully formulated. You do not want to convey to staff that you plan to control their off-the-job activities. If such relationships interfere with job performance or create the possibility of a third-party sexual harassment lawsuit, however, then an organization has the right to enforce a "no-dating" policy. This can be particularly troublesome when a supervisor is romantically involved with one of his or her employees and other employees under his or her jurisdiction complain of favored treatment. Your response has to be fair and consistent. You cannot fire an employee for dating the supervisor and not punish the supervisor. If the romance is causing a problem, document it before taking action so that you can deal with a potential lawsuit.[27]

A no-dating policy is difficult to enforce when coworkers are involved with each other. The focus has to be on whether romance affects job behavior. For example, if coworkers are overtly romantic and this is causing agency clients to be concerned, or if they are involved in a lovers quarrel that affects their ability to communicate, these behaviors must be dealt with directly.

ADDRESSING COMPLACENCY AND STAGNATION

Like all living systems, organizations have a tendency to wind down over time. Borrowing from the physical sciences, social systems theory uses the term *entropy* to describe this tendency of organizations to move toward disintegration.[28] To offset this natural process of decline, organizations must be constantly infused with new ideas, new people, and new ways of doing things. Otherwise, individuals and the organization as a whole stagnate.

Sometimes, members of the organization are not even aware of stagnation. Staff become entrenched and comfortable in performing the routines of the organization, managers concentrate on preserving their positions and power, and supervisors become complacent about the quality of the work performed by their staff. Successful organizations are especially prone to complacency because everyone rests on the good feelings that come from having achieved the organization's goals. Like a tree in full bloom that is suffering from dry rot, a successful organization can look good from the outside while experiencing inner decay.

The antidote to becoming stale on a personal level involves self-renewal and revitalization. Sometimes this can take the form of changing your routine, such as gathering data differently or experimenting with different approaches to carry out your activities. Sometimes the process of self-examination will stimulate you to ask yourself questions such as the following: "What have I learned from the past year's experience that can be applied to what I want to accomplish this year?" "How can I make a special impact on the organization and the people I serve?" and "What skills do I need to truly improve my job performance?"

Sometimes, seeking self-renewal by taking on a special assignment engenders new ways of performing your usual activities. The change of pace pushes you out of a rut. The key to this effort is that the responsibility for seeking change rests within you. Self-renewal must be viewed as an important personal value that keeps you from "retiring on the job."

Be cautious, however, in the quest for self-renewal. Although personal growth or new experiences may contribute to the work of the organization, other efforts may be diversionary. For example, consider the manager who attends more than five or six out-of-town meetings each year. Is the primary purpose to use these meetings as a perquisite ("perk") to get out of town or truly to add value to the work of the local organization? Both the individual and the organization need to scrutinize the self-renewal process to determine if it will add value.

Just as individuals must change and adapt, so too must organizations. It is an interesting phenomenon that both profit and nonprofit organizations can go out of business if they do not continually strive to be relevant to the changing needs of their customers and clients. Adaptation, innovation, and experimentation are used by organizations to evolve to meet changing conditions.

How can an organization keep from becoming unresponsive and inflexible? It can hire dedicated, motivated staff. It can promote qualified, high-energy, enthusiastic, prudent risk takers instead of tired, burnt-out staff (keeping in mind seniority rules). It can foster constructive competition among various units. It can establish a special unit designed to create innovative pilot projects without requiring the initial acceptance of other parts of the organization. It can create a climate of calculated risk taking in which failures are accepted and even honored as "good tries." It can seek partnerships or joint ventures with other organizations to handle a new problem or deal with an old one in a different way. All these efforts are designed to counter organizational paralysis.

BEING SENSITIVE TO INEQUITIES

One of the factors that distinguishes human service staff from their counterparts in private industry is that they are attracted to their work because of their idealism and their desire to help improve the lives of vulnerable people. They have high expectations that their organization will operate with integrity and high-mindedness. Many have had professional education and are imbued with values that may occasionally be in conflict with expedient measures taken by their organization.

When actions of the organization's management run counter to staff's professional values and expectations, the staff may become deflated, disillusioned, and hostile. This is especially likely to occur when management makes decisions not so much to benefit clients but to make their own jobs easier. Disgruntled staff become less invested in their work because they have lost the caring spirit that originally attracted them to the organization.

It is useful here to distinguish between staff dissatisfaction and low morale. Staff discontent and unhappiness can be based on many ongoing organizational concerns: low wages, periodic conflicts, and difficulties in working with clients with severe problems. This unhappiness usually results from conditions over which management has little control and is something to be endured equally by all who work in the organization. People can live with their unhappiness and still try and do the best they can do.

Low morale, however, is based on a sense of injustice, whether perceived or real. Staff who think they are operating under inequitable conditions have an increasing disaffection and even distrust of the organization. In this atmosphere, expect staff productivity to decline.[29]

It is not difficult to find examples of inequities. The following are a few actual examples drawn from several community organizations:

- A staff committee requests flextime from management. After considerable discussion, management decides to provide this special arrangement for the managers but not for counselors and support staff. The result: bitterness, jealousy, and divisiveness.
- Eleven staff are terminated and their clients reassigned to other already overburdened colleagues on the basis that a financial crisis needs to be averted. A month later, top managers are given raises from $2,000 to $5,000. The result: Staff are bewildered and resentful at the deceptive approach used to curtail client services.
- Staff in one agency complain that their furniture is old and dilapidated. They are told that no funds are available to buy new furniture. Several months later, a manager buys a $700 desk. The result: An anonymous staff memorandum is circulated throughout the organization detailing this inequitable action.
- Supervisors in one organization use support staff to type term papers for their children, pick up laundry, and bring in their lunches. Support staff are referred to as "girls." The result: Staff feel exploited, and the organization is shortchanged because of time tied up in non-work-related tasks.[30]
- In an organization dealing with delinquents, a special unit is established to provide intensive counseling to a caseload of no more than 30 juveniles. The remaining staff have to take on their additional cases, resulting in their caseloads numbering more than 200. The result: The overburdened staff feel resentful and demoralized.
- Job changes are fairly common in the organization, but a supervisor learns through the grapevine that she is being replaced by the director's longtime friend.

The result: Rumors of cronyism run rampant throughout the agency, and staff wonder whether competency counts.

- Hoping to provide greater challenge to a select number of employees, one agency establishes a pilot program that gives increased autonomy and responsibility to the staff. No effort, however, is made to provide increased pay to accompany the increased responsibilities, nor is there any explanation given about whether increased pay will be forthcoming. The result: Staff believe they are being exploited, and their productivity declines.

The previous examples have in common a lack of evenhandedness in organizational decisions. Inappropriately favoring some staff over others, providing perquisites, treating staff unfairly, inappropriately discriminating, and exploiting staff may or may not be intentional. The result is that staff will probably perceive that the organization is operating with diminished integrity, and this affects their attitudes and professional performances. Because staff are acutely aware of possible injustices, effective managers must be sensitive to staff's perceptions of unequal treatment while doing all they can to prevent inequitable decision making. Employees must believe that they are working in an organization that treats all employees fairly, equitably, and consistently.

NOTES

1. L. Moss, *Management stress* (Reading, MA: Addison-Wesley, 1981), pp. 94-95.
2. R. E. Herman, *Keeping good people: Strategies for solving the dilemma of the decade* (Cleveland, OH: Oakhill, 1990), pp. 160-162.
3. R. R. Middleman & G. B. Rhodes, *Competent supervision: Making imaginative judgments* (Englewood Cliffs, NJ: Prentice Hall, 1985), pp. 132-135; A. W. Schaef & D. Fassel, *The addictive organization* (San Francisco: Harper & Row, 1990).
4. L. Moss, pp. 101-102.
5. R. T. Crow & C. A. Odewahn, *Management for the human services* (Englewood Cliffs, NJ: Prentice Hall, 1987), p. 144.
6. M. Bramnall & S. Ezell, How burned are you? *Public Welfare, 1* (1981), p. 24.
7. M. L. Kaplan, Labor of love: The joys and stresses of nonprofit management, *Nonprofit World, 3* (1990), p. 28.
8. L. Moss, pp. 200-202.
9. R. B. Flannery, The stress resistant person, *HMS Health Letter* (1989, February), p. 6; J. S. Shepherd, Manage the 5 c's of stress, *Personal Journal, 4* (1990), pp. 64-69.
10. R. B. Flannery, p. 7.
11. M. L. Kaplan, p. 28.

12. R. R. Thomas, *Beyond race and gender: Unleashing the power of your total workforce by managing diversity* (New York: AMACOM, 1991), p. 174.

13. R. R. Thomas, p. 109.

14. R. R. Thomas, pp. 10-15.

15. R. R. Thomas, pp. 15, 167; D. A. Thomas & R. J. Ely, Making differences matter: A new paradigm for managing diversity, *Harvard Business Review, 74* (1996, September/October), p. 80.

16. L. Copeland, Learning to manage a multicultural work force, *Training* (1988, May), pp. 1-5; B. Geber, Managing diversity, *Training* (1990, July), pp. 23-30; C. M. Solomon, Careers under glass, *Personnel Journal, 4* (1990), pp. 96-105; R. R. Thomas, From affirmative action to affirming diversity, *Harvard Business Review, 2* (1990), pp. 107-117; K. Hildebrand, Use leadership training to increase diversity, *Harvard Business Review, 41*(8) (1996, August), pp. 53-58.

17. D. A. Thomas & R. J. Ely, p. 90.

18. D. S. Evans & M. Y. Oh, A tailored approach to diversity planning, *Harvard Business Review, 41*(6) (1996, June), p. 131.

19. Alexander Hamilton Institute, *What every manager must know to prevent sexual harassment* (Ramsey, NJ: Author, 1997), pp. 33-35.

20. Alexander Hamilton Institute, pp. 9-10.

21. K. L. Lloyd, *Sexual harassment: How to keep your company out of court* (New York: Panel, 1991), p. 7.

22. Alexander Hamilton Institute, pp. 10-11.

23. Alexander Hamilton Institute, pp. 8-9.

24. R. B. McAfee & D. L. Deadrick, Teach employees to just say "no!" *Human Resource Management, 41*(2) (1996, February), pp. 86-89.

25. Alexander Hamilton Institute, pp. 18-19; E. Cassedy & K. Nussbaum, *9 to 5: The working woman's guide to office survival* (New York: Penguin, 1983), p. 38; K. L. Lloyd, pp. 47-58; National Institute of Business Management, *Fire at will: Terminating your employees legally* (New York: Author, 1991), p. 29.

26. 9 to 5, *Sexual harassment* [Brochure] (Cleveland, OH: Author, 1990); R. Sandroff, Sexual harassment: The inside story, *Working Woman* (1992, June), p. 51.

27. Alexander Hamilton Institute, pp. 19-20.

28. F. K. Barrien, *General and social systems* (New Brunswick, NJ: Rutgers University Press, 1968), pp. 16-53.

29. T. Caplow, *How to run any organization (Hinsdale*, IL: Dryden), p. 157.

30. E. Cassedy & K. Nussbaum, p. 25.

Part III Review

ENHANCING EMPLOYEE PRODUCTIVITY

6. TIME MANAGEMENT

- Through time records, diagnose how time is being spent. Plan how you will use time by setting priorities and placing activities in high, medium, low, and posterior categories.
- Concentrate on those activities that have the potential for highest impact (80/20 principle) and those that deviate from standards (exception principle).
- Block out time to work on demanding assignments requiring concentration.
- Develop techniques to deal with time-wasting activities involving paperwork, conversations, and telephone calls.
- Deal with procrastination tendencies by facing the fear of failure, pushing yourself to do uncomfortable tasks first, and dividing overwhelming assignments into manageable, short-term tasks.

7. GETTING AND KEEPING PRODUCTIVE EMPLOYEES

- Staff are the social capital of an organization, and continuous investment in them is essential.
- Match competent people to the requirements of the job. If feasible, hire from within. If hiring from outside, check references carefully.
- Be careful to conduct nondiscriminatory interviews with potential employees. The only focus in an employment interview should be on bona fide job requirements.

- By being clear about job expectations and demands, you are more likely to find a suitable candidate who will last.
- Staff training should be related to strategies and objectives of the organization.
- A parallel effort to train supervisors should accompany staff training so they can handle new challenges.
- Training works best when trainees have opportunities to practice their new skills.
- The organization's structure should be based on the services it provides or work it is intended to do.
- To coordinate the work of the organization, institute hierarchical, market, or matrix formats or a combination thereof.

8. DEALING WITH UNPRODUCTIVE EMPLOYEES

- Determine whether an employee's lack of productivity resides in the person or in organizational practices and procedures.
- Effective supervisors work with staff whose problems interfere with their productivity.
- Formulate policies to deal with special issues that could affect productivity, such as AIDS and substance abuse in the workplace.
- For those staff who must face the consequences of their work behavior, apply progressive discipline.
- Establish clear procedures for terminating employees.
- If, in exceptional circumstances, you are forced to retain an unproductive employee, take action to minimize his or her damage to the organization's productivity.
- The Americans With Disabilities Act makes it unlawful to discriminate against individuals with respect to hiring, firing, compensation, training, and advancement. In these situations, do not focus on the disability as a reason for your decision.
- Carefully document with a paper trail all disciplinary action taken regarding a poorly performing employee.

9. HUMANIZING THE ORGANIZATION

- Determine whether the organization is unduly contributing to work stress. Help staff anticipate problems and develop realistic expectations.
- Take proactive measures to deal with staff diversity to ensure productivity of a heterogeneous workforce.

- Manage cultural diversity so that all staff members have the opportunity to achieve their highest potential.
- Harassment in the workplace can involve both sexual and nonsexual attitudes and behaviors.
- Sexual harassment cannot be permitted in the workplace. All staff must believe that organizational culture and policies permit them to work in a nonthreatening environment.
- Provide training so that staff can feel more comfortable in confronting harassers in a timely manner.
- Organizations should consider developing no-dating policies, especially in regard to a supervisor dating a staff member in the same unit.
- Management should support efforts at self-renewal and revitalization, both for individuals and for the organization as a whole.
- Managers who violate staff expectations on evenhandedness invite disillusionment, hostility, and work disinvestment. Effective managers guard against favoritism, unfair treatment, and self-serving actions.

Part IV

SUPERVISING STAFF, ASSESSING PERFORMANCE, AND PROVIDING REWARDS

In this part, you will learn how to

- Manage the multiple roles of management
- Delegate effectively
- Apply motivational theories to influence performance
- Convey supervisory expectations
- Consider the advantages of measuring performance
- Develop specific appraisal methods to assess performance
- Use management by objectives to appraise results
- Prepare an evaluation narrative
- Prepare for an appraisal conference
- Consider the advantages and disadvantages of job classification and skill-based pay systems
- Weigh the pros and cons of pay as a means of rewarding performance
- Be aware of cautions in implementing pay for performance and how to deal with them
- Consider using bonuses and gain-sharing
- Provide symbolic rewards and recognition as a way of influencing behavior

Chapter 10

SUPERVISING STAFF

Managers face a tremendous challenge in dealing with different supervisory aspects of their jobs, including reconciling the expectations of superiors with the needs of subordinates, integrating the many roles they must play, and determining when and in what ways to delegate assignments. To help them supervise more effectively, managers should consider applying motivational theories to staff behavior. This chapter concludes with a review of elements of good supervisory practice.

THE PICKLE IN THE MIDDLE

In a children's game, one player runs between two bases while trying not to be tagged by the catchers on either side. That child is "the pickle in the middle." Managers are frequently the pickle in the middle, caught between the conflicting expectations of their bosses and those who work under their supervision. They are often called on to reconcile the expectations and policies of the organization with the concerns and needs of their subordinates.[1]

Whether a supervisor in a local welfare office, a director in a mental health clinic, or a unit head of a foster care program, the effective manager must deal with value conflicts and differing perspectives. To handle this diversity, these middle managers must be able to truly understand and accept that there is validity in different points of view. For example, if, as a middle manager, you understand and are committed to the mission and goals of the organization, you will appreciate why it has regulations to restrict some client services. Simultaneously, you understand that staff often want to "bend the rules" to increase eligibility for those with whom they come in contact.[2]

Through this appreciation of different perspectives, managerial loyalties can be pulled in several directions. Managers' abilities to connect the needs and requirements of one level of the organization to those of another ultimately determine their effectiveness. Effective managers work to diminish a "we-they" atmosphere, replacing it with an emphasis on teamwork. Managers could explain to staff, for example, why they must complete the monthly reporting forms that the top administration requires and also work with the administration to modify these report requirements so that staff can complete these forms with greater ease.

Certainly, being part of a team is not always easy for middle managers. Occasionally, they will be caught in a conflict and want to advocate for staff because most middle managers have moved up through the ranks and therefore naturally identify with their former peers. They may believe that to sustain staff loyalty they must be willing to advocate for staff concerns. As a result, managers may try to convince the administration to make changes based on the experiences of their staff.

Even if middle managers question a particular change made by top administrators, however, after making their case they are obligated to help staff understand why the change is necessary and help them implement the new arrangements. Hence, middle managers are the ultimate facilitators of communications between different staff levels of an organization.

Because middle managers have to report to superiors, it is important that they tune in to their bosses. It is essential that middle managers determine their bosses' strengths, work performance, and values. This is the secret of "managing" the boss.[3]

Sometimes, employees who work in a department may "go above the head" of their own supervisor to complain directly to his or her manager. Perhaps the supervisor has a personality conflict or a work style that may cause problems with staff. In these circumstances, it is important to convey to employees that they need to respect the chain of command and try to work out their problems with their immediate supervisor. Simultaneously, the supervisor may need special coaching or training to build relationships with his or her subordinates. The goal is to avoid undermining the supervisor's authority while working to resolve problems.[4]

THE MULTIPLE LIVES OF THE MANAGER

Imagine being in a play in which you are the only actor. First, you are the mother, then the uncle, the hero, and finally the villain. Managers' daily performances are no less taxing. Each day, managers at all levels of the organization are called on to play multiple roles. Just as they must reconcile working with different parts of the organization, so too must they reconcile major managerial roles: coach, judge, explorer, warrior, treasure hunter, media expert, and advocate.

Coach

One of the most demanding roles of a manager is that of coaching his or her staff. As a coach, a manager's primary responsibility is to train staff to help attain the goals of both the organization and the unit. The coach must recognize that each employee has a different array of strengths and weaknesses. He or she provides feedback to staff, encourages them to devise their own plans for performance and improvement, and supports their growth. As the situation demands, the coach may provide support and counseling or confront staff with the consequences of their behavior. Throughout all these activities, the coach conveys a combination of genuine concern for the employee and an expectation that tasks will be accomplished well.[5]

You can be an effective supervisor if you practice the following coaching techniques:

- Actively listen to subordinates so that the staff members know you truly understand their ideas and concerns. Listening will enable you to clarify any misunderstandings.
- Help subordinates reflect on what is happening. For example, in a coaching meeting, you might ask, "What do you think happened and why?" "What feedback did you receive?" and "How have others reacted to the employee?"
- In helping staff to develop skills, start with those that are easy to master and proceed to those that are more difficult.
- Expect a certain amount of trial and error; if changes require several different behaviors, work on the easiest ones first.
- Set intermediate objectives that lead to an ultimate objective. For example, if a staff member needs to reduce controlling behavior, he or she might be encouraged to hold back opinions at meetings until others have had a chance to express their ideas.

- Practice role-playing situations that are particularly troublesome for the subordinate.

Behavioral change occurs in small increments, and people do not move forward in a straight line. Allow for an occasional slip backward. Developing these techniques can become both challenging and rewarding.[6]

Judge

As judge, the manager must evaluate the extent to which staff achieve their goals. If they are not achieved, the manager must diagnose whether the problem is with the staff, the work environment, or the nature of the task. Moreover, if the problem is with staff, the judge must determine whether the solution involves skill training or other measures.

To carry out this role, staff should be monitored through formal review procedures (e.g., computerized data or evaluation sessions) or informal, but purposeful, contacts with staff. Closely linked to this judging role is the ability to evaluate and then influence the distribution of resources. Pay increases, promotions, or symbolic rewards are connected to employee assessments. In the role of judge, a manager may also be called on to handle disturbances and resolve differences between staff or units of the organization.[7] The judge must also be willing to make difficult and often painful professional decisions. Committed to acting fairly and consistently, the middle manager will be able to embrace tough decisions and find the right balancing points.[8]

Explorer

The manager frequently engages employees as partners in searching for solutions to problems. By involving employees in this process of mutual problem solving, managers build the confidence and commitment of their staff. As an explorer, the manager seeks to understand the basis of the problem but resists making decisions quickly, instead encouraging staff to search out constructive options. By encouraging staff to develop their own ideas and communicating genuine belief that staff are capable of developing creative solutions, the explorer fosters a commitment to exploration from the entire staff.[9]

Communication with staff is a major part of the explorer's job; therefore, the manager must seek out and disseminate information to staff. To be an effective communicator, therefore, the explorer must have a network of contacts both within and outside of the organization.[10]

Warrior

The term *warrior* is a metaphor for the manager as a person of action. If productivity is decreasing, this alerts the manager to take action to improve it. To be an effective warrior, the manager must persevere in the face of obstacles. He or she must often deal with others in the organization—subordinates, colleagues, or top administrators, who all have their own agendas—and must be coaxed to correct their end of the problem. The warrior must continually, but gently, goad staff to do better. If certain operations are inefficient or unproductive, the manager may have to make the painful decision to discontinue them. If the organization or the unit experiences a crisis, the warrior must respond without hesitation.[11]

Treasure Hunter

Effective managers must be ever mindful that the organization's survivability depends on the capacity to generate resources. Fund raising is an essential ongoing activity of managerial staff, who must constantly be on the lookout for new funding. They must also work continuously to preserve the funding that they have previously garnered. Much of Part VI focuses on this important role.

Media Expert

Human service managers frequently have to obtain the support of the public for their programs. In turn, this need requires them to be knowledgeable about ways to communicate their messages that are easily understood.[12] Managers know that working with the media involves gaining access to the media by developing newsworthy items that include sensation, conflict, mystery, celebrity, deviance, and tragedy.[13] A story about middle-aged men teaching swimming at the YMCA is not news; a 92-year-old man who rides his motorbike to volunteer to provide swimming instruction is news. Second, managers must frame the issue so that it can be easily understood by the public. Human service managers are well aware that their clients have problems that are complex and interrelated. They can seek simple solutions or more comprehensive ones. Reducing teen pregnancy, helping battered women, or assisting homeless persons to find independent living will require more than memorable slogans. These and other complex issues call for educating the public about factors that significantly contribute to the problem and using the media to communicate the right messages and stories that the public can understand.

Advocate

To produce change, human service managers may need to engage in various forms of advocacy. Occasionally, management staff may need to be at the forefront of public controversy because this is one of the best ways to get the media to report on an issue. As a result of controversy, the issues raise people's levels of conscious awareness.[14] Getting rid of alcohol billboards in the inner city, challenging the school system to do a better job educating students, and leading the effort to make agencies more culturally sensitive to the minority populations they serve all affect the lives of agency clients and must be confronted and addressed by both business leaders and policymakers.

Legislative advocacy is another important activity. Often, major funding for human services is derived from legislative bodies (county commissioners, city councils, and state legislators). Forming coalitions, developing constituent support, identifying legislative sponsors, working with the administration to include a budget item, developing relationships with legislators, using the Internet to get your message out, and mounting a grassroots campaign are some of the approaches that the advocate must take to influence change in the legislative process.[15]

These different roles are carried out by different levels of managerial staff. In large organizations, executive managers may concentrate their energies outside the organization—focusing on dealing with the legislature, communicating with the media, and working with publicly elected officials. At the supervisory level, middle managers ensure that staff are carrying out their roles properly, that clients are flowing through the system and proper referrals are being made, and follow up on troubleshooting assignments. In smaller agencies, managers must continually juggle various roles, often simultaneously.

Handling Multiple Roles

Each role must be handled judiciously and not be carried to such an extreme that it interferes or becomes incompatible with the other roles.[16] For example, managers should not be so focused on the encouraging and supportive functions of the coaching role that they are unable to fulfill the roles of objective judge and distributor of resources. When sorting out problems, the explorer role is appropriate, but when dealing with a crisis a manager may need to become a warrior, able to make intrepid decisions.

These different roles are sometimes incompatible because every manager has both strengths and limitations. Some are good at being evaluative, whereas others prefer to be supportive. It is important to assume the proper role as circumstances warrant. The inability to fire an incompetent bookkeeper whose error costs the agency $30,000 reflects a reluctance to carry out the major and necessary managerial role of judge called for by the situation.

Managers need to understand these different roles, assess their own ability to carry them out, and obtain guidance where they are deficient. This counsel could be obtained either from a formal training program or, more likely, through a mentoring process in which a manager has an opportunity to associate with a role model from within or outside the organization. Handling various and complex roles is difficult; seeking guidance is not a sign of weakness but demonstrates true commitment to addressing concerns.

Although managers can do much to enhance their own productivity and job satisfaction, the organizations for which they work must also be sensitive to the level of satisfaction that supervisors are deriving from their jobs. Administrators need to support supervisors who work with staff who provide direct service to the public. The following specific steps can be taken:

- Increasing the autonomy of managers so that they can have greater control and influence over their job tasks
- Increasing salary benefits, professional development, and opportunities for growth for all staff
- Providing adequate organization resources, including adequate support staff and professional backup staff
- Providing an organizational climate that visibly displays respect for the direct services and supervisory staff

Clearly, the job satisfaction of supervisors plays an important role in a productive organization.[17] Agency administrators can enhance their sensitivity to line supervisors by periodically spending time in direct contact with the basic work of the organization.

DELEGATING ASSIGNMENTS

If managing is the art of getting things done through working with others, then delegating is the process of giving others assignments to complete. Delegation is no simple matter, however; it requires considerable thought, planning, and follow-through.

Both managers and staff can be resistant to delegation. Some managers do not delegate because they fear that their subordinates may upstage them. These managers have an inordinate need to reap full credit. They may fear losing control, do not want to take the time to guide the process, prefer doing the assignment themselves (even when they are pressed for time), or perhaps do not want to invest in developing their subordinates. These problems reside in the delegator. On the other side, staff may resist responsibility because they lack the necessary experience or training, are overloaded with work, or are poorly organized.

These problems must be addressed if staff are to grow in their capabilities and if the work is to get done. By developing staff, effective managers increase the organization's flexibility. Also, by shifting responsibilities from one level of the organization to another, managers can free up staff to take on new assignments and expand their skills.

Of course, it is not desirable to delegate every task. Some responsibilities are simply too complicated or controversial to pass along. Some tasks require such advanced technical knowledge and judgment that they cannot be easily delegated. Also, some are so sensitive, such as handling budget information or disciplining staff, that delegation is inadvisable.

Therefore, the issue of "when to delegate" is clearly a delicate one. Delegation must be used judiciously and with careful consideration of the following criteria:

- Select the right people: Delegate according to realistic assessments of strengths, limitations, and task preferences.[18]
- Ensure that assignments are fair and realistic by maintaining continuous communication with staff.
- Distinguish between delegating and dumping. If the assignment is boring, unpleasant, or exceedingly difficult, you could potentially cause ill will if you give it to someone else. The best reason to delegate is because the delegatee can do the job better, and the assignment has the potential to spark interest and stimulate growth.[19]

- Make the assignments clear. Staff must understand what the organization expects of them. They should have a clearly defined work plan complete with deadlines.[20]
- Delegate tasks to the lowest possible level at which they can be performed satisfactorily to make the most efficient use of organizational resources.[21] Resist making a decision that your staff could make just as easily—even though it might be different than yours—if the result is likely to be a positive one.
- State the constraints (if any) within which staff must operate—for example, a budgetary constraint.
- Determine criteria for selecting employees to take responsibilities on the basis of who can best do the job, who can use time most productively, who wants more responsibility, and who would experience the most professional growth.
- Give staff a voice in the assignment. The delegation process should be a dialogue, not a monologue.[22] Being sensitive to staff preferences is more likely to ensure their enthusiasm in completing assignments.
- Determine how thoroughly staff understand the task and, based on that understanding, communicate all necessary knowledge to assist them in completing it. Provide specific instructions about what the result should be, and clarify the limits of the employee's responsibility. Anticipate problems that are likely to occur, such as requests for more funding or more staff to carry out the assignment, and establish ground rules for what resources are available (or not) to carry out the project.
- Convey your expectation that if staff encounter problems they will consider one or more solutions before coming to you. This conveys your confidence that they will work hard to resolve problems and will not become unduly dependent on you as their ultimate problem solver. Some managers subscribe to the parachute principle of "You pack it, you jump with it." On their own, people are forced to think like entrepreneurs and to implement the assignment without interference. There is a fine line between no interference and lack of guidance, however. Occasionally, everyone needs some guidance and some support.[23] Make yourself available in the event that staff encounter particularly difficult challenges. Find the right balancing point between letting staff work out their problems and interceding when vexing problems occur.
- Grant authority to get the task done. Responsibility without authority never works. You may have to give your imprimatur to the employee who is carrying out the assignment so that others are aware of your backing.

The following is an example of a conversation in which a supervisor is effectively delegating an assignment to a staff member:

Maria: Ann, I am pleased that in our last two sessions together you have come in with good ideas about managing your new responsibilities. I'm also delighted that you are willing to meet the challenge of increasing the number of outreach contacts to women of childbearing age. We have agreed that, within the next 4 months, your unit will reach a minimum of 350 women.

Ann: As we agreed, I am planning to hire two outreach staff, and I will be developing a reporting form within 2 weeks.

Maria: You have this assignment well under control. Can we meet every Tuesday, say, at 10:00, to discuss any problems and your proposed alternatives? Do you have any questions about this assignment? I'll send you a memo outlining our mutual decisions about this assignment.

Given that managers who delegate assignments are ultimately responsible for the work of those under their supervision, it is vitally important that they maintain control without limiting the freedom of staff to think and act. If you have made assignments clear and have mutually determined outcomes, then tracking progress should be fairly easy. Moreover, if you have defined a method of feedback, including a reporting schedule and checkpoints, then you help ensure proper control of the project. On the one hand, you do not want to "micromanage" the project or overindulge your own need for information and data. On the other hand, you must not assume too passive a role so that you receive needed information too late to take corrective action. You must clarify that staff must tell you about any unexpected developments, delays, or problems.

Managers should be aware that even when staff members demonstrate the ability to manage a situation on their own, they should not be abandoned to figure out how to deal with discouragement that may be part of the process. Not working with people as they encounter major challenges could potentially set them up for failure. Hence, tracking people to determine appropriate times for providing guidance is essential.[24]

If done well, delegation can release a powerful force that may be latent within staff. Through their newfound sense of challenge and freedom, staff will invest as never before.

APPLYING MOTIVATIONAL THEORIES

There are several theories that can help explain what motivates people to work. If supervisors are familiar with them, these theories can be helpful in improving job performance.[25] It is probably accurate to state that no one theory can be used exclusively to explain how best to motivate work performance. It may be more useful to use an eclectic approach that draws on several motivational theories in working with staff.

Maslow's Need Hierarchy

This theory is familiar to most supervisors. Individuals are motivated to satisfy the following needs: (a) physiological, (b) safety, (c) social, (d) esteem, and (e) self-actualization. The concept that an individual must fulfill a lower need before a higher need is intuitively appealing, although not necessarily confirmed by empirical studies.[26] The value of the theory is that, for highly skilled professionals, self-actualization plays a significant role in motivating behavior—assuming that the other more basic needs have been satisfied.[27] Effective managers therefore strive to provide projects and activities that can enrich professional growth.

McGregor's Theory X and Theory Y

According to this model, two different assumptions may influence work behavior. Theory X assumes that, unless managers are controlling and directive, staff will tend to be passive and disinvested. Thus, managerial tasks are to persuade, reward, and punish. Theory Y is based on the managerial assumption that staff are not basically passive or resistant but capable of and enthusiastic about assuming responsibility. Hence, the managerial task is to engage staff in taking responsibility and initiative for their work performance. Most forward-looking organizations prefer Theory Y.[28]

McClelland's Need for Achievement Theory

This theory attempts to explain how employees differ in their desire for self-fulfillment. Some have a great need to achieve entrepreneurial success by accomplishing tasks and even keep score by how much money they make. They tend to be independent, high risk takers. Others in the organization may have a strong need for affiliation—social relationships are more important to them than feelings of accomplishment. Still others have a strong need for power and control over others. McClelland's theory highlights the importance of matching individual needs to job roles. For example, achievement-oriented employees will require extraordinary challenges and special recognition for success to sustain their work motivation.[29]

Vroom's Expectancy Theory

Vroom postulated that motivation is influenced by the individual's perception that better performance means greater rewards. Furthermore, these rewards must hold value to the individual. The theory helps us understand that various outcomes are important to different employees. Levels of performance should be challenging but attainable, and the reward system should be accurate, prompt, visible, and significant.[30]

Herzberg's Hygiene-Motivator Theory

This model is based on two frameworks that influence job behavior. The first involves hygiene (external) factors—supervision, salary, working conditions, job security, status, and fringe benefits. They are called "hygiene" factors because they represent preventive or maintenance needs. Their impact on motivation is minimal, but if absent staff can become dissatisfied. The second framework involves motivational (intrinsic) factors and includes the actual work, growth, and responsibility. These are conditions that directly influence motivation. Unsatisfying work factors will also lead to general dissatisfaction but are not solely responsible for motivational loss.[31]

Empirical research conducted since Herzberg's theory was formulated has shown that certain external factors can indeed motivate behavior. For example, increases in pay do affect motivation.[32] The significance of the theory, however, is that it focuses attention on the importance of making the work more meaningful and more interesting. Job enrichment is viewed as a major motivator for employee behavior.

These motivational theories can provide helpful guidelines in working with staff:

- Expect staff to be genuinely motivated to do a good job. Assume they want to succeed and perform well—if they operate in an atmosphere that helps them succeed.
- Staff are more likely to be motivated toward goals and objectives that are meaningful to them. The more they can participate in establishing their own goals and performance standards, the more likely they will be to carry them out.
- Staff should know what is expected of them. They need to understand how the organization in general, and their supervisors in particular, determine that a job is well done. Through expectations, staff will gain clarity about the challenges they must meet.

- Staff members are motivated in individual and unique ways. They all have different needs—status, affiliation, a sense of accomplishment, financial rewards, and praise. Therefore, it is important to tune in to their individual motivations to determine what they want and, if reasonable, to do your best to help them achieve it.

ELEMENTS OF GOOD SUPERVISION

Chapter 1 discussed aspects of effective management and good leadership, which are qualities that can be applied to front-line supervisors. After all, they are on the firing line with their staff. These supervisors, however, also have the unique responsibility of dealing one-on-one with staff. To bring out the best in each employee, supervisors must focus on enhancing their supervisory relationships, providing constructive criticism, and clearly conveying expectations.

Enhancing the Supervisory Relationship

Good supervisors follow the guidelines presented in the following paragraphs to help foster positive and productive relationships with staff.

Set or identify positive examples in your organization. This enthusiasm and dedication can be contagious. Staff are keenly aware of whether the supervisor is committed to the work or is merely filling in time. The process of providing positive examples, sometimes known as "reflective modeling," is based on setting a work ethic that employees can emulate. You set a positive example for your staff, and acknowledge those who make attempts to follow the example. Furthermore, you communicate respect to your staff and colleagues, deemphasize your own personal goals and individual recognition in the spirit of being a team player, and take on some of the less desirable assignments to convey that all employees have to pitch in.[33]

Sometimes, other staff convey behaviors and performance that you would like to see emulated. This is the process of identifying and praising the best behavior patterns in your organization. In industry, the term *benchmarking* means finding the best practices and emulating them. In effect, you are identifying individual performance as benchmarks. By praising those individuals who set high standards, you convey a strong message of what is important.[34]

Take time to know staff. Good supervisors meet with their staff both formally and informally on a regular basis. They take time to find out if staff are satisfied with their jobs and what gives them feelings of achievement. In turn, staff trust their supervisor as one who is responsive to their concerns.[35]

Give clear instructions. Supervisors need to convey specifically what needs to be done, within what time period, and what factors will be considered in evaluating the success of the project.

"Sell" rather than "tell." To gain the enthusiastic support of staff, supervisors' requests should be accompanied by an explanation of potential benefits for the staff, the unit, or the organization as a whole. The staff should be persuaded, not ordered. In this sense, people are not managed but are led by capitalizing on their strengths and their knowledge.[36]

Foster a collaborative spirit. Get used to saying, "We are on the same team, so, when things go well, we will share the credit and, when problems occur, we will work together to resolve them." Some organizations foster this spirit by referring to their staff as associates, not subordinates. This term conveys a respect for the knowledge and expertise that the staff members bring to their positions.[37]

Draw the line between supervision and therapy. Being a good listener and being empathic are important, as long as the focus remains on improving service to clients. An effective supervisor acknowledges, but does not take responsibility for, personal problems of the staff. If personal problems are interfering with job performance and are disruptive to other employees, supervisors must take action, such as referring the employee to a counseling agency or an employee assistance program.

Engage staff in problem solving. Good supervisors actively seek ideas and suggestions from staff to improve productivity. They understand, for example, that direct service staff can probably make helpful suggestions on how best to handle client complaints.[38]

Providing Constructive Criticism

One of the major responsibilities of supervisors is telling staff when their performance is not measuring up to standards. It is tempting to confront staff with what they are doing wrong, but people do not easily change their behavior on the basis of explicit criticism. Sentences that begin "Do you realize that . . . ," "You have a problem with . . . ," or "What you are doing is unacceptable . . ." cause staff to feel inadequate rather than help them improve their performance. Unfortunately, some supervisors derive great personal satisfaction from putting staff down and being insensitive to their feelings and concerns.

Such a self-serving attitude does little to change behavior but much to foster resentment and resistance.

Certainly, the supervisor does have an obligation to engage staff in improving their performance. The best way to provide effective and constructive criticism is to observe the following:[39]

- Criticism can best be tolerated within a trusting relationship. If the relationship is based on mutual respect, then your staff will know that you can accept mistakes, that criticism is not equated with failure, and that you expect people to learn from their mistakes and grow professionally.
- Provide feedback that is descriptive and specific rather than evaluative and vague. For example, instead of saying "You are gaining a reputation for being rude with the other staff," you might point out specific instances in which the staff member behaved inappropriately with his or her coworkers. By being specific, you allow your subordinate to consider with you whether a destructive pattern is emerging.
- Concentrate on behavior that the staff members can change. There is little value in criticizing abilities or behavior patterns over which staff have no control. It will only increase their frustration and heighten insecurities about shortcomings.
- Use the "sandwich technique" to convey constructive criticism. Soften the impact of criticism by sandwiching it between appreciation for good work. Find a reason to acknowledge the positive contribution before expressing a concern. After expressing criticism, indicate that the employee will make an even greater contribution once the concern is corrected.
- Time the criticism to be most effective. Usually, you should meet with the staff member as soon as possible after a given behavior occurs. Sometimes, however, you may decide to delay discussion to permit a cooling-off period. For example, you might say, "Our emotions are running high at the moment. Let's take a day to mull it over and then review it."
- Be careful about misinterpreting staff's motivation or intentions because this tends to contribute to resentment and distrust. It is the height of arrogance to assume that you know why a person said or did something. This may be a difficult suggestion to follow, particularly for those in the helping profession who spend their waking moments thinking about the causes of behavior, but it will help you communicate more openly with your staff.
- Be aware that sentences that begin with "You should . . ." immediately cause staff to become defensive. For example, statements such as "You shouldn't be so intolerant of your client's behavior" or "You should complete your assignments on time" may cause staff to feel they must defend their positions and deny the problem is theirs. Use "I would suggest that . . ." as an alternative.
- Consider statements that convey how the staff's behavior affects you and the organization. For example, you might say "When you do not complete your assign-

ments on time, then I cannot be in a position to assist you" or "When you are intolerant of clients, you reflect badly on the organization, which is intended to provide the best possible services to those who need them." You are challenging the behavior but in such a way as to reduce the employee's need to defend and justify it.

Avoiding Coaching Mistakes

Several guidelines should be followed when coaching your staff:

- Do not overcontrol your staff because this conveys little trust in them. By micromanaging your employees, you deny them the opportunity to grow and develop.
- Do not set your employees up for failure by assigning them projects they may not be qualified to handle. Overestimating staff's experience and abilities and then letting them flounder will lead to poor performance.
- Do not play with the truth. Even the smallest of lies can effect your credibility. Staff must be able to trust your integrity.
- Do not play favorites. If your staff thinks that you are not objective or that you value some members more than others, they will lose the common team spirit you are trying to develop.
- Do not create an environment in which there is only one way to do things. Identify the unique perspective and skills of each of your staff members and build on them.[40]

By avoiding these pitfalls, you are more likely to ensure a positive atmosphere that will contribute to your being accepted as a coaching supervisor.

Conveying Expectations

With so much emphasis on participation, decision making, and the need for diplomacy in conveying criticism, the reader might easily be misled to believe that supervisors should avoid making demands on staff. Some supervisors may be reluctant to push for growth, to make tough demands on their staff, and to request higher levels of performance. In fact, they may be asking too little from staff out of fear of inviting rejection or causing resistance. For some, a relaxed, congenial atmosphere with low expectations is a way to keep work life pleasant and anxiety free. It is certainly not conducive to creating productive organizations, however.

To counteract complacency, supervisors must convey their expectations. The best way to approach this is to identify an urgent problem, one for which it is imperative to obtain results. Are the staff not seeing as many clients as they should? Is there a shortfall in the number of foster homes? Are staff conducting fewer interviews this month compared with the last? These are questions that cry out for action and that demand urgently needed improvements. Supervisors, in their special role of leader, have a responsibility to mobilize their staff to face tough, frustrating challenges. Although sometimes it may be necessary to protect staff, at other times you will want to keep people in a productive growth mode even if it causes some anxiety.[41] When holding discussions with staff, it is the supervisor's responsibility to communicate and agree on expectations about the tasks at hand. In a climate of identifying and successfully meeting specific objectives, staff can expand their horizons to identify other issues and problems requiring their attention.[42]

Sometimes, the culture and climate of the organization is such that staff tend to cover up problems with "persistent positiveness."[43] People try to be positive even though they are aware that issues exist, and they look to top management to take responsibility that they should be handling. The consequence of this poor communication, of feigning positive thinking, is that staff do not take the opportunity to explore how their own actions may contribute to the problem. For example, employees may not be completing their record keeping on time but they deny that this is a problem. When they feel pressured at the end of the month or quarter, they attribute the problem to management's not giving them sufficient time. Good communication could result in exploring why staff do not want to take the time to take on the arduous task of writing. Both management and staff have to admit together, in frank discussion, that a problem exists and needs to be addressed.

Sometimes, poor performance is the result of poor communication between management and staff. If managers' expectations are vague and employees have to guess at what they are supposed to be doing, then their performance is likely to suffer. Clarifying expectations is not simply a matter of setting formal performance standards and measuring accomplishments. It requires extensive and continuous collaboration between management and staff to elicit staff ideas on reasonable performance expectations. The following six-part, mutual-interaction process can help the supervisor convey expectations and monitor staff progress:

1. Determine what the staff member is capable of achieving.

2. Decide whether the staff person's abilities are sufficient to complete the task.
3. Define the work that must be performed.
4. Communicate the assignment.
5. Assess whether the performance matches ability.
6. Identify, where necessary, why the performance was inadequate.

Supervisors must convey their expectations because staff who understand precisely how they must perform will work better than those who do not. Managers should continually reinforce expectations in frequent reviews, in formal evaluations, and even in writing.

Management by expectations is a two-way street. Managers should not only convey expectations to staff but also understand what staff expect of them. By doing so, managers gain insights on what they need to do to improve overall performance. One interesting approach to obtaining staff feedback is called the "upward performance appraisal."[44] Managers provide employees with an anonymous questionnaire asking for ratings on managerial performance in key areas such as communication, team building, motivation, suitability of assignments, and support. In a climate of mutual trust and respect, personal discussions focusing on such questions as "What am I doing that helps you with your work?" and "What am I doing that hampers you?" can be enlightening.[45] On the manager's part, this requires a great deal of personal security and an ability to react positively to constructive criticism. Being open to ideas from staff brings new insights into improving productivity and helps managers develop closer relationships with their staff.

NOTES

1. H. M. Havassy, Effective second-story bureaucrats: Mastering the paradox of diversity, *Social Work, 2* (1990), pp. 103-109.

2. A. Kadushin, *Supervision in social work* (2nd ed.) (New York: Columbia University Press, 1985), pp. 117-333.

3. P. Drucker, *Management challenges for the 21st century* (New York: HarperBusiness, 1999), pp. 184-185.

4. Alexander Hamilton Institute, *Coaching & counseling: Managers' secrets for improving employee performance* (Ramsey, NJ: Author, 1998), pp. 3-7.

5. A. Kadushin, pp. 145-164; A. Lauffer, *Working in social work* (Newbury Park, CA: Sage, 1987), p. 278; R. R. Middleman & G. B. Rhodes, *Competent supervision: Making imaginative judgments* (Englewood Cliffs, NJ: Prentice Hall, 1985), p. 6.

6. J. Waldroop & T. Butler, The executive as coach, *Harvard Business Review* (1996, November/December), pp. 111-117.

7. Bureau of Business Practice, *Front line supervisor's standard manual* (Waterford, CT: Author, 1989), p. 79; S. Cohen, *The effective public manager: Achieving success in government* (San Francisco: Jossey-Bass, 1988), p. 117; R. E. Herman, *Keeping good people: Strategies for solving the dilemma of the decade* (Cleveland, OH: Oakhill, 1990), p. 192; R. E. McCreight, A five role system for motivating improved performance, *Personnel Journal, 1* (1983), p. 24; H. Mintzberg, The manager's job: Folklore and fact, *Harvard Business Review, 2* (1990), p. 171.

8. D. C. Martin, Performance appraisal, 2: Improving the rater's effectiveness, in *Performance appraisal* (New York: American Management Association, 1989), p. 25 (reprinted from *Personnel,* 1986, August), pp. 28-33; M. S. Peck, *The road less traveled* (New York: Touchstone/Simon & Schuster, 1978), pp. 76-77.

9. T. Kirby, *The can-do manager* (New York: AMACOM, 1989), pp. 49-54.

10. H. Mintzberg, p. 169.

11. R. Brown, *The practical manager's guide to excellence in management* (New York: AMACOM, 1979), p. 113; T. Caplow, *How to run any organization* (Hinsdale, IL: Dryden, 1976), p. 44; A. Lauffer, *Working in social work,* pp. 283-284; R. von Oech, *A kick in the seat of the pants* (New York: Harper & Row, 1986), pp. 115-135.

12. L. Wallack, L. Dorfman, D. Jernigan, & M. Themba, *Media advocacy and public health* (Newbury Park, CA: Sage, 1993), p. 47.

13. L. Wallack et al., p. 80.

14. L. Wallack et al., p. 121.

15. R. Brody, M. Goodman, & J. Ferrante, *The legislative process: An action handbook for Ohio Citizens' Group* (3rd ed.) (Cleveland, OH: Federation for Community Planning, 1985).

16. D. C. Martin, p. 25.

17. J. E. Poulin, Job satisfaction of social work supervisors and administrators, *Administration in Social Work, 19*(4) (1995), pp. 35-49.

18. S. Cohen, pp. 71-72.

19. M. McCormack, A fine line separates dumping & delegating tasks, *The Plain Dealer* (1999, March 9), p. 5C.

20. P. Drucker, *The effective executive* (New York: Harper & Row, 1985), p. 182; M. McCormack, Giving instructions that make things happen, *The Plain Dealer* (1997, November 25), p. 3C.

21. R. Brown, p. 11.

22. S. Cohen, p. 72.

23. M. McCormack, *Mark H. McCormack on managing* (West Hollywood, CA: Dove, 1996), pp. 93-96.

24. K. Blanchard, J. P. Carlos, & A. Randolph, *The 3 keys to empowerment* (San Francisco: Berrett-Koehler, 1999), p. 30.

25. R. T. Crow & C. A. Odewahn, *Management for the human services* (Englewood Cliffs, NJ: Prentice Hall, 1987), pp. 63-67; A. Lauffer, *Careers, colleagues, and conflicts: Understanding gender, race, and ethnicity in the workplace* (Beverly Hills, CA: Sage, 1985), pp. 21-32; G. T. Milkovich & J. W. Boudreau, *Personnel/human resource manage-*

ment (5th ed.) (Plano, TX: Business Publications, 1988), pp. 167-172; D. Sanzotta, *Motivational theories and applications for managers* (New York: AMACOM, 1977), pp. 17-28; D. E. Terpstra, Theories of motivation: Borrowing the best, *Personnel Journal, 6* (1979), pp. 15-18.

26. D. E. Terpstra, p. 15.

27. A. H. Maslow, *Motivation and personality* (New York: Harper & Row, 1954).

28. D. McGregor, *The human side of enterprise* (New York: McGraw-Hill, 1960).

29. D. C. McClelland & D. Burnham, Power is the great motivator, *Harvard Business Review, 2* (1976), pp. 100-111.

30. V. H. Vroom, *Choosing a leadership style: Applying the Vroom & Yetton Model* (New York: AMACOM, 1973).

31. F. Herzberg, B. Mausner, & B. Synderman, *The motivation to work* (New York: John Wiley, 1959).

32. D. E. Terpstra, p. 16.

33. Alexander Hamilton Institute, pp. 21-23.

34. M. McCormack, *On communicating* (Los Angeles: Dove, 1998), pp. 37-38.

35. R. Brown, p. 62.

36. P. Drucker, Management's new paradigms, *Forbes* (1998, October), p. 166.

37. P. Drucker, Management's new paradigms, p. 164.

38. Bureau of Business Practice, Get the best from your employees, *Front Line Supervisor's Bulletin, 157* (1991), pp. 1-2.

39. S. Ford, *The ABC's of managing with employee teams* (Campbell, CA: Sondra Ford, 1983), pp. 77-79; T. Gordon, *Leader effectiveness training* (New York: Bantam, 1977); M. S. Peck, pp. 150-153; R. S. Schuler, *Personnel and human resource management* (3rd ed.) (St. Paul, MN: West, 1987), pp. 261-262; Alexander Hamilton Institute, pp. 10-15.

40. Alexander Hamilton Institute, pp. 29-31.

41. W. C. Taylor, The leader of the future, *Fast Company* (1999, June), p. 136.

42. R. H. Schaffer, Demand better results and get them, *Harvard Business Review, 2* (1991), pp. 145-149.

43. C. Argyris, Good communication that blocks learning, *Harvard Business Review* (1994, July/August), p. 82.

44. Bureau of Business Practice, The performance appraisal: Yours, *Front Line Supervisor's Bulletin, 151* (1990), pp. 1-3.

45. P. Drucker, *Managing the nonprofit organization* (New York: HarperCollins, 1990), p. 184.

Chapter 11

APPRAISING STAFF PERFORMANCE

Effective managers in human service organizations, like their counterparts in profit-making enterprises, use performance appraisals as a means of accomplishing several objectives. Appraisals are an important means of connecting staff performance to the organization's mission and goals.[1] They are useful in focusing on areas requiring staff improvement and training. They contribute to decisions requiring disciplinary action or termination. Also, they provide feedback on performance that could result in salary increases or staff promotions.[2] It is difficult to imagine any effective organization not conducting appraisals of its staff. Because appraisals can have such a profound impact on staff performance, effective managers must periodically review the appraisal content and process to determine its usefulness to both staff and the organization.

APPRAISAL METHODS

Because no universal appraisal format exists, each organization must develop a customized method to meet its special needs and circumstances. In establishing or revising a particular performance system, consider the following questions:

- Does it embrace organizational values and goals?
- Does it apply qualitative or quantitative standards or both?

- Is it used primarily for analyzing performance or for other purposes such as salary determination, promotions, reassignments, disciplinary action, or layoffs?
- Are the performance standards acceptable to directors, supervisors, and staff?
- Is the method easy to use?
- Is it both reliable (i.e., consistent over time and across the unit or organization) and valid (i.e., does it actually measure what it is intended to measure)?
- Is it likely to motivate appropriate behavior?

Human service organizations face the continuous problem of whether to focus on behaviors (activities) or outcomes (results). Ideally, effective managers should focus on outcomes; in reality, these can be difficult to measure and can be contaminated by forces outside of staff's control. Frequently, organizations will devise evaluation systems that encompass a review of both behaviors and results.

Organizations typically use one or more of the following appraisal methods: graphic rating scales, critical incidents, behaviorally anchored rating scales, and management by objectives.

Graphic Rating Scales

This appraisal method is used more frequently in evaluating performance than are others. Organizations select key characteristics—initiatives, creativity, job knowledge, dependability, cooperation, reliability, perseverance, and adaptability—that are identified as being most relevant to accomplishing their overall mission and goals.[3]

Ratings can be discrete, such as "outstanding," "good," acceptable," or "unacceptable," or they can be scaled along a continuum from 1 (poor) to 10 (outstanding). Often, scores are given without precise definitions provided so that evaluators rely on their own subjective sense in their ratings, as shown in Figure 11. 1.

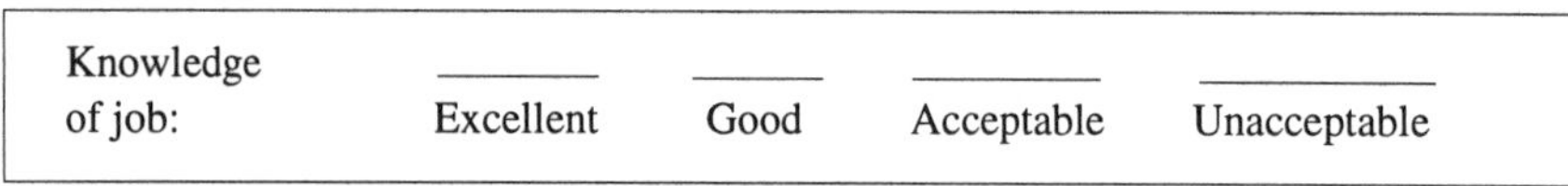

Figure 11.1. Rating Scale

Sometimes, organizations will define each characteristic. For example, the characteristic "initiative" might be defined as "carries out assignments with minimum instruction; willing to take risks and experiment with new ideas."

The advantage of graphic rating scales is their convenience and simplicity. If numerical values are given, they can be easily scored and are subject to statistical computations. Each employee can be scored against all others.

The disadvantages include selecting inappropriate characteristics, incorrectly scaling them, and giving the illusion of precision when numbers are used to reflect subjective opinions.[4]

Critical Incidents

These are descriptions by supervisors or other qualified observers of staff behaviors that are especially effective or ineffective. After the various accounts are recorded and studied, a group rates them on a scale in relation to contributions to the organization. In reality, few human service organizations go to the trouble of identifying a large number of critical incidents to form a scale. Instead, supervisors would use this approach to record incidents of behavior that reflect a pattern. For example, the evaluator might note that a staff member met 12 times with various units to develop a workable referral system, or the evaluator would observe that "uncooperativeness" was reflected in the way the employee failed to respond to several staff's requests for information.[5] The value of this method is that it can be used to supplement existing scales to highlight outstanding or poor performance.

Behaviorally Anchored Rating Scales

The behaviorally anchored rating scales (BARS) method is similar to the graphic rating scales method, except that BARS is quite specific in defining behaviors. Each point along an evaluation continuum is defined in behavioral terms. For example, if one of the behaviors is "relationship to clients," then the rating of "excellent" would be defined as "always responding appropriately and being helpful to clients." The rating of "poor" would be defined as "acting with hostility and rejection toward clients." The organization would determine how it wants to define "excellent," "competent," and "poor" for each of the qualities being evaluated.[6] A variety of characteristics can be identified, such as commitment to tasks, response to supervision, communication skills, initiative, and analytic ability. Each organization would determine what behavioral characteristics it wants to evaluate and also how it would define the ratings for each behavior.

For example, a manager might use the following criteria for evaluating an employee's "knowledge of job":

- Outstanding: has exceptionally thorough knowledge about all facets of the job and its relationships to other jobs
- Good: has above-average knowledge about most aspects of the job; requires only limited supervision on the more complex tasks
- Average: knows the necessary elements of the job to meet the requirements of the job; requires periodic supervision
- Poor: knowledge of job is limited; needs additional training or experience in several phases; makes frequent mistakes and requires extremely close supervision

The advantage of BARS is that it reduces bias among evaluators because the ratings are related to behaviors established by the organization. Evaluators will still be influenced by their subjective impressions, although presumably this subjectivity will be reduced by their having specific behavioral definitions. Of course, the organization must devote considerable time and effort to developing a customized scale.

Management by Objectives

Recall that in Chapter 4 organizational objectives were developed to hold the organization accountable for results. This same approach, usually referred to as management by objectives (MBO), can be used to guide individual staff performance and accountability. Preferably, individual performance objectives and their standards should be mutually developed by staff and their supervisors so that both will have a clear idea of how the staff will work to achieve the organization's mission and goals. The advantage of MBO is its flexibility and adaptability in responding to different agency situations and individual staff circumstances.

Before evaluating individual employees, the organization should define key results (or goals) it wants to accomplish during the following year, such as providing information, increasing revenue, developing an XYZ system, recruiting foster parents, reuniting families, and serving *X* number of clients.

Typically, individual objectives are then linked to selected key results, which can include both normal work expectations and innovations or special areas of improvement. For example, key results in a human service unit within a public housing authority could include

increasing referrals to ancillary services,

mobilizing community resources,

counseling individuals, and

preparing reports.

Attached to each key result would be specific performance objectives that staff are expected to accomplish annually to achieve the result. For example, connected with the key result "increasing referrals to ancillary services" would be the following individual staff objectives:

- Make an average of 20 referrals each month.
- Ensure that clients positively connect with a referral organization 60% of the time.

Similarly, connected with the key result "preparing reports" would be the following individual staff objectives:

- Complete reports on clients within an average of 5 working days.
- Complete all administrative report requirements within the schedule specified.

Table 11.1 illustrates examples of management and staff objectives.

The previously discussed objectives are illustrative; each organization and each job category will require careful examination to determine which results should be measured. Some organizations make a distinction between routine and exceptional or innovative objectives. Routine objectives usually remain the same from year to year and reflect the ongoing work expected of staff. Innovative objectives are set when developing new projects or new programs for the year if new circumstances occur. Also, some effective managers make a distinction in a given job between the objectives established for experienced staff and those for novices.

To be useful, objectives should be determined from an interactive process in which managers, supervisors, and staff collectively decide on them.

Table 11.1
Examples of Management and Staff Objectives

Management objectives

- Maintain an average program capacity of *X* consumers.
- Implement *X* program.
- Cross-train *X* staff.
- Develop *X* objectives for each staff person.
- Write *X* grants for *Y* funding during the course of the year.
- Administer customer satisfaction surveys.
- Reduce deficit in *X* program by *Y* amount.
- Provide documentation that illustrates *X* cooperative arrangements with other units.
- Reduce cost per unit of client service by *X* %.
- Reduce staff absenteeism by *X* %.
- Reduce staff grievances by *X* %.
- Implement a plan for promoting the organization.
- Increase gross operating income by *X* %.
- Complete the quarter with no more than *X* audit exceptions to all contracts.

Staff objectives

- Conduct *X* group activity sessions.
- Increase number of clients served by *X* %.
- Match *X* volunteers with clients.
- Give *X* presentations during the course of the year.
- Conduct *X* home visits.
- Contact *X* service providers for progress reports each month.
- Increase average starting wage of job program clients from *X* to *Y*.
- Increase number of completed placements by *X* %.
- Increase the number of clients completing the program from *X* % to *Y* %.
- Increase acceptances of recommendations by referral source from *X* % to *Y* %.
- Increase client satisfaction from *X* % to *Y* %.

For example, in a children's institution, management and staff mutually determine that monitoring the distribution of medication is an important objective, and therefore they establish quantifiable objectives for this activity. Because they created the process together (continually modifying it, if necessary), staff will deem it equitable. Staff involvement is essential because no appraisal system will be completely objective, and everyone must live with the results.

The following guidelines will help to develop performance objectives:

- Use an achievement-oriented action verb (e.g., "implement," "complete," and "write").
- Specify a target date or time period for each objective.
- State objectives that are realistically attainable and yet challenge staff.
- Include a process that requires both supervisors and their staffs to mutually agree on the objectives.
- Set objectives that are consistent with resources available, that provide the best return on the investment of time and resources, and that are clear and understandable to employees.
- Be certain that your objectives reflect what you truly want to accomplish. For example, if "increasing job placements" is a key result your organization has selected, include in the objectives a performance criterion to secure jobs for clients, not just obtain job interviews for them.[7]
- Prepare action plans that are sufficiently detailed to provide clear guidelines for staff behavior.
- Be prepared to renegotiate objectives if circumstances warrant.

Because of the possibility that objectives may be vague and ambiguous, it is important to establish measurement indicators in advance. For example, if management is concerned about the lack of cooperation between units, then "enhancing cooperation" becomes a key result and would include specific objectives such as "conferring with other units before decisions are made," "holding joint meetings," and "obtaining feedback from colleagues."

Some organizations establish an elaborate point system to rate quantifiably how people are performing. For example, foster home placement staff may earn points for having returned children to their biological parents within a designated time. Caseworkers may be given points based on the number of referrals they make and bonus points for the number of referrals that become contacts. By quantifying results, the organization can more systematically rank staff performance. The organization, however, has to be confident that an objective is truly measurable and does not force staff into being so concerned about achieving points that they ignore other important, but not easily measurable, activities.

Although MBO has the potential for distinguishing mediocre from outstanding employees, it is understandable that an organization may not want to rely solely on it as a means of appraising performance because of inherent measurement problems. Are measurement indicators true reflections of performance? What if an employee's performance is dependent on factors that may not be entirely controllable? These are questions that are bound to be raised in an MBO appraisal program and for which there may not be ready answers.

Some organizations see value in combining a rating system that emphasizes staff qualities such as interpersonal relationships and knowledge with an MBO appraisal system that emphasizes achievement of results. This provides an evaluation of both staff qualities and accomplishments. In addition, the organization may wish to provide a rating of the contribution the individual makes to the achievement of the department's or the organization's objectives that is above and beyond the individual's objectives. Table 11.2 demonstrates this combination of personal traits and achievement of objectives.

USE OF NARRATIVE

Regardless of the specific appraisal method an organization uses to obtain a more rounded assessment, it is generally a good idea to encourage supervisors and staff to engage in discussions about staff performance. The following questions might help to facilitate such a dialogue:

- What has the employee done to improve performance since the last evaluation?
- What specific performance areas should receive special attention in the following year?
- What can the employee do to strengthen job performance?
- What are the employee's highest priorities for the following year?
- What career goals does the employee have?
- What additional training does the employee want to achieve these goals?
- What does the employee think the organization should do to improve?

By discussing these broader issues, staff have an opportunity to think about and articulate how they can enhance their own professional growth and contribute to the organization's productivity. These observations by both the

Table 11.2
Combined Performance Appraisal Process

Factors	*Maximum Points*
Individual factors based on supervisor's assessment:	50
Job knowledge	
Interpersonal relationships	
Work quality	
Analytical ability	
Initiative	
Dependability	
Achievement of individual objectives	30
Assistance in achieving department's and organization's objectives	20
Total	100

SOURCE: Adapted from Nelson (1991).[8]

staff member and the supervisor are written and become part of the employee's permanent record.

CONDUCTING AN APPRAISAL CONFERENCE

Prior to the appraisal conference, and even at the beginning of a staff member's probationary period, the staff member should be given a copy of the appraisal form that will be used to evaluate performance. In this way, the employee will know, long before the appraisal session, what the specific expectations are regarding performance and what behavioral and attitudinal qualities will be reviewed.

Effective managers are aware that, regardless of the format used to evaluate staff, they must carefully prepare for appraisal conferences. They must gather relevant information about performance and compare it with objectives that have been established. Staff should be expected to attend the appraisal conference with information documenting their achievements. In addition, consider the guidelines discussed in the following paragraphs in conducting the appraisal conference.

Connect the employee's work to unit objectives and organizational values. Effective managers use the appraisal conference to transmit the values of the organization and what it is trying to achieve (see Chapter 2). Staff should understand how their efforts tie in with the mission of the organization and the objectives of their department (see Chapter 3). They need to see how their individual efforts relate to the "big picture." The measures that apply to the individual must fit within the context of his or her unit.[9]

Conduct appraisals throughout the year. The year-end appraisal should provide an opportunity for reviewing previous discussions. Continuous appraisals are far better for changing behavior than a one-time, annual review session that may contain surprises. The annual review should be used to summarize performance, not shock the employee.[10] In addition to conferences held throughout the year to deal with special problems, it is desirable that formal appraisal conferences occur at least twice annually. The advantage of semiannual or even quarterly formal appraisal conferences is that corrective action can be prescribed and then monitored before the next appraisal conference.

Determine desired outcomes in advance. Effective managers prepare for the interview by thinking through what they want to accomplish: What information do you want to impart? What objectives for the following year do you want to see achieved? What skills do you want staff to develop, and how will they develop them? What steps are you prepared to take if the employee does not agree to change his or her performance? How is the employee likely to react, and how might you respond to that reaction? Always enter an appraisal session with an agenda, and be clear on what you want to achieve.

Foster mutual problem solving. Staff should be encouraged to take an active role in the discussion. The atmosphere during the appraisal conference should be one of mutual problem solving. Before jumping to conclusions about the cause of a problem, ask open-ended questions that can elicit ideas from the staff. For example, ask what the employee thinks is causing a downturn in performance.[11] Identify together what specific steps the staff member must take to improve performance. For example, if you have conveyed concern about "lack of initiative," mutually develop specific actions the employee must take to foster more proactive work behavior.

In most performance reviews, encourage employees to do most of the talking. By asking open-ended questions that require thoughtful responses, you encourage the staff member to fully engage in thinking through issues. The following are examples of open-ended questions:

"How would you describe your progress this past year?"

"Why do you think the problem is occurring?"

"What areas do you think need strengthening?"

"What concerns do you have about accomplishing your goals and objectives?"

By actively listening, you convey respect for your staff's ideas. Only after you have heard what your staff has to say—fully and completely—would you begin to express your own thoughts.[12] It is appropriate for a manager to use the appraisal discussion to offer his or her own interpretations and judgments of the employee's performance. In this regard, it is important to use "I" statements that are behaviorally specific. For example, instead of using the vague, judgmental statement, "You should be more responsible," you might say, "I'd like you to take more time preparing for your group counseling sessions each week."

Sometimes, staff will use the appraisal interview to express their concerns or complain about other staff members or about policies and procedures of the organization that they perceive interfere with their work performance. The best approach is to let the staff discuss their concerns and to consider together some options to deal with the issue. Especially focus on those aspects that impinge on the staff member's performance. Show your understanding and your empathy, seek as many facts as possible, avoid quick decisions, and then determine together what steps might be taken.[13]

By the end of the session, supervisor and staff should develop an action plan with clear objectives, specific target dates, and plans for following up.[14] By emphasizing shared problem solving, you help staff maintain their sense of dignity and respect, thus reducing their defensiveness and making them more responsive to your suggestions for growth and improvement.[15]

Be aware that the following appraisal defects can enter into the appraisal process:[16]

1. The *recency tendency* focuses on the most recent performance rather than on behavior during the entire rating period.
2. The *halo effect* is based on one characteristic or performance rather than a complete view of the employee.
3. The *average tendency* results in supervisors assessing everyone toward the average as a way of avoiding exceptional ratings they may have to defend.

4. The *forced choice tendency* occurs when supervisors believe they must balance those staff given positive ratings with an equal number of staff given negative ones, whether deserved or not.

5. The *inflation tendency* occurs when supervisors give all their staff indiscriminately high ratings.

Provide meaningful feedback. Discussions about how an employee's personality characteristics negatively affect performance are usually not helpful because they are loaded with value judgments, will probably make the employee feel defensive, and rarely result in personality change. The emphasis should be on improper behavior that affects the employee's performance.

The best feedback is clear and descriptive, not vague and judgmental. Support general statements with concrete examples that illustrate thematic concerns. The descriptions "Does not take sufficient initiative" or "Fails to follow agency procedures" are too vague, but "Needed constant supervision during X project" or "On three occasions, reports were submitted after the deadline" clearly define the problem. Set up a file folder for each staff member, and throughout the year, when episodes occur, record information on special achievements or failures or evaluative comments made by other professionals. These data provide specific backup to general observations.

Put major points of the appraisal in writing. It is especially important to write objectives for the following year, any changes in duties and expectations, and observations that relate to performance. Note particularly agreements and disagreements you as supervisor have with the staff. Writing these ideas will greatly reduce misunderstandings.

Some managers are especially uncomfortable about criticizing their subordinates, either verbally or in writing. Their written record of underperforming employees contains instead only positive or neutral observations. Then, when an employee's performance deteriorates to the point at which the person must be terminated, the supervisor belatedly writes observations that had never been fully shared with the staff member. This process can surely backfire in court proceedings. It is therefore important to ensure that the written appraisal contains objective statements about performance and that employees are aware of everything that goes into their files.[17]

Mutually determine staff priorities. This is important if the supervisor or the organization wants to augment a staff member's responsibilities. Determine which assignments can be postponed if staff are overloaded. The appraisal conference provides the opportunity to assess how to balance multiple assignments.

Be positive and constructive, not negative and punitive. Be especially watchful of how you express criticism; staff generally think they are performing at their best level. Convey, when it is meaningful to do so, improvements that staff are making or the positive results they are achieving as a prelude to constructive criticism. Be aware, however, that the "good news-bad news" approach can become ritualistic, and depending on the person you may want to vary the pattern. The important point is that staff are more amenable to criticism when you can genuinely recognize their positive attributes in the context of criticism.

The appraisal conference should provide a positive opportunity to assess past performance and future directions. Effective managers use the conference to provide a forward thrust, a sense that progress has been or can be made, and an affirmation that employees have been contributing and will continue to contribute positively to the goals of the organization.

It may be a good idea in the appraisal interview to establish intermediate objectives that can be measured within the next few weeks or months rather than waiting until the end of the year to determine whether progress has been made.[18] For example, if tardiness is a problem, you would want to establish objectives that would be met within the next month. During the appraisal interview, you would clarify that an employee's job might be in jeopardy unless his or her performance improves. It is hoped that the employee will improve by the next assessment; if not, the appraisal will provide docu- mentation for future review and action.

If staff performance has improved following the appraisal conference, then positive feedback—genuine and sincere praise—can be meaningful to your employee. Reinforcing good performance will help sustain this improvement.

NOTES

1. Design for peak performance, *Nonprofit Management Strategies, 4* (1991), pp. 1-4.
2. D. Cherrington, *Personnel management: The management of human resources* (2nd ed.) (Dubuque, IA: William C. Brown, 1987), pp. 237-238.
3. G. T. Milkovich & J. W. Boudreau, *Personnel/human resource management* (5th ed.) (Plano, TX: Business Publications, 1988), pp. 195-196.
4. D. Cherrington, pp. 248-249.

5. G. T. Milkovich & J. W. Boundreau, pp. 200-203; P. J. Pecora & M. J. Austin, *Managing human services personnel* (Newbury Park, CA: Sage, 1987), pp. 77-84.

6. D. Cherrington, p. 252.

7. D. D McConkey, *MBO for nonprofit organizations* (New York: AMACOM, 1975); P. J. Pecora & M. J. Austin, p. 75.

8. W. C. Nelson, Incentive based management for nonprofit organizations, *Nonprofit Management and Leadership, 1* (1991), p. 63.

9. J. H. Boyett & H. P. Conn, Developing white-collar performance measurement, *National Productivity Review* (1988, Summer), pp. 209-218; Tarkenton Productivity Group, *Motivational theories and applications for managers* (New York: AMACON, 1977), pp. 1-2.

10. D. Sanzotta, *Motivational theories and applications for managers* (New York: AMACOM, 1977), p. 89.

11. Alexander Hamilton Institute, *Conducting successful appraisal interviews* (Maywood, NJ: Author, 1991), p. 16.

12. Alexander Hamilton Institute, *Conducting successful appraisal interviews: The right way to discuss employee performance* (Ramsey, NJ: Author, 1998), pp. 10-11.

13. Alexander Hamilton Institute, *Conducting successful appraisal interviews: The right way,* pp. 13-17.

14. S. D. Bruce, *Face to face: Every manager's guide to better appraisal and discipline interviewing* (Madison, CT: Business and Legal Reports, 1989), p. 223.

15. D. C. Martin, Performance appraisal, 2: Improving the rater's effectiveness, in *Performance appraisal* (New York: American Management Association, 1989), pp. 26-28 (Reprinted from *Personnel,* 1986, August, pp. 28-33).

16. S. D. Bruce, pp. 16-17; D. Cherrington, pp. 238-239; R. I. Henderson, *Compensation management: Rewarding performance* (Englewood Cliffs, NJ: Prentice Hall, 1989), p. 318.

17. Alexander Hamilton Institute, *Conducting successful appraisal interviews: The right way,* pp. 30-31.

18. Alexander Hamilton Institute, *Conducting successful appraisal interviews: The right way,* p. 12.

Chapter 12

COMPENSATING WORK AND REWARDING PERFORMANCE

In almost every study asking employees about what is important to them, pay is at the top of the list. An opinion-polling organization that reviewed data found that pay and benefits ranked among the most important rewards for employees in different job classifications—managers, professionals, clerical staff, and hourly workers.[1]

In human service organizations, pay as a reward for work is certainly an important factor. Effective managers are aware that many staff hold their jobs out of a deep sense of commitment and a desire to have an impact on the lives of other people. Managers also know, however, that it would be a mistake to take advantage of staff's goodwill by compensating them at a rate lower than what they are worth. The work must be inherently interesting, but staff must have extrinsic (pay) rewards as well.

This chapter reviews various ways that salary can be used to compensate staff for work: pay based on job, on skills, and on performance—whether by individuals or groups. Because "pay for performance" is of particular interest to managers, it will be given special attention. The importance of symbolic rewards will also be discussed.

JOB CLASSIFICATION PAY SYSTEM

In most human service organizations, the usual method of determining pay level is to analyze the value of a job based on criteria such as education required, technical knowledge, degree of autonomy, and importance of the job to the organization. A rating is made for each factor, and jobs are ranked in a hierarchy. A job salary survey is conducted by the agency, by a national body of which the local agency is an affiliate, or by a local health and human services planning agency to determine what other organizations are paying for similarly rated jobs. On the basis of this analysis, administrators develop pay ranges for job categories, which are then adjusted for inflation and other market factors.[2]

Many organizations using job classification systems pay staff within an established salary range, usually on the basis of seniority. Typically, organizations bound by union agreement, or those that have difficulty in measuring performance, cannot objectively distinguish highly productive from average employees and so are likely to base salaries on length of service in classified jobs. To remain competitive in the job marketplace, they sometimes rely on local or national surveys to provide guidance in offering comparable pay for similar positions in the community. Employees are slotted into specific classifications, each with its own salary range. More experienced staff tend to be at the middle to upper range of their classification; newer, less experienced staff tend to be at the lower end.

As the traditional method of compensation, pay based on job classification remunerates staff for their job responsibilities, taking into consideration the relationship of a particular job to others both within and outside the organization. The advantage of job classification is that it is a useful way of maintaining equity because the relative value of the job can be established with some degree of objectivity.[3]

Increases in pay are often made "across the board" and are intended to keep pace with cost-of-living increases. Thus, if inflation is 4%, pay increases are likely to average the same. Consistency and equity are hallmarks of the job classification system, and the majority of staff are not likely to express dissatisfaction. Under this system, those who demonstrate outstanding performance may be promoted to supervisory positions. Movement up the hierarchy, with accompanying responsibilities and increased compensation, is one way exemplary performance is rewarded.

One of the problems with the job classification system is that pay inequities can occur. Organizations may tend to reward seniority over merit so that longtime workers receive more pay even if they are less productive than their younger colleagues. Length of time on the job, not merit, becomes a primary criterion for pay level.

Another problem is that staff receive significant increases in pay primarily through promotions. A highly skilled counselor may not receive much more in pay than one less skilled because of his or her classification; only by moving up to supervisor can the counselor achieve a significant increase. By far the greatest problem associated with job classification systems is that they do not emphasize outstanding achievement of results. If you know you will receive a modest pay increase just by remaining on the job another year and there are no other values operating to stimulate excellent performance, what incentive is there for excelling in the job? Superperformers and high achievers can feel frustrated because monetary rewards ultimately do not reflect their achievements. In some instances, agencies establish a two-track system so that highly skilled staff may be eligible for pay equal to that of supervisors.

Some organizations establish a culture of high-performance expectations instead of relying on financial incentives. They communicate to staff that they are special people hired to do a special job. Staff are expected to be dedicated to their work and have a strong service commitment. In organizations that are new, have charismatic leadership, promise future opportunities, or provide intrinsically satisfying jobs, this value orientation can be a significant incentive. Be mindful, however, of the inherent danger of relying on charisma, promises, and cheerleading as means of dealing with the absence of adequate financial compensation.

Effective managers work especially hard in a job classification system to change staff mentality from that of "I'm owed it" to that of "I've earned it."[4]

SKILL-BASED PAY SYSTEM

Some organizations base pay ranges on a hierarchy of the least skilled to the most skilled. The skill-based evaluation system encourages staff to acquire new skills through on-the-job training or through special internal or external training programs. Staff can move upward through the hierarchy and thereby increase their pay based on increased talent rather than having to take a management position. Providing for growth in skills accompanied by pay increases allows upward mobility in organizations that want to reduce management hierarchy and maintain a "flat" structure. Staff grow within their current positions rather than moving up the organizational structure.

In addition to increasing the skills in a single specialty area or job classification, some organizations provide the opportunity for staff to obtain skills in many different jobs across the organization. For example, a secretary might be encouraged to obtain bookkeeping skills. A public relations representative may develop fund-raising skills through a process of "cross-training." By achieving these new skills, staff become more valuable to the organization. They are then able to fill in when needed, and the organization benefits further by having greater flexibility. Managers give increased pay to those employees who develop a breadth of skills useful to the organization.

Many human service organizations do not necessarily reward staff for obtaining new skills but expect them to grow on the job. Professional staff who attend conferences and workshops for continuing education credits do not receive extra pay because the organization distinguishes this ordinary and expected professional growth from that which is extraordinary, demanding, and may require several years of specialized training. The latter is more likely to be financially rewarded. An example is increasing the pay of an employee who attains a master's degree, although his or her duties remain the same.

One of the problems with a skill-based system is that some staff may reach the top of their skill level and find themselves with no place to go after several years in the same position. In addition, staff who obtain university degrees or special technical training may become more marketable and decide to leave, thereby causing a "brain drain" on the organization. Despite these problems, an organization that emphasizes a skill-based system can benefit from staff who seek constant upgrading in their technical skill levels. In general, human service organizations use pay increases when staff in technical and blue-collar positions (e.g., maintenance personnel) achieve certain technical milestones.

PAY FOR PERFORMANCE

Pay for performance (PFP) systems adjust the salary based on appraisals of staff performance. Variations will occur depending on the extent to which the organization emphasizes rewards. For example, some organizations provide across-the-board increases for union staff and PFP for nonunion, management staff.

The fundamental purpose of PFP systems is to reward staff for their expenditure of effort, the quality of their work, and, most important, the results they achieve. It provides special motivation to work hard because staff know that the highest financial rewards will go to those whose performance is outstanding.[5] Particularly for achievement-oriented staff, PFP provides extra incentive for them to function at their optimum level, whereas it conveys to unproductive employees that they will receive little or no financial gain.

PFP both permits management to reward those staff whose performance contributes to the overall achievement of the organization's goals and objectives and helps staff to focus on management priorities. Staff have an incentive to give attention to activities (e.g., completing records) that may not be as appealing as others they might choose (e.g., working with clients). Financial incentives may motivate staff to perform "boring" or "routine" administrative chores they might otherwise put on a back burner.

Some organizations establish an elaborate point system based on well-defined appraisal measurements that provide for a range of percentage increases. These increases in pay are incorporated in the staff's base salary. An employee paid $30,000 who receives a 5% increase in Year A will have a base salary of $31,500 in Year B. Specific expectations are defined for each position, and management makes weighted judgments based on points assigned to each work category. In a vocational employment program for disabled and disadvantaged persons, staff might be measured as shown in Figure 12.1.

Note that in Figure 12.1 the vocational employment agency has developed objective and measurable standards to evaluate a vocational counselor. These standards include number of clients served, number placed, wage rates, and achievement of concrete objectives. A client satisfaction survey is also incorporated. The point system can result in 0% to 9% salary increases.

As another illustration, a mental health organization establishes PFP for its nonunion, managerial staff. The executive staff establish concrete objectives in discussion with each of the managers. Together, they determine that staff performance will be measured on the basis of achieving one of two major performance rankings: standard or outstanding. To be eligible for an outstanding performance rating, supervisory staff must meet superior performance objectives. Staff who achieve standard performance receive a 5% increase; those few who achieve a superior performance rating (e.g., by obtaining special funding or conducting two additional training programs) can receive as high as a 9% increase. These extraordinary merit increases are applicable until the base salary reaches the salary ceiling for a particular job classification.

Staff and management jointly develop measurable outcomes so that the definition of success will be clear to everyone in advance. A combination of

Key Result Area	*Weight*	*Points Earned*
a. Number of clients served		8
1. 250-300	10	
2. 225-249	8	
3. 200-224	5	
4. Less than 200	2	
b. Number of clients placed		20
1. 150-175	20	
2. 125-149	15	
3. 100-124	10	
4. 75-99	5	
c. Average starting wage		15
1. $5.50 and up	15	
2. $5.25-5.49	10	
3. $5.00-5.24	7	
4. $4.25-4.99	5	
d. Supplementary objectives		
1. Provide quality quarterly reports	5-15	12
2. Obtain additional funding ranging between $25,000 and $100,000	5-15	11
3. Conduct four quality training programs	5-15	14
e. Consumer satisfaction survey results		5
1. Fully satisfied	10	
2. Highly satisfied	7	
3. Moderately satisfied	5	
4. Poorly satisfied	0	
Total		85

In this hypothetical example, the employee received 85 out of a possible 100 points. The employee would be eligible for a pay increase between 5.0% and 6.9%, based on a formula applied to a rating scale. 85 is 50% of the difference between 80% and 89%. The raise is therefore 50% of the difference between 5.0% and 6.9%, or 5.95%.

Rating	Performance Rating (%)	Salary Increase (%)
Exceptional	90-100	7.0-9.0
Highly qualified	80-89	5.0-6.9
Competent	70-79	3.0-4.9
Conditional	60-69	0

Figure 12.1. Performance Rating Objectives: Vocational Placement Counselor

objective and subjective measures is used, although the key to success is the achievement of results. Consequently, staff buy into the prospect of earning a higher pay level based on their performance, and pay based on accomplishments ultimately becomes a highly regarded value of the organization's culture. Staff also accept that management may exercise a certain amount of judgment in their final decisions on salary increases.

Cautions About Pay for Performance

As increasingly more corporations develop PFP systems, volunteer business leaders will be encouraging human service organizations to follow suit. This pressure, along with the inherent appeal of rewarding outstanding performers and using pay as a primary motivator, may propel agencies to move prematurely without considering all the ramifications. Several caveats should be kept in mind.

There is a natural tendency for staff to overrate themselves and then feel upset when they are not evaluated in the highest category.[6] If the PFP focuses primarily on merit, it could cause all but the superstars to have negative reactions. Studies show that most employees rate their performance in the 80th percentile when they compare themselves with others in the organization. Given the fact that an organization cannot pay everyone in the 80th percentile, it is not surprising that many employees who work in organizations that provide differential pay rewards believe they are underpaid relative to their coworkers.[7]

One reason why employees tend to overrate themselves is because supervisors may not provide candid performance evaluations. Knowing that their assessments could have a direct impact on the pay of their subordinates, they may tend to inflate their evaluations; consequently, staff develop unrealistic views of themselves and become dissatisfied with their pay.[8] Obviously, for PFP to succeed, employees must understand that they will most likely fall in the middle range of pay increases, with only a few receiving substantive increases. Moreover, supervisors should realize that their evaluations will be taken seriously, and that they themselves will be evaluated on the basis of their ability to judge staff performance. Of course, if goals are quantified, there is less possibility that employees will overrate themselves; the numbers will speak for themselves.

The comparative worth of staff is difficult to measure, and staff could perceive PFP as benefiting some while unfairly hurting others. Staff may think that their objectives are more difficult to achieve than those of others in the organization. Moreover, they may resent the fact that their jobs do not demonstrate their value as clearly as others in the organization. An accountant's worth may not be as demonstrable as a fund raiser's or a job placement counselor's in determining pay increases. This presents a special dilemma that the organization must confront. Either certain jobs must be designated as outside the PFP system because they do not produce easily measurable accomplishments or the measurement system has to factor in ways that all jobs can be equitably assessed.

In addition, a PFP program assumes that staff do have control over the results of their performance. There are, however, few outcomes in human service organizations that are not dependent on other factors or individuals, and there are even fewer that are not subject to external variables.[9] For example, in a juvenile justice program, when probationers get jobs in a growing economy and stay out of jail, juvenile counselors understandably will want to take credit and be rewarded financially for success. When recidivism is high, however, in part because probationers cannot find jobs, then staff must operate under a disincentive of no financial rewards. Staff may perceive the PFP as being unfair when factors beyond their control influence outcomes.

PFP may not be flexible enough to respond to important changes. Staff evaluations and pay in some agencies are based on meeting predetermined objectives that, during the course of the year, may be set aside for other emerging priorities. The remedy for this situation, of course, is a flexible PFP that will permit both employee and supervisor to negotiate objectives to be calculated into the PFP system.

If PFP becomes a primary motivator, it could subvert other important organizational values. If staff become psychologically consumed by the pay reward system, their self-worth and motivation may become based almost exclusively on this tangible measure. Consequently, monetary compensation becomes the central driving force for performance and tends to overshadow other desired values. For example, employees may become highly competitive and place their own interests over those of their team or unit.[10]

Organizations should take this caution seriously and work to keep PFP from becoming the dominant motivator. They need to give continuous attention to the importance of interpersonal relationships, job enrichment, and the significance of providing high-quality service to consumers. Pay incentives cannot be a substitute for good employment practices; rather, they should be used to reinforce positive work behavior. PFP should be a secondary, not a primary, method of influencing behavior.[11]

Serious measurement problems can affect PFP systems. In the private sector, considerable evidence exists that in most enterprises merit pay systems fail to create a close relationship between pay and performance and, as a result, fail to motivate employees. In large part, this failure is due to the lack of credible, comprehensive measures of performance. Because objective measures of individual performance typically do not exist, most organizations rely on the judgment of managers. These judgments are sometimes viewed by subordinates as invalid, unfair, and discriminatory. To many employees, merit pay is a fiction—a myth that managers try to perpetuate for the purpose of influencing behavior.[12] This concern about measurement limitations in the private sector needs to be considered by managers in human service organizations.

Objective measures, such as counting interviews or job placements, can appropriately be used in PFP. Organizations must give considerable thought to measuring more subjective accomplishments. This is especially true in organizations that provide some type of counseling as their primary service. It is difficult to measure the extent to which child-parent or marital relationships improve on an aggregated caseload basis. Because of the difficulty in measuring "soft" services, organizations may either not use a PFP system or develop more appropriate measurements, such as the number of interviews conducted or response from consumer surveys.

As noted in Chapter 11, methods of appraising staff may be subject to supervisory bias. When presented with a scale ranging from "poor" to "outstanding," some supervisors tend to rate staff at the upper end of the scale, and others rate at the lower end. To avoid skewed ratings, the organization could set strict guidelines for rating staff—for example, only a certain percentage of staff will be eligible for the highest pay increases. Even under this arrangement, however, it is possible that the best member of the worst group is given a higher pay increase than the worst member of the best group. If this is likely, top management must take responsibility for overseeing the totality of the PFP system to determine whether it is in fact identifying outstanding employees. Supervisors must review the evaluation process with their own managers to understand their own biases.

Basing the reward system on individual achievements may not be appropriate when much of the work in human service organizations occurs as a result of cooperative interrelationships. Frequently, work performance (e.g., referrals to other staff) depends on other staffs' skills and motivations.[13]

A PFP system is no insurance for continued high performance. Over time, previous pay increases based on high performance become a permanent part of the base pay and are paid in perpetuity.[14] Last year's outstanding performance, however, gives no assurance that this year's will be equally outstanding. Previous high performers may tend to coast. Of course, this criticism also applies to job classification systems in which seniority, rather than merit, is built into the base pay. At least the PFP system allows for limiting of financial rewards for those who do not perform, even though they may have done so in the past. The disadvantages of building increases into the base pay under a PFP system could be mitigated through a one-time bonus system, which will be discussed in the next section.

PFP places a strain on supervisors and managers because it is time-consuming and emotionally demanding. Preparation of evaluation materials can be challenging because both staff and management feel pressure to carefully document performance and productivity. Evaluation takes on even greater significance when increases (or decreases) depend on it. Staff will want to negotiate objectives and will likely challenge those that their supervisors have established.

Moreover, staff may refuse to embark on a vital new activity during the course of the year, fearing that it could jeopardize other previously established objectives. Also, staff may think that supervisors are not giving enough weight to their current activities. These complications mean that supervisors may need to invest themselves as never before in negotiating and renegotiating with their staff. This investment is not necessarily wrong and, in fact, may be essential to fill the supervisory role properly; it is noted here as a caveat to acknowledge that PFP can be quite a demanding challenge for supervisors.

In addition, supervisors must understand that, if objective measures are limited, the PFP system thrusts them into a more judgmental role, which could affect their usual role as coach and supporter. This may place strains on the relationship with staff, who are well aware that their supervisors have the power to determine whether they receive a $200 or a $1,200 pay increase.

Sufficient funds may not be available to fulfill PFP goals. The PFP system may be appropriate when an organization has additional discretionary funds or when staff salaries lag behind those paid for comparable positions in other human service organizations. When funds are limited or when long-time, high-achieving staff reach the highest level of their salary scales, however, PFP becomes more difficult to carry out. When there is only a finite amount of money to distribute, other demands on the pay system such as cost-of-living increases and maintaining salary competitiveness may have to take precedence.[15]

One way to deal with these conflicting demands is to reduce across-the-board pay increases based on the conviction that poor performers should receive no or limited increases (or even layoffs), leaving additional funding available for high performers. Of course, the culture of the organization must clearly support this conviction. When top performers reach the maximum of their pay scales after several years of above-average increases, special arrangements must be made so that they do not lose their incentive, such as providing them with a bonus that allows them to be paid more than the maximum for their classification.

Special organizational constraints may inhibit the development of PFP. In situations in which unions work out contractual arrangements, PFP may be limited to managerial staff. In some instances, an organization may initiate special negotiations with a union. For example, an organization serving the mentally retarded could work out an agreement with the bus drivers' union in which members will receive additional funding based on their improved driving records and the resultant insurance cost savings.

Dealing with the board of trustees presents another constraint. Many trustees appreciate improving productivity and increasing efficiency but balk at giving incentive pay. They think this detracts from the dedication of staff. Because board acceptance is usually required, it is advisable that trustees participate with management in developing a PFP system.

The best advice for organizations considering PFP is to be prepared to invest a maximum degree of managerial, staff, and board time. Although much can be learned from other organizations, each agency must go through its own intense process and prepare a customized program geared to its particular situation. At the very minimum, an incentive system can only be effective if managers assure their staffs that the organization has a clearly defined mission, long-range goals, carefully constructed objectives, good job designs, a performance appraisal system that clearly demonstrates individual accomplishments, and sufficient funds to provide financial rewards.[16]

Bonuses

The advantage of bonuses is that they do not automatically become part of the base pay the following year. Organizations award them only in special circumstances with no guarantee that they will be repeated. One way of designing a bonus system is to pay a flat rate to everyone in a particular job category and then establish a merit bonus range and pool of money to increase some individuals' rates substantially higher than the rate for the job category. Each year, the system would require new appraisals, and the total bonus range would be open to each individual so that past performance gives no assurance of future total pay or bonus.[17]

Although bonuses are usually identified with profit-making organizations, many human service organizations (especially those that do not have unions or do not operate under civil service restrictions) have some flexibility in providing bonuses. For example, a bonus might be given to child care workers who conduct special outreach. A secretary might receive extra pay for taking on an assignment that normally would require the experience or expertise of program staff. Also, one might give a bonus to a career counselor who places an extraordinary number of clients in jobs.

A bonus, then, often rewards a one-time accomplishment. It sends a clear message that the salary an employee earns is based strictly on demonstrated competencies and effort in the current job.[18] It will likely have more impact if it is given all at once; a lump sum of $500 has greater significance than $10 payments spread over 50 weeks. Increasingly, private sector companies are establishing bonus plans based on specific performance goals.[19]

Consider this variation on the use of a bonus that motivates staff to sustain positive work behavior. Staff receive a bonus in recognition of the work done in Year 1. Their base pay remains unchanged in Year 2, but at the beginning of Year 3 the Year 1 bonus is added to their base rate. Hence, there is a 1-year delay in increasing the base salary, although they are eligible for another year-end bonus. Of course, staff who do not perform satisfactorily in Year 2 will not have the bonus included in the following year's base rate.

Of course, there are concerns about giving bonuses. They raise questions about equity because there may be subjectivity involved in the decision of who gets rewarded and who does not. Establishing criteria based on a consensus of staff and management is essential. In addition, unless base salaries reflect staff worth, promoting a bonus program may cause resentment throughout most of the organization. This is likely to happen if the majority believe that a few privileged employees receive unwarranted, set-aside income that could have been spread throughout the staff. Then, too, high performance is more evident in some staff than in others. Does the staff person who recruited the most volunteers deserve a bonus more than the accountant who competently kept the financial records? Perhaps for this reason, some organizations treat bonuses confidentially, although in doing so they run the risk of staff finding out anyway, thereby creating even more resentment.

One additional concern: Despite all the disclaimers to the contrary, employees do expect bonuses to be repeated year after year, and when they are not, either because of the lack of discretionary money or because someone else in the organization becomes eligible for it, staff feel let down. For example, staff who received a 3% bonus 2 years in a row may resent not receiving one the following year. If they believe that they worked just as hard and were just as productive this year as in the previous two, they may be offended by the "demotion."

A bonus plan can best function if it is clearly understood by staff, is easy to calculate, is based on definable results, involves staff in developing the plan, and results in a feeling of fairness among staff.[20] The bonus plan must operate within a context of trust between staff and management. It should be viewed as an added incentive that cannot replace an internalized commitment to providing good service.

UNIT- AND ORGANIZATIONWIDE PAY PLANS (GAIN-SHARING PLANS)

Gain-sharing plans, which are being used more frequently in industry, provide extra funding for particular staff if a unit within the organization or the entire organization meets or exceeds its objectives. Occasionally, a human service organization may find that it has a positive fund balance ("surplus") because of staff effort to keep expenses to a minimum or increase income. The extra proceeds are then distributed to the staff as a way of celebrating the organization's achievements. This special distribution might be especially welcome if staff have not had salary increases for 1 or 2 years. Staff receive this special compensation with the understanding that it is not likely to occur annually.

Gain-sharing can stimulate staff to work harder and cooperate with one another. It encourages staff to make suggestions on improving economies and to share ideas that can lead to more effective programs.[21] It works best in a climate of involvement among all levels of staff.[22]

In some organizations, one or more units may generate income above and beyond the costs required to run the unit. By selling the organization's products or services or raising new endowment funds, staff may believe that they, and only they, should receive special financial rewards. This presents a dilemma that some organizations handle by stipulating a certain minimum income expectation; beyond this, members of the unit receive rewards. Other organizations, in keeping with their culture, do not provide special rewards based on the expectation that some units will produce income and other units will produce other nonmonetary beneficial results.

THE IMPACT OF A MONETARY REWARD

In the absence of empirical evidence, it is difficult to know unequivocally the extent to which special monetary rewards motivate behavior. For staff who are self-starting, achievement oriented, and willing to put in extra time, monetary rewards are appealing. For those who want to leave at 5:00 p.m., give a good day's work but not overinvest, and be valued for their seniority, financial incentives may not be significant motivators. What may be satisfying and motivating to one person may be stressful and discouraging to another.[23]

In some organizations, highly committed staff may claim they are not primarily motivated by the money incentive, although they like receiving the lump sum bonus. They strive for a good evaluation—money is a way of keeping score, a gauge of how well they are doing. What may be most important to committed staff is that they are paid fairly and are earning a competitive salary compared with that of others doing similar work.

Because research on the impact of using money as a reward for productivity is limited, organizations may need to consider experimenting with their compensation systems.[24] Using pay as an incentive requires thoughtful and deliberate examination of both its potential positive impact on staff and its possible pernicious consequences.

The implication of this discussion is that financial rewards can work in certain human service organizations in which the cultural values are conducive to it. Financial incentives can induce achievements where (a) staff have participated in their creation, (b) staff accept the idea that they can be rewarded on a graduated basis, (c) increased efforts can potentially be translated into higher income for the organization, and (d) objective measurements can distinguish staff performance.

A pay incentive system should not be used in every organization, however. It should not be undertaken if performance is difficult to measure in any objective way, if staff are likely to believe that the payment system is unfair, if staff have limited control over the outcomes, or if financial constraints limit the amount of money available for superperformers.

Because the availability of money is a very important factor in a PFP system, it warrants special attention. In for-profit organizations, if employees work harder, they presumably attract more customers and consequently there are more profits to be shared. In human service organizations, however, staff do not necessarily reap the rewards of hard work because "customers" often are not able to pay enough to provide extra funds. The organization relies on third-party payments, usually in the form of public funds and private donations. Working harder does not necessarily result in more funds for the agency to be distributed among the staff. What works in the private sector—extraordinary efforts resulting in more income from paying customers—is not necessarily the same formula for financial success in the nonprofit, human service field.

Organizations receiving reimbursement from external funders that require results as a condition for payment (performance contracting) may find pay incentives to be a useful approach. Just as the organization can be rewarded for achievements by its funder under a performance contract, so too can those superachievers be rewarded by the organization. For example, if an organization is in the business of placing low-income persons in jobs, and its local department of human services provides funding on the basis of the number placed in a given quarter, then, when the organization exceeds its goals and is funded at a higher amount, it can pass this extra funding on to staff. Of course, the reverse can be true as well: If the organization does not achieve its goals, then staff may have to take a cut in pay.

When an organization is committed to pay incentives but has only a limited pool of funds to distribute, then the actual amounts that high-performing staff receive may be more symbolic than substantive. The pay difference could amount to only $200, hardly enough to be noticed during a period of 50 paychecks. Some would argue that such increases are too small to have an impact on staff motivation, particularly given the potential of PFP to damage the self-esteem of those who do not receive a pay increase at all.[25]

Rather than thinking of pay incentives as an "either-or" system, consider their possible use on a continuum. For some organizations, rewarding a few outstanding individuals on an occasional, ad hoc basis may make sense within the context of a job classification system that provides most of the staff with across-the-board raises. For other organizations, an ongoing bonus program can provide lump sums to outstanding individuals without increasing base salaries. Still other organizations can establish a formal pay incentive system that applies to some, but not all, positions within the organization. Moreover, some organizations may develop an appraisal system that combines the subjective judgments of supervisors with the achievement of concrete, measurable objectives. Finally, some human service organizations could develop an elaborate point system that qualifies everyone for PFP on a graduated basis. There will no doubt be considerable experimentation occurring in human service organizations. Effective managers must consider both positive and negative aspects of pay incentives before embarking on a course of action.

SYMBOLIC REWARDS

Because compensating staff for accomplishments may present special difficulties, human service organizations should consider other ways of rewarding staff for their performance. The values and the ethos of the organization may require it to use nonfinancial or symbolic methods of influencing employee behavior. Rewarding good performance increases the likelihood that it will continue and provides long-term benefits for the organization.[26]

Because beliefs about rewards can be highly subjective, it is important to tune in to what is important to various staff. For example, a "Worker of the Month" award may motivate paraprofessional staff but may be inappropriate for higher-level program specialists in the same organization. Inviting staff to a dinner with the boss may cause some staff to feel anxious, whereas others may welcome it as a special opportunity.[27]

Of course, although employees' wishes are important, the reward system must also consider the needs of the organization. For example, staff may express a preference for time off as a reward for a job well done. Because productivity will suffer if good people are given too much time off, however, staff and management may need to agree on other rewards.

Rewarding productive behavior need not wait for final achievements, such as the completion of a project. People need to believe that they are making good progress toward achieving an objective. Celebrate milestone achievements toward the major goal.[28] When acknowledging staff progress, observe more than just the superstars. There are plenty of people backstage—accountants, receptionists, and support staff whose daily acts are worthy of praise. Your attitude should be one of "let's catch people doing something right."[29] It is an unfortunate part of workday experiences that people receive so little acknowledgment for what they do. Informal, ongoing pat-on-the-back expressions of appreciation can be done regularly and are always welcome.

Some organizations establish a "complimentary interview" procedure in which the employee receives formal commendation for superior performance.[30] Other organizations encourage the practice of sending thank-you notes. An especially good newsletter, an outstanding report, or the delivery of services in trying circumstances are the kinds of events that warrant written notes of acknowledgment. Such notes are tremendously meaningful to employees because they convey that their work is not taken for granted and that someone in the organization is pleased with it. Whether structured or informal, if the appreciation is sincere and based on noteworthy achievement, then you cannot err by giving too much praise.

Some organizations establish public acknowledgment of performance. The YMCA, for example, establishes a nominating process in which staff rate their colleagues, and then supervisors submit selected names with accomplishments to a central office. Through this "competition," staff are designated as "heroes" or "happy warriors." To the outsider, this competition might seem hokey, but to the staff who receive the happy warrior award, it is a special sign of recognition for a job well done.

Many organizations provide an annual awards program that acknowledges staff in various units for their work. Effective managers make these formal ceremonies a priority in their busy schedules to recognize those staff who have made special contributions.

In one organization, staff were elated to receive certificates of appreciation. The director of the organization remarked, "I can't believe how many of my staff placed these certificates on their desks. Obviously, they had more meaning than I anticipated." Because previously there had been so little acknowledgment of staff contribution, a certificate ceremony caused morale to surge. Be mindful, however, that across-the-board acknowledgments can lose their potency if they are repeated too often.

To avoid the monotony of providing rewards on a routine basis, consider altering the pattern by spontaneously and intermittently proffering symbolic rewards—taking a staff member to lunch, buying a small gift of appreciation, or acknowledging their good performance to their peers in the next staff meeting. When staff are truly surprised by thanks, they appreciate it all the more.[31]

Sometimes, unfortunately, a meaningful acknowledgment practice dies out because of the lack of commitment to keep it going. Too many offices have only half-filled Employee-of-the-Month plaques adorning the walls because new administrations discontinued the practice.

One way to provide staff with formal public acknowledgment is to have them make a presentation of their work to the board of trustees or to public officials. Providing them with this audience allows them to gain recognition in the community because it broadens the circle of significant people who are aware of what they have done. Giving staff this opportunity assumes they have the confidence and communication skills to make a good presentation. If they do not, it could backfire.

The following are other ways to recognize performance:[32]

- An important assignment
- A celebratory party
- A gift certificate for merchandise
- Modest financial rewards (e.g., $50)
- An article in the organization's newsletter
- A status symbol, such as a new title or a special parking spot
- Assignment to serve as acting head of a unit in the supervisor's temporary absence
- Opportunity to attend workshops
- A memo to your own boss citing your subordinate's accomplishment
- A move to a more prestigious office
- Appointment as chair of a special project
- An informal breakfast with the executive director and one or more staff members who have done something special
- Encouragement of coworkers to post congratulatory notes on a "thank-you" bulletin board to acknowledge helpful deeds
- Provision of a "personal touch," such as bringing flowers from your garden or homemade cookies, which conveys special personalized appreciation

A significant way of rewarding staff for good performance is to provide them with growth opportunities. This is important because not only does the individual benefit from the new opportunity but also the organization becomes invigorated with new ideas and ways of doing things. Staff can be rewarded by being sent to conferences, being invited to participate in decision-making meetings, or having their job responsibilities expanded. These become opportunities for growth and learning. It helps to convey to the staff that these special opportunities are being provided in response to their good performance.

The issue of nonmonetary rewards may seem to be a self-evident one, but unfortunately many organizations fail to regularly give any appreciation to staff for the work they perform. Effective managers in highly productive organizations give considerable attention to this issue. As Peters and Waterman indicate in their study of profit-making organizations, "We were struck by the wealth of nonmonetary incentives used by excellent companies. Nothing is more powerful than positive reinforcement. Everybody uses it. But top performers, almost alone, use it extensively."[33] Through explicit acknowledgment of successful performance, you reinforce the notion that staff are winners, and this will likely enhance their positive sense of self-worth and encourage continued high performance.

NOTES

1. M. Beer, B. Spector, P. R. Lawrence, D. Q. Mills, & R. E. Walton, *Managing human assets* (New York: Free Press, 1984), p. 118.

2. M. Beer et al., pp. 131-132; J. H. Boyett & H. P. Conn, *Maximum performance management* (Macomb, IL: Glenbridge, 1988), p. 178; M. C. Haller, The new balancing act: Variable but equitable pay, *Human Resources Professional* (1989, July/August), p. 31.

3. G. T. Milkovich & J. W. Boudreau, *Personnel/human resource management* (5th ed.) (Plano, TX: Business Publications, 1988), pp. 716-717.

4. R. I. Henderson, *Compensation management: Rewarding performance* (Englewood Cliffs, NJ: Prentice Hall, 1989), p. 286.

5. W. C. Nelson, Incentive based management for nonprofit organizations, *Nonprofit Management and Leadership, 1* (1991), pp. 59-69.

6. T. Caplow, *How to run any organization* (Hinsdale, IL: Dryden, 1976), pp. 153-156.

7. M. Beer et al., p. 119; T. Rollins, Pay for performance: Is it worth the trouble? in *Performance and rewards: Linking pay to performance* (The HR Magazine Series) (Alexandria, VA: Society for Human Resource Management, 1989), p. 12.

8. M. Beer et al., p. 120.

9. M. Beer et al., p. 141.

10. J. H. Boyett & H. P. Conn, p. 195; P. C. Jordan, Effects of an extrinsic reward on intrinsic motivation: A field experiment, *Academy of Management Journal, 29*(2) (1986), pp. 405-412; E. E. Lawler, III, Pay for performance: A strategic analysis, in *Compensation and benefits* (L. Gomez-Mejia, Ed.) (Washington, DC: Bureau of National Affairs, 1989), p. 150.

11. W. C. Nelson, pp. 58-59; A. Pileggi & D. T. Hickey, Incentive pay plans, *Nonprofit Management Strategies, 6* (1991), pp. 1-3.

12. E. E. Lawler, III, p. 151.

13. R. I. Henderson, p. 288.

14. B. P. Maclean, Value added pay beats traditional merit programs, *Personnel Journal, 9* (1990), p. 46.

15. W. L. Mihal, More research is needed; Goals may motivate better, *Personnel Administrator* (1983, October), pp. 63-68.

16. E. E. Lawler, III, p. 155; W. C. Nelson, pp. 59-69.

17. E. E. Lawler, III, p. 153.

18. B. P. Maclean, pp. 46-51.

19. R. I. Henderson, p. 298.

20. R. S. Schuler, *Personnel and human resource management* (3rd ed.) (St. Paul, MN: West, 1987), p. 349.

21. E. E. Lawler, III, p. 152.

22. M. Beer et al., p. 145; J. H. Boyett & H. P. Conn, p. 198.

23. R. I. Henderson, p. 292.

24. R. Steinberg, Profits and incentive compensation in nonprofit firms, *Nonprofit Management and Leadership, 2* (1990), pp. 137-149.

25. M. Beer et al., p. 143.

26. J. H. Boyett & H. P. Conn, pp. 144-170.

27. J. H. Boyett & H. P. Conn, p. 143.

28. Alexander Hamilton Institute, *A manager's guide to motivating without money* (Ramsey, NJ: Author, 1999), pp. 5-6.

29. R. E. Herman, *Keeping good people: Strategies for solving the dilemma of the decade* (Cleveland, OH: Oakhill, 1990), p. 132.

30. J. P. Cangemi & J. C. Claypool, Complimentary interviews: A system for rewarding outstanding employees, *Personnel Journal, 2* (1978), pp. 87-90.

31. Alexander Hamilton Institute, p. 15.

32. S. Cohen, *The effective public manager: Achieving success in government* (San Francisco: Jossey-Bass, 1988), p. 41; R. E. Herman, pp. 134-135; W. Nord & J. L. McAdams, Performance-based reward systems: Which will work best for you? *Human Resources Professional* (1989, May/June), p. 32; Alexander Hamilton Institute, pp. 9-38.

33. T. J. Peters & R. H. Waterman, *In search of excellence: Lessons from America's best run companies* (New York: Harper & Row, 1982), p. 269.

Part IV Review

ASSESSING AND REWARDING PERFORMANCE

10. SUPERVISING STAFF

- Middle managers must reconcile conflicting expectations and requirements of their superiors and subordinates.
- Managers take on several roles—coach, judge, explorer, warrior, treasure hunter, and advocate—that must be handled judiciously.
- Delegate assignments so that staff have proper autonomy for decision making and implementation, but you as manager retain ultimate oversight and accountability.
- Good supervision requires an ongoing investment in staff and a spirit of collaborative problem solving.

11. APPRAISING STAFF PERFORMANCE

- Staff welcome evaluations that measure their performance.
- A good appraisal process requires supervisors and staff to agree jointly on specific performance expectations.
- Evaluating staff on the basis of traits such as independence, interpersonal skills, knowledge, judgment, and resourcefulness is useful, but this should be combined with an evaluation of accomplishments.
- Evaluation instruments that define and scale a continuum of behavior increase the consistency of supervisory evaluations.
- Management by objectives provides for review of the extent to which staff achieve previously agreed-on results. Establish objectives that are based on de-

sired key results; identify measurable outcomes that are realistically attainable within a specified time period and that can be monitored.

- Because each staff member performs differently and has unique strengths and weaknesses, it is generally useful to write a brief narrative on staff performance.
- To ensure professional growth, conduct performance appraisals at least annually, preferably more often.
- Good appraisals engage staff in determining objectives, connect organizational goals with individual efforts, provide constructive criticism, treat staff with respect, and formulate specific action plans.

12. COMPENSATING WORK AND REWARDING PERFORMANCE

- Staff are motivated by being recognized and rewarded financially and symbolically for their work.
- Typically, human service organizations reward staff based on their particular job classification, and increased compensation is based primarily on seniority.
- Skill-based reward systems encourage staff to upgrade talents needed for the job.
- Cautions about pay for performance include the need to establish an objective appraisal system, training for supervisory staff, and a commitment to invest extensively in the process.
- Bonuses reward one-time accomplishments and are not necessarily part of the base pay.
- Pay for performance (PFP) can be undertaken if clear measurement indicators are available, if staff perceive the system as being fair and perceive that they have control over outcomes, and if sufficient funding is available to keep pace with inflation and provide extra income for high achievers.
- Modified versions of PFP can be used to reward a few outstanding individuals on an ad hoc basis.
- Gain-sharing can be used when a unit of the organization is capable of producing more income than expenses. It may be desirable to reward these individuals for their efforts, unless this causes serious repercussions in other parts of the organization.
- Symbolic rewards can have tremendous meaning to staff. Be mindful of the highly subjective nature of these rewards, however, because what is meaningful for some staff may not be for others.
- Generally, staff are not praised often enough. Do not be stingy with compliments, because they are the best way to reinforce staff efforts to sustain their good work.

Part V

EFFECTIVE INTERACTIONS: INTERNAL AND EXTERNAL

In this part, you will learn how to

- Decide when a meeting is needed
- Improve the way meetings are conducted
- Ask the right questions to facilitate ideas
- Use consensus to make decisions
- Use creative techniques to stimulate fresh thinking
- Develop task forces to gain focus
- Avoid problem communications
- Develop various ways to foster top-down and bottom-up communications
- Listen more effectively
- Prepare writing materials
- Reconcile conflicting expectations of superiors and subordinates
- Develop well-functioning teams
- Facilitate alliances with other agencies
- Identify different collaborative structures
- Work with a board of trustees and its committees

Chapter 13

MAKING MEETINGS PRODUCTIVE

Poorly planned and poorly managed meetings waste staff time and can cost the organization a great deal of money. Think of the value of meeting time in dollars and cents: Suppose a staff meeting is held once weekly for 2 hours. Also suppose that the average hourly wage of the 12 professional staff who attend is $15. This translates to $300 per meeting (12 staff × $15 × 2 hours). During a 40-week period, the cost for this 2-hour weekly meeting is $12,000. The cost to the organization could be half this amount if the meeting were reduced to 1 hour per week, held biweekly, or involved half the number of staff. Because managers spend much of their time leading or participating in meetings, they need to be quite purposeful in their goal of increasing the organization's productive use of this activity.

CONSIDERING WHETHER OR NOT TO HOLD A MEETING

Meetings should be called when it is essential to deal with important matters that cannot be handled on a one-to-one basis.[1] They should not be used to conduct individual supervisory conferences with others in the group being passive observers.[2] In addition, it is generally not a good idea to hold a meeting when one or more of the following situations exists:

- You can communicate better by telephone, memo, fax, or e-mail.
- The issue is so confidential that it cannot be shared with others, such as hiring, firing, or negotiating salaries.
- There are inadequate data or poor preparation.
- There is no compelling reason to hold a regularly scheduled meeting.

Holding a meeting, however, is a good idea when

- You want to reinforce the organization's essential values (e.g., emphasizing cooperative efforts) or relate staff efforts to the organization's mission, goals, or objectives
- You are dealing with a complex problem involving several options, and you consider staff interaction essential to solve the problem or make a decision
- You need the expertise or advice of selected individuals
- You need to share concerns or clarify an organizational issue
- You want to share with or obtain information from group members about a current project or event, and you want to improve the accuracy of information so that everyone receives the same data in the same way
- You want to coordinate activities of various units
- You want to provide training or use the session for questions and answers
- You want to publicly recognize an achievement, build morale, or encourage teamwork
- You expect resistance from some individuals and think their participation in a group process will ameliorate their concerns

To enhance the effectiveness of the meetings, make sure you have considered the following questions:

- What do you want to accomplish by the end of the meeting?
- On the basis of your expectations, who should attend and what kind of involvement do you want from them?
- What will be on the agenda? How much time should be allowed for each item?
- What specific tasks, deadlines, and responsibilities will you communicate?
- Who will be responsible for decisions?
- With whom should you meet before the meeting?
- What materials must be prepared in advance of the meeting?[3]

MAKING THE BEST USE OF TIME

You cannot control the outcome of a meeting without being perceived as manipulative. You can guide possible outcomes and plan accordingly, however. Have a definite reason for every meeting. Think "reason" first, then "meeting." By doing this, you can avoid the malady of "meetingitis"—the tendency to have regularly scheduled meetings whether they are necessary or not. By letting the participants know up front what you are hoping to achieve by the end of the meeting, you will be able to facilitate the discussion more easily.

You should also plan the meeting in detail. Think in advance about who, what, when, why, where, and how. Send out in advance any pertinent reading material, such as minutes of previous meetings or special reports. Print out the agenda so everyone knows what will be discussed. Set a specific ending time, and violate it only in extraordinary circumstances. Normally, meetings should last no longer than 1 or 2 hours. If a meeting is extended beyond that, the group runs the risk of cutting into others' schedules. As a result, staff who must leave before the meeting ends may believe that their departure prevents them from participating in significant decisions.

Set a time limit for each topic on the agenda and stick to it. In exceptional circumstances, the group could agree to extend the time period of one item by subtracting time from another. Appoint someone to serve as timekeeper (or let the chairperson retain the role) if the group tends to wander and needs the discipline of being reminded about time. To keep meetings on target, the leader should establish the ground rule that the group must avoid distracting and irrelevant ideas so that they can conduct the main business of the meeting within the agreed-on time limit.

If the meeting has a function other than providing information, such as coordinating work or solving problems, participants should be selected on the basis of their potential for contributions. Limit attendance to those directly involved with topics on the agenda to make the best use of everyone's time. The larger the group, the more discussion you will have, and the longer the meeting will run. Schedule some participants to attend only that part of the meeting to which they can contribute. When they complete their item, they may leave the meeting.[4]

It is better to delay a proposed agenda topic until you have the appropriate staff to deal with the issue. For example, if, in a children's treatment center, a meeting is called to handle discipline problems among the children, and the group inadvertently excludes the recreation counselor and the night supervisor, not all of the appropriate staff are present to address these concerns.

Always begin a meeting on time, regardless of late arrivals. If at every meeting you wait until latecomers arrive, those who do arrive on time will develop the habit of tardiness, and the late ones will become even tardier. There is an old saying: "People do not miss trains that leave on time."

Send out a meeting notice well in advance with background material related to items on the agenda so that participants attend the meeting well prepared. Indicate under each agenda item whether it is for the purpose of information, discussion, or decision making.[5] This procedure avoids the time-consuming distribution of documents at a meeting and encourages group members to do their homework. By specifying each agenda item in advance, you create a working structure for the meeting. To make the best use of meeting time, you could hold a premeeting with two or three people to analyze the issues in-depth and determine a proposed course of action based on their review of several options. The larger group should have an opportunity to examine the options and to understand the rationale for the option being proposed.

Some organizations provide an annotated meeting agenda called a "docket." Not only does a docket list the items to be discussed but also it provides a paragraph or two of explanation after each item to save time during the meeting. The docket is a useful technique for covering many items in a short time period.

FUNCTIONS OF MEETINGS

It is critical that both the chairperson and the group understand the central function of a group session. The following are some of the functions:

Coordinating: Gather several participants to work on the same issue and develop ways to complement their efforts.

Distributing work: Clarify and distribute assignments to group members.

Team building: Establish an esprit de corps and mutual support among participants. Emphasize working cooperatively.

Reporting information: Provide the necessary background that later may become the basis for decision making. Reports can include facts and other findings gathered in recent studies.

Studying a problem: Undertake precise problem analyses.

Making decisions: Make a decision or recommendation from among alternatives. Group members may or may not be the same as those who study the problem.

Ratifying decisions: Propose a recommendation to a decision-making body.

Monitoring: Review progress toward resolving the problem.

A group can be established to undertake only one of these primary functions, but most carry out more than one, although not necessarily simultaneously. That is, a group may study a problem, then gather facts, then decide on recommendations, then act on a decision, and, finally, monitor results. Moreover, identifying, analyzing, and solving problems can take several weeks or even months. In the meeting, it is important that the group always be aware of its primary function(s) because by doing so discussions will be kept on track and irrelevant or peripheral issues can be dealt with in an objective manner.

DEALING WITH MEETING PROBLEMS

Whether a meeting is a failure or a success can be highly subjective. Some would consider a meeting a failure if considerable conflict occurred without resolution. Others at the same meeting might say that the meeting was productive because participants aired long-festering concerns. Some might be concerned that the group did not accomplish specific objectives, whereas others might view the session as a first step in an extended process that will eventually lead to results. Hence, the success or failure of a meeting can be in the eyes of the beholder.

There are times, however, when there is a clear sense that a meeting was a waste of time. The following sections discuss some reasons that meetings can be unsuccessful and result in frustration.

Group Size

There is value in having mass meetings to announce new developments or provide information to a large number of people. If, however, the purpose of the meeting is to engage in problem solving, limit the number to 6 to 10 people to allow for maximum participation. Use mass meetings only when you want to make innocuous announcements or communicate quickly to the entire organization.

One-Person Domination

When a high-level executive takes over a meeting, there can be trouble. He or she may exert influence by sending messages—subtle or otherwise—to members of the group about what should and should not be discussed. When, as a result, members "clam up," their withdrawal is viewed as assent. Afterward, participants may express their disgruntlement and frustration to each other. If members of the group are uncomfortable communicating that they wish to participate more, they may need to designate a spokesperson from either within or outside the group to clarify differing expectations.[6]

Pulling in Different Directions

Sometimes, leadership passivity results in members competing for control of the meeting. Lack of leadership creates a void that is filled by more active, powerful participants, and the session may end in confusion or unresolved conflict. In this situation, stronger leadership is necessary to help clarify where discrepancies and differences exist and to inspire resolution. In addition, if discussions tend to drift from one topic to another without resolution, the leader must help the group focus on one issue at a time.[7]

Problem Participants

The free flow of ideas in meetings may be hampered by the attitudes and behaviors of some participants. Some people, for example, like to say something about every topic, whether their statements are relevant or not. You may need to remind them to remain on topic and to suggest that others need to be heard from. Other people may go through an entire meeting without saying anything, and the group misses out on possible valuable input. You may need to call on them to seek new insights. Some participants may appear condescending and even hostile toward other people's ideas. If they do not respond to the ground rules that "put-downs" are out of bounds, you may need to take them aside and discuss how their behavior is disruptive. Ask them to work on searching for constructive suggestions for building on people's ideas. The chair of the meeting thus has to be ever mindful of how participants contribute to or distract from the flow of the meeting.[8]

Conformity Through "Groupthink"

Some members of a group believe they must show loyalty by agreeing with the group's position even though they inwardly have serious concerns with the direction of the meeting. This groupthink occurs when members want to avoid what they fear will be harsh judgments by their peers. Consequently, they keep criticism of the position to themselves. "Groupthinkers" choose acceptance over their need to express fundamental differences. Groupthink is most likely to occur in strongly cohesive groups in which criticism is not the norm. Members suppress their differences of opinion and may minimize, even to themselves, their own misgivings. As a result, the group develops the illusion of unanimity.[9]

One danger of groupthink is when members are pressured to give in, and the resulting diluted decision greatly weakens what might otherwise have been a strong stand, position, or program. Another danger is that unvoiced criticisms may later result in some form of sabotage because of some members' deep-rooted reservations. A third danger is that the desire for conformity may squelch a valid criticism that could prevent a poor decision. Ways to prevent groupthink include the following:

- Propose alternative choices that are presented to the group.
- Establish the ground rule that ideas are to be based on their merit, not on who presents them.
- Recognize that there are many appropriate paths that can lead to desired results. Encourage members to play "devil's advocates" to ensure positions are defensible from a variety of positions.
- Talk with people who are not part of the deliberations, including knowledgeable people outside the organization who can suggest other options and ideas.
- Think through scenarios about how different people would probably react to the ideas under discussion.
- Encourage members to express reservations if they have them.[10]

QUESTIONS THAT FACILITATE DISCUSSION

If participants believe their ideas and thinking will contribute to common objectives, they are more likely to address the problem at hand and participate in its solution. One of the most useful techniques to enrich discussions is to elicit responses through targeted questions. Although the group facilitator is primarily responsible for directing the flow of ideas through questions, any member of a group can ask questions. The following kinds of questions can stimulate discussion:

If You Want To	*Then Ask*
Focus the group on an issue	What information do we need to explore the problem?
Redirect the group's thinking	Are there other ways we can go about this?
Stimulate the group and bolster their arguments	What makes you think this will work?
Inject your own ideas	What do you think would happen if we . . .?
Encourage alternative solutions	What other options should we consider?
Focus on one idea	Which approach do you think is best?
Clarify an issue	Could you explain your position further?
Make an abstract idea more understandable	Would you walk us through this process?
Shift from the details to the essence of an idea	Before we get into the details, shouldn't we consider our main objective?
Stimulate new ideas	Are there new approaches we can consider?
Encourage participation	What do each of you think about this idea?
Consider next steps	Where do we go from here?
Come to closure	Have we agreed on the following . . .?
Assist the group in assessing itself	How can we improve our discussion process?

These questions do not exhaust all the possibilities. They illustrate that, through the questioning process, you can guide the discussion without being perceived as manipulative. One of the main attributes of a good discussion leader is the ability to continuously pose questions that help the group with its decision-making process.

FORMING A CONSENSUS

A group arrives at a consensus after all members have had an opportunity to voice their opinions. A consensus is a solution that everyone can live with—

one that does not violate any strong convictions or needs. The process of arriving at a consensus is a free and open exchange of ideas that continues until the group reaches a conclusion based on criteria, agreed on in advance, that will guide the decision. This process ensures that each individual's concerns are heard and understood, and that the group will make a sincere attempt to take everyone's ideas into consideration while searching for a solution. The final resolution may not reflect the exact wishes of every member, but because it does not violate the concerns of any one participant it can be agreed on by all.[11] In fact, some members may even "agree to disagree" and be willing to cooperate because their differences are not tremendously deep and they are committed to the spirit of working together.

Consensus, then, is a cooperative effort to find a sound solution acceptable to everyone. It is not a voting process or a competitive struggle in which an unacceptable solution is forced on the losers. Usually, those who initially express disagreement finally consent to go along with the prevailing viewpoint even though they may not fully endorse it. With consensus as the pattern of interaction, members need not fear being outsmarted or outmaneuvered. They can be frank in the decision-making process, knowing that different viewpoints can be expressed.[12]

In some cases, decisions are postponed until there is a "Quaker consensus," in which not even one member of the group vetoes the action. If someone dissents, discussion continues until he or she acquiesces or the group delays its action. Typically, however, complete unanimity of opinion is not absolutely essential and is rarely achieved when seeking consensus.

In some staff situations, however, even when decisions do not have to be unanimous, there still exists the ground rule that supervisors or managers must approve decisions. Their vetoes can block action. If this criterion for accepting or rejecting a plan is understood in advance, the reactions of a manager unexpectedly blocking a group's decision can be minimized.

If the group is not able to agree on a solution that everyone supports enthusiastically, then the matter may be placed in the hands of a manager to make an executive "win/lose" decision. If the group clearly understands that a manager will make the final decision if a consensus cannot be developed within the time limit, participants may work harder to develop a decision that all can accept.

Decision making by consensus works best when members of a group trust each other. In a trusting climate, disagreements are a natural and acceptable means of fostering opinions and ideas rather than a reflection of interpersonal hostility or rivalry.

In summary, the need to arrive at a consensus encourages group members to listen to each other and try to understand viewpoints that may differ from their own. It also encourages people who disagree to continue hammering out their differences. A consensus discourages an "I win—you lose" mentality and promotes a climate that allows everyone to benefit.

USING THE GROUP PROCESS TO GENERATE IDEAS

Occasionally, group meetings become mired in ritualistic patterns. Problems may persist because fresh perspectives and new ideas are absent. Conventional solutions seem inadequate to address unfamiliar or complex issues. The challenge facing the group is to set in motion ways of breaking out of the mold, explore new paths, and view problems and possible resolutions from different perspectives. Taking risks, exploring unusual connections, and taking nothing for granted are ways of generating fresh approaches.[13] To foster this kind of thinking, groups can use several techniques: brainstorming, nominal group technique (NGT), pro-con discussions, creative questioning, and analogous thinking.

Brainstorming

This procedure is used to encourage creativity that generates ideas while suspending judgment and evaluation of them. Nothing is too strange or funny to say; the goal is to express as many ideas as possible within a short period of time. Participants are encouraged to build on previous ideas. The theory behind brainstorming is that by discouraging evaluation the group expands the number and quality of ideas.

Groups should consider brainstorming when (a) conventional discussions lack fresh ideas or approaches, (b) individuals working independently need the stimulation of other people's ideas, (c) a group has become so hypercritical that ideas are being stifled, or (d) information needed for solving a problem is scattered among different people. Brainstorming does not work for all problems. It works best for those issues that require new ideas because current modes of thinking are not sufficient. A problem best solved through a brainstorming session should hold the potential for many alternative solutions.

Participants who have experience with or knowledge of the issue should be engaged in brainstorming, although you may purposefully wish to include some people who are not knowledgeable based on the premise that they may offer fresh perspectives. The size of the group should range from 4 to 12; groups larger than 12 are too large for meaningful exchange. The group facilitator should define the problem, stimulate ideas, prevent evaluative comments, keep the group on the subject, and end the discussion after an appropriate period of time (usually 15-30 minutes). A recorder should write all ideas on a chalkboard or on chart paper taped to a wall for easy viewing.[14] The group should be reminded that only a small percentage of the ideas are likely to be accepted.

Following this idea-generating session, a separate phase of idea evaluation should occur. The evaluation panel can consist of all those involved in the brainstorming session, a mix of members and nonmembers of the brainstorming group, or a completely different group of people. Those involved in the evaluation and selection of the ideas should be people who will deal directly with the problem or who will be involved in implementing the suggested solutions. This panel must establish standards or criteria by which they will evaluate ideas, such as in terms of financial constraints, political acceptability, and staff availability. This panel could rate the brainstormed ideas as immediately applicable, worthy of further exploration, or not useful.

Nominal Group Technique

The term *nominal group* means that it is a group in name only. It is a form of silent brainstorming in which members submit their written ideas anonymously to the leader and therefore have minimal interaction with each other. The purpose of this approach is to deter aggressive members from dominating the discussion and to elicit a wide variety of ideas from all participants.

Each member is asked to generate as many ideas as possible on a given subject. For example, participants might be asked to consider a variety of ways to improve lunchroom facilities. Each person then contributes one idea in writing in round-robin fashion. After all ideas are presented and listed, the group pursues a discussion to clarify, defend, or challenge ideas. "Hitchhiking" is encouraged: If an item mentioned by one member encourages someone else to think of another idea that has not been suggested, then that new idea can be presented at the end of the round-robin procedure. Through a voting process, the group narrows the list to three or four major ideas to pursue.

The advantage of NGT is that it draws out everyone's ideas. As with brainstorming, the initial list will probably require further evaluation and analysis. Some of the most creative ideas may later prove too difficult to implement or may require more resources than feasible. Hence, ideas generated by NGT should be subject to additional, careful analysis.[15]

Pro-Con Discussions

To stimulate good thinking and prevent premature emphasis on any one idea, use a pro-con approach. Ask the group to generate different alternative ideas for a particular problem. For example, a staff group concerned with how to reduce "client no-shows" might generate the following possibilities:

- Send outreach staff to the homes of clients who are habitual no-shows.
- Telephone each client before their scheduled appointment to verify attendance.
- Always send an appointment reminder letter.
- Discontinue clients after three no-shows.

For each suggestion, the group would be divided into four task groups, each one debating the pros and cons and summarizing their ideas before the plenary discussion.

Creative Questioning

Another method designed to generate creative ideas is to use a checklist similar to the following:

1. Can the idea be copied?
   ~ What other organization is doing something like this?
   ~ Has this been done before?
2. How can the idea be modified?
   ~ Should we try a new twist?
   ~ Should we change the format?
   ~ Should we develop new procedures?

3. Can the idea be expanded?
   - ~ What can we add?
   - ~ What can be done more frequently?
   - ~ Can it be strengthened?
   - ~ Can it be multiplied?
4. Can the idea be reduced?
   - ~ Can elements be subtracted, condensed, made shorter, streamlined, or split up?
5. What can be substituted for the idea?
   - ~ Who else could do it?
   - ~ In what other place or time could it be conducted?
   - ~ Could different resources be used?
   - ~ What other approaches could be considered in its place?
6. Can the idea be rearranged?
   - ~ Are components interchangeable?
   - ~ Can the sequence be altered?
   - ~ Is the pace or schedule flexible?
7. Can the idea be reversed?
   - ~ Can roles be reversed?
   - ~ Can potentially negative aspects be turned into positive ones?
8. Can ideas be combined?
   - ~ Can units be combined?
   - ~ Can purposes be joined?

The following are examples of how the checklist can be used to stimulate different approaches:

> An organization wants to reach out to older people in the community but realizes that its limited staff resources prevent it from doing so. It considers the following alternative methods of expanding its resources: (a) hire neighborhood people to reach out, (b) arrange to have elderly volunteers provide current in-home services in exchange for future home services, and (c) expand volunteer participation through a "Volunteers of Distinction" campaign.

An organization is concerned that junior high school students who have failed more than one grade are potential dropouts. They can, however, read and do math problems at a sixth-grade level. Considering the idea of reversal, the organization devises a program in which these adolescents become "big buddies" to elementary school students who require tutoring and companionship.

Analogous Thinking

When an organization is bogged down with a problem and is seeking fresh perspectives, thinking with analogies can be useful. Analogies compare one situation with another that is similar but not identical. By comparing a problem situation with something else that is in some way like it, you begin to view the problem from a different perspective. For example, you notice at the airport how passengers are processed when their flights are canceled. Are there not similarities in processing clients when a service breakdown occurs, such as approaches in handling inconveniences or developing alternative routing? Also, you might think of combining chemotherapy and radiology treatment for their cumulative effect on cancer cells and then ask, "Are there similar combined treatment programs for dealing with drug addicts in which cumulative effects might also be effective?" Consider applying the rules of a basketball game with penalties for infractions in dealing with gang rivalries. Analogies can be drawn from gardening, astronomy, cooking, machine functioning, and so on. The analogies may seem far-fetched and may not directly lead to a solution, but they are mind stretching and offer new perspectives that can ultimately yield results.

Therefore, the value of being creative is to encourage fresh perspectives. In doing so, some of the ideas may initially seem zany but may contain elements that can be built on. In some instances, the group may become quite enthused about a brainstorming suggestion or an analogous idea. Now that it has opened up to a new approach, it is time to apply critical thinking. Suppose, for example, the group considers tutoring for elementary school students to be an appealing and fresh approach to dealing with the high school dropout problem. The group must critically analyze who would benefit from the project, in what circumstances, with what backup support, and at what costs. To be truly effective, creative thinking must always be accompanied by critical assessment so as to avoid the danger of sharing ignorance and implementing superficial ideas. Creative ideas, especially those you are enamored with, must be subjected to analytic scrutiny.

RECORDING THE MEETING PROCESS

Meetings rich in information that present many facts and ideas can cause groups to experience data overload. A powerful tool for keeping track of ideas and assisting the collective memory of the group is to use a chalkboard or an easel with a large newsprint pad. A recorder writes down key words or basic ideas. As sheets fill up, they are taped around the room. These sheets allow the group to recall what has transpired. The advantage of this technique is that the group can (a) communicate many ideas at the same time; (b) visualize all the ideas at all times; (c) change the wording of ideas; (d) easily determine gaps in, and overlap of, ideas; (e) focus, if the group wishes, on one idea at a time; and (f) prevent the same idea from being repeated.[16] Sustaining the group memory helps to keep the meeting on track.[17]

Groups often take minutes as a way of preserving the ideas and actions agreed on during the meeting. At the next meeting, the chairperson ensures that the minutes accurately reflect the essence of the previous session by providing an opportunity for corrections. Sometimes, the actions taken by the group can be lost in the verbiage of the text. For clarity, some groups highlight each decision. Alternatively, a format that distinguishes discussion from action can be used for minutes:

> Discussion: Juvenile court staff expressed interest in developing formal procedures for addressing the special needs of mentally retarded offenders.
>
> Action: Mental retardation staff agreed to prepare, in writing, procedures by April 15.

An alternative to minutes is a group action report, used only when one or two major topics are discussed. It contains the following sections:

1. The issue—that is, how participants analyzed it and what alternatives they considered
2. The group's decision
3. Who will carry out which tasks and when

Figure 13.1 illustrates a group action report. The special advantage of this kind of recording is that it captures the essence of the meeting and pin-

Name of group:	Day Care Coalition	Date: May 25
Chairperson:	Fred Heim	
Present:	Ahom, Botelli, Callder, Slenk, McVelan	
Meeting purpose:	To consider ways of passing legislation in the state assembly on funding for day care for mentally and physically disabled children.	
Problem/issue:	Legislation on special-needs day care is encountering considerable resistance in the Human Resources Committee of the House.	
Major points of the discussion:	Major opposition appears to be those legislators who are pressing to keep a lid on spending for human services.	
Decision:	The group agreed that committee members must undertake a vigorous advocacy campaign between now and June 12, when public hearings will be held.	
Action steps:	Group to be divided into task forces.	

Assignments	*Responsible Person*	*By When*
1. Undertake letter-writing campaign	Tod Lortz	June 2
2. Obtain editorial support of local papers	Murry Niar	June 5
3. Have a newspaper reporter write a human-interest story	Agie Johnson	June 7
4. Have a busload of people appear before hearings	Ramone Alben	June 12
5. Day Care Coalition to meet	Dale Heatherfork	June 20

Figure 13.1. Group Action Report

points responsibilities for follow-up, without requiring people to read extensive narrative.

THE ROLE OF THE LEADER

Whether the chairperson is a supervisor or manager, or has been specially designated by the supervisor to lead the group, he or she should assume the following responsibilities:

State the purpose of the meeting: It is helpful for the chairperson to establish the goal of a meeting or series of meetings by articulating expectations. These expectations may be formulated by the organization's management, or the group may be given discretion to formulate its own charge. The following is an example:

> The charge to the personnel committee is to formulate a recommendation on a drug policy for the staff of the organization. To achieve this objective, you will examine what similar organizations have adopted and engage in discussions with key staff and board members. The policy must be nonpunitive but reflect the organization's mission to provide the highest quality services to our clients.

Prepare the agenda for the meeting: It is preferable for this to be in writing and submitted in advance, as discussed previously.

Clarify ground rules: The chairperson identifies expectations for how members are to interact with each other and how the business of the meeting will be conducted. This includes clarifying the process for decision making.

Make assignments: Assignments should specify what is to be done, by whom, and within what time frame.

Deal with conflict: Conflicts sometimes surface at staff meetings as participants express differences about priorities and use of resources. The chairperson must work to keep competing forces under control by exploring ways in which staff members can reconcile their different interests. The chairperson can neither ignore these battles nor take sides without jeopardizing the leadership role. The primary recourse is to seek a genuine compromise based on a synthesis of positions.

Summarize discussion: The group leader should continually review the points that have been discussed, identifying where there are differences of opinion and where there are agreements. By synthesizing different views, the chairperson suggests where there is consensus. Summarizing is especially important at the end of a meeting, when the chairperson should clarify what decisions were made and what the next steps will be.[18]

In summary, effective managers are keenly aware that staff meetings are where the organization's domestic commerce occurs. They can be either a waste of time or highly productive. If they are conducted with good preparation and considerable purpose, they can contribute to the productivity of the group and the organization as a whole.

NOTES

1. R. Brody, *Problem solving* (New York: Human Services Press, 1982), p. 51; M. Doyle & D. Straus, *How to make meetings work* (New York: Berkley, 1976), p. 158; Alexander Hamilton Institute, *A manager's guide to productive meetings* (Ramsey, NJ: Author, 1997), pp. 1-5.

2. H. Reynolds & M. E. Tramel, *Executive time management* (Englewood Cliffs, NJ: Prentice Hall, 1979), pp. 115-117.

3. M. Doyle & D. Straus, p. 84; Alexander Hamilton Institute, p. 7.

4. Alexander Hamilton Institute, p. 4.

5. S. Albert, Eight steps to productive committees, *Nonprofit World, 4* (1988), p. 25.

6. J. D. Jorgenson, I. H. Scheier, & T. F. Fautsko, *Solving problems in meetings* (Chicago: Nelson-Hall, 1981), pp. 9-17.

7. F. Pryor, Manage your meetings effectively, *The Nonprofit Executive* (1985, March), p. 7.

8. Alexander Hamilton Institute, pp. 21-24.

9. I. L. Janis, Groupthink, *Psychology Today* (1971, November), pp. 43-46, 74-76.

10. R. Brody, pp. 68-69.

11. E. H. Schein, *Organizational psychology* (New York: Prentice Hall, 1970).

12. T. Caplow, *How to run any organization* (Hinsdale, IL: Dryden, 1976), p. 58.

13. E. de Bono, *Lateral thinking* (New York: Harper Colophon, 1973), pp. 21-22; A. T. Hollingsworth, Creativity in nonprofit organizations: Preparing for the future, *Nonprofit World, 3* (1989), pp. 21-22.

14. A. E. Schwartz, When good ideas are needed fast, *Nonprofit World, 6* (1989), pp. 22-23.

15. A. L. Delbecq, A. Van de Ven, & D. H. Gustafson, *Group techniques for program planning* (Glenview, IL: Scott, Foresman, 1976); A. Lauffer, *Assessment tools for practitioners, managers, and trainers* (Beverly Hills, CA: Sage, 1982), pp. 63-89; C. M. Moore, *Group techniques for idea building* (Newbury Park, CA: Sage, 1987), pp. 24-36.

16. R. Brody, p. 81.

17. M. Doyle & D. Straus, pp. 40-44.

18. J. E. Tropman, *Effective meetings: Improving group decision-making* (Beverly Hills, CA: Sage, 1980), pp. 39-42.

Chapter 14

COMMUNICATION AND CONFLICT

When employees are adequately informed about their organization and have opportunities to convey their ideas, they are likely to be more involved and more invested in their work. This chapter discusses ways in which effective managers can improve communication to heighten staff's commitment to the organization.

Good communications occur when staff believe their concerns will be listened to and dealt with promptly, when mistakes can be quickly identified and corrected, and when staff understand what is taking place in the organization without feeling inundated with messages. In other words, communication involves upward, downward, and across movement of ideas, suggestions, and values. It is a process of continuously sharing and transmitting important information throughout the organization. A positive flow of information is the result of an attitude that respects people for their ideas and that views information not as a source of power but as a tool for accomplishing the organization's important work. As discussed in Chapter 2, good communications can make the organization's culture more meaningful.

Although communication is generally desirable, in certain circumstances it is absolutely essential. When an organization is considering changes in strategy or structure, communication takes on special significance. The greater the change, the greater the need for communication.[1] Even when the basic structure of the organization is not changing, the tendency for organizations to delegate responsibilities to the lowest practical level means that every staff member will be involved in making choices. To make good decisions, staff must share in the basic understanding and purpose of the organization.

In a time of crisis, communication is absolutely essential. For example, when an organization goes through a period of severe retrenchment, discussions must be held openly with staff to encourage their input regarding the situation. To do otherwise runs the risk of creating discontent in employees who remain with the organization but who believe that management cannot be trusted.[2]

Communication is also vitally important when staff are expected to implement important projects. The more they understand the significance of the project to the organization and to the community, the more willing they will be to dedicate themselves to it.

Finally, as discussed in Chapter 2, communication is essential in enhancing staff loyalty to the organization. Staff may appreciate the work of their own unit but may not be aware of how it must mesh with other parts of the organization to accomplish the overall mission. By understanding their part in the whole picture, they will feel pride in their organization. Proud people are committed people.

FACTORS THAT INTERFERE WITH GOOD COMMUNICATIONS

Because communications are so significant in the organization's life, effective managers must be alert to situations that inhibit the positive flow of information.

Poor Use of Written Documents

Communicating to staff through memos and written announcements is a valuable tool for managers. First, the process of writing forces you to discipline your thinking. By putting messages on paper, you clarify your own thoughts and become aware of gaps in what you want to say. Second, written materials have the power to focus attention on a single issue, more so than verbal communication. By putting your inquiry or request in a memo, you encourage the recipient to give the matter special attention. Moreover, memos are useful to disseminate easily understood and noncontroversial information. If you want staff to remember your message, use written communication. (Because the process of writing can be an arduous task, the boxed text contains a discussion on overcoming writer's block.)

CONQUERING WRITER'S BLOCK

Every manager is faced with communicating through the arduous task of writing reports. For some, this can cause overwhelming anxiety. For both managers and staff, writer's block is a common malady. The fact is that writing for most of us is not fun, but it is an essential part of what we do.

There are many factors that directly affect our ability to complete a writing assignment. If we expect it will produce anxiety and frustration, or if we feel insecure about it, we will probably complete it late, if at all. If the results of the writing process lead to a sense of pride and are rewarding, however, we look forward to the undertaking. Hence, our attitude about success or failure can greatly influence the degree to which we experience writer's block. The following are suggestions of ways to get out of the writer's rut:[28]

1. Approach the task with expectations of success. Accentuate the positive by stressing that you can give the time and effort to complete the assignment.
2. Visualize what you want to have happen as a result of the writing. By specifying what you want to achieve—whether more funds for your organization, motivating your staff, or developing new procedures—your clarity of purpose will be a powerful motivator.
3. Be clear about your audience. Form a profile in your mind of the readers so that you are communicating directly to them. Your writing must be geared to their level of understanding and to meeting their needs.
4. Have a quiet place and adequate time to write. This involves writing in an area that is comfortable for you at a time that permits uninterrupted thinking. If your day is filled with interruptions, you may need to find a "hideaway" to allow time for concentration. Try to block out at least 60-minute segments.
5. Become proficient in using the word processor so that you can easily and quickly make changes in your drafts; this technology is a tremendous time saver.
6. Organize your material. Usually, you will want to prepare an outline, but consider it tentative and modify it as your writing proceeds.

7. Keep a note pad or 3 × 5 card in your car or on your nightstand at home to write down ideas at odd times.
8. Prepare a "zero draft." If you are having a difficult time getting started, force yourself to write nonstop to get the words on paper. Known as "free writing," the purpose of this train-of-thought writing pushes you to get words on the paper without concern for spelling, clarity, or even coherence. This is not the time to be critical but to generate ideas to use later in preparing your first draft. The value of this zero draft exercise is to loosen you up and reduce your perfectionist tendencies.
9. Begin your writing project wherever you feel like starting. This may mean commencing in the middle rather than at the beginning. The actual process of writing will allow you to determine what you want to say. You may then want to write the introduction.
10. If you feel confident in where you want to end up, write the conclusion first. By doing so, you will be guided in preparing the rest of your writing assignment.
11. Talk out your writing. By reading it out loud, your ear will assist you in communicating better. Phrases that are trite, awkward, or filled with jargon are more easily discovered when spoken aloud.
12. When you have a difficult time expressing your thoughts in writing, pause for a moment and ask yourself, "What am I really trying to say?" Think through what your point is and then work to get it on paper.
13. Put space between yourself and your first draft. Take a break of hours or preferably days so that you develop detachment and return to the assignment refreshed and ready to be critical. Knowing up front that you will have time for revision can allow you to be less self-demanding when you prepare the early drafts.
14. Before you go public with a report, you may want to show it to one or more trusted persons for their critique. The advantage of this step is that outsiders may alert you to ambiguous ideas of which you were not aware. You may assume that you have stated something clearly, but the words themselves may not communicate precisely what you had in mind.
15. If, after the first or second draft, you still have some degree of discomfort about sharing it, even to obtain preliminary criticism, you might try splattering coffee or stamping heel marks on the paper to emphasize that the writing is truly a draft, or mark "DRAFT" on the paper to convey that you expect it to be revised. Knowing in advance that your intent is not to present a perfect and final piece of writing may help lighten your burden. (Interestingly, some read-

ers give more attention to a document stamped DRAFT than they do to a final document, so be mindful of this possibility.)

16. Because of time pressures, you may sometimes have to forego massaging a document until it is perfect. Of course, you do not want shoddy work going out under your name, but you may have to make the decision that the press of other important work may keep you from achieving a perfect document. You may have to reconsider which writing tasks require obsessive attention to detail and which do not.[29]
17. During the revision process, keep uppermost in mind that good communication is your primary objective. Ask whether the writing is clear, well organized, and easy to follow. An important part of the editing process is getting rid of wordiness.

Hence, dealing with writer's block requires time and effort. Writing requires disciplined thinking, which is inherently hard work. For most people, writing will always involve a degree of struggle and challenge, but, like all other challenges, writer's block can be overcome by following the previous suggestions and having a willingness to commit to the process.

If you want your reader to pay attention to your written message, announce in your first sentence what you want to communicate. If you are asking for a new computer, want to draw your reader's attention to a special problem, or have a request, say so at the beginning. Also, keep your memos short and to the point. The reader does not need to know all your thought processes. Short words, short sentences, and short paragraphs work.[3]

Even a well-written message, however, can have its drawbacks. Because it is a one-way message, you are unable to obtain the immediate feedback you need—the reaction and questions that ensure that your ideas are understood.[4] Merely making written pronouncements does not guarantee that staff will understand issues or policies, particularly complex ones.

Some managers resort to memos to protect themselves. They want to be on record as having taken a position so they are not blamed if something goes wrong. This is a poor way of handling the negotiating process; it is far better to engage in face-to-face discussions. Other managers are afflicted with "memo-itis," not an uncommon disease among those who desire minimal contact with staff. Still others write memos on unimportant, even trivial, matters so that staff, buried in paper, eventually view the paper that comes across their desk as meaningless. If you want attention paid to your memos, make certain each one is significant.

Moreover, some managers use paper as a way of exchanging barbs. They resort to arguing by memo. Such paper grenades serve to intensify hostilities, with each side working hard to cleverly defend a position while attacking the other.[5] The paper exchange serves to impede, rather than facilitate, the resolution of differences. Again, a face-to-face exchange is superior to the written word.

With the availability of faxes and e-mail, communication has become much faster and easier. New technologies of communication, however, can have their own special issues. One of the main concerns is that of confidentiality. A sensitive message on a fax can be read by others. E-mails can be stored and retrieved; therefore, make certain that your system provides for a high degree of privacy, or caution staff about how confidentiality can be compromised with new communication technologies.

With the ease of communicating through e-mail and voice mail, there is a tendency for people to resort to this medium of communicating rather than face-to-face contact when dealing with highly sensitive issues. Like a memo, an e-mail is unambiguous and may be more harsh and more blunt than might be conveyed when people get together and look into each other's eyes.[6] Similarly, voice mail provides a medium for angry people to conduct a one-way diatribe. Their hostile monologue is not conducive to working out problems.

Therefore, as a general rule, when you have to explain ideas, when there exists the potential for hostility, when you want to influence behavior, or when you need to negotiate, arrange to communicate directly rather than send a piece of paper or e-mail or use voice mail.

Misperceptions

The possibility always exists that staff will misinterpret what you intend to communicate. For example, you offer to meet with secretarial staff to discuss agency policies. They, however, resent that you are dealing with them separately from the rest of the staff and believe they are being treated as "second-class citizens." As another example, you temporarily hire a consultant, and staff misinterpret this as dissatisfaction with their own performances. Asking staff members to write a report detailing their current activities makes them wonder why you are singling them out. In all these instances, staff perception is quite different than your intention.

In addition, nonverbal communications can have special interpretive meaning. Rolling your eyes, reading a report when an employee is speaking, failing to make eye contact, and ignoring a greeting are cues that convey lack of interest or even disapproval. Be aware that your reactions are constantly being observed and interpreted by each member of the staff in a very personal way. To avoid misperceptions, take careful note of how your nonverbal messages could be perceived by others. You need this sensitivity and empathy to ensure that people do not read more into what you are saying or doing than you intend. Take the time to obtain feedback from staff so you can counter any misinterpreted reactions.

The problem with communication is the illusion that what you convey has been received by the other party. You have said one thing, but they have heard quite another. That is why it is important to ask for feedback by requesting their response and their understanding of what you have conveyed. Sometimes, for example, a supervisor may request that an activity be accomplished but fail to indicate a specific time frame and a specific course of action.

Sometimes, failure of communication occurs because silence gives the illusion of agreement. This is referred to as "the disagreement fallacy." Just because people do not express their disagreement does not mean they automatically agree with you. The opposite can also be true: Just because someone argues with some aspects of your position does not mean that they are opposed to the fundamental idea—or to the person proposing it. Arguments can occur within an atmosphere in which people respect each other and afterward go to lunch together.[7]

Insensitivity to Staff Feelings

A good communications process requires managers to be especially clear with staff during times of organizational change. Insufficient attention to communicating with staff may result in rumors, low morale, and even antagonism. For example, suppose you decide to hire a new supervisor. Because you may be focusing primarily on the hiring process, which requires many interviews and discussions, you may be giving inadequate energy to talking with staff about the role of the new supervisor and how it might affect their work. Be aware that every major organizational action gives fodder to the rumor mill.

In summary, effective managers pay close attention to factors that interfere with good communication. Because managers can so easily take the communication process for granted, the likelihood of poor communications occurring is an ever-present danger that can quickly spoil a positive organizational climate. Once that happens, tremendous energy has to go into undoing the unintended harm. Therefore, be prepared to focus on the interactions between you and the staff.

HANDLING CONFLICT

In every organization, staff interactions produce inevitable conflict; there is no conceivable way of avoiding it. Most of the conflicts do not threaten productivity and are not very painful to the people involved. In fact, constructive conflict can bring about genuine growth as participants gain new insights and perspectives different than their own. Positive conflict can be used to explore opposing ideas so that outmoded ideas can be challenged and the group can discover new ways of working.[8] In many instances, disagreements should be encouraged if they provide alternatives that should be examined before decisions are made.[9]

Conflicts, if they have gotten out of hand, can be devastating and waste huge amounts of the organization's energy. The normal pattern of cooperation is disrupted, the organization may even undergo a great loss of resources, and its own survival may be at stake. Those who are forced to concede in a conflict situation are not inclined to remain with the organization or, if they do, are not committed to the organization as before. Morale is likely to deteriorate throughout the organization. For these reasons, it is much better to address conflicts before they escalate to the point of being destructive.

Types of Conflict

In most human service organizations, certain conflict situations commonly occur: personal feuds, the alleged persecution of a subordinate by a superior, and struggles between two units of the organization.

Personal feuds between key members of an organization usually occur when they have mutual grievances, and the feuds can lead to suspicion and hostility. Each party wants others in the organization to take sides. In some circumstances involving low-level conflicts, it may be desirable for the manager to take one side to quickly resolve an issue so that staff can get back to work.[10] Because arbitrarily taking sides can produce long-term animosities, however, a better approach is to meet with the participants, individually and together, to sort out their grievances and reach a mutually agreeable resolution.[11]

The alleged persecution of a subordinate by a supervisor presents a special dilemma. If the manager sides with the supervisor, there appears to be unjust bias, whereas if the manager sides with the subordinate he or she risks losing the loyalty of not only the supervisor involved in the incident but also other supervisors. Some managers have an open-door policy that allows anyone in the organization to communicate a grievance. Because this can be a time-consuming process, and because of the possibility of perceived bias, some organizations arrange for impartial third parties to handle grievances in a reasonable, objective manner.

In the private sector, delegating the responsibility for investigating and settling a complaint to an impartial agent is a common practice. At IBM, for example, employees can take their grievances to any manager, including the chief executive; the manager must take time to investigate the problem. Another alternative is to have a committee of peers review grievances. At General Electric, a five-member panel of both management and hourly employees is available to investigate grievances. Some organizations use an ombudsperson who investigates complaints, listens to all sides, and works with participants to arrive at a solution they all can accept. Regardless of whether managers, peers, or an ombudsperson is used to resolve conflict, employees must believe they are treated fairly, that the resolution is reached in a timely manner, and that they are protected from recrimination.[12]

Struggles between two units of an organization occur when one believes the other is encroaching on its sphere of responsibility. This is commonly known as a "turf battle." Unit A refuses to cooperate with Unit B as a way of protesting or even stopping the intrusion into its territory or functions. When such a rivalry occurs, the best approach is to clarify roles and assignments. If this is not successful, it may be necessary to reorganize the functions of each unit so that their boundaries are made quite clear. This is not a time for indecisiveness or ambiguity.

Units within an organization can conflict with each other in different ways: They fight because the staff perceive different objectives to be achieved, they compete for scarce resources, or they believe other units are being treated more favorably.[13] In general, these conflicts are best handled when the feuding units or parties work out their own solutions. If this is not possible, effective managers must play a more vigorous role in helping the units reach a resolution, particularly if the conflict becomes highly disruptive.

The Manager's Response to Conflict

Basic differences involving major organizational change are, by their very nature, controversial. Honest disagreements emerge because well-intentioned staff feel strongly about fundamental directions.[14] For example, expect disagreements to occur among staff about whether to serve primarily paying or nonpaying clients. Why shouldn't there be controversy over such a profound difference in emphasis? In keeping their eyes on the larger picture, managers welcome these major debates as a means of stimulating the organization to come to terms with significantly different directions. Such controversy is healthy for the organization and must be worked out before final decisions are made.

Because each conflict has its own unique characteristics and nuances, effective managers must be cautious about responding in a set pattern, as if following a prescription. The suggestions in the following paragraphs may be useful whether a conflict occurs between individuals, between staff and their superiors, or between units.

Confront conflicts as soon as they occur. Immediate response is especially important in dealing with office politics; people are inclined to take sides, and political intrigue disrupts the work of the organization. If conflicts are allowed to fester, you can expect more severe problems later. The best approach is to bring them out in the open and deal with them directly.[15]

Accept the reality that there are two sides to every issue. It is important that all parties involved in a conflict believe that they will have their "day in court" and a fair and impartial hearing of their concerns.

Be aware that conflict resolution takes time and thought. Whoever is assigned to examine a conflict must be willing to invest in the process. Conflict resolution should not be viewed as an appendage to managers' duties but as an integral part of their responsibilities.

Expect that most incidents eventually will be known in various parts of the organization. Although some conflicts may prove embarrassing to the parties involved, and confidentiality must be respected, news tends to travel among staff. For this reason, do not attempt to cover up a controversy; this will only draw more attention to it.

Promote an atmosphere of decorum. Set explicit ground rules so there is a clear sense of fairness perceived by the parties involved.[16] If emotions are running exceedingly high, call for a "cooling off period" (e.g., overnight) before attempting to resolve matters.

Establish a collaborative problem-solving process in which the conflicting parties seek a mutually beneficial resolution. Both parties strive to work through their differences by engaging in a win-win strategy. If this is not possible, then a compromise strategy involving some form of exchange ("quid pro quo"—this for that) may be needed. Through this form of "horse trading," parties can seek a resolution that satisfies both sides.

PERSUASIVE COMMUNICATIONS

Selling ideas and persuading people occur continuously in organizations. Supervisors frequently try to convince their superiors, colleagues, or staff of their opinions. Persuading and being persuaded are vital parts of the commerce of every organization.

The following is one example of the selling process: You have received a brochure inviting you to an out-of-town professional conference, but you know that the agency's budget is tight and the conference occurs 2 weeks before a major budget must be prepared. It is not a good time to be going. As a middle manager in your agency, you consider the conference a unique opportunity to enhance your managerial skills, but you realize you will have to be very persuasive with the organization's executive in order to go. What are some of the approaches or techniques you can consider? To answer this question, I borrow from techniques used by good salespeople in selling their products.[17] In the business world, the term *customer* is used to describe someone who is on the receiving end of a sales presentation. For our purposes, the term customer is the person you are trying to persuade.

Preparation is the key to making a persuasive case. Every good salesperson takes time before making a call to become highly knowledgeable about the product and potential customer. In the case of the conference, you would gather details about costs and benefits to the organization prior to meeting with your executive. There is no substitute for knowing your facts and doing your homework. Moreover, as part of your preparation you should think through what is central to your concerns and what is secondary, or even peripheral. In advance of the negotiating session, learn as much as you can about the position of the person with whom you are dealing. For example, in this situation develop an understanding of your boss's position regarding staff development and conferences.[18]

Be prepared to assert your position in a clear, succinct, and unequivocal manner. You need to communicate what you want and why you think it makes good sense. You must convey your own sense of conviction about the value of the conference. In any proposal, your belief in the product and your enthusiasm for how it can benefit the other party (your supervisor or your organization) can be a deciding factor in making a convincing case. Certainly, any uncertainty or feelings of ambiguity can detract from being persuasive. You have to be convinced that your project is worthwhile before you can convince others.

Convey both data and an emotional story to get your point across. If you are proposing a new plan, provide evidence of how it will cut costs or add clients. Supplement numerical data with examples, stories, and analogies to make your story come alive. Paint a vivid picture to give compelling credibility and to make an emotional impact.[19]

Tune in with genuine empathy to your audience by understanding what is important and of high priority. Is staff development of major importance to your superior? If the answer is yes, you still must realize that the budget needs to be completed on time and financial constraints must be addressed. Putting yourself in the other person's shoes helps tremendously in determining how you might present your case. As a result of carefully listening to your audience, you may be willing to alter or compromise your own plans, which in turn will make your case more appealing to the other side.

Anticipate and deal with objections. Sometimes, an objection may be a disguised way of asking for more information. For example, if your executive states that your being away will keep you from completing your part of the budget assignment, then you could formulate a question—for example, "Could we figure out a way that I could complete my assignment in time for me to attend the conference?"

Sometimes, it is better to anticipate objections in advance of their being voiced by your audience. You might say, for example, "Although I see some major advantages to attending the conference, I also recognize that my leaving might affect our being able to properly work out the budget." By acknowledging the objection in advance, you gain the opportunity to defang it. Suppose you anticipate that the costs will be a factor in the decision of whether or not you can attend the conference. Knowing this likely objection, you can convey how your attendance will allow you to deal more effectively with a certain category of clients, thereby bringing in more revenue to your organization.

In responding to an objection, it is generally a good idea to cushion your response with such comments as "I can appreciate and understand why you might feel this way, but I would like you to consider . . ." You can disagree without being disagreeable. Your objective is to remove or neutralize the roadblock without making your audience feel defensive.

Be specific about the advantages of your proposal to your audience. You would not give as a reason for going to the conference that you need a break from your daily work. The needs of the organization, not your own, must be paramount. Also, in conveying how you will meet those needs, you need to be specific. For example, you would indicate which particular workshops would be helpful. You might even offer to train other staff on your return. The point is that your proposal should demonstrate in concrete terms how attending the conference will add value to the organization.

To gain closure, provide options for your audience to consider. Having tuned in to your audience and heard some of their objections, you should offer alternatives or even compromises that will help you "close the deal." If cost is a factor in your attending the workshop, you might offer to pay for half or arrange for out-of-town housing with a friend. If time away from the office is a factor, you may need to work weekends to complete your part of the budget assignment or take work with you and complete it by the time you return.

These options can provide a win-win decision. Your willingness to make adjustments shows your commitment to the organization. In conveying options, you are providing your executive with choices: "Would you prefer that I attend 2 days instead of 5 to keep the costs down?" By using the choice format, you encourage your audience to make a decision rather than let it hang in the air. Of course, providing options requires a degree of flexibility and a willingness to make adjustments in your original proposal. The most effective persuaders seem to share common traits: They are open-minded, never dogmatic, and they begin the persuasion process prepared to adjust their views and incorporate others' ideas. When your colleagues (or your manager) realize that you want to understand their views and are willing to make changes in response to their concerns, they will not feel manipulated.[20]

This is an example of attending a conference, but the same approach could be used in considering whether to buy an additional computer or embark on a new program. In all instances, you are identifying a gap between what exists now and what could be accomplished as a result of your proposal.

In the final analysis, persuasive communication satisfies a need; it solves a problem. You should first crystallize what that need is and then show how your proposal will answer that need. You must either neutralize objections or show how your solution will provide overwhelming benefits. Persuading people to your point of view is not so much a matter of selling them but of tuning in to their issues and negotiating constructive solutions.

WAYS TO IMPROVE COMMUNICATION

No single method of communication is useful for all situations. If staff number in the hundreds, formal written communications may be necessary, but this would likely be inappropriate in communicating to a staff of 10. Usually, the chief executive will communicate through a network of key staff people, who in turn communicate with their staff, and so on throughout the organization. To further clarify ways to enhance communication, consider the suggestions in the following sections.

Top-Down Communications

A common complaint among staff is that they lack information about developments in their organization. This can be quite demoralizing to staff who want to believe they are a part of and contribute to the organization. Thus, communication must be given high priority. Communication should not be limited to "professionals" but should include every staff member. By communicating with all staff, you indicate that everyone is important and plays a significant role in accomplishing the organization's mission.

In large organizations, communication flows down from the top of the structure. Usually, the agency is organized so that top management is responsible for formulating positions or carrying out policies of outside funders or policymakers. Typically, the span of control involves four to seven managers who then meet with division heads under their supervision. This hierarchy can be quite extensive, depending on the size of the organization. The more complex the structure, the more each manager is a key link in the communication network. Breakdowns in communication can easily occur when messages are lost or poorly conveyed, especially when middle managers feel free to add their subjective interpretations, which can engender problematic reactions. The results can be disastrous for the organization.

Communiqués to staff about a change in assignments or procedures should always be accompanied by clear explanations about the reasons for the change. Staff should understand the rationale behind the change; otherwise, they may resent what appears to be an arbitrary and capricious decision, ultimately preventing them from carrying out the request. They need to have clear, candid explanations about how the change will benefit them, their clients, or the organization.

For example, suppose that management decides that staff who work with foster children must see the children at least once a week. Managers should communicate to staff that the children will benefit from the increased continuity that results from these visits. To ensure that staff understand and accept the top-down communication, a monitoring system should be established so that supervisors can determine whether the children are actually being seen once a week.

In addition to this hierarchical network, there are other ways of communicating from the top of the organization. Organizational newsletters, public announcements, bulletin boards, and large staff meetings are among the ways that staff can learn about the latest developments.

Bottom-Up Communications

Staff should have ample opportunity to communicate ideas and give reactions to their immediate supervisors and top management. This upward communication network can help managers determine whether staff understand and accept requests or whether they have concerns or problems. Furthermore, a bottom-up approach can solicit valuable suggestions and provide information from those directly on the firing line. Most important, when staff are encouraged to send information to top management, they feel better about their own role in the organization.

Unfortunately, some organizations give the illusion of being an information network while treating staff ideas in a cavalier fashion or ignoring them altogether. If staff sense an insincere gesture, expect an even more demoralizing atmosphere than if no effort was made in the first place.[21] If you cannot carry forward staff ideas, at least make certain that you give staff an explanation. Nothing is more frustrating to staff than when management claims their ideas will be taken seriously but then does not follow through.

Obtaining Key Information

Certain events and certain activities demand information on which decisions have to be made. For example, the information may have to deal with the progress of projects, the development of a new service, or staff performance. Certain activities or events become particularly crucial when they go beyond a particular threshold. For example, if there has been a substantial increase in client no-shows, it is important to understand why this trend is occurring. Similarly, if there is a major decrease in client participation in group counseling sessions, this information must be made known. If there is a reduction in an expected income category, this information should also be made clear. Managers seek to know if something unusual, unexpected, or exceptional is occurring. It is important to obtain data about trends before they turn into major problems. Weekly and monthly reports should distinguish general information from that which is key and exceptional to foster managerial decisions. The term *management by exception* conveys the idea of concentrating on out-of-the-ordinary events.[22]

Employee Surveys

One way to encourage good communication is to take an opinion survey when a new policy is under consideration or a program needs to be implemented. Staff can be of particular help in identifying the problems they are encountering with a new program idea. They may not have the answers, but their ability to articulate problems can be invaluable to management.

Surveys are fairly common because they are inexpensive to use, they collect information from everyone in the organization, and they permit management to see trends. Management could ask staff questions such as "What in this organization would you retain?" "What would you want to see discontinued?" "What do you think the organization expects of you?" and "What do you expect of the organization?" Answers to these questions can provide insight about what is uppermost on the minds of the staff and permit management to consider new directions. Surveys, however, have the disadvantages of inviting bias in the way they are worded and of causing staff to become disenchanted if they see little response to their feedback.[23]

Suggestion Systems

To identify concerns from the entire staff, try the old-fashioned suggestion box. This permits people to communicate their concerns anonymously and could reveal festering problems. The suggestion box allows staff to present their complaints and concerns without feeling intimidated. Perhaps staff are talking too loudly in the corridors. Perhaps clients in the waiting room are not being treated courteously. Perhaps there is concern about the consistency of the staff in dress for work. Normally, without a suggestion box, these concerns might go undetected and therefore unaddressed. Through the anonymity of the suggestion box, everyone—telephone operator, mail clerk, computer programmer, and manager—can express concerns or make suggestions.

The manager, of course, should determine whether the suggestions are helpful or are in fact so vague and undeveloped that they cannot be addressed. As with surveys, respond to the entire staff so that employees know management hears and values their suggestions. Otherwise, the box becomes a receptacle for gum wrappers.

Another way to encourage communication is to have an open-door policy in which top management is available either on a continuous basis or for scheduled appointments. For example, some managers formally schedule an "open house" on a certain weekday afternoon. Staff welcome the opportunity to talk with top managers on matters that bother them. This approach may create problems for supervisors who believe that their subordinates "go over their heads," and it may tempt top management to try to resolve matters that are better left within the units. Still, safeguards can be built in so that staff do not inappropriately bypass supervisors. For instance, a manager could suggest that employees follow up the issue with their supervisors, or that supervisors form ad hoc task groups to address staff concerns. Furthermore, discussion could be limited to systemic rather than interpersonal or individual issues.

Active one-on-one consultation with subordinates is another way to foster good communications. Individual consultation with several staff, however, can result in delays between the formulation and execution of a top-management idea, sometimes elicits irrelevant suggestions, and even invites criticism. By actively soliciting advice and information, however, you can determine if there are mistakes in your plan and whether and how a decision might work.[24] If particularly interested in staff productivity, then supervisors can individually determine what makes staff feel productive by asking them questions such as the following:

When do you work at your peak?

What do you like most about your job?

What bothers you about your work?

What resources do you need to be more productive?

What policies and procedures should be modified so you can be more productive?

From the responses, you can determine what is highly individualized and idiosyncratic and what concerns are held in common.

A variation of one-on-one consultation consists of management meeting with small groups of employees. These face-to-face meetings, sometimes comprising staff from several different sections, can provide helpful responses to policies under consideration. These meetings can be time-consuming but worthwhile not only for obtaining valuable input but also for squelching rumors.[25]

Informal Communications

One of the best ways to keep in touch with staff is through informal contacts. In the hallways, on the elevator, and in the lunchroom, you can take a few moments to ask how a project is going, how the copy machine is working, or how a spouse is recuperating. Sometimes, these spontaneous communications occur immediately after a formal meeting and, interestingly, can be even more important than the meeting. By asking people about their jobs as you walk through the building, you obtain ideas and suggestions that you would never obtain by sitting at your desk. The tag name for this is MBWA—management by walking around.[26] Some managers make a point of regularly scheduling time to walk through their unit so they can obtain feedback from their staff. Be careful, however, because when you make a daily walk you may be perceived as a prison guard making rounds. An alternative is to engage in impromptu discussions to and from your office.

If your schedule is too demanding during the workday, arrange to greet people as they arrive at work or go home. Informal staff functions such as picnics provide a chance to get to know staff on a more personal level.

Good Feedback

At the heart of any communication is feedback, a process that requires a reaction to actions or situations in the organization. High reliance must be placed on good feedback because it is the basis for taking necessary corrective actions. To encourage good feedback, the ability and the commitment to listen are absolutely essential.

Unfortunately, meaningful listening, although often subscribed to, is often breached. We all have a tendency to concentrate on our own agendas and concerns so that we resort at times to "pretend" or selective listening. Meaningful listening requires tremendous effort and total concentration.[27]

It is quite human for all of us to want to hear only what we are doing right and to avoid hearing negative responses. For example, some supervisors avoid listening to employees complain because it spoils their own good moods. By taking the time to listen, however, a minor complaint can be handled with minimal energy or a hidden problem can surface. Nothing is worse than for a staff member to express a concern only to later feel that no one cared enough to respond to it. If nothing can be done, for whatever reason, staff should be given an explanation and a sense of appreciation for having raised the concern. This paves the way for improved communication in the future. Only when staff know that they will be taken seriously will they feel positive about communicating their concerns.

Occasionally, Staff A may complain about Staff B: "He's goofing off on the job" or "She offended a client." Staff A, however, requests that the information be kept confidential, thus making it difficult to communicate directly to Staff B without divulging the source of information. Confrontation of Staff B with a rumor has elements of a witch-hunt and will usually result in defensive denials. This sensitive communication issue can be dealt with in one of three ways. Either request Staff A communicate the concerns directly to Staff B or request that Staff A give permission to give the source of information. If neither of these two options is agreeable, you may be forced to communicate to Staff B that this matter has been brought to your attention in confidence.

In summary, effective managers must ensure good communication to convey the organization's values, promote staff commitment, and handle conflict. Be mindful that communicating is a two-way process of transmitting ideas and tuning in to staff's thinking and feelings. Good communicators are good listeners.

NOTES

1. D. H. Gaylin, Break down barriers by communicating your company's strategy, *The Human Resources Professional* (1990, Summer), pp. 20-21.

2. G. M. Barton, Manage words effectively, *Personnel Journal, 1* (1990), pp. 32-33.

3. M. H. McCormack, *On communicating* (Los Angeles: Dove, 1998), pp. 142-143.

4. E. Bliss, *Getting things done* (New York: Bantam, 1976), p. 93.

5. R. Townsend, *Further up the organization* (New York: Knopf, 1984), p. 134.

6. M. McCormack, Reliance on e-mail may erode the quality of communication, *The Plain Dealer* (1999, August 3), p. 8C.

7. M. McCormack, *On communicating,* pp. 15-28.

8. D. Tjosvold, *The conflict-positive organization* (Reading, MA: Addison-Wesley, 1991), p. 11.

9. P. Drucker, *The effective executive* (New York: Harper & Row, 1985), pp. 150-153; A. Lauffer, *Careers, colleagues, and conflicts: Understanding gender, race, and ethnicity in the workplace* (Beverly Hills, CA: Sage, 1985), pp. 145-146.

10. T. Caplow, *How to run any organization* (Hinsdale, IL: Dryden, 1976), p. 170.

11. H. Bisno, *Managing conflict* (Newbury Park, CA: Sage, 1988), p. 66.

12. G. T. Milkovich & J. W. Boudreau, *Personnel/human resource management* (5th ed.) (Plano, TX: Business Publications, 1988), pp. 614-617.

13. R. T. Crow & C. A. Odewahn, *Management for the human services* (Englewood Cliffs, NJ: Prentice Hall, 1987), pp. 145-146.

14. P. Drucker, pp. 122-123.

15. D. Tjosvold, p. 4.

16. H. Bisno, p. 56.

17. J. Carew, *You'll never get no for an answer* (New York: Simon & Schuster, 1987); J. Gubkin, *Persuasive communication* (Cleveland, OH: J. Gubkin, 1985), pp. 1-82.

18. R. N. Haas, *The power to persuade* (New York: Houghton Mifflin, 1994), pp. 171-174.

19. J. A. Conger, The necessary art of persuasion, *Harvard Business Review, 76* (1998, May/June), p. 92.

20. J. A. Conger, p. 87.

21. A. Zaremba, Communication: The upward network, *Personnel Journal, 3* (1989), p. 36.

22. P. Drucker, *Management challenges for the 21st century* (New York: HarperBusiness, 1999), pp. 127-130.

23. J. H. Boyett & H. P. Conn, *Maximum performance measurement* (Macomb, IL: Glenbridge, 1988), p. 256.

24. T. Caplow, p. 55.

25. G. M. Barton, p. 32.

26. R. E. Herman, *Keeping good people: Strategies for solving the dilemma of the decade* (Cleveland, OH: Oakhill, 1990), p. 140.

27. M. S. Peck, *The road less traveled* (New York: Touchstone/Simon & Schuster, 1978), p. 125.

28. B. Joseph, Writer's block: Is there a cure? *Nonprofit World, 3* (1986), pp. 27-28.

29. M. McCormack, *Mark H. McCormack on managing* (West Hollywood, CA: Dove, 1996), pp. 47-48.

Chapter 15

TEAM BUILDING AND COALITION BUILDING

Managers of human service organizations must continuously work with others both inside and outside their agencies. These collaborative relationships involve striving to achieve mutual goals while respecting separate identities and different roles. In working together with others, managers seek common ground, but they appreciate it when it is appropriate for colleagues to take separate paths. This chapter explores how managers can work collaboratively with individuals and groups—internally and externally—to further the goals of their organization. Specifically, this chapter focuses on (a) building teams and task forces within the agency and (b) working with collateral organizations.

THE IMPORTANCE OF TEAM BUILDING

Increasingly, organizations—whether in the corporate world, voluntary agencies, or governmental bodies—are moving away from hierarchical, top-down decision making to bottom-up decision making that makes for greater involvement of their staff members. This trend is especially true in the human service field, in which many staff members actively participate in the operation of the agency. Effective administrators turn to staff members at all levels for information, for opinions, and for carrying out administrative decisions. Because those who are actively involved in decision making are most likely to have the enthusiasm for implementing those decisions, agency managers should seek meaningful ways to foster staff participation. Forming staff into teams is one of the most effective methods of developing staff commitment.

Merely putting a group of people together in the same room does not guarantee a team. As distinct from a group of individuals who may lack a common purpose, a team strives for unified goals. Team members use the group process to generate a diversity of ideas and experiences that can address organizational problems. The combined contributions of members equals more than the sum of their individual efforts. This group synergy results from staff members working cooperatively to produce results that are qualitatively better than what each individual member could produce on his or her own.[1]

Teams can be manager led or self-managing.[2] Typically, manager-led teams are those responsible for implementing assigned work. For example, in a children's institution, staff assigned to individual cottages would work as a team under the supervisor. In turn, each cottage team would be part of a larger residential unit team that would meet periodically to work on problems of common concern. In this format, the supervisor assumes the role of team leader, and the individual members work together on common concerns.

Under a self-managing team, members assume responsibility for determining their own process and monitoring results. They may select their own team leader, who may or may not be a manager. The team deemphasizes formal supervisory roles and encourages members to substitute group decision making and consensus for the direction of a supervisor. Management, however, can still retain responsibility for the overall direction and provide some degree of coaching as needed. Self-managing teams may be ongoing or operate as task forces with a time-limited schedule (discussed later).

Teams Respond to Circumstances

To borrow from a sports analogy, different circumstances promote greater or lesser degrees of team interaction. A basketball, football, or hockey team may require much interaction and interdependence among its members. A tennis team, and to even a greater extent a golf team, requires its players to function relatively independently of each other. So, too, in human service agencies, circumstances may dictate the need for different degrees of interdependence. For example, a counseling agency requires its practitioners to perform most of their activities in separate offices with individual clients. It may also want heightened interaction, however, at a time when it is being reviewed for reaccreditation.

Creating Team Spirit

Highly productive teams share the following characteristics:[3]

1. They develop and communicate a shared vision and work toward common goals.
2. They deemphasize hierarchy because every team member works to make the idea or plan succeed. With few exceptions, no one pulls rank.
3. They encourage open communication. Although they may discuss complaints openly among themselves, they are discreet about what they share with those outside the team.
4. They develop trust in each other and respect their teammates both for their skills and as people.
5. They are comfortable with each other, and they enjoy playing and working together.
6. They are task oriented and focus on producing results. They are not just a discussion group; rather, they have identifiable objectives that they want to accomplish. They establish specific performance objectives—for example, developing a new service or responding to client requests within 24 hours.
7. They establish clear rules and behavior, such as attendance requirements, confidentiality, respect for each other, constructive confrontation, and full participation. These rules promote focus, openness, commitment, and trust.[4]
8. Members of the team are interdependent. They recognize that they are trying to achieve something that would not be possible for them to do as individuals. Team members build on each other's contributions instead of duplicating or interfering with them. They are willing to sacrifice their own interests for the good of the whole team.
9. Team members are constantly aware of the team's performance. On the basis of continual feedback, they make self-correcting adjustments to improve performance.
10. They develop a high level of commitment to and ownership of the work of the team and do whatever it takes to complete team tasks. Sometimes, this commitment involves working more hours than those in the usual work week.

11. Depending on the team assignment, members take responsibility for areas outside their immediate sphere. Working as a team member, a counselor may have suggestions for the marketing department, or a support staff may have thoughts on how maintenance can be improved. The most important factors in selecting team members are their credibility, expertise, and the ability to connect to important constituencies within the organization.[5] The consensus is not based on the need for everyone to conform; rather, people argue, debate, and work their way to a common decision.
12. They make decisions by consensus, which is made possible because of an agreement on goals. Generally, votes are not taken, and majority rule is not applied.
13. They have a period of training, especially if they are new at working on a team. This training could include team problem solving, managing meetings, and conflict management. Team training helps people understand that consensus decision making means people might have different opinions about the best solution to a problem, even after considerable discussion. Everyone is willing to support one option to make it work, however.

Overcoming Barriers to Winning Teams

Initially, not all participants on the team may be good team players. Even those who lack traits that would make them effective team members, however, may eventually become team contributors if they are given the right motivation and training. For example, some may want to work independently, preferring to receive credit or even criticism for their own individual efforts. They may believe that being part of the team interferes with their ability to complete their own individual work. They may need time to adjust to the team. Encourage their participation in meetings so that other members of the team can appreciate how their expertise can contribute to achieving team goals.

Two other problems can occur among members of a team. First, one or more members may tend to dominate the team process, attempting to dictate directions and unduly influence the thinking of the group. Other team members can then become dissatisfied and frustrated. The leader needs to communicate with these "prima donnas" that their personal attitude is disrupting the team spirit, and that their overall work performance will be measured on the extent to which they participate as a team member. A second, and opposite, problem is the tendency for some members to disengage. An effective team leader will understand that the disengaged team members may feel insecure and may be afraid to say something that may make them appear foolish and be wrong. In both instances, the team leader needs to take members aside to talk about how their behaviors need to change for the benefit of the organization.[6]

Occasionally, you may encounter a team member who is unwilling to respond to training and who is unable to work with other members of the team. Their mistrust is so profound that they poison the ability of the team to work together. If these staff members do not respond to training or coaching, they should be transferred out of the team.

Becoming an Effective Team Leader

Not all team leaders are inherently effective: Their own personal style can negatively affect the team, or the atmosphere of the organization may not truly support team efforts. Team leadership, however, can be enhanced in several ways. First, team leaders need clear directives from senior managers regarding their role. At the very least, their roles should be legitimized with a formal title and job description that clarifies how this differs from usual supervisory roles. Team leaders must also understand the boundaries of their decision making and the parameters within which their team can function. How much initiative can they take? How innovative can their team be? These are questions that must be understood at the beginning of the team process. Second, team leaders should develop leadership skills that can enhance the functioning of their team, including negotiating, communicating, agenda setting, goal development, and action planning. Third, a team leader creates a safe environment in which people can communicate whatever needs to be said without fear of reprisal. In the course of discussions, a team leader pulls together divergent ideas and identifies themes that may have connections.[7]

Handling Conflict

Conflict can significantly affect a team's decision-making effectiveness. Inevitably, team members will have incompatible wishes or irreconcilable desires. Two kinds of conflict can occur in teams. Relationship conflict can involve tension and even dislike among group members. This form of conflict is detrimental to group performance and member satisfaction. Because relationship conflicts distract people from their tasks, both leaders and group members must work hard at controlling personal animosities. Team leaders must bring the antagonistic parties together to resolve their concerns—or help them work together as professionals despite their personal animosities.

Task conflict involves differences of viewpoints and opinions related to how the group is to accomplish tasks. Moderate levels of conflict over tasks can enhance group performance and further the development of new perspectives.[8] Teams whose members challenge each other's thinking develop a more in-depth awareness of choices, create a rich range of alternatives, and ultimately make the kinds of effective decisions required in today's turbulent environment.[9] Task conflicts can reduce apathy and generate a higher level of team investment. Managers can ask members to take opposing viewpoints. Members who suggest different and useful ideas should be given special acknowledgment. Debate within the team can reduce the dangers of "groupthink" (discussed in Chapter 13).

The key to managing conflict is to encourage people to debate their ideas, to have strong differences of opinions, and simultaneously maintain a high level of civility. Team members must know that they can feel strongly about an issue and fight hard for it without questioning the competence or integrity of those with opposing views.[10] They avoid becoming personally hostile or angry with their colleagues. When conflict is managed well, it becomes an effective tool for exchanging ideas and making better organizational decisions.

The most common type of conflict relates to work problems. For example, one faction may want to change to a whole new procedure, whereas the other opposes major change. Another kind of conflict occurs when some members believe that they have to carry the load of others. This kind of conflict can destroy a team if it is not resolved quickly. Pinpoint whether the persons not carrying their load lack skills or need additional training or coaching. A more serious problem is apathy in relation to achieving the team's goals. Still another type of problem relates to individuals forming clicks. These issues must be dealt with quickly if the team is to continue working together.

In all these conflict situations, team leaders must determine the source of the conflict and then take proactive steps to deal with it. Initially, the team leader may wish to meet with those who are complaining to determine the nature of their concerns and then meet individually with those who are the target of their annoyances. It is important, however, that the team leader air these concerns to the full team.[11] If conflict is not discussed candidly, upset members will continue to corrode the team process. Moreover, the team leader must help those that are in conflict to listen to each other, especially if each side is intent only on winning its own point. Asking key members to paraphrase what the other is saying is one way of opening up their minds. It is also helpful for each faction to convey how its position will help the team achieve its goals. If both can see that everybody is working toward the same goal, there may be room for flexibility and compromise.

The team leader must encourage differences while discouraging interpersonal hostility. Ground rules for discussion must be clearly established in advance: "There are to be no personal attacks, no disparaging comments, no personalizing of the issue." Another helpful ground rule is that changing a position is not a sign of weakness but of strength. Finally, people can express their feelings because positions are usually a combination of both intellectual thought and emotional reactions. Understanding how other people feel about an issue, and the depth of their feelings, is an important part of teamwork.

One approach a team leader can use to foster a more open negotiating process is to have each faction prepare a list of what it believes the other side should do and then have the parties exchange lists and determine the compromises to which they might agree. Another approach is to ask the conflicting members to write questions that require answers from the other side. Out of this process can come a mutually agreed-on position.

Having a Good Fight While Getting Along

Understanding how group members can have fundamental disagreements and still get along without resorting to destructive conflicts with one another is vital. It is instructive to understand the following specific tactics that can be taken to achieve this goal:[12]

- Frame the choice as a collaborative, rather than a competitive, effort. Successful teams develop a position that collaboration works for everybody's best interest. Having a shared vision and working toward a common goal will further the team process.
- Obtain facts. The more current data that can be made available, the more likely team members will focus on issues, not personalities. In the absence of good data, a tendency will be to debate opinions—some ill formed. Facts allow people to move quickly to the central issues and reduce reliance on guesses or self-serving desires. Therefore, it is important that preparation for team meetings be devoted to obtaining good information.
- Develop multiple alternatives. Having many options for the group encourages creative thinking and may allow participants to consider combining elements from each of the choices. Sometimes, members are encouraged to present a range of options just to have more choices for the group.

- Put people in a positive mood. It helps to have people loosen up before embarking on the seriousness of the team's agenda. Maybe they can tell humorous episodes that happened to them during the week or describe some positive personal experiences. Jokes and humor help lighten the atmosphere and provide a psychological mood for blunting the threatening edge of criticisms or negative information.
- Seek consensus with qualification. This particular tactic may be more suitable in manager-led teams. It involves a two-step process in which team members talk about an issue and try to reach a consensus leading to a decision. If they cannot, the most senior manager makes the decision.

For example, a children's institution staff team may have different opinions about whether an adolescent is ready for discharge. The residential director in these special circumstances makes the ultimate decision with the guidance of various members' input. The other members of the team accept this decision as long as they believe the process is a fair one and that they have had ample opportunity to express their ideas. Most people want their opinions to be considered seriously, but they accept that these opinions cannot always prevail. The key is that the ultimate decision is based on open and honest communication and not on a hidden agenda known only to the team leader. This approach permits decisions to be made fairly quickly.

Interactive Team Exercises

Learning to be an effective team member takes work and a considerable amount of introspection. Team members need to be aware of how they are doing as a member of a team and be able to help their fellow team members function appropriately. One way of fostering this understanding and enhancing team skills is to ask team members to participate in preliminary exercises that allow them to simulate roles in a nonthreatening manner. The following are exercises team leaders can use to stimulate team understanding:

1. Ask two factions to debate an issue relevant to your agency. For example, a neighborhood center could debate the question, "Should we take youngsters to an outside playground?" Give each group starting arguments for their position for and against. Provide members of each group with disparaging remarks that they might convey in regard to the other group's position. Discuss afterward how the designated leader and other group members might have better resolved their differences. Also identify some of the positive ideas that were conveyed and how these might be replicated in regular team meetings.

2. Divide the group into those who will be wearing blindfolds and those who will be leading the blindfolded around obstacles and down stairs. Discuss afterward how supportive (or not) the coaches were to those who had to wear the blindfolds. Also discuss what would foster trust or lack of trust in team discussions.
3. Ask people to spend 30 minutes drawing together on a large roll of paper their individual thoughts about how they perceive their team functioning and their role in the team. Obviously, artistic talent is not the essential aspect of this exercise, so stick figures or use of color may be ways of expressing people's thoughts. For example, one person may draw a swing without ropes, indicating his or her feelings of lack of support. Another may draw an octopus, conveying concerns about the team going in many different directions and lacking central focus. No one is to talk during the drawing, but afterward each uses the drawing to reflect on his or her position. This becomes an opportunity for people to examine what procedures need to be altered for team members to believe that they can contribute more.

Aside from the fun of doing these exercises, their value is for staff to take time to consider how their team is functioning and what they can do to improve it. Once people feel more comfortable, time can be set aside periodically for team members to reflect on how their team is working. Among the questions members can ask are the following:[13]

- Are members contributing suggestions about how the group can improve?
- How well do members of the team understand problems?
- How often do members ask for—and give—support to each other?
- How willing are members to finish the work that was assigned to individuals?
- Do group members respect each other's ideas?
- Is everyone pulling his or her weight?
- Is there a strong sense of collaboration, even when there are differences?
- Is there a tolerance for individuals functioning on their own, when this seems to be a good idea?
- Are innovative ideas encouraged?
- Are people encouraged to try new roles and have growth experiences?

Positive answers to these questions indicate that teams are working constructively and collaboratively to resolve issues.

TASK FORCES

Sometimes, teams are designated as task forces, which implies carrying out a specific assignment on a time-limited basis. The term *ad hoc task force* suggests that when the group accomplishes its purpose, it will disband. The advantage of an ad hoc task force (sometimes known as an "action team") is that it has a clear mandate to deal with a particular problem and is disbanded once the problem is solved. Usually, members are asked to participate voluntarily based on their experience and expertise.[14] As discussed previously, the group may establish its own timetable and set its own pace. The supervisor can be team leader, or the role may be assigned to different members of the staff for different issues. If task force members are drawn from different units of the organization, then problem analysis has the advantage of different perspectives.[15] Moreover, there is the possibility of developing a network as task force members communicate to their home-base units.

Five caveats should be kept in mind to keep task forces from becoming counterproductive. First, the staff who develop an action plan may not necessarily implement it. The group formed to carry out the plan may need to be reconstituted with top management and participants from other units. Because newcomers may not have participated in the planning process, they will need time to develop ownership of the undertaking.

Second, it is possible that staff will identify so much with their task force that they become elitist and exclusionary in their outlook. Others in the organization may become resentful because they perceive this task force to be a clique. Members of the group must understand that they have a responsibility to share their experiences with others. Time limits and rotation to different groups help diminish cliques.

Third, in establishing the task force, it is important to clarify roles, responsibilities, and ground rules under which it will function. Otherwise, the group will be unclear about its function and decision-making boundaries. Is it only advisory? Is it responsible for carrying out its own recommendations? Is it designed to initiate ideas or react passively to ideas being generated by management? Can its decisions be overridden and, if so, by whom? It is also important to clarify the role of the "taskmaster." Is the chairperson responsible for following through, or is his or her role limited to facilitating the group discussion process? Thus, the task force must be given clear and detailed guidance about the job it will carry out.[16]

Fourth, staff involvement on task forces must be meaningful; unfortunately, it can be superficial when staff appear to have an input into the organization's decision-making process but management ultimately ignores or belittles their ideas. If staff are limited to making trivial decisions, they will not invest in the process.[17] People sense when their ideas are genuinely desired and when the organization is resorting to gimmickry.

Finally, if several task groups are organized simultaneously to deal with different issues, they must be coordinated. Unless the various parts of the organization coalesce on issues, serious problems can result. For example, if one set of members is working to change the reward system, while another set studies personnel practices and a third group considers the organization's tasks, much confusion can result if there is no attempt to unify these group's efforts and findings. Hence, task groups must keep lines of communication open and work to achieve a collaborative effort. It may be helpful to appoint a "traffic cop" to oversee the various task forces.

COALITION BUILDING

If team building requires that effective managers focus on developing strong internal staff relationships, coalition building requires managers to look outward to build collateral relationships and to partner with other agencies. To maximize the impact of their organization in the community, effective managers periodically join with collateral organizations in forming strategic alliances. This collaboration occurs when two or more organizations perceive that their own goals can be achieved most effectively and efficiently with the assistance and the resources of others. The relationship involves a commitment to a mutual relationship, a jointly developed structure and shared responsibility, mutual accountability, and the sharing of responsibilities, resources, and rewards.[18] Thus, collaboration is a mutually beneficial and well-defined relationship that two or more organizations enter into to achieve better results than they are likely to achieve on their own.[19]

Alliances of organizations offer the possibility of pooling funds, sharing staff and volunteer time, and involving talent and expertise that may not be available in one group.[20] The term *synergy* conveys that the sum is greater than the parts, meaning that more clout and power can emerge when groups work together than when they work alone. By forming alliances, they increase the availability of people power. Not surprisingly, politicians and other public officials discern the difference between a group of 50 and one that represents a coalition of 5,000.[21]

Forming a coalition does not necessarily occur easily. Members of organizations generally want to control their own destiny and decision-making process, develop a sense of identity, and convey to the world their particular efforts and accomplishments. This need for autonomy and identity can be so profound that some organizations purposefully avoid interaction. They want to preserve their independence and think they can achieve their goals without relating to others. They want to be unencumbered, free to pursue their objectives without compromising. For example, a child advocacy organization may decide not to participate in a cooperative community effort to improve foster care because it wants to preserve its advocacy, "gadfly" role in relation to human service agencies.

Despite this tendency to be independent, organizations that work on complex community problems find it necessary—even essential—to deal with other organizations. A collaborative approach requires organizations to harmonize ways of working together on many community problems—such as unemployment, inadequate housing, and delinquency—that are complex and interrelated. Often, organizations become highly specialized and concentrate on a given aspect of a problem. As specialization has increased, so too has the need for interaction among organizations. For example, establishing an employment program requires more than setting up training programs: Health services, transportation, day care, counseling, and housing services all become necessary components. Hence, although many organizations strongly desire to preserve a high degree of decision-making authority and power, the complexity of problems and the need for funds, skills, staff, community support, and other resources may compel them to interact cooperatively to form strategic alliances.[22]

Factors Facilitating Strategic Alliances

Certain key capabilities should exist for strategic alliances to function successfully.

Goal Compatibility

Organizations forming an alliance should share a clear vision of their mutual goals. Through this common vision, organizations should determine that they can maximize their respective goals. Goals of different organizations can be similar, such as when several of them decide to work together to reduce crime in a neighborhood. Goals also can be complementary, such as when one agency decides to serve clients it ordinarily would not serve because it will be paid by another agency for doing so. Sometimes, goals can even be dissimilar, such as when "strange bedfellow" organizations harmonize their efforts to achieve their respective goals.[23]

Development of Resources

Organizations will collaborate when sufficient resources exist to reduce competition or when they can agree on how resources are to be divided. Collaboration is less likely to occur when organizations must compete for scarce resources. Organizations can be involved in an exchange of resources that are tangible (involving funding, facilities, personnel, clients, and services) or intangible (involving prestige and good will). Sometimes, the exchange is immediately reciprocal: Organization A agrees to serve the clients of Organization B in exchange for funding. At other times, the exchange is initially unilateral: Organization A agrees to assist Organization B on child welfare legislation in anticipation of Organization B assisting Organization A in passing a mental health levy the following year. Organizations thus weigh anticipated costs of the exchange against present or future benefits.

Role of Higher Authority

When state or national organizations encourage coordination of their local units, they are likely to work together. Similarly, foundations sometimes require (as a condition of a local grant) that agencies demonstrate that they will work together to achieve their joint program's goals. For example, Salvation Army, Catholic Charities Services, Neighborhood Family Center, and the Hispanic Drug Prevention Program may join together in a community proposal to provide comprehensive services to a target population at the request of a community foundation.

Governance

Organizations will collaborate successfully when they can work out agreements about who can make decisions and what type of decisions can be made. A written protocol can define (a) when Organization A can make a decision independent of other organizations, (b) when it must consult with the others but not require their approval, and (c) when Organization A can act only with the consensus of the collaborating partners.[24] Furthermore, the decision-making process should include procedures for resolving conflict. For example, suppose that a mental health agency and a substance abuse agency are working together to address the needs of homeless persons. What procedures might they develop should individual staff members disagree on how they should work with a particular mentally ill, substance-abusing client? These mechanisms need to be clarified in the beginning to avoid later interorganizational problems.

Domain of Activities and Target Population

Organizations need to come to terms with how they will work with clients whom they will serve. When the roles are complementary, such as when an employment organization provides a different set of activities from those of a day care organization, then collaboration will be facilitated. When a substance abuse agency decides to find jobs for its clients, however, then its participation in an employment alliance may come into question. When one agency begins to encroach on another's activities or their target population, collaboration will be impeded.

Cultural Compatibility

Although each organization in an alliance may have its own culture, these cultures should be sufficiently compatible so that they can develop a distinct culture within the alliance that can support their mutual mission.[25] This development requires thinking through how individual organizations can affect other members of the alliance. Furthermore, it requires a mind-set of negotiating and cooperating. Also, it means considering what is best for the alliance and the community, not just one agency.[26]

Power and Prestige

When an organization perceives that it can influence changes that it thinks are important, and when it senses that others will not be overbearing, then it is more likely to collaborate. Furthermore, when this organization and its partners perceive that their prestige is enhanced and when others are not gaining prestige at their expense, they will continue to collaborate. When parties have equal status and respect for each other, their relationships are likely to be more effective than when they do not have equal status or respect for each other.[27] People involved in successful collaborative ventures find ways to balance the unequal positions among all members.[28]

Communication Infrastructure

Open, consistent communication can lead to clear expectations of performance. By determining specific objectives with a clear timetable of the alliance, organizations can avoid later problems of ambiguity. Information systems and up-to-date technologies (e.g., conference calls, faxes, and e-mail) can facilitate communications.

Trust

Perhaps the most intangible factor, but the one that is most indispensable, is that members of the respective organizations basically trust others to honor their commitments. Over time, this trust is most likely to increase. As organizations have opportunities for successfully conducting joint programs, greater willingness develops to accept new forms of interdependence. In summary, whether or not two or more organizations collaborate will depend on how committed they are to working together to achieve their common goals.

Collaborative Structures

Structures developed as a result of collaborative efforts can vary depending on the desired goals. Where the situation requires autonomous agencies to retain a high degree of independence while linking temporarily on a specific issue or situation, the collaborative process is ad hoc and limited. A special crisis (e.g., a hurricane) may require organizations to temporarily mesh their programs, but once the crisis recedes and in the absence of provisions for an ongoing structure organizational relationships can evaporate as autonomous groups return to their independent activities.

Sometimes, organizations with different goals will work together informally through a loose coalition on a temporary basis. Coalitions emerge from the joining of two or more organizations that discover they have more to gain by collaboration on an issue or activity than by pursuing independent courses of action. When the project is completed, the coalition is dissolved. For example, 10 mental health agencies form a coalition to pass a mental health levy. For a period of 3 months, these mental health agencies send representatives to meet weekly to develop strategies for the campaign. When the campaign is concluded, the group is dismantled. Four years later, a new coalition is formed for the next levy campaign.

Organizations may also establish a formal ongoing relationship through a federation. Each organization is self-directing; neither is entirely dependent on or completely responsible to the federated body. Organizations within the federation remain primarily accountable to themselves and only in a limited way to the federation. Usually, actions proposed by a federation must be approved by the constituency groups. Because one of the major purposes of the federation is to harmonize and integrate different groups, controversial issues that might cause a breakup are often avoided.

If a collaborative organization is ongoing, then as it resolves one problem or issue it prepares to move on to the next. For example, suppose that organizations form a coalition to combat neighborhood crime. They decide that their first project will be to secure better street lighting for various neighborhoods. After succeeding with this first project, the group then is able to move on to other compelling issues, such as speedier police response.

Organizations may also form a consortium—a formal partnership to undertake joint activities or programs. The following are ways two or more organizations can coordinate their efforts:[29]

Joint planning

- ~ Planning coordinated delivery of services
- ~ Information sharing of resources or policies
- ~ Joint evaluation of program effectiveness
- ~ Joint program design

Example: The County Department of Human Services and the County Mental Health Board develop a coordinated effort to assist families with special mental health needs.

Administrative services

- ~ Central record keeping on clients seen in more than one organization
- ~ Centralized purchasing and use of equipment
- ~ Joint advertising
- ~ Sharing facilities and equipment

Example: Two separate agencies in the same building form an interagency committee to purchase supplies together, thus reducing their respective costs.

Service coordination

~ Joint outreach of clients
~ Common intake and diagnosis
~ Formal referral patterns
~ Follow-up with clients receiving common services
~ Combined transportation
~ Combined case conferences on families seen by different organizations
~ Case management to coordinate services by different agencies

Example: A children's cluster is formed consisting of the alcohol and drug addiction board, juvenile court, mental retardation and disabilities board, public schools, and youth services for the purpose of ensuring service for children who have multiple needs and for whom appropriate local services are not accessible. The organization develops individual service plans, ensures proper management, and arranges for shared funding for multiple-need children.

Personnel coordination

~ Colocation of staff in a commonly shared facility
~ Out-stationing of staff by one organization to that of another
~ Lend-lease of staff from one organization to function under the administration of another organization for a specified time
~ Joint training
~ Interagency staff teams
~ Compacts involving formal staff cooperative agreements, although no funds are exchanged

Example: An elementary school arranges for a mental health agency to colocate a staff member in the school. The counselor meets with students referred by teachers in a group counseling session and works with them to improve their school performance. The counselor is accountable to both the principal and a mental health agency supervisor.

Financial coordination

~ Joint fund raising
~ Purchase of service to provide a specified service in exchange for funds
~ Joint project funding

> Example: Three organizations in the local community related to day care, youth counseling, and vocational training sponsor a community event designed to publicize their services and raise money for their respective organizations.

The previous examples illustrate that the structural format of the coalition can vary depending on the nature of the task to be accomplished. Similarly, the structural format can be customized in relation to various participants. In some instances, leadership of the coalition will rotate over time from one organization to another, or various tasks may be rotated among members. One agency may be designated to take fiscal responsibility, another might be responsible for intake, and a third might be responsible for marketing the services of the coalition. Finally, an organization may be designated as the lead organization to ensure that services are completed, evaluated, and supported.[30]

Whatever the structural arrangement, collaborative alliances leverage resources to accomplish member agency goals. The synergy that is created by joining together with others results in a greater impact on the clients of the respective agencies.

NOTES

1. K. J. Blanchard, P. Carlos, & A. Randolph, *The 3 keys to empowerment* (San Francisco: Berrett-Koehler, 1999), pp. 103-104; R. Skidmore, The nature of dynamic teamship, in *Social work administration* (Needham Heights, MA: Allyn & Bacon, 1995), p. 169.

2. A. Seers, M. M. Petty, & J. F. Cashman, Team-member exchange under team & traditional management, *Group & Organizational Management, 20* (1995, March), p. 19.

3. H. A. Rosso, *Achieving excellence in fund raising* (San Francisco: Jossey-Bass, 1991); Alexander Hamilton Institute, *Making teams succeed at work* (Ramsey, NJ: Author, 1997), pp. 1-38; C. Joinson, Getting the best results from teams requires work on the teams themselves, *Human Resource Management, 44*(5) (1999, May), pp. 30-36.

4. J. R. Katzenbach & D. K. Smith, *The wisdom of teams* (New York: HarperCollins, 1993), p. 123.

5. M. H. McCormack, *Mark H. McCormack on managing* (West Hollywood, CA: Dove, 1996), p. 185.

6. Alexander Hamilton Institute, pp. 6-8.

7. B. Gummer, Go team go! The growing importance of teamwork in organizational life, *Administration in Social Work, 19*(4) (1995), pp. 93-94.

8. R. Wageman & E. A. Mannix, *Power & influence in organizations* (R. M. Kramer & M. A. Neale, Eds.) (Thousand Oaks, CA: Sage, 1998), pp. 270-271.

9. K. M. Eisenhardt, J. L. Kahwajy, & L. J. Bourgeois, III, How management teams can have a good fight, *Harvard Business Review* (1997, July/August), p. 77.

10. Alexander Hamilton Institute, p. 21.

11. Alexander Hamilton Institute, pp. 23-27.

12. K. M. Eisenhardt et al., pp. 77-85.

13. A. Seers et al., p. 37.

14. R. B. Campbell, *The process,* public address at Higbee's Annual Meeting, Cleveland, OH, May 1982.

15. D. C. Eadie, *Changing by design* (San Francisco: Jossey-Bass, 1997), p. 165.

16. D. C. Eadie, p. 167.

17. E. E. Lawler, *High involvement management* (San Francisco: Jossey-Bass, 1986), pp. 53-59.

18. P. W. Mattessich & B. R. Monsey, *Collaboration: What makes it work* (St. Paul, MN: Wilder Research, 1993), p. 7.

19. M. Winer & K. Roy, *Collaboration handbook* (St. Paul, MN: Amherst H. Wilder Foundation, 1997), p. 24.

20. J. Rothman, J. L. Erlich, & J. G. Teresa, *Promoting innovation and change in organizations and communities* (New York: Macmillan, 1976), p. 314.

21. R. Brody & M. D. Nair, *Macro practice: A generalist approach* (4th ed.) (Wheaton, IL: Gregory, 1998), p. 325.

22. R. Brody & M. D. Nair, p. 324.

23. R. Brody & M. D. Nair, p. 325.

24. M. Winer & K. Roy, pp. 88-89.

25. PricewaterhouseCoopers, Building high-performing strategic alliances, *Growing Your Business* (1999, July/August), p. 3.

26. M. Winer & K. Roy, pp. 99-100.

27. J. K. Butler, Jr., Behaviors, trust, & goal achievement in a win-win negotiating role play, *Group & Organizational Management, 20*(4) (1995, December), p. 499.

28. M. Winer & K. Roy, p. 25.

29. R. Brody & M. D. Nair, pp. 328-330; A. Lauffer, *Grantsmanship and fund raising* (Beverly Hills, CA: Sage, 1984), pp. 62-71.

30. M. Winer & K. Roy, pp. 102-104.

Chapter 16

WORKING WITH A BOARD OF TRUSTEES

An effectively managed human service organization requires a governing body that actively works with the executive director and management team to provide organizational stewardship. By working in a collaborative partnership, executive staff and board can achieve their common goals of providing an effective service for their community.

Two major problems can affect a true collaborative partnership between executive staff and board. These problems relate to possible confusion about the respective roles and responsibilities of staff and board. At one extreme, an executive may use the board of trustees to affirm decisions and policies that staff have predetermined. For example, staff may screen out important information, offer limited or no options for decision making, use board meetings only to report how well they are doing, and have the expectation that the board will not challenge or question policies or program. In this scenario, the chairperson is weak and malleable; trustees are passive and disengaged. When support must be marshalled during a special crisis, the board is incapable of action. Because of their disengagement, board financial support is limited.

At the other extreme, a board may become excessively involved in day-to-day operations, make decisions about hiring and firing staff, and become overly direct in telling staff how to administer programs. These kinds of interventions undermine professional staff and can result in a less effectively run organization. In some circumstances, extraordinary board intervention conveys serious warning signs that the board lacks sufficient confidence in professional decision making or the ability of the executive staff to carry out their functions properly. For example, if a board loses confidence in the executive's staff's ability to maintain a proper balance of income and expenses, then it is more likely to want to have a detailed accounting of expenditures. In this scenario, the executive and the board experience considerable tension—or the executive is reduced to an ineffectual administrator.

To achieve a high-level working relationship, executive and board need to understand clearly (a) the various roles that a board must fulfill, (b) the dynamic relationship between executive and board, and (c) ways to improve board functioning.

ROLES AND RESPONSIBILITIES OF A BOARD OF TRUSTEES

Determining the Organization's Mission and Goals

The board's fundamental concern is to ensure that the organization fulfills its mission. Although the staff may assist in writing and implementing the mission, it is the board that ultimately is responsible. As discussed in Chapter 3, the purpose of the mission is to articulate the organization's purpose. It should explain what makes the organization distinctive and provide a compelling rationale for financial support. In determining whether to take new directions or to discard programs, the board's responsibility is to make certain that the primary mission is foremost. Periodically (annually or biannually), the board should take time to review the mission to assess its adequacy and validity.[1]

Selecting the Executive Director

This process is undoubtedly one of the most important functions of a board. Conducting a good search process may take several months and may be a responsibility of a search committee, but the final choice rests with the board as a whole. As part of this process, the board would prepare a comprehensive job description, including clarity about the distinctive roles between the professional head and the volunteer chair of the board of trustees. Also, the board would need to delineate its expectations of the director and be clear that the executive has exclusive responsibility to select and supervise a management team without board interference.[2]

Providing Financial Oversight

The responsibility for submitting the organization's annual budget ultimately rests with the executive director. It is the board's responsibility, usually on the recommendation of its finance committee, to approve the budget and take responsibility for being fiscally responsible for the organization's clients. Monthly or at least quarterly reports should be submitted to the full board or its designated committee. In its oversight capacity, the board actively asks questions to ensure appropriate use of funds, payment of bills, and placement of fiscal policies. The board pays particular attention to audit reports and management letters to determine that the proper fiscal checks and balances are in place.[3] The board also monitors the organization's financial reserves and, where appropriate, develops an investment strategy.

Some boards permit the executive director to have considerable discretion in spending money without board approval. Having provided general guidelines for the expenditure of funds and having approved a budget, these boards encourage executive autonomy in financial decision making. Other boards place constraints on the executive by requiring that any expenditures more than a certain amount (e.g., $1,000) require board approval through cosignature of the board chairperson or treasurer. Usually, the larger the organization, the greater the executive discretion of expenditures. Also, boards may require that no check be written unless monies are available from the appropriate fund for that specific expense.

Supporting and Evaluating the Executive

Either the board as a whole or a designated committee is responsible for providing frequent and constructive feedback to the executive. Both the board and the executive should agree on the process under which an evaluation will occur. Properly done, the annual performance evaluation should be equally beneficial to the executive director and the board. It should be an opportunity not only for constructive criticism but also for praise for exceptional initiatives and performance. It can also be an opportunity for the executive to provide feedback to the board in regard to board performance that affects the progress of the organization. The board and executive accept the fact that their effectiveness is interdependent; neither can be assessed completely independently of the other.[4]

The performance evaluation process should be based on a mutually agreed-on job description and on objectives that the executive director is responsible for achieving. A useful approach is for the director to identify programmatic and administrative objectives at the beginning of each fiscal year that are approved by the board. At the beginning of the following fiscal year, the director provides a document that discusses the extent to which each of these objectives has or has not been achieved. For example, the executive might include the following (partial) objectives:

1. Update the computer system by establishing an office network.
2. Develop a new agency brochure.
3. Obtain two foundation grants of $30,000 each.
4. Increase the annual membership by 10%.

The extent to which these objectives are achieved—fully, partially, or not at all—would be reported to the board with an explanation as part of the executive's assessment process.

There is a tendency for boards not to conduct an annual evaluation either because they are reluctant to be put in a position of criticizing a well-regarded director or because conducting an evaluation takes more time than board members want to commit. It is in the interest of both the director and the organization, however, that the board be convinced to carry out this important responsibility.[5]

Assisting With Public Information

The board is responsible for building the organization's image in the community. This is a responsibility that may be shared with staff, as trustees interpret the agency's mission and explain its functions in both informal conversations and formal presentations. Trustees are truly ambassadors in interpreting the mission of the institution, defending it when it is under pressure and representing it to their constituencies.[6]

Making Organizational Planning Decisions

Board members must participate extensively in strategic planning so that they can assume ownership of plans and implement goals through the development of new resources. Their role in the planning process is to ask good questions, expect good answers, and serve as resources in their own individual areas of expertise. Of course, they cannot be full-time experts on programmatic or managerial issues, but they can provide objective judgments on the organization and assess the quality of the program goals.

In reviewing a program, the board can responsibly inquire into the following:

1. How do the costs of the program compare with its benefits?
2. Which programs are so central that they must be retained, and which are peripheral to accomplishing the organization's mission?
3. How can the organization reach more clients?
4. Are the programs adequately staffed?
5. Can the quality of the programs be improved?
6. What kind of resources will be necessary to sustain current programs or mount new ones?

In its role of making policy decisions, the trustees cannot be concerned with details of operations or in "micromanaging." They should be interested in results. Programs that depart from the organization's primary purpose or mission require close scrutiny. Board members help to determine whether the organization should be moving in new directions.

Policies involve three aspects in which the management staff and the board intersect. First, formulating the policy can involve a series of suggestions or recommendations and can be initiated by either the staff or the board. Second, policy determination usually resides with the board. Although staff may have input into board deliberations, the board, not the staff, ultimately determines policies. Third, policy implementation typically, although not always, is a responsibility of staff. When an organization lacks adequate staff, it may rely on trustees to carry out certain activities. It is usually useful for the board, working with the executive, to make clear who is responsible for implementing the decision within a given time frame.[7]

Developing Personnel Policies

It is the executive director's responsibility to hire, supervise, evaluate, make compensation decisions within the parameters set by the board, and (if necessary) terminate employees. The board is responsible for approving personnel policies such as wage scales, fringe benefits, vacation plans, and sick leave. The board also ensures that a staff grievance procedure is in place. Occasionally, a personnel committee of the board may provide a grievance process for an employee who has an unresolved dispute with the executive director and who seeks relief from some higher authority. Personnel practices should deal with this possibility.

Although the executive director has responsibility for hiring staff, he or she may wish to consult with the board before hiring those staff who may have direct connections with the board. For example, the hiring of a development director or a chief financial officer might benefit from board consultation. Sometimes, a board member will seek out the executive with a suggestion for hiring a friend or relative. Such efforts, if intended to put pressure on the executive director, should be discouraged by the chair of the board.

Conducting Fund Raising

Whether the board or the staff takes primary responsibility for fund raising depends mostly on the source of funding. If most of the organization's financial support is derived from foundation grants or state or federal subsidies, management staff will likely have major responsibility. In these circumstances, the board would serve in a supportive or oversight role.

If, however, the organization needs to rely on community support through annual campaigns, United Way funding, capital campaigns, or endowment funding, the board of trustees must provide leadership and carry most of the load, with staff serving in a supportive role. This active approach is needed because effective fund raising in the community is usually best implemented by peers in the community. If occasionally the organization must seek community support to supplement public or foundation grants, board members will be needed who can raise funds or who have links to those who can provide funding. Even if the bulk of the money is raised through public support, foundation grants, or the United Way, these funding entities will want assurances that the organization has a board of trustees that is well regarded and that shows evidence of genuine commitment to the organization.[8] Board members need to understand that each one of them must make an annual contribution to be able to manifest to outside funders the commitment of the board.

Ensuring Proper Legal and Financial Obligations

In certain circumstances, and depending on the particular laws of the state, trustees can be held legally accountable for actions of their nonprofit organization. Trustees have the legal responsibility to meet the purposes of the nonprofit in substantial ways. Many states have enacted legislation to protect trustees of nonprofit organizations. In circumstances in which a court determines that trustees did not act in good faith (and with the care an ordinary prudent person would exercise in similar circumstances), trustees can be held personally liable. For example, if trustees expend funds in excess of expected income and without proper cost controls, they could be sued.[9] Trustees must provide proper oversight to ensure that the organization complies with laws governing nonprofits.

Moreover, trustees must avoid conflicts of interest or being compensated beyond reimbursement for expenses as part of their board function. Conflicts of interest can occur when a trustee is involved in a transaction that provides some personal benefit. In addition, trustees are responsible for conducting the organization's efforts in such a way as to avoid harm to those who come in contact with the agency. Trustees are also obligated to ensure the personal safety—physical and emotional—of those who come into contact with the agency.

Trustees can be held accountable and taken to court for gross negligence; therefore, they must have directors' or officers' liability insurance. It is rare that a judgment will be rendered against a trustee, but insurance is necessary to defray the expense of defending lawsuits.[10]

The Dynamic Relationship Between the Board and Staff

Normally, the executive director is the principal staff person who interacts with the board of trustees. In ideal circumstances, the board and chief executive work closely together in determining directions and policies. The traditional formulation (i.e., the board enacts policy and the executive and staff carry it out) has given way to a more dynamic partnership requiring more flexible interactions between board and executive and even board and the staff. Also, occasionally the trustees will become engaged in operations because it makes sense to do so.[11] For example, if an organization plans to add an addition to its nursing home facility, board members may become involved in selecting architectural plans and working out loan arrangements because they may have the expertise to carry out these functions.

Just as the relationship between the executive and the board is becoming more dynamic, so too is the traditional approach of keeping staff at a distance from the board changing. Clearly, the executive will want certain appropriate staff to have a relationship with the board. For example, staff members responsible for fund raising may work with the board's development committee. Financial staff must work with the board's treasurer, and program staff will need to be in close communication with the board's program committee. When the organization undertakes a strategic plan review, staff members could be in a position to make significant contributions. Thus, although the board maintains ultimate policy, staff input is essential in helping the board make good decisions. This intermingling of staff and board can greatly reduce a "we-they" adversarial mentality.

To carry out the board's many functions, it will typically organize into committees. Although each organization will form its committee structure based on its own unique functions, the following are common:[12]

An *executive committee* includes the officers and the chairs from the other committees. It usually can take actions in emergencies or when the board does not meet, and it coordinates the work of other committees. A board of fewer than 15 people may not need an executive committee. The executive committee must be careful not to usurp the roles and decision making of the board because if this happens board involvement will wither away.

The *finance committee* reviews the organization's budget and provides financial oversight, usually on a monthly basis. It is advisable for the chair of this committee to be someone who is highly knowledgeable about accounting procedures and finances so that reports to the board are credible. It develops and regularly updates a long-range financial plan for the organization.

The *resource development committee* develops the financial resources of the organization. Its activities can include annual campaigns, fundraising events, and securing grants. For such vital activities, board members are especially recruited.

The *human resources committee,* sometimes referred to as the personnel committee, develops the personnel policies and also promotes staff development and training. It may occasionally handle grievances.

The *public information committee* promotes the agency through oversight on annual reports, newsletters, and other public information. It may also organize speakers for public functions and develop relationships with political figures at the local and state level.

The *committee on trustees,* sometimes known as a nominating committee, has primary responsibility for identifying and recruiting new trustees. This activity is not a one-time event but should be carried out year-round. In addition to cultivating new trustees, this committee develops an orientation package for new members, provides for mentors to new trustees, and encourages ongoing board education. It also develops a leadership succession plan. Finally, it assesses how well the board is functioning.

As stated previously, different organizations will establish ongoing committees unique to their needs. For example, a mental health board might establish an agency relations committee, or a neighborhood organization might create a board program committee. In addition to ongoing committees, boards establish strategic or ad hoc (time-limited) committees that focus on issues identified through the strategic planning process and require ongoing attention. Other special committees will occasionally be created to deal with specific, time-limited tasks.

Whether a committee is ongoing or ad hoc, it is usually helpful for the chair, in consultation with the executive director, to formulate a charge that will guide committee deliberations. This charge would state what the committee is expected to accomplish in the course of the year. For example, the committee on trustees may have as one of its charges the cultivating of 15 people, from which 5 would ultimately be selected to serve on the board. The finance committee might be charged with responding to concerns raised in the previous year's management letter regarding how finances are handled. Of course, in addition to the charges formulated by the chair, each committee may establish its own objectives that would be shared and agreed on by the board.

Depending on the organization, board committees can function with or without staff support. If the chair of the board and the executive determine that staff support is needed, the following functions would be appropriate:

- Give advice, information, and direction based on expertise (In giving their opinions, staff members do not assume the roles of committee members and do not manipulate the discussion.)
- Work with the board chair, executive director, and committee chair to formulate committee goals and objectives (The staff member may help formulate the charge to the committee.)

- Serve as a liaison to a committee and other parts of the organization, especially staff units
- Assist the committee chair in constructing the agenda that provides ample opportunity for committee discussion and decision making
- Take minutes of the meeting if volunteers are unable to do so
- Work with the committee chair to prepare committee reports

In summary, the staff liaisons work closely with the committee chair to ensure that the committee understands its function, has the correct information with which to make its decisions, and has a process that fosters full participation.

Improving the Functioning of Boards

A major criticism of nonprofit boards is that they tend to make low-level decisions. A board's contribution is meant to be strategic—the talented product of high-level achieving people who use their collective knowledge to address the major challenges facing the organization. Instead, board members often feel discouraged and underused. These high-powered people lose their energy as they focus on mundane issues such as what kind of carpeting should be selected for the new offices or what the new logo should look like. At board meetings, they listen to executive directors or staff drone on about what the staff have been doing the previous month. Trustees are relegated to approving committee reports that may be the result of intensive debate, and these same reports are bland and distilled by the time the trustees read them. Trustees become polite but bored and passive listeners.

Obvious problems can occur when a board is encouraged to be passive. First, a passive board tends to fall into a mode of neglecting organizational operations and finances and fails to properly manage and supervise activities. Periodically, the media report on members of a board of directors who have failed in their collective duty to govern and have abdicated their responsibility by delegating their obligation for oversight to the executive director.[13] Second, an inactive board cannot be expected to enthusiastically generate needed financial support. Finally, an inactive board will greatly underuse the rich talent and expertise that high-level members can provide.

A poorly functioning, passive board can be detected by the following list of symptoms:[14]

- Unprepared trustees who do not keep current on organizational developments

- Unwillingness of trustees to make decisions because of lack of participation
- Agenda set solely by the executive director
- Rubber stamping of the executive's recommendation without discussion
- Perpetuation of trustees over many years
- Inability to evaluate the executive
- Lack of clarification of the respective roles of board and staff

To change the role of a board from a passive, reactive one to one that is highly invested and empowered, the agency's executive director should[15]

1. Meet with the board chair on an ongoing basis to clarify roles and discuss joint or separate responsibilities. Clarifying their respective roles up front prevents later misunderstandings.
2. Work with the board chair to develop clear goals for each of the board's committees. If possible, these goals should be in writing. The executive director should ensure that each committee has developed a clear set of objectives of what it wants to (or needs to) accomplish in the following year.
3. Work with the board chair to facilitate board meetings. Obviously, it is improper for an executive director to run a board meeting or to dominate it. In a supportive role, the executive director can ensure that necessary materials are sent out before the meeting and work with the board executive to set the agenda. In some organizations, the executive or some other staff member (instead of the board secretary) takes minutes of meetings since this is a task that many volunteers do not relish.
4. Facilitate board committee functioning by providing staff assistance (where feasible). This assistance, of course, will depend on the availability of staff to help with meeting notices, preparation of agendas, taking minutes, and writing reports.
5. Work with the board to hold an annual retreat involving the management team and the board. The meeting should be used as an opportunity to review the strategic plan and discuss major initiatives. The executive should be responsive to the board's request to articulate key issues and strategic challenges that the organization faces. He or she should apprise the board of changes in the environment and of new opportunities or crises that require organizational adaptation.

6. Encourage the board to provide strong oversight, especially in relation to the budget. The executive should work with the board chair to specify a charge to each committee. Moreover, he or she should work with the board chair to ensure that the board committees are completing their tasks and meeting their deadlines.

7. Ensure a good code of regulations or set of bylaws, which will contain provisions for turnover of trustees, frequency of meetings, committee functions, and election of officers. In addition, the executive, working with the board chair, should compile a list of board policies that have been enacted throughout the years so that all board members become aware of board positions.

8. Assist the board chair in setting up a proper orientation for new board members. If possible, written material that covers the organization's history, programs, and finances should be prepared. As part of an ongoing orientation, the executive should arrange for board members to make contact with clients or to see program activities firsthand.

9. Keep a pool of potential candidates for the nominating committee (if requested).

10. Involve board members, where appropriate, in providing expertise in the area of their competence. For example, a trustee who is a public relations professional might assist an organization in its marketing strategies. An architect might give guidance to the building design. The executive must take time to become aware of each board member's commitment and interests so that he or she can be placed on appropriate assignments and committees.

11. Work with the board chair and resource development committee to enhance organizational resources. It is essential that the executive work in a partnership arrangement with various board members on fund-raising activities. These activities could include jointly developing a capital campaign, identifying and calling on potential contributors, and preparing proposals for funding.

12. Prepare reports for the board, including budget reports, program service data, and community developments. It is the executive's responsibility to shape this information so that the board can be in a better position to make decisions that are relevant and timely.

SUMMARY

Elements of a Well-Functioning Board

The following can serve as a checklist for whether a board is functioning properly:[16]

- Does the organization have a clearly defined process for selecting, recruiting, and orienting new board members?
- In the orientation of new board members, is supporting information (e.g., board manual) provided? Does this information contain the history of the organization, description of current programs, fiscal data, bylaws, committee assignments, trustee job descriptions, and a review of major board policies?
- Are the expectations of being a trustee, including a job description, available?
- Does the board have a process for evaluating board members' activities?
- Does the committee on trustees work throughout the year to identify and cultivate candidates for consideration?
- Does the organization provide for the resignation of trustees before their normal term due to poor attendance or lack of involvement?
- Are board meetings well organized and focused on priority issues? Are routine matters handled quickly, and is the major emphasis on strategic issues and trends?
- Do trustees work with the executives to develop annual plans with specific objectives?
- Does the board monitor agency progress in relation to goals and objectives?
- Does the board receive periodic reports about agency progress (and sufficient data) prior to meetings?
- Are minutes of meetings concise and distributed following each meeting?
- Does the board have active committees whose responsibilities are clearly articulated and that develop an annual work plan based on strategic planning with both specific assignments and a timetable?
- Does the board evaluate its own procedures, attendance, and participation?
- Do trustees recognize that they are expected to provide an annual financial gift to the best of their personal ability and to participate in a fund-raising activity?
- Does the board receive periodic financial reports that indicate whether the agency is meeting its budgetary targets? Does the board formally approve an annual operating budget and monitor the organization's ability to adhere to this budget?

Pursuing answers to these questions will result in an empowered board, which in turn will ensure a viable organization.

NOTES

1. R. T. Ingram, *Ten basic responsibilities of nonprofit boards* (Governance series booklet) (Washington, DC: National Center for Nonprofit Boards, 1995), pp. 1-7.

2. R. T. Ingram, pp. 1-7.

3. P. C. Brinkerhoff, *Financial empowerment* (Dillon, CO: Alpine Guild, 1996), pp. 178-190; A. Swanson, Who's in charge here? *Nonprofit World, 4*(4) (1986, July/August), p. 16.

4. R. T. Ingram, pp. 1-7; A. Swanson, p. 18.

5. D. C. Eadie, *Changing by design* (San Francisco: Jossey-Bass, 1997), pp. 92-93.

6. P. F. Drucker, *Managing the nonprofit organization* (New York: HarperCollins, 1990); A. Swanson, p. 16.

7. A. Swanson, pp. 16-18.

8. A. Swanson, pp. 15-16.

9. T. A. Croxton, Liability & risk management, in *Nonprofit boards* (J. E. Tropman & E. J. Tropman, Eds.) (Washington, DC: CWLA Press, 1999), pp. 225-233.

10. W. R. Joseph, Trustee liability a practical view, *Weston Hurd Fallon Paisley & Howley L.L.P.* (1998), pp. 1-4.

11. D. C. Eadie, p. 30; B. E. Taylor, R. P. Chait, & T. P. Holland, The new work of the nonprofit board, *Harvard Business Review, 74* (1996, September/October), p. 42.

12. J. E. Tropman & E. J. Tropman, pp. 96-99.

13. M. Gibelman, S. R. Gelman, & D. Pollack, The credibility of nonprofit boards: A view from the 1990s and beyond, *Administration in Social Work, 21*(2) (1997), pp. 21-40.

14. M. Gibelman et al., p. 32.

15. B. E. Taylor et al., pp. 36-46; D. C. Eadie, pp. 30, 72-95; R. D. Herman & R. D. Heimovics, The effective nonprofit executive: Leader of the board, *Nonprofit Management & Leadership, 1*(2) (1990, Winter), pp. 167-180.

16. S. P. Joyaux, *Strategic fund development* (Gaithersberg, MD: Aspen, 1997), pp. 85-89.

Part V Review

EFFECTIVE INTERACTIONS INTERNAL AND EXTERNAL

13. MAKING MEETINGS PRODUCTIVE

- Staff spend much time in meetings: Hold meetings when they are essential, and prepare for them carefully.
- Determine what you ultimately want to achieve from a meeting.
- Improve meetings by limiting group size, controlling overbearing members, helping the group decide on a common purpose, and avoiding excessive conformity.
- Ask appropriate questions to facilitate the flow of ideas.
- Use brainstorming, the nominal group technique, provocative questions, pro-con discussions, and analogies to stimulate a creative group process.
- Conduct a critical analysis of ideas following creative thinking.
- Record meetings by means of group action reports (abbreviated minutes).
- Strive to achieve a consensus that allows everyone to participate in a final decision.
- Clarify the meeting's purpose, prepare agendas, establish acceptable ground rules for discussion and decision making, distribute assignments, resolve conflicts, and summarize the discussions leading to closure.

14. COMMUNICATION AND CONFLICT

- Give special attention to communication when the organization is in transition.
- Be mindful of problems such as poor use of written documents, unwarranted staff meetings, misperceptions, and insensitivity to staff feelings.
- Communication can be conducted from the top down or bottom up through employee surveys, use of suggestion boxes, "open-door" appointments, and informal encounters.
- Communication is a two-way process. Make the effort to listen meaningfully to staff.
- To conduct persuasive communications, show how your proposed idea satisfies a need or adds value to your unit, the organization, clients you serve, or the community.

15. TEAM BUILDING AND COALITION BUILDING

- Increasingly, agencies organize work groups or teams to focus on special issues.
- Highly productive teams make allowances for individual styles while fostering a shared vision. The following qualities contribute to a successfully functioning team: open communication, interdependence, clear rules governing behavior, high commitment, a climate of generating and then challenging ideas, training, and trust.
- When interpersonal conflicts occur in teams, they must be immediately addressed. Expect and encourage ideas to be debated, however.
- Use ad hoc task forces to achieve specific assignments.
- Alliances among agencies require them to work together collaboratively in a mutually satisfying exchange.
- Certain factors facilitate agency collaboration. Alliances are most likely to occur when organizations share the same goals, discern that they can garner resources through mutual efforts, need to respond to their national organizations or funding bodies to collaborate, work out a satisfactory governance process, develop complementary roles, are satisfied in sharing power and prestige, readily communicate with each other, and, most important, develop trust in each other.
- Collaborative structures can take different forms, involving the coordination of planning, administration, services and personnel, financial management, and fund raising.

16. WORKING WITH A BOARD OF TRUSTEES

- Executives and trustees must be clear about their respective roles.
- Organizations are weakened if, on the one hand, boards are passive and reactive or, on the other hand, boards are overbearing and intrusive. Executives and their boards need to effect a true collaborative partnership.
- An effective board of trustees determines the organization's mission, selects the executive director, provides financial oversight, supports and evaluates the executive director, carries out a public information function, makes planning decisions, develops personnel policies, and conducts fund raising.
- The board of trustees ensures that the organization complies with all laws, and that trustees do not engage in conflict of interest activities.
- Boards normally parcel out the work of the organization to various standing or special committees. Staff may be assigned to assist these committees. The executive director works closely with the board chairperson to facilitate the work of the board.

Part VI

ENHANCING AGENCY SURVIVABILITY

In this part, you will learn how to

- Prepare a budget
- Monitor income and expenses
- Determine what managerial decisions need to be made based on variances
- Consider a variety of cost-cutting measures
- Develop specific approaches to resource development, including writing a case statement, preparing an annual fund drive, working on a capital campaign, soliciting major gifts, raising funds from corporations, and mounting a planned giving program
- Write an effective funding proposal
- Review criteria that funders use to evaluate proposals
- Search for funding in the governmental and private sectors
- Conduct a fund-raising event

Chapter 17

FINANCIAL MANAGEMENT

UNDERSTANDING THE BUDGETING PROCESS

No matter how well you perform your nonfinancial managerial responsibilities, if the "money is funny" and if the budget is off kilter, you are heading for trouble. In a turbulent economic environment, human service managers must develop a keen understanding of the budgeting process to manage their resources more effectively. This chapter will help you understand the budgeting process to gain managerial mastery of it. The primary purpose of this chapter is to focus on the expense aspect of the budget. Revenue considerations will be discussed in subsequent chapters.

A budget is a plan for anticipating income and expenses to achieve specific objectives within a certain time period. To mount an effective budgeting process, you need to consider past financial experiences, be aware of current information about organizational programs, and identify future assumptions. Budgets guide you in implementing policies, allow you to determine the organization's financial health, give direction to acquiring and using resources, anticipate operational expenses and the income needed to pay for these expenses, and offer ways to control spending to avoid deficits.[1]

The budgeting process should involve the perspectives, priorities, and needs of several constituencies: the board of trustees, staff, donors, clients, and public officials. Budgeting is also an ongoing process; data are continuously being gathered and analyzed, and projections and assumptions are continually being revised. New information can lead to budget changes.

Human service agencies use several different budgeting formats to reflect projected income and expenses. These formats are not mutually exclusive and can be combined in various ways. The most commonly used budget formats are line item, program, operating, incremental, and zero based. In addition, it is important to understand the categories capital budgeting and cash flow budgeting that will be discussed subsequently.

The *line-item budget* is widely used in both public and voluntary human service agencies because of its simplicity in reporting. It allows for managerial control over each income and expense. By itself, however, a line-item budget does not provide sufficient information about how various programs are faring in relation to the objectives they are intended to achieve.

The *program budget* identifies income and expenses related to the organization's services or programs. Examples of programs include counseling, day care services, foster home care, or employment services. The value of identifying these separate categories is that they can be linked to program objectives. For example, an objective of a foster care program is to reunite 50 children with their biological parents in a given year. If the total budget for foster care is $170,000, it is possible to link the cost of the service with the objective to be achieved. Both the agency and its funders can now be in a position to answer the question, "How does the expenditure of $170,000 to return 50 children to their biological families (an expenditure of $3,400 per child) compare with previous costs of this agency and with foster care programs of other agencies?"

The *support service budget* involves expenditures required to administer agency services or to conduct fund-raising activities for the entire organization. The *operating budget* is a composite of the program budget and the support services budget.

The budget model shown in Table 17.1 for the Hypothetical Agency, Inc. Operating Budget—Expenses reflects a combination of line-item, program, and operating budgets.

Most of the organization's expenses should be related to program services. The agency's funders will want assurance that the greater portion of the budget is devoted to programs rather than to supporting services. The operating budget of the Hypothetical Agency, Inc., totals $1,176,600. Of this amount, $358,700 is devoted to support services, which represents 30.5% of the total budget ($358,700 ÷ $1,176,600). To some outside funders, devoting 30.5% of the total budget for support services may seem excessive unless it can be justified that extraordinary fund-raising expenses are being incurred

Table 17.1

Hypothetical Agency, Inc., Operating Budget—Expenses 20XX

	Program Services ($)				*Support Services ($)*			
	Day Care	*Foster Home Care*	*Counseling*	*Total*	*Management and General*	*Fund Raising*	*Total*	*Total Agency ($)*
Salaries	121,000	73,300	210,000	404,300	120,300	87,400	207,700	612,000
Fringe benefits and payroll taxes	34,100	18,600	57,600	110,300	28,300	24,100	52,400	162,700
Total salaries and fringe benefits	155,100	91,900	267,600	514,600	148,600	111,500	260,100	774,700
Supplies	29,300	18,300	3,600	51,200	5,000	4,900	9,900	61,100
Telephone	19,600	2,900	3,200	25,700	4,000	10,100	14,100	39,800
Postage	7,000	3,700	9,700	20,400	2,100	21,200	23,300	43,700
Occupancy	47,100	17,800	25,700	90,600	4,400	3,500	7,900	98,500
Equipment	8,700	3,300	3,500	15,500	4,200	2,000	6,200	21,700
Printing	12,700	12,800	14,900	40,400	1,400	6,600	8,000	48,400
Travel	2,700	5,100	5,700	13,500	6,000	3,600	9,600	23,100
Conferences	1,400	2,400	7,100	10,900	11,000	1,900	12,900	23,800
Membership dues	700	400	0	1,100	0	0	0	1,100
Insurance	12,200	9,500	7,300	29,000	1,800	1,100	2,900	31,900
Depreciation	1,600	1,900	1,500	5,000	2,000	1,800	3,800	8,800
Total nonsalary	143,000	78,100	82,200	303,300	41,900	56,700	98,600	401,900
Total expenses	**298,100**	**170,000**	**349,800**	**817,900**	**190,500**	**168,200**	**358,700**	**1,176,600**

for future development of the agency. There is no magic formula for the "proper" balance between support services and program services; therefore, one may need to make a case to justify the amount being spent on administration and fund raising. Both management and board need to be especially focused on this issue.[2]

An *incremental budget* involves increasing (or, occasionally, decreasing) the various budget items by a small amount every year. Agencies with a fairly stable funding base typically practice incremental budgeting. For example, depending on inflationary or other circumstances, expenses such as salaries or utilities could increase (or decrease) 3% to 5% annually.

A *zero-based budget* (ZBB) is based on the premise that annually every program and every item starts from zero. It requires managers to assess whether each particular activity or unit should continue; they must justify each item rather than merely build incrementally on the previous year's budget. Perhaps a particular unit should be discontinued or at least modified in some major way. Nothing is taken for granted. If a program or item can be justified, however, it would be included in the budget.

ZBB can be quite threatening to both managers and staff because it involves critical challenges of the budget and possible radical change. Moreover, cost calculations based on detailed information must be made available, which is not always possible. Despite these problems, ZBB disciplines managers to explore more options than they would if they limited themselves to incremental budgeting. Many managers use a modified form of ZBB: Most of the budget is done on an incremental basis, but certain program expenses are identified for closer scrutiny and challenge.

Capital budgeting requires fairly large, one-time expenditures for items such as major building repairs, equipment purchases (e.g., computers or furniture replacement), or buying agency vehicles. Usually, capital projects entail making an expenditure in 1 year, although the income needed to support the expenditure may be set aside for several years either before or after the actual expenditure. For example, the organization might anticipate needing to set aside money for the next 3 years to pay for an expected major roof repair. The value of developing a capital budget is that it helps alert the organization to future major expenditures for which fund raising or long-term borrowing may be necessary.[3]

Cash flow budgeting records the difference in the amount of actual cash coming into the organization and the amount of cash expended. This kind of budgeting requires agencies to project the schedule of actual revenues and expenses and is essential to both the day-to-day and long-term fiscal health of an organization. When income lags behind expenditures, the agency could experience a crisis. For example, if an agency is not reimbursed for its contracted services for several months, it could experience a cash flow problem.[4] In these circumstances, staff salaries and other expenses need to be paid from some other sources while waiting for cash reimbursement. Negative cash flow occurs when a gap exists between projected disbursements and cash on hand. Conversely, when more cash is available than is needed, the agency experiences a positive cash flow. By having a cash flow projection, the agency has an early warning mechanism to prevent cash reserves from becoming too low to meet cash needs.

During times when negative cash flow is expected, the organization needs to generate more cash, reduce cash outlays, or both. A projection may show, for example, that a negative cash flow will exist in the 7th and 10th months of the year. Knowing this, the organization may delay purchases, move up the date for planned fund raising, consider short-term borrowing, or transfer funds from reserve accounts, if available. Of course, any decision will require careful planning to ensure that the organization is not getting deeper in debt or potentially violating its contractual obligations. Thus, it is an effective procedure to conduct cash flow projections for the following fiscal year and update monthly projections throughout the year.[5]

Understanding Types of Income and Expenses

Managers should understand the basic income and expense terms discussed in this section that are used in fiscal management.

Unrestricted funds are not restricted for any specific purpose. A funding source permits the agency to use its funding in whatever way it deems appropriate. Hence, the organization makes its own decision about how and when to expend unrestricted income. For example, it can allocate funding from one item to another. Money raised through the annual campaign or membership dues is classified in this "no strings attached" category.

Donor-restricted funding means that donors have specified restrictions on how the funding is to be used. For example, those setting aside money in their wills may restrict funding for certain purposes, such as a scholarship. Annual contributors may designate that their pledges be used for the purchase of an agency vehicle, the addition of a new office, or specific programs.

Contract or grant funding can restrict funding for a specific purpose. Those served by the program may have to meet eligibility requirements, expenses may be limited to those specifically identified in the budget proposal, and approvals may be required to modify the budget. The organization may be audited to ensure compliance with funding requirements. Sources may be public or private funding or agencies.

Income from service or business activities can involve fees charged for services rendered. Usually based on a sliding scale, the aggregated income is calculated based on the previous year's data. A tax adviser may be necessary to determine whether taxes need to be paid on income derived from products or services that may be deemed to be unrelated to the main purpose of the agency. *Asset-generated income* can come from existing assets, such as investments or rental income.

Endowment income could be unrestricted or restricted funding. These are funds set up by donors in a specific name—for example, the Smith Family Endowment Fund. Funds may be set up in several ways: (a) endowment in perpetuity—the principal of the fund may never be expended; (b) time-limited endowment—the principal may be expended after a given date or time period; and (c) general endowment—the principal may be expended either on passage of an event or on agency discretion (see Chapter 18).

Pledged income involves anticipated income during a period of time. People do not always pay what they have pledged, and therefore the budget will factor in a percentage of attrition and periodically be updated based on an evaluation of whether pledges can be collected.

Cash or in-kind matching funds can take the form of a challenge grant, which requires the agency to raise a certain amount to be eligible for additional outside funding. A noncash or in-kind matching involves goods, facilities, services, or equipment worth a specified amount to support a program. This matching share would be included in the budget, and the method of determining value would be indicated.

Fixed revenues are based on a constant income flow, commonly referred to as "hard money." Examples are regularly received income from United Way or interest from an endowment fund.

Variable revenues fluctuate from year to year. Revenues from special events, foundation grants, and annual pledges are considered variable or "soft money."[6]

Fixed expenses would be based on recurring expenditures—for example, staff salaries, fringe benefits, payroll taxes, and rent. *Variable expenses* fluctuate, depending on the increases or decreases in services used. Changes in supplies and travel could depend, for example, on the kind and frequency of programs the agency provides.

It is a good idea to have fixed expenses be funded by fixed-income sources, such as income from endowment or reasonably ensured government funding. Similarly, variable expenses should be matched with variable revenues.[7] For example, if staff are hired to fulfill a 2-year foundation grant, their salaries will be tied to the length of the grant. When the grant runs out and there are no other sources of funding, these staff may need to be discontinued.

Administrative overhead (indirect costs) is all expenses connected to operating expenses that involve more than one program within the organization. Examples include salaries for senior management, shared facilities, central accounting, and use of common conference rooms. Sometimes, administrative overhead and other shared costs are allocated on a predetermined basis to specific programs. This produces a budget that accurately reflects the full costs of the agency. If a particular program is eliminated, the administrative or other shared costs must either be reallocated or reduced. Funders may be more inclined to support overhead costs of a program if the budget clearly reflects that these costs are an essential part of the proposed program.

It is important to develop a rational and justifiable written costs allocation plan. A simplified method of allocating operating costs uses a percentage share of the total budget or the total salary budget. For example, if the total budget is $2 million, a 10% overhead cost would be $200,000. This $200,000 could be spread across all items in the budget or, as illustrated in Table 17.1, the operating budget can be identified as a separate category.[8]

Indirect costs include expenditures that are shared by various programs' cost centers in an agency, such as costs incurred for the use of utilities and supplies, telephone, and photocopying. When it is not possible to keep track of individual staff expenses without imposing excessive monitoring, it is simpler to divide these expenses among the various staff members. For example, if the telephone bill is $600, it would be divided evenly among four staff in different programs for $150 each. Similarly, the costs of supplies would be divided evenly among the four staff as with the photocopying costs.[9]

To obtain a more accurate assessment of the costs of a particular program, actual monitoring would occur so that specific telephone costs, photocopying costs, and use of supplies would be tracked and attributed to the particular cost center. In this case, the costs would be a direct cost rather than an indirect cost. Certain general costs, such as the cost of rent, a portion of the administrator's salary, and a portion of the accounting and marketing costs, would be categorized under general administration expenses. Hence, the designation of whether costs are to be considered direct or indirect is based mostly on the agency's ability to keep track of actual program costs.

CONDUCTING THE BUDGETING PROCESS

Preparing an Organization-Wide Budget

Organizations with multiple programs require an organization-wide budget. This budget involves all income and expenses needed for the following year, including the cost for employees, programs, facilities, and all other elements necessary to carry out the organization's activities.

The size and the complexity of an organization will determine the extent to which the budget resembles a pyramid with each level representing a budgeting unit or cost center. For example, the lowest level might involve all the programs of the agency. The second level might involve the department budgets of which they are a part, and finally the organization-wide budget can be at the top of the pyramid. Each agency will determine the number of cost centers (i.e., primary fiscal units) for which it wants to keep track. Each of these self-contained cost centers would have an income and expense budget.

To establish an organization-wide budget, the steps discussed in the following sections need to be considered.

Step 1: Set Organizational Objectives

The fundamental purpose of an overall budget is to help the organization achieve its goals and objectives. The budget is a means to an end, not an end in itself. Hence, the organization must first determine what it wants to accomplish and then build a budget to help achieve its objectives. See chapter 3 on setting organizational goals and objectives.

Step 2: Establish Organizational Budgeting Policies and Procedures

Prior to setting income and expense targets, it is important to establish responsibilities and timetables in a budgeting schedule. Determine who will be responsible for collecting data on income and expenses. Also discuss with the board of trustees or public officials what your overall budgeting parameters are going to be. Develop guidelines about staff expansions or reductions, make estimates regarding inflation, and anticipate certain organization-wide extraordinary expenses.

You would also determine your fiscal year. Many organizations select a fiscal year that coincides with the receipt of major funding. For example, if major funding is from the federal government, the fiscal year might be from October through September. If the organization provides most of its programming during a certain part of the year, it may select a fiscal year that ends after its busiest season. For example, an agency providing day care services that end in June might select a fiscal year that begins on July 1.

Step 3: Set Annual Income and Expense Targets for the Entire Organization

This initial calculation provides the units with an advance understanding of income that is either available or can be expected to be generated for the following year. The projected expenses give guidance to the units of the expense constraints within which they must operate.

Step 4: Each Unit Establishes Draft Budgets That Indicate Its Priorities

Reflecting an incremental budgeting process, some organizations require departmental units to prepare three variations of cost center budgets for review. Draft Budget A reflects no changes from the previous year's budget. (A budget total that is required to be the same from one year to the next, however, actually may have reductions in some items to account for automatic inflationary increases in other items.) Draft Budget B represents an incremental increase (e.g., 5% increase). Draft Budget C represents a percentage decrease (e.g., 5% decrease). This review of options allows managers to assess the consequences of budget variations. Unit managers would relate their budget to program goals and objectives and also supply a rationale for major changes in the projected budget compared to the current year's budget. For example, the program manager would justify significant salary changes or needed changes in supplies, travel, and printing. Detailed information justifying projected costs for any new or expanded programs or positions must be provided. Hence, unit managers must do a considerable amount of research to justify expenses in their program budget.

Step 5: Management Team Proposes a Budget for Board Approval

When all the program draft budgets are received, the finance staff prepares a summary for management staff so that they will have an idea of the resources needed for the total budget. The chief executive officer would then determine if the draft budgets must be trimmed prior to sending the budget to the board or public officials for approval. These recommendations are based on calculations of income and expenses, aggregated for each unit. If the organization is a nonprofit, the board's finance committee will carefully scrutinize this projected budget. In the public sector, the budget office will examine the agency's budget prior to review by the top public official. Where conflicts exist, the management team works with the finance committee to resolve them. Assumptions about expected incomes and expenses are communicated. In the voluntary sector, the board of trustees approves the final budget; in the public sector, elected public officials are the ultimate decision makers.

Developing Program and Unit Budgets

In some agencies, financial statements are regarded as closely guarded secrets, with staff often being told that a request cannot be honored because "it's not in the budget." Preparing a program budget (see Step 4) is so fundamental to the overall budgeting process that this will be reviewed in more detail. Other organizations, however, place great emphasis on "bottom-up" budgeting. The essence of bottom-up budgeting is that staff nearest to providing direct services can and should have more budgeting involvement, which is in contrast to the concept that top management always knows best.[10]

Four components are essential for bottom-up budgeting to work:

1. Train staff to read financial statements. They may be puzzled at first about certain elements, but they can learn easily how the agency is working to balance its budget and remain financially viable.
2. Give staff responsibility to develop budgets and the authority to spend them. This assumes that people who provide services know what they need to do their jobs. Staff will feel more involved, experience ownership of their work, and be motivated to achieve their objectives. Over time, staff who might feel overwhelmed initially by the responsibility of proposing and managing a budget will grow in their confidence to make the right decisions.

~ Example: In a children's institution, staff assigned to cottages are given budget responsibility for items such as food, allowances, monthly personal need shopping, weekend recreational activity money, clothing, and birthday celebrations. Over time, they begin to determine where they are overspending on certain items, which prevents them from spending as much as they would like on other items. They have to make difficult decisions about how they are going to adjust for shortfalls in various categories.

3. Provide risk and reward based on successful accomplishment (or failure). When staff spend less than the budget or bring in more income than was budgeted, they get to use the additional net income for purposes they designate. Drawing from the previous example from a children's institution, net savings can be used for a special event such as an amusement park outing. If, however, staff spend more than their budgeted expenses for a given month, they would have to make alterations in their plans for the following month. They must then explain their decisions and may have to carry forward the deficit to the next year, resulting in a reduction for the following year. Providing this risk and reward encourages staff to make the extra effort to save money or bring in new income.
4. Provide for regular monitoring, and share information openly. Staff need to be informed about how they are doing. Where there are major deviations from the agreed-on budget, determine with staff why this is the case and what can be done about it.

The previous suggestions on involving staff in bottom-up budget planning can be tried on an experimental basis with certain programs and, if successful, be implemented in other parts of the organization. Identify those units that are most likely to succeed before moving to other areas.

Relating the Unit's Budget to Its Work Plan and Objectives

Whether organization-wide or related to a particular unit, a budget is a means by which the organization accomplishes its objectives, and therefore there must be a clear connection between the budget and a work plan. Recall Chapter 4 on implementing objectives and the timeline chart on foster care recruitment (see Figure 4.2). In specifying the details of activities that must be performed to achieve foster care placements, the manager and his or her staff need to document expenses that may be involved, such as personnel, supplies, transportation, and equipment.

It is a good idea to provide a budget justification or documentation of costs, especially if the cost item is unusually large or may be open to question. For example, if travel expenses are high, you might need to indicate how staff mileage was derived and why out-of-town trips are essential to achieve program objectives. Personnel costs should be based on the rates that other agencies are paying for staff in the same positions. This can be determined in consultation with other agencies, through the local governmental funding body, or through the local United Way.

Prior to estimating budget expenses, the manager would determine various policy decisions affecting these expenses. Is there to be an increase in salary for all positions or designated ones? Will overtime be permitted? Will part-time staff be hired? Should all positions in a new program be budgeted for the entire year or just part of the year? Clarifying policy decisions and budget assumptions will make the budgetary process more efficient.

Projecting fringe benefits requires review of applicable state and local laws affecting minimum benefits. Use government publications to identify the employer's share of social security, Medicare, and unemployment insurance. Insurance carriers can provide estimated costs of health, life, and worker's compensation insurance.

Estimating other operating costs involves review of leases and contracts, estimated price changes in services and supplies, and estimated annual rate of inflation. If significant cost increases are projected (e.g., printing costs or travel expenses), obtain specific estimated increases. If a significant expansion is expected in a particular program, estimate the costs involved in that expansion. Prepare an annual summary of major changes.

In developing the budget, managers must pay attention to pricing services to ensure proper reimbursement for actual costs. Because funders may not reimburse for overhead expenditures and instead only reimburse for direct costs related to the project, you may find that you are actually underpricing your services. If you have no other means of subsidizing the service, then you may want to decline the project.[11]

For example, a counseling service agency is offered the opportunity to provide counseling services to severely disturbed substance-abusing youth. Each adolescent is to receive three intensive counseling sessions per week, which the agency estimates will cost $150 ($120 direct costs + $30 indirect costs). The contracting agency, however, is able to provide only $100 per adolescent per week, which is $20 less than the direct costs and $30 less than the indirect costs. Although the counseling agency wants to provide the service, it decides not to do so because of the discrepancy between what it needs to be paid for the cost of service and what the government is willing to reimburse. It does not have sufficient funds from other charitable contributions to make up for the shortfall.

USING THE BUDGET AS A MANAGEMENT TOOL

Monitoring and Modifying Budgets

The best way to monitor a budget is to systematically compare the projected organization managers' budgets to actual financial reports. You must identify income shortfalls, expense overruns, or operational problems that will require corrective action. By receiving reports on a monthly basis, you can focus on discrepancies or variances that invite closer scrutiny. If these variances are identified early enough, mild corrections, such as postponing filling a vacant position, deferring nonessential purchases, or searching for new sources of revenues, may be possible. If, however, the variance is very large or discovered late in the year, more severe action may be required, such as reducing staff.[12] It is extremely important that the organization take action immediately when major variances between budgeted income or expenses are discovered. Most problems worsen over time, and delays can lead to quite serious deficits and potential difficulties with funders. (See the discussion at the end of the chapter on cost reductions.)

During the year, as you obtain new expenses and income information, you should revise your budget estimates. For example, if an anticipated program is not funded, then the income and expenses connected with that program would be eliminated from the budget. Similarly, if an unanticipated new program is acquired during the year, then the revised budget would contain these new income and expenses. The organization should determine in advance how programs are to be modified and who has the approving authority.

Managers need to guard against two dangers in reviewing the budget on a monthly or quarterly basis. The first is giving equal attention to all items no matter how small the variances, which can be an overwhelming task. The second is not paying sufficient attention to the most important variances requiring managerial attention. The best way to manage a budget review is to conduct a variance analysis that helps you determine which variances require special focus of attention. If you develop a percentage figure that indicates the degree of fluctuation you can tolerate, then reviewing cash income and expense items need only vary from that percentage figure for you to take corrective action.[13] Using Excel or another spreadsheet program will assist in predetermining threshold percentages or dollar amounts requiring possible corrective action.

Table 17.2 provides the Hypothetical Agency, Inc., Management Income/Expense Report for the month ended March 31, 20XX. This report also provides information on the quarter (year-to-date [YTD]) January 1 to March 31, 20XX. For both the month and YTD, a variance column indicates the difference between the actual budget and budgeted amounts. The percentage variance reflects the degree to which the budgeted amounts differ from the actual amounts. Note that a favorable variance for income reflects income received in excess of the budget. A favorable variance for expenses reflects expenses incurred below budget. For purposes of this example, the monthly budget is approximately 1/12 the annual budget, and the quarterly budget is approximately 3/12 the annual budget. In the real world, income and expense streams would be budgeted based on the best available information rather than on a mathematical formula. For example, printing expenses may be higher in certain months because of special printing costs, and these months would be budgeted accordingly.

In Table 17.2 under the income category, United Way funds are being received by the agency as projected, and government funding is actually showing a favorable variance. Although fees are down by 5.13% in March, they are only down by 1.37% for YTD. Of greater concern is the fact that both foun-should alert management that more effort may be needed to secure grants, and an aggressive campaign needs to be mounted regarding contributions.

For expenses, several line items do not require special attention because either the variance is favorable (i.e., the expenses incurred are below budget) or, if there is a negative percentage variance, the dollar amount is low (e.g., postage, equipment, printing, membership dues, insurance, and depreciation). Management can quickly determine which items do not require attention so that they can spend more time analyzing those items that are unfavorably out of line with expectations.

Table 17.2
Hypothetical Agency, Inc. Management Income/Expense Report, Month Ended March 31, 20XX

	Monthly				Quarterly				
			Variance				Variance		
Line Item	*Monthly Actual ($)*	*Monthly Budget ($)*	*Favorable ($)*	*Unfavorable (%)*	*YTD Actual ($)*	*YTD Budget ($)*	*Favorable ($)*	*Unfavorable (%)*	*Annual Budget ($)*
Income									
United Way	12,000	12,000	0	0.00	36,000	36,000	0	0.00	144,000
Government funding	50,000	43,000	7,000	16.28	136,200	129,000	7,200	5.58	516,000
Foundation grants	3,500	12,500	(9,000)	(72.00)	36,000	37,500	(1,500)	(4.00)	150,000
Contributions	3,400	11,300	(7,900)	(69.91)	14,800	34,000	(19,200)	(56.47)	136,000
Fees	18,500	19,500	(1,000)	(5.13)	57,700	58,500	(800)	(1.37)	234,000
Total income	**87,400**	**98,300**	**(10,900)**	**(11.09)**	**280,700**	**295,000**	**(14,300)**	**(4.85)**	**1,118,0000**
Expenses									
Salaries	52,500	51,000	(1,500)	(2.94)	187,500	153,000	(34,500)	(22.55)	612,000
Fringe benefits and payroll taxes	14,900	13,600	(1,300)	(9.56)	44,900	40,700	4,200	10.32	162,700
Total salary expense	67,400	64,600	(2,800)	(4.33)	232,400	193,700	(38,700)	(19.98)	774,700
Supplies	4,000	5,100	1,100	21.57	25,000	15,300	(9,700)	(63.40)	61,100
Telephone	4,300	3,300	(1,000)	(30.30)	9,900	10,000	100	1.00	40,100
Postage	3,700	3,600	(100)	(2.78)	10,000	10,900	900	8.26	43,700
Occupancy	9,900	8,200	(1,700)	(20.73)	30,300	24,600	(5,700)	(23.17)	98,500
Equipment	1,000	1,800	800	44.44	5,400	5,400	0	0.00	21,400
Printing	5,200	4,000	(1,200)	(30.00)	10,000	12,100	2,100	17.36	48,400
Travel	2,800	1,900	(900)	(47.37)	8,400	5,800	(2,600)	(44.83)	23,100
Conferences	2,100	2,000	(100)	(5.00)	5,700	5,900	200	3.39	23,800
Membership dues	100	100	0	0.00	600	300	(300)	(100.00)	1,100
Insurance	2,700	2,700	0	0.00	8,200	8,000	(200)	(2.50)	31,900
Depreciation	700	700	0	0.00	2,200	2,200	0	0.00	8,800
Total nonsalary	36,500	33,400	(3,100)	(9.28)	115,700	100,500	(15,200)	(15.12)	401,900
Total expenses	**103,900**	**98,000**	**(5,900)**	**(6.02)**	**348,100**	**294,200**	**(53,900)**	**(18.32)**	**1,176,600**
Excess (deficiency) income over (under) expenses	(16,500)	300	(16,800)		(67,400)	800	(68,200)		3,400

NOTE: Parentheses indicate a negative number or percentage.

Managers should be alerted to specific items in this hypothetical budget. Although supplies is under budget for the month, it is considerably over budget for YTD and will require ongoing attention. Salaries and fringe benefits are only 4.33% over budget for the month, but for YTD they are almost 20% over budget. This item should be of serious concern because of both the unfavorable percentage variance and the relatively high unfavorable dollar amount. Telephone for the month is considerably over budget and should require special attention even though YTD is on target. This may indicate the beginning of a negative trend. Occupancy costs are over budget for both the month and YTD and should alert management that this is a problem that requires action. Staff travel is 47% over budget for the month and 44% over budget for the first quarter, indicating that either the allocation to this line item has to be modified considerably or travel limitations need to be put into place.

In determining which items should require special attention, it may be desirable to establish certain threshold percentages, such as 5% or 10%, which would alert management and a board finance oversight committee that the budget is heading for trouble. Management could also identify certain dollar amounts (e.g., unfavorable variances that are higher than $1,000). Whether using percentages or dollar amounts, managers need to establish thresholds that require exploration, decision making, and corrective action.

In some instances, there may be good reasons for unfavorable variances. As mentioned previously, certain costs may be unusually high and have to do with the timing and flow of program activities. A conference may be held during a particular month that may put pressure on the travel budget, but, if possible, this strain should be anticipated in the budget. Backup work sheets for each month should allow managers to calculate more precisely when unusual expenses or revenues are expected.

Although there may be good explanations for the reasons why income and expenses are worse than expected, it may also be that the agency is hemorrhaging and that management must take steps to reduce expenses or significantly increase income. At the very least, questions must be asked, and corrective action must be considered early in the fiscal year to avoid more severe measures later on in the year. For example, it may be painful to lay off one staff member at the beginning of the year when it is apparent that salary costs are exceeding budget. If a tough decision is not made then, however, a more difficult decision will have to be made later to lay off two or three employees because of budget overruns. The advantage of having this income expense report is that it provides an early warning of a problem that can become much more serious.

It is a good idea for managers to complete a variance report for their board of trustees' review or for review by public officials that would explain why variances are occurring and what steps the manager is planning to take to deal with them. Such a report will give funders confidence that management is in control of the budget.

Because the budget represents an understanding between the agency's administration and its funders, board, or public officials to whom it is accountable, managers are obligated to work to keep the budget in balance. Managers get into trouble because, in their quest to meet the needs of their clients, they develop an overly optimistic attitude that somehow their board or the public officials will find the money to meet necessary expenses. Certainly, hope and optimism have a place in the budgeting process, but if these are carried too far managers can develop a reputation for being irresponsible.

Although it is essential to strive for a balanced budget, it is also important to recognize that the budget should have some flexibility. After all, the budget is based on yearly estimates, which in turn are based on certain assumptions about inflation and other information that is available at the time the budget is prepared. During the course of the year, you may need to revise the budget. For example, you obtain an unexpected grant, which also requires budgeting new expenses. Be prepared to revise the budget as circumstances change. Using Excel or other spreadsheet software makes it easy to make budget adjustments on individual items that will then alter total amounts.

FIFTY CONSIDERATIONS FOR REDUCING COSTS

One of the most demanding and challenging responsibilities a manager faces is determining how to reduce costs to bring budget expenses in line with anticipated income. To reduce costs, the following steps can be taken:[14]

1. Form a cost-cutting team that will examine the options contained in this section and generate additional ideas. The team may be able to develop enough austerity so that you can avoid more drastic measures—or it may not, in which case your proposal to cut staff may be understandable.

2. Reward staff for cost-saving ideas. Staff are a good source for ways to save money. A $25 reward to a staff member for suggesting ways to recycle paper, for example, could reduce hundreds of dollars in paper costs.

3. Postpone filling new or vacant positions. If cuts require reducing current staff, anticipate expenses connected with terminating positions—for example, unemployment compensation, severance pay, or continuation of fringe benefits for a specified period. Also be certain that by reducing staff the organization is able to meet its obligations.

4. Examine whether needed services such as payroll preparation or public information materials can be contracted with an outside vendor (called outsourcing) instead of hiring additional staff.

5. Eliminating positions can provide a quick fix to balancing a budget. Referred to euphemistically as "downsizing" or "organizational restructuring," the disadvantage is that scaling back employees can create more work for those remaining, which contributes to stress, resentment, and poor-quality work. Downsizing should be related to those individuals and those units of the organization that are least productive. It is possible that you could be both downsizing and "upsizing" simultaneously. It may be difficult, but nevertheless necessary, that as you lay off people in one section you may need to expand other, more productive units of the organization.[15]

6. Use contract employees or consultants for specific projects. Working with a consultant during the period of a specific project can help to match project and staffing needs. This may eliminate the need to reduce staff once a project is completed. Be aware, however, of the possible "employee versus independent contractor" issues for employment taxes.

7. Request staff to consider working part-time (especially during off-season periods such as summer months). Some organizations have instituted voluntarily sharing positions—that is, two full-time staff agreeing to cut their work time in half.

8. Delay starting new activities or expanding existing ones, such as buying new equipment. Defer or eliminate low-priority purchase programs. Prioritize their requested purchases. Those designated low priority would either be postponed or not included in the budget.[16]

9. Reduce services and programs. For example, instead of providing individual counseling to 400 clients in a substance abuse reduction program, you could

serve 220 and provide group counseling for the others. Be aware, however, that you may be shortchanging your clients.

10. Delay salary increases or reduce employee benefits. Personnel costs, including salaries and benefits, are usually the largest items in the budget (as much as 70-80%) and therefore are an understandable target for cost cutting. The disadvantage is that these measures can have serious effects on the morale of the organization and could cause undesired staff turnover.

11. Reducing costs related to fee-for-service contracts may also reduce the total amount of reimbursement an organization is eligible to receive. Carefully review contracts and grant agreements before cutting costs.

12. Explore the advantage or disadvantage of leasing rather than purchasing equipment such as a copying machine. In the long term, you may pay more, but leasing may help with cash flow and provide short-term budget relief.

13. Determine whether there are ways that departments can share resources. For example, can support staff be shared? Can the copying machine be shared? Can the number of conference rooms be reduced as different units coordinate their use?

14. Create an in-house printing operation to produce stationery, newsletters, and other printed materials.

15. Obtain bids to produce competitive pricing on purchases, such as equipment, supplies, and other work-related materials. It is especially important to initiate a bidding process for vendors with whom you have been doing business for a long time. They may be willing to lower their price when they experience competition.[17]

16. Inquire about a discount. Ask your vendors if they provide discounts to nonprofit agencies. Also, request whether a discount might be provided on guaranteed purchases over an extended period of time. For example, your printer might quote a volume price for all stationary, newsletters, and forms that you might need for the next 2 years. Also, inquire whether your vendor could provide a discount when you pay with cash up front. Check with your phone company to see if it gives a discount to nonprofit organizations.

17. Take advantage of "economies of scale" by making bulk purchases. Bundling purchases, currently made separately, could result in lower prices. It may be possible to join with other agencies in contracting for a bulk purchase arrangement. Be aware, however, that a large amount of supplies can disappear quickly unless you have proper controls on distribution. Inquire

if there are any purchasing "co-ops" in your area. Some co-ops offer purchase opportunities for medical supplies and capital items as well as general items, such as office supplies and paper disposables.

18. Give staff responsibility for site-based decision making. Staff responsible for department and program budgets can be more accountable for expenditures.
19. Use ZBB to determine whether programs should continue based on their demonstrated value and their contribution to the mission and goals of the organization. As discussed previously, ZBB requires you to justify expenses each year rather than build on last year's budget. The drawback of this approach is that it is extremely time-consuming and can create considerable anxiety, especially when related to popular programs that are difficult to justify fiscally.
20. Seek donated items, such as furniture and equipment. Companies that are moving their offices are a good source of usable furniture and equipment.
21. Purchase items or services at the right time of year. For example, winter items can be purchased in early spring for the following winter.
22. Change the fiscal year from January-December to October-September to purchase auditing services at a reduced rate because this is an off time for auditing organizations.
23. Use volunteers to provide services, perform clerical tasks, and assist in running programs. Companies sometimes "lend-lease" their staff for a specific time period or a specific purpose. For example, a company might release its controller to assist your bookkeeping department in setting up a computerized accounting system. Many attorneys, business people, accountants, and carpenters will donate their time to nonprofits. Also check with local universities that offer course credits for service experience.
24. Check in your community whether the local criminal justice system can provide "volunteer" assistance. Instead of serving time in jail, persons convicted of nonviolent crimes have the option of providing community service. Services range from carpentry to computer programming and maintenance work. Also consider involving Welfare to Work participants and senior citizens participating in retraining programs.
25. Negotiate contracts carefully to determine whether there are any hidden costs. For example, foundation grants may not sufficiently cover administrative costs or overhead. A government contract might require financial reporting and have audit requirements. Preparing reports will require someone's

time; therefore, assess whether this time can be fiscally justified and be included in the grant request.

26. Review personnel policies to ensure compliance with legal requirements, and train staff to follow these policies with no exceptions. A wrongful termination or harassment judgment can be extremely expensive (see Chapter 8).

27. Hire staff carefully. This admonition is especially important when supervisors are tempted to hire staff out of desperation to fill a position. A mismatch between the person and the job can be very costly in the long run (see Chapter 7).

28. Reduce staff turnover. It is an expensive hidden cost because you have to devote time to hiring new staff and training them. Conduct exit interviews with staff to determine why they are leaving. It may be more cost efficient to increase salaries and benefits to stop employees from moving to more competitive agencies.

29. Invest cash in short-term instruments, such as certificates of deposit, an interest-bearing checking account, or a savings account that is linked to a checking account. Many banks will offer special interest-bearing accounts to not-for-profit organizations that are not available to for-profit organizations.

30. Set up a system to track all equipment and building usage. Examine whether moving to a smaller set of offices can reduce expenses. Sharing facilities such as conference rooms with other agencies may be cost-effective. You may need to consider the cost of breaking leases or renegotiating for space compared to the cost of a move.

31. Review current staff positions and assignments to determine whether all activities are essential, whether some assignments conducted by a highly paid employee can be delegated to a lesser paid staff member, or whether work can be performed by a part-time employee.

32. Review personnel practices to reduce carryover of unused vacation or sick leave time. Many agencies require staff to take all or most of their vacation each year and set an upper limit on accrued sick leave.

33. Consider offering staff an improvement in their benefits (e.g., time off and health, dental, and life insurance) in lieu of cost of living pay increases. This idea will require considerable dialogue with staff.

34. Review unemployment compensation claims for those employees who quit. Your state unemployment insurance office will request an explanation, which you should provide so that if there is any question about your former employee's eligibility this statement can be considered.

35. Explore the use of tax-deferred annuities and flexible spending accounts ("Section 125 plan") that allow the organization to reduce taxes while still providing (or even increasing) benefits. Due to the complexities involved, check with an expert.

36. Encourage employees to opt out of benefits when their spouses already have medical and dental benefits that could cover them. Offer incentives, such as cash or more vacation days.

37. Ask the landlord for a rent deduction by paying the rent in full but then requesting the landlord donate a portion of it. This exchange preserves the landlord's ability to show the property at its true market value based on rents collected and simultaneously provides your organization with unrestricted funding.

38. Consolidate your office space, and sublet unused space to a compatible group.

39. Negotiate free use of space for meetings and events. Sometimes, banks, hotels, and corporations offer conference rooms for nonprofit meetings and special events.

40. Arrange to have an organizational supporter purchase equipment and then have it leased to your organization through an accounting method called "asset conversion." The supporter can depreciate the equipment and take a tax deduction, and the cost of leasing to the organization will be less than the full cost of the equipment. At the end of the designated period, the organization can purchase the equipment at a nominal cost. Check with a tax adviser to determine compliance with tax laws.

41. Regarding your travel budget, determine whether hotels offer a discount. Some hotel chains offer a government discount; inquire whether they would provide a special discount for a nonprofit organization. Use Internet sites to identify low-cost hotels and airlines. Limit staff attendance only to trips that can truly add value to achieving your mission.

42. Reimburse board members for travel, especially to an out-of-town meeting, with the expectation that the members can donate the money and obtain a tax write-off.

43. Regarding insurance, negotiate a fee that is limited to approximately 15%, and select an agent that works with nonprofits. Consider using the Nonprofits Insurance Alliance (*http://www.niac.org*).

44. Strongly encourage the board of directors to authorize purchase of officers' and directors' insurance, which will pay for the cost of defending a lawsuit and also the cost of any settlement.

45. Use e-mail instead of long-distance phone calls or faxes. With only a small monthly access fee, e-mail communications are free. E-mail can also be used to obtain information about grants and other essential information. If you are planning to hook up to the Internet for e-mail communications, consider using an Internet access provider that will give you a free World Wide Web site. You can then create a web page that can be viewed by those interested in your activities, including potential donors. In addition, newsletters can be sent by e-mail, thus saving printing and postage costs.

46. If you have a large volume of mail, use discounted postage rates; contact the National Federation of Nonprofits in Washington, D.C. (202-628-4380) for more information.

47. Examine potential local tax savings. Check with your local tax authority to determine if your agency qualifies for a tax exemption on all or a portion of the equipment and furnishings your organization owns. Check your lease to determine that you are not paying this tax as part of your rental. Also, determine whether you are exempt from real estate taxes. Have a knowledgeable professional review whether you have possible tax overpayments. You should not be paying tax on any purchases (office supplies, etc.). Your accounting department should routinely be reviewing all invoices for possible erroneous taxes.

48. Periodically prune mailing lists and eliminate those whose mailing addresses are unknown or who are no longer part of your organization.

49. Calculate salary increases based on anniversary dates. This calculation will reduce salary costs but should be done in conjunction with the organization's personnel policies and union contract. (This change may add a level of complexity of administrative paperwork.)

50. Consider using service agreements for maintenance and repair of equipment instead of paying repair costs for each occurrence.

ACHIEVING LONG-RANGE FINANCIAL STABILITY

Effective managers are committed not only to the current economic health of their agencies but also to their long-term viability. To continually strengthen their organization, managers must (a) establish working capital or cash reserves, (b) ensure cost-effectiveness, and (c) seek diversified funding.

Establishing Working Capital

A few organizations make the mistake of hoarding resources for potential future use, thus denying benefits to those who currently need services. For example, an organization may choose not to expend the interest endowment funds received for a period of years so that it can build up its principal. The more common problem, however, is that some agencies do not adequately prepare for the future because of their desire to provide for current service needs. They do not allow for future inflation adjustments. They put little value on building a financial base and erode their cash reserves, hoping that the future will take care of itself.

Understandably, human service organizations want to use all the money available to provide services rather than set aside funding for unknown future needs. Some provide even more services (even though funding is not ensured) in the hope that, if the program is good enough, funders or their trustees will eventually bail out the agency. They would even argue that it is immoral to set aside cash when needs are so great. Unfortunately, organizations that live "hand-to-mouth" must spend an inordinate amount of time searching for the next bailout and not focusing on long-term issues. Trying to be all things to all people is a formula for eventual poor services and possible financial decline.

Generally, it is a good idea to have approximately 90 days of cash reserves or approximately 10% of the overall budget, depending on the organization's need, for cash reserves. For example, if an organization provides counseling services and a Medicaid contract delays payments for 4 months, the organization must have sufficient working capital to meet its payroll while waiting for cost reimbursement.[18] An agency that has a regular income and predictable expenditures will need less reserves than one that experiences a continuous turnover of grants and has much more unpredictability connected to its income and expenditures. The greater the unpredictability, the greater the need for a large amount of cash reserves.

Another reason to develop working capital is the ability to respond quickly to unmet needs. Having this flexibility allows the agency to deal with changes in the environment and to avoid staying rooted in the present instead of moving into the future. As program trends change or funders convey new priorities, so too agencies must develop the flexibility to be responsive. An effectively run agency must be able to take advantage of new opportunities to fulfill its goals. A well-developed strategic plan can anticipate how the agency might seek out opportunities for expansion and consider a budget that is practical and feasible. Some agencies even develop an "opportunity budget" that identifies where and when the agency will need to invest in new staff, training, and equipment. For example, in anticipation of new employment training legislation, an agency may want to invest in a 6-month pilot training program that will demonstrate its effectiveness in this area. It is now in a position to take advantage of new legislation. To create this desired cash reserve, an agency must have more years with positive revenue than it has years in which the net revenue was negative.

Although it is desirable to build up a cash reserve, be mindful that some funders may have reservations about building up too large a cash reserve fund. For example, some United Way budget committees frown on agency cash reserves, considering that United Way funding is supposed to be "last money in." They would prefer that United Way money not be used until an agency is without much cash reserves. Agencies with greatly fluctuating income and expenses must have a reserve fund to provide financial stability, and the United Way budget panel must be convinced that this is necessary. Budget panels, however, may be justified in questioning when a reserve fund becomes inordinately large (however this is defined). Therefore, be prepared to make your case for cash reserves.

Ensuring Cost-Effectiveness

An effectively run organization can further its long-term financial strength by demonstrating its ability to achieve its objectives at reasonable costs. Developing a cost-effective program is not the same as developing a program at minimum cost. Sometimes, high costs are necessary to achieve sustained improvement. For example, one employment program may cost $1,000 per participant, but most participants will be employed in menial jobs for an average of only 6 months. Another employment program may require costs of $7,000 per participant, but the results of extensive job training will result in the people keeping their job for more than 1 year and being paid at a higher rate. Hence, cost-effectiveness must be related to the desired objectives.[19]

Cost-effectiveness is defined as the measure of how effectively resources are used—results obtained for each unit of cost. To carry out cost- effectiveness analysis, organizations track the cost of a program and record its results; then they compare the two to determine whether the results justify the costs.[20]

To carry out a cost-effectiveness analysis, the agency has to record both costs and results. Obviously, a good accounting system would track actual costs, including both direct and indirect expenditures. For example, a calculation would be made in a tutoring program of the cost of administering volunteer tutors. Recording results may be much more difficult than recording costs. Most agencies will readily identify output results—that is, efforts expended on behalf of clients. These include the number of clients served, the number of training sessions provided, and the number of youth participating in a recreation program. Outcomes are more difficult to measure. For example, we could more easily know how many youngsters participated in a recreation program than how many we helped prevent going to jail. Measuring both costs and benefits remains a major challenge for human service managers.

To further the agency's cost-effectiveness, managers must focus on agency productivity. Frequently, productivity indicators are expressed through the agency's quantitative objective statements. For example, an agency providing group counseling services would want to track the number of participants in each session on a weekly or monthly basis. An agency that provides recreation services for older persons will have a different set of numbers relevant to its services. These numbers should not be collected primarily as a public relations effort; rather, they should be relevant for managerial review of productivity.

Reviewing quantitative information allows managers to ask the following questions:

- How does the number of staff hours compare from one month to another?
- How many new clients does the agency have each month?
- How many clients are able to pay for services?
- How many billable hours do we have this month compared to the previous month?
- What is the cumulative total of different clients seen in the agency during this period?

Each organization must determine its own productivity standards against which monthly quantitative information can be assessed. Periodically, managers should report to their funders, public officials, or trustees regarding the productivity of their organizations' operations.

Seeking Diversified Funding

Excessive dependence on a particular funding source is a major problem in sustaining any organization. Such concentration puts the organization unduly at risk because if the funding resource dries up, the organization becomes highly vulnerable. An organization that has relied primarily on United Way funding may experience pressure to raise its own money or risk losing its portion of United Way funds. A mental health agency that depends almost entirely on state mental health funding for its prevention services may find that its mental health board has shifted its priorities to other essential services not provided by the agency. A neighborhood organization that has received 5 years of foundation grant funding may belatedly realize that this funding cannot continue indefinitely and that it must seek other funding if it is to survive. An agency that has built up its endowment funds is much better off than a nonprofit that has long ignored its dependence on a particular funder. Even so, a sudden decrease in the stock market will influence an agency's program capability; therefore, it is important to diversify the organization's portfolio to spread its risks.[21] Fund raising is so important that the remainder of Part VI is devoted to identifying funding alternatives.

NOTES

1. M. Dropkin & B. LaTouche, *The budget-building book for non profits* (San Francisco: Jossey-Bass, 1998), pp. 3-5.
2. R. Herzlinger, Effective oversight: A guide for nonprofit directors, *Harvard Business Review* (1994, July/August), p. 56.
3. P. C. Brinckerhoff, *Financial empowerment* (Dillon, CO: Alpine Guild, 1996), pp. 48-49.
4. M. Dropkin & B. LaTouche, pp. 8-9.
5. M. Dropkin & B. LaTouche, pp. 89-90.
6. M. D. Feit & P. Li, *Financial management in human services* (New York: Haworth, 1998), pp. 39-40.
7. R. Herzlinger, p. 57; M. D. Feit & P. Li, pp. 39-40.

8. M. D. Feit & P. Li, pp. 46-47.

9. M. D. Feit & P. Li, p. 143.

10. P. C. Brinckerhoff, pp. 120-125.

11. P. C. Brinckerhoff, p. 140.

12. M. Dropkin & B. LaTouche, pp. 86-89.

13. P. C. Brinckerhoff, pp. 92-94.

14. G. J. Dabel, *Saving money in nonprofit organizations* (San Francisco: Jossey-Bass, 1998); M. Dropkin & B. LaTouche, pp. 75, 84; M. H. McCormack, *Mark H. McCormack on managing* (West Hollywood, CA: Dove, 1996), pp. 192-200.

15. M. H. McCormack, pp. 193-194.

16. M. Dropkin & B. LaTouche, p. 74.

17. M. H. McCormack, pp. 199-200.

18. P. C. Brinckerhoff, pp. 49-50.

19. M. Browman, J. Baanante, T. Dichter, S. Londner, & P. Reiling, Measuring our impact: Determining cost-effectiveness of non-governmental organization development projects, in *Cost-effectiveness in the nonprofit sector* (G. L. Schmaedick, Ed.) (Westport, CT: Quorum, 1993), pp. 93-118.

20. G. L. Schmaedick (Ed.), *Cost-effectiveness in the nonprofit sector* (Westport, CT: Quorum, 1993), pp. 3-15.

21. R. Herzlinger, p. 57.

Chapter 18

STRATEGIC FUND RAISING

To be effective as a manager, you have to develop an organization that can raise funds strategically. Strategic fund raising requires long-term planning that is diversified and builds a base of involved, supportive contributors. It is not based on a series of isolated, haphazard events. Desperately attempting to deal with a major budget deficit by a last-minute appeal, hastily preparing a special event, or requesting foundations provide bailout funds can result in very limited success. Begging for money is not the way to conduct fund raising.[1]

Some organizations that receive funding from several sources (which generate large amounts of income) hire part-time or full-time fund development staff. These development staff, however, cannot operate in isolation and must rely on other staff and volunteers to contribute ideas and make important contacts. Smaller organizations and those that look to only one or two income sources require their management staff to be their principal fund raisers. Fund raising is an inescapable and essential part of every effective manager's job in both large and small organizations.

This chapter provides a framework for fund-raising activities by discussing the need for an integrated fund-raising plan and the importance of preparing a case statement. Then, the chapter highlights four major fund-raising endeavors: the annual fund drive, major gifts, corporate giving, and planned giving. In the subsequent chapters, preparing proposals, searching for funding, and conducting effective fund-raising events will be discussed.

DEVELOPING AN INTEGRATED FUND PLAN

All fund-raising activities should fit within the organization's overall strategic plan and be related to the goals and objectives of the organization. The organization must first decide what it must do to achieve its goals and then determine how it will raise the necessary funds to achieve them. Moreover, as part of its comprehensive planning, an organization will examine various funding options to determine which ones are most suitable and how the various funding activities can build on each other.

Organizations must determine which funding approaches are suitable for the organization. An organization established to provide innovative programs will be continuously involved in writing proposals for government or foundation funding. Those agencies that receive the major source of their funding from a government agency, such as a mental health board or drug and alcohol board, will want to develop a close working relationship and be responsive to these government entities.

Each organization must conduct a careful review of its funding options based on an in-depth understanding of its past performance in fund raising and its strengths and weaknesses. A grassroots organization, whose constituents have limited discretionary funds, might determine that a neighborhood carnival or bake sale is appropriate because of its ability to attract large numbers of people to this kind of event. In contrast, a hospital might offer a five-star cooking event and charge a limited number of patrons $300 a ticket because it is capable of attracting affluent people to this special event. Both approaches are sound because both build on the strengths of the organization and an assessment of its donors.

An effective fund-raising campaign works to combine various fund-raising endeavors so that they are part of a total integrated plan. For example, a special event might provide the names of potential contributors to an annual campaign. An annual campaign can produce the names of those contributors who might be solicited for special large contributions or for making gift commitments in their wills. Before submitting a funding request to a foundation, an organization may conduct an internal fund-raising campaign to demonstrate its own trustee commitment. Hence, it is very important to determine how the various fund-raising efforts interrelate and build on each other.

If an organization is involved in several different kinds of fund-raising activities, it is desirable to establish a committee that gives general oversight and plans strategically to implement various funding endeavors. Typically, organizations appoint a development committee, often consisting of both trustees and community volunteers, to provide this oversight. Depending on the complexity of funding efforts, this committee could be limited to planning, to carrying out each fund-raising activity (e.g., special event, annual campaign, or proposal), or to delegating each activity to a special task group.

Before a fund-raising program is undertaken, an organization would do well to get its house in order by ensuring that the following are in place:[2] First, the board and the staff must articulate their shared vision in a mission statement.[3] Chapter 3 discussed the importance of developing a mission statement and a strategic plan. One of the dangers that organizations face is that the mission may become obsolete if it is not reviewed (and, if appropriate, revised) regularly. To determine if its mission is current and realistic, the organization must engage in ongoing market research to identify emerging issues or conditions that must be addressed. The mission must be understandable to outsiders and potential funders.

Second, the organization's management and board must be able to demonstrate how they complement each other and work together in a collaborative partnership. The organization's volunteers should be actively engaged and committed to raising funds and providing financial stewardship. Board members must feel a personal ownership for the organization's functioning. (See Chapter 16 for a discussion on developing a strong management-board collaborative partnership.)

Third, the organization must be able to articulate a meaningful and significant rationale for its fund raising. Its goals and objectives must be clearly defined so that the results of its interventions are readily apparent. It must show that its programs are responsive to community needs and document measurable outcomes. (See Chapter 4 for a discussion on setting goals and objectives.) Typically, a case statement will be the vehicle for communicating the reason for fund raising.

Clarity of mission, engaged staff and board members in a collaborative partnership, and a well-prepared case statement provide a powerful backdrop to any fund raising that is undertaken.

PREPARING A CASE STATEMENT

Organizations prepare a case statement to articulate a clear and compelling reason why people should consider making a contribution.[4] The case statement expresses why the organization is important to the community, how the organization will meet urgent community needs, how contributions will make a difference, how the agency will measure results, and how it will responsibly manage its funds.

To attract community support, the case statement should express a strong reason for contributing money. For example, the goal could be to reduce hunger, to help people become self-sustaining, to help children learn better, or to improve health care. It should be client focused and contain an inspiring message, such as striving to achieve social justice or improving the quality of life of the agency's clients.[5] In addition to these lofty statements, it should specify the number of people that will be served and the impact the program will have on them.

Effective managers will want to promote two parallel case statements. An *internal case statement* is the organization's planning document, and an *external case statement* informs outside constituencies. Through the planning document, the organization clarifies how the project will be staffed, what facilities will be required, how the finances will be managed, and how the program will be evaluated. By being clear about these programmatic issues, the organization is in a better position to respond to questions and concerns from potential donors.

The external case statement focuses on how the program will resolve problems or take advantage of new opportunities. Potential contributors will enthusiastically support programs that meet a compelling community—not agency—need. For example, expanding the number of offices is not in itself a sufficiently compelling case. The fact that this expansion will enable the organization to serve more people in its literacy program, however, provides an urgent rationale for financial support.

The case appeal should be both rational and emotional because people give with both their hearts and their minds. An anecdote about how a child will benefit from a counseling service needs to be accompanied with an explanation about the organization's finances and accountability. In addition, the case needs to identify the variety of gift opportunities that are available. For example, each donor could designate a specific category for giving ($25, $50, or $100). If a tax deduction is possible, this would also be made known, although tax deductibility is not usually a primary motivation for giving.

The form that the case takes will be based on the particular audience you are trying to reach. It could be an annual report sent to the organization's members. Elements of it could be included in a speech to a service club from which funds are being requested. It could be included in a brochure. Regardless of the form it takes, it is helpful to involve as many organization members, particularly from the board, as is feasible because people who have an opportunity to shape the case in the process learn more about the program and increase their sense of ownership. Of course, one or two people will ultimately be responsible for actually writing the case statement since it is impossible for a committee to design a case statement.

Assume that your organization has developed a strategic plan, and you are now ready to prepare a case statement. In discussion among board members and staff, you could consider the following questions:

1. What is the community problem that our organization wants to address?
2. What are the causes of the problem, and what are the consequences to both our individual clients and our community?
3. How does our organization propose to address the problem?
4. Why are we the best organization to deal with the problem?
5. What are the major messages we want to convey in a fund-raising program?
6. What specific objectives have our agency developed? To what extent have we achieved them? What remains to be done?
7. What are some profound, personal stories we can tell about our success? How can we make the data become more real by attaching a personal face to them?
8. Who are the target audiences we want to reach?

After the case statement is prepared, use it to educate your trustees and volunteers. Do not just hand them the document. Walk them through it, set up role-playing opportunities, and encourage them to ask questions that they may need to answer in the course of their fund-raising activities.

In summary, the case informs, inspires, and motivates constituencies to become involved as advocates, contributors, and volunteers.

THE ANNUAL CAMPAIGN

The primary purpose of an annual campaign is to raise money to support the organization's general operations. Usually, the annual campaign is time limited and is held at the same time each year for a few weeks or more. Through the annual campaign, the organization identifies a base of donors that can be expanded over time and that includes donors who may eventually make major gifts. First-time donors can be identified through direct-mail or telephone solicitation. Renewed donors may receive telephone solicitation or personalized letters. Some of these donors will increase their donations from one year to the next through personal contact. The annual fund is thus designed to acquire, maintain, and upgrade many donors who give a relatively small contribution on an annual basis.[6] If done well, however, an annual campaign can be a vehicle for developing committed and dedicated members who want to contribute to the organization's work. These members become informed and bond together in a common purpose; they develop a habit of giving for both general operating funds and special programs.

Building the Campaign Team

To have a successful annual campaign, the organization needs to recruit a team of volunteers and staff who will undertake the campaign. (This same approach to building a team can also be applied to a capital campaign.) This team commits itself to developing a fund-raising plan, implementing it, and evaluating it on an ongoing basis. It is essential that trustees be actively involved in planning; their acceptance will lead them to accept responsibility and ask others to participate in improving the financial stability of the organization.[7] Before commencing the annual campaign, solicit advance gifts from board members. You should expect 100% contributions, with the expectation that trustees will make their own gift a top priority.[8]

The annual fund can be organized in the form of a volunteer solicitation pyramid or hierarchy. At the head will be the chairperson, who in turn will recruit campaign division captains who are then responsible for division coordinators. At the bottom of the pyramid will be division solicitors who actively approach donors. This division of responsibility ensures good campaign follow-up and accountability.[9] The role of the chairperson is crucial for the success of an annual campaign. Other members of the committee and perspective donors will be motivated by the chair and will seek the chair's acknowledgment and approval. Campaign leaders lend credibility and motivate enthusiasm. Their commitment and investment will largely determine the campaign's success. The leaders' own financial commitment needs to be made up front to convey dedication to the cause.[10]

People are willing to join the annual campaign team if the organization has developed a compelling case and inspiring vision, and if they think they will be on a winning team.[11] Ideally, members of the committee should have the potential to be major donors, and they should have a reputation that will lend credibility to the campaign. Identifying significant people initially to serve on the committee will make it easier to later recruit other credible people to serve.[12]

Constructing a Gift Chart

Planning the fund-raising campaign requires establishing a reasonable goal based on evidence of recent fund-raising experience and an understanding of the potential contributor pool.[13] Suppose you have decided on an annual goal of raising $50,000. To determine whether this is realistic, you would identify specific prospect names and consider how much money each one could contribute toward that goal. Note that the gift range chart (Table 18.1) calculates the projected gift range categories, the number of actual gifts from expected contributors, the pool of prospects needed, and expected totals in each category. In this example, less than 10% of the contributors will provide 60% of the projected funds raised. Note that to obtain two gifts of $2,000 each, 8 prospects would have been identified who are capable of making this kind of specific contribution—a ratio of 4 to 1. The organization anticipates that 4 prospects would need to be contacted to achieve these major gifts. Similarly, 24 prospects would be contacted to achieve eight gifts of $1,000—a ratio of 3 to 1. At the lowest end of giving, a mailing to 1,600 people is expected to achieve a return from 400.

Constructing a gift chart for both annual and major gifts programs helps the organization anticipate the challenge ahead and permits the organization to make a realistic assessment of whether it can achieve the anticipated fund-raising goal. The development of the gift chart disciplines the organization's fund raisers to identify specific individuals who may be capable of making large gifts. It also fosters discussion about which persons who have given previously might be capable of upgrading their gifts. Those that have given over a long period of time and have tended to upgrade their gifts are candidates for a larger solicitation—and for personal attention.[14]

Fund raisers have determined that certain solicitation activities are more effective than others. The following are methods used to solicit annual gifts:

1. A personal visit by one person or a team composed of a volunteer and a staff member (This is by far the most effective way of obtaining a large annual gift.)

Table 18.1
Gift Range Chart for a $50,000 Annual Fund Program

Gift Range ($)	*Number of Gifts*	*Pool of Prospects Needed (Ratio)*	*Expected Totals ($)*
2,000	2	8 (4:1)	4,000
1,500	3	12 (4:1)	4,500
1,000	8	24 (3:1)	8,000
500	12	36 (3:1)	6,000
250	30	90 (3:1)	7,500
100	50	200 (4:1)	5,000
50	100	400 (4:1)	5,000
25	400	1,600 (4:1)	10,000
Total	605		50,000

2. Solicitation by personal letter with a follow-up telephone call
3. Solicitation by a personal note at the end of an annual form letter
4. A personal phone call followed by a letter with an enclosed self-addressed return envelope
5. Phone-a-thons in which volunteer solicitors conduct a telephone campaign
6. Door-to-door solicitations
7. Direct mail campaign

In general, emphasize personal contacts for those individuals identified as potential major contributors to the annual campaign. Referring to the previous list, note that the broader the appeal, the more impersonal it becomes. In the first few years of developing an annual campaign, if you primarily solicit by mail expect to raise only a minimal amount—and maybe to only break even. As you expand to a phone-a-thon, you will do better. Some businesses or law offices may be willing to let you use their phones if your own organization has limited capacity.[15] In some instances, you may be surprised to receive a larger than expected gift from a few people. These donors should be put on the list for major gift solicitation at another time. They may also be considered as candidates for planned giving (discussed later).

In summary, the annual fund seeks to build a strong donor base by reaching out and inviting the organization's constituencies to give a gift, renew their gift, or upgrade their gift to meet the organization's needs.

CAPITAL CAMPAIGNS AND MAJOR GIFTS

One of the best ways to secure major gifts is through a capital campaign. These campaigns differ from annual fund raising in that they usually enable an organization to raise a significant amount of money in a limited time for a special project—for example, building a new facility, adding equipment, or developing a major new program. Capital campaigns do not fund current operations. They have clearly defined timetables, occur infrequently (once every 5 or 10 years), and enable the organization to accomplish specific project goals. Capital campaigns often evolve from a strategic planning process because they are intended to fund major new initiatives.[16]

Certain principles that apply to fund raising in general can be reiterated in regard to capital campaigns:

1. The organization should conduct a precampaign analysis or feasibility study to determine its readiness to ask and the communities' willingness to give. Certain key people would be interviewed to determine whether the case for a capital campaign is sufficiently appealing and the needs sufficiently valid. During this feasibility phase, campaign leaders would be identified, and proper timing would be considered.[17]
2. People give to make a difference to those programs that are particularly important to them. Make certain that your case statement provides an inspirational message to your potential contributors.
3. The personal relationship between solicitor and donor is extremely important. People give to those with whom they have a relationship.
4. The more involved people are in the organization and the more they are interested in the organization, the more significant their gift will be.
5. As in an annual campaign, carefully select a chairperson who can attract high-level participation.[18]

6. The campaign must be built on a compelling need that benefits the community. Merely expressing the need to purchase a building is not sufficient. A campaign must be able to convey how the use of a building will contribute to meeting the needs of those the agency serves.

7. The financial goal should be realistic and based on previous fund-raising experiences, the number of qualified prospects, and the commitment of volunteer and board leadership who are willing to make personal solicitations. The goal is based on the gift range chart previously discussed. This format emphasizes that a few people at the top will provide the pacesetting or lead gifts to raise a high percentage of the funding.

   Of course, each organization will modify the chart based on its particular circumstances. For example, a small organization with a few potentially committed wealthy donors could have a higher percentage of contributors at the top, in contrast to an organization with several thousand annual donors and no history of major gift funding. In the latter instance, a smaller percentage might be raised from a few major contributors. Although the gift range chart should be customized to the organization, if a lead gift(s) of at least 10% of the financial goal cannot be obtained, then the capital campaign may need to be delayed to allow time for cultivating a few crucial, high-contributing donors.

   By establishing clear and realistic goals, the agency's managers and volunteers can ensure a successful outcome to the campaign. They can thus avoid the possibility of mutual disappointment and accusatory "finger pointing" when the results are far less than could possibly be achieved.

8. Top gifts are of such importance that these donors are solicited before the campaign becomes public so that at the time of a campaign kickoff approximately 25% of the money has already been raised. These initial gifts—called "pacesetters"—serve as an example to other potential donors that the campaign cause is worth contributing to.[19]

9. Successful campaigns build enthusiasm for the cause by initiating the solicitation process from the inside. People closest to the organization make the first contributions. In effect, these become the advance gifts.

10. Although the campaign relies heavily on the contributions of top donors, these donors do not want to feel totally responsible for the success of the campaign. A broad base gives them confidence that they are not alone in being responsible for the success of the program, and that they are contributing to a cause that has general commitment.[20]

Developing a Donor Base

Developing a donor base profile is absolutely essential because it reveals information trends on each person's contribution. With the use of a computer, the database can preserve information and provide feedback on which donors are repeating and even adding to their contributions. These people become good prospects for a major gift or upgrading.[21]

It is helpful to distinguish between a genuine potential contributor and a vague prospect. Someone who is well-known in the community and who has considerable assets but is not connected with the organization is a vague prospect. Any attempt to secure a gift without access to that person is probably a wasted effort. Similarly, conducting a mail campaign or telephone solicitation campaign with the general public that has no awareness will provide limited financial return for the amount of effort expended.

Potential contributors are those who have a good likelihood of donating funds to your organization. In this connection, it is helpful to draw on the "linkage-ability-interest" principle. Fund raisers have long used this principle to distinguish potential prospects from potential contributors:

Linkage relates to having access directly or through a peer to the potential donor.

Ability means that the potential donor has discretionary income and is psychologically committed to making a philanthropic contribution.

Interest is based on the potential contributor's having knowledge of and commitment to the organization's mission and accomplishment.

Without all these elements, it is difficult to secure a significant donor gift.[22]

Fund raisers face a major challenge of identifying donors with the ability to give a substantial gift and establishing proper linkages with them. Think of your major contributors as being in the center of a circle and constituting those who are most strongly committed to the organization: members of the board, staff management, founding members, and major past contributors. Outside this central ring, in the second ring, are those who are committed because they are annual contributors, employees, volunteers, or clients with discretionary funds. The third ring might consist of former board members, vendors, and people who have a general philanthropic interest and some awareness of the organization. The farther one moves out from the center, the less committed and the lower the potential for contributions. The task of the organization is to engage these various constituencies as much as possible and help them feel a connection to the work of the agency.

It is tempting to identify people of wealth in a community (those with ability) and try to determine how they can be induced to make substantial contributions. The wealthy widow with assets of more than $40 million, the CEO whose annual salary is more than $1 million, and the well-known celebrity may each be potentially capable of making a substantial contribution. Until a meaningful connection occurs, however, these hoped-for contributions will not occur. Therefore, the challenge for a fund raiser who wants to attract affluent philanthropic people is to identify ways to attract those with discretionary income to the organization.

For example, an organization providing research and planning on health and human service issues is interested in raising funds to provide ongoing staffing for health issues. The former director of the agency approaches a retired industrialist who had formerly chaired a health committee from the organization. Because of his past interest and because of the linkage with the former director, the industrialist agrees to fund a permanent position in health planning.

Contrast this approach with that of an organization interested in attracting a celebrity who would help raise money for its AIDS programs. The local organization is aware of the celebrity's commitment to AIDS research but recognizes that probably hundreds of AIDS organizations throughout the country will be seeking this celebrity's donation. The odds of securing this donation through a mail solicitation and without linkages may be only slightly better than winning the lottery. The hour that it takes to compose and transmit the letter may not be much of an investment, but a big payoff without a linkage should not be expected.

The question remains: "How can we create linkages to affluent donors?" Some organizations can more easily do this because of their very nature. Typically, wealthy donors participate in organizations that attract their peers, such as boards of hospitals, universities, local United Ways, and museums. Therefore, you might select people on your board who have relationships with those who serve on these elite boards. For example, one of your board members is involved in a university fund-raising campaign and, through this involvement, talks with his or her new friends. It is fairly common that a "quid pro quo" or exchange mentality operates among those who are involved in different charitable organizations. Often, people will call each other and say, "I gave to your campaign last year, now I would appreciate you contributing to my campaign."

Sometimes, the linkages are indirect but nevertheless significant. The head of the bank may not be a member of your board, but certainly a neighborhood bank manager could provide you linkage with the top management of the bank. The vice president of a major corporation may not show interest in your children's agency, but the spouse or adult child may become heavily committed and eventually obtain a donation from the vice president's company.

Of course, linkage alone is not sufficient. Affluent people have to be shown why they should be interested in donating to your organization. Your organization has to have a credible mission and a track record to appeal to potential donors (case statement). For example, suppose your organization is working to reduce crime and drug activities in selected neighborhoods. Your approach to the head of the grocery chain is to convey how your work will make it safe for shoppers. Clearly, the self-interests of the head of the grocery chain can result in a significant contribution to your agency. Similarly, knowing that an affluent person has a mentally challenged grandchild will open up the possibility of a donation. In these examples, having a direct linkage to your children's agency increases the odds of obtaining more than just a token donation. Furthermore, you need good communication that will convey what you are trying to achieve and your degree of success. Those with linkages to potential donors need to convey that an investment in your agency will produce valued results.

Soliciting Major Gifts

A major gift contribution will be different for each organization. For those agencies that customarily do not receive more than a few hundred dollars from their loyal contributors, a gift of $5,000 would be considered major. A mega-institution, such as a hospital or university, would likely have its sights set much higher. In either case, organizations seek out those few people who have the ability and the commitment to make a difference. Here, the "80/20 rule" can be applied and perhaps even modified. This rule posits that 80% of the dollars will come from 20% of the donors. For many organizations, a more likely scenario is that 90% of the money raised will come from 10% of the donors.[23]

Recognizing the importance of focusing on a few potential donors requires organizations to limit expending huge amounts of time and energy on reaching out to every potential contributor. The focus instead would be on those few who could make a substantial contribution. This means that someone—management staff, volunteer, or professional fund raiser—must concentrate at least weekly on cultivating those who are on the "major donor" list.

How does one identify potential major gift givers? Typically, they are in the inner circle. These are the "family": board members, alumni (former board members, former clients, and former employees), volunteers, and top contributors to the annual fund. In addition, major donors are also those with financial ability who may be in the second or third circle—that is, vendors and community leaders who have expressed an interest in your organization. Each organization has to identify and develop its own customized list of potential major givers.

It is usually helpful to develop a file on each potential major contributor that identifies not only demographic information but also his or her previous giving pattern and interests. The most effective way of reaching major contributors is through face-to-face solicitation. The process may begin with a personal letter or a phone call asking for a meeting, at which time a personal solicitation will occur. Before the meeting, you should find out about the potential donor's interests that could be related to your organization's activities. For example, someone on your solicitation team or board of trustees may be aware that the prospect has grandchildren who are the same age as those who are being tutored in your tutoring program. Perhaps your prospective donor has contributed to organizations similar to yours and therefore may be receptive to your special project.

Assuming that you have done proper research and that you know about the interest and commitment of the potential donor, you would use the meeting to discuss common interests, highlight the plans the organization has for the future, and then close the discussion with an "ask."[24] It is important that the discussion conclude with a specific request or a suggested contribution range, such as "Would you consider providing a leadership gift of $5,000 toward our new tutoring program?," or the following statement could be made: "It is not our purpose to tell you what to do, but we had hoped you would consider a gift in the range of $5,000 a year for the next 3 years as your contribution."[25] After you convey the ask, it is best not to say anything. Allow time for the potential contributor to consider the idea, but encourage him or her to make the decision during the time of the interview rather than at an indefinite later time.

Developing a Mind-Set for Soliciting Major Gifts

Usually, volunteers or members of the board of trustees will be making the direct solicitation request. Their request for money will be viewed as a genuine commitment to the organization. If, however, only a staff member is involved in soliciting, then the potential contributor might perceive the request as self-serving. Knowing that a volunteer is committed to raising funds sends a message that the organization is worthy of volunteer support. The job of the administrative staff is to assist in the recruitment of these volunteer solicitors. Recruitment of volunteers is no easy matter, however, because those soliciting for money, even though they are committed to the work of the organization, may feel uncomfortable about asking their peers to make a contribution. They may fear being turned down. Staff need to help volunteers deal with their concerns and work with them to achieve a positive and even joyful experience. Help them understand that being turned down "goes with the territory." Keep them focused on your main purpose and on realizing that rejections are only temporary obstacles on the route to the main goal.[26]

Three factors contribute to a good solicitation process. First, solicitors must make a contribution before they ask others to do so. Only by making their own contribution do solicitors convey their own personal commitment. A generous gift allows the solicitor to be able to say, "I am so dedicated that I gave a generous gift and I hope you would consider this also." Of course, the solicitor would not necessarily state the gift amount but could convey the conviction that it was in proportion to his or her income or assets.[27]

Second, it is helpful for the solicitors to develop a positive attitude that they are providing prospects with the opportunity to give a donation. Without the solicitation, that person is denied the privilege of saying "yes." The best attitude is that giving is not an obligation or responsibility. Nobody can be forced to give. Rather, it is a privilege. The emphasis is not on giving money so much as investing discretionary, philanthropic dollars in a special organization that is making a contribution to the community.[28] You may need to provide special training to bolster the confidence of your solicitors. Provide them with role-playing opportunities. Anticipate how they might handle questions or concerns. Give them a campaign manual or information sheets that discuss the campaign in-depth. Also, offer them an opportunity to see firsthand the work of the agency.[29]

A third factor to consider is that the meeting involves a dialogue, which includes an understanding of the prospect's interests, possible objections and complaints, and genuine listening to what is important to him or her and his or her philanthropic giving. Serious attention must be given to the donor's concerns. The art of soliciting involves both talking and listening.[30] In the solicitation process, you are not selling but instead conveying knowledge and personal interest. It is important that people not feel manipulated or be "sold" on an organization. By being sensitive to the donor's views and attending to his or her concerns, the solicitor conveys a respect for the donor. The prospect may need time to make a decision, in which case you would offer an opportunity for a follow-up discussion.[31]

Continuously Cultivate Donors

Developing a significant relationship with prospects is fundamental to effective fund raising. It involves high-quality, frequent communications—both formal and informal—between the organization and potential contributors. Newsletters, invitational tours, luncheons, and events allow people to understand firsthand the work of the agency and help you to develop a pool of prospects from which potential contributors can be drawn. Every organization has to consider whether to expend limited volunteer and staff resources in reaching out to large numbers of people who may provide only limited, nominal gifts or to focus on more committed and more affluent potential donors who could make substantial gifts.[32]

In the long term, a donor renewal program is more cost-effective, efficient, and meaningful to an organization than short-term gains that might be obtained through extraordinary efforts through new donor acquisition. In the commercial world, businesses have learned to cultivate their current customers. For example, airlines know that their best customers are repeat customers; hence the widespread use of frequent-flyer mileage programs. It is more cost-efficient and financially productive to work on keeping a donor than to acquire a new one.[33] A renewal program would focus on those donors who have contributed for several years and who have been active participants in the work of the organization. They are the ones that would benefit from a peer volunteer soliciting an increased donation.[34]

To move to a higher level of contribution, donors must believe that they are investing in something that will provide large returns. They want to know whether their investment can truly make a difference and therefore are entitled to information about how their investment has paid off. How many books were provided? How many children learned to swim? How many houses were rehabilitated? The more concrete and specific an organization can be about its results, the better. If an organization can establish some measurable baseline, then it can document more accurately for potential contributors exactly how much progress has been made or could be made with additional funding.

Keeping open and continuous communication with your existing donors is perhaps the most important way of cultivating them. In your strategic planning, include them on a reacting panel or send them a draft plan asking them for their comments. They may respond with important ideas that you may want to take into consideration. Periodically, invite them to an agency update session. If the newspapers have a positive story about your program, send them a copy. They should be recipients of your newsletters and annual reports. They like to hear good news about your program. Even if the news is not good, however, your contributors need to know, preferably before anyone else. If your bookkeeper has embezzled funds or a staff member has committed a criminal act, communicate with your contributors to indicate how you are addressing the situation. Funders will appreciate being informed promptly about the problem and learning what corrective actions you are taking.

PLANNED GIVING

Increasingly, organizations are using a planned giving program (PGP) as a way of seeking additional resources for their programs and ensuring their ongoing stability. The primary purpose of planned giving is to help provide the organization with long-term financial security and survival capability. It helps the organization keep pace with inflation, compensates for funds lost from other sources, permits expansion of programs that otherwise could not be funded, and provides for unusual emergency situations for which other resources are not available. In general, planned giving is not designed to meet short-term, operational needs of the organization.

Planned giving is a gift legally provided by contributors during their lifetimes. The gift can be in the form of money, securities, or other property. Usually, the benefit of the gift is not available to the organization until a future date involving the death of the contributor or a surviving beneficiary or the end of a specific term. The gift is made from a contributor's accumulated assets and is part of an overall estate plan. This is in contrast to annual gifts, which are derived from current income. For donors who want to contribute to a PGP, there are many options for making gifts.[35]

Types of Gifts

Outright gifts of appreciated property permit donors to save on taxes by making an outright gift of stocks or bonds that have increased in value. Donors who itemize deductions can achieve tax savings. For example, suppose that the value of a stock or mutual fund has increased from $2,000 to $10,000. Instead of making a cash contribution of only $2,000, the donor can give $10,000 of appreciated stock shares and deduct the entire $10,000 from his or her income tax.

Bequests are will commitments that provide a gift of money or property at the time of the owner's death or a subsequent death of a designated prior recipient. The bequest could be a specific dollar amount, a percentage of the entire estate, or specific items such as shares of stock. It is deductible from estate taxes. If an irrevocable plan is selected (i.e., the contributor gives up ownership of the assets), then the donor receives an income tax deduction and any additional payments of premiums can be charitable income tax deductions.

Life income gifts provide financial and estate planning benefits and are increasingly popular. The donor makes an irrevocable gift of cash or property and yet retains a life income for one or more beneficiaries. When the last income beneficiary dies, the assets that produce the income will go to the charity. The donor enjoys a charitable deduction in the year that the gift is made, or the deduction can be carried forward for several years.

Charitable remainder trusts entitle the donor or another named person to income for life (or for a period of years), at the end of which time the named charity can have the "remainder" of the original gift. Under this arrangement, the donor can receive either a variable amount of income based on increases or decreases in the market value of a percentage of the trust assets (unitrust) or a fixed income (annuity trust). The income can be specified for the lifetime of one or more individuals, or it can be for a fixed period of years. This latter trust arrangement is particularly suitable to meet the income needs of elderly beneficiaries. The trust income is fully taxable to the beneficiary, unless the trust is invested entirely in tax-exempt bonds.

Pooled-income funds allow donors to join together and create a pool of investments similar to a mutual fund. The donor or his or her designee receives a regular pro rata share in interest payments based on the earnings of the pooled fund. After all the designated beneficiaries die, the organization receives the principal.

Charitable gift annuities are a combination of an income gift and an investment. The organization accepts the gift and agrees to pay a specified fixed amount (annuity) to the donor or another recipient. It is an irrevocable gift and immediately becomes the property of the organization, which is then legally responsible to pay income for the lifetime of the donor. The advantages to donors are that they obtain a charitable deduction for their gift and receive a fixed income, partly tax free. The advantage to the organization is that it is ensured the principal sometime in the future.

Charitable lead trusts are directed to the organization for many years, often 10 or more. At the end of this period, the principal reverts back to the donor or someone else who has been designated. The lead trust differs from the unitrust or annuity trust in that the charitable organization receives the income from the trust during the trust period rather than receiving the principal at the end of the trust period. Donors experience the satisfaction of giving cash donations during their lifetime. The organization has the advantage of an immediate income flow, but it has to be prepared to lose this designated income at the end of the designated period.

A *life insurance policy* allows the donor to incur a modest out-of-pocket cost while being able to provide a significant charitable gift. Donors have an opportunity to make a larger gift than would normally be possible and pay for it on an installment basis through annual premiums. If the donor assigns ownership of a policy to the organization, then the donor has available an immediate federal income tax charitable deduction.

Aspects of a Planned Giving Program

The process of raising money through planned giving is not mysterious. The essential aspects of a PGP consist of five major qualities, summarized in the acronym IMRIP:[36] integration, motivation, relationships, innovation, and persistence.

PGP is not an isolated activity. It has to be an *integrated* part of the organization. It should emerge from an organization's strategic plan, reflect the ability to raise needed resources, and be integrated with other fund-raising endeavors. Furthermore, the PGP must be an integral part of an organization that has excellent management and outstanding services that meet significant community needs. If your organization is perceived positively for its ability to help people effectively, your efforts at planned giving will be much easier.

Motivation has to be heightened by your belief that a PGP gift will truly benefit the community long into the future for staff and volunteers to put in the time and effort needed to achieve your objectives. The motivation of the contributors is also essential. The contributors' needs must always be highest priority. They may want to preserve their assets so that they will be able to provide for their spouse or heirs or for their own financial future. They have to understand that planned giving can help them achieve these objectives.

Developing positive *relationships* with potential donors is a key element in a successful PGP. Many people may feel positively about the contributions of various organizations in their community. These positive feelings, however, do not automatically translate into significant donations. People generally give because someone they like and respect talks with them about their gift.

Innovation is also important because there is usually no simple formula for working with people who may be potential contributors. You need to think about new ways to reach them. After all, you are not only meeting the needs of the organization but also the needs of the contributors; therefore, you must think constantly about how you can best be responsive. Also, you must be innovative and perceptive in regard to timing the requests.

Persistence is another key quality. Invariably, the things you predict will happen do not occur. People will make commitments and then postpone their decisions. It is not unusual to devote between 3 months and 2 years to cultivating a potential contributor. Continuous contact and establishing a true bonding are essential in effective planned giving. Because events will occur that will sidetrack the attainment of your objectives, you must be persistent in your efforts to reach out to potential donors.

Identifying Potential Contributors

Meeting directly with individuals is at the heart of a successful PGP. Although general announcements in your newsletter or even target mailing may be useful to alert people to planned giving, the most effective way to reach prospective donors is through individual contacts.[37]

Because the organization's management staff and trustees must devote considerable personal investment to making individual contacts, give careful thought to narrowing a broad list of prospects to a manageable few. Suppose you have a potential pool of 1,000 people who have been, at one time or another, connected with your organization and are on your mailing list. Presumably, many of these people would have contributed to your annual campaign in the past few years. Without an annual campaign, it is probably unrealistic for a PGP to be initiated; people must have demonstrated their commitment to the organization through a habit of giving.

You narrow this list to a smaller number of approximately 100 people who have made actual contributions to the organization by participating on committees or volunteering their services as indications of their interest in supporting the organization.[38] This list needs to be narrowed further to perhaps 40 individuals who are your most likely prospects based on commitment, age, resources, and family situation. For these 40 prospects, you need to conduct ongoing research and develop individual profiles. In each file, you should include basic information such as address, phone numbers, family members, birth date, marital status, donation history, estimated worth, names of friends, and space for notations regarding contacts or other special information. These data can be put into a computer file for easy reference and updating. Your profile research may provide important information that will indicate where to concentrate your efforts. For example, you may want to focus more effort on a wealthy retired couple than on a couple in their forties who have a growing family and a moderate income.

Occasionally, it is possible that people could be on your list who have had limited, if any, connection with your organization. For example, a wealthy businessperson may have expressed concern about educational needs of young children in the inner city, which is what your organization has been set up to address. To encourage this individual to consider a planned giving gift would likely require many contacts during which the donor would be encouraged to give to the annual campaign or to a special program. Once the donor shows interest in the work of the organization, it would be appropriate to ask for a planned giving donation.

It is more likely that a planned gift will come from those people who have been connected with your agency for a long period of time and who will make a moderately substantial gift. The senior citizen of modest means participating in a senior citizen program, the veteran housekeeper for a children's institution, and the agency secretary who has been with the agency for 30 years and has no heirs are likely candidates for planned giving contributions. Those people who have contributed in the past and who have upgraded their gifts have conveyed how much they value the organization and are also likely candidates for planned giving. Their emotional attachments to the organization and their habit of giving are strong indications that they are interested in providing a gift for the long term.

Maintaining Ongoing Contact

It is extremely important that you maintain ongoing contact with donors because if you do not they may lose interest or feel neglected and even resentful. If they have made a will commitment and then believe that they are unimportant, they may reconsider their financial commitment to the organization. Continually seek ways to maintain relationships. Notes reminding donors of the power of their contributions show respect for and keep donors aware of their legacy. Because of the demands of other responsibilities, it is easy to relegate keeping in touch with those who have made a planned giving commitment to a low-priority activity. Establishing a schedule of contacting three or four donors or potential donors on a regular basis will preserve these important relationships.[39]

Administering Planned Giving Programs

Income from planned giving can be developed into three kinds of reserve funds for your organization: beneficial trust income, board-designated fund, and endowment income.[40]

Beneficial trust income is distributed to the organization based on the donor's wish. The principal, however, is controlled not by the organization but by community foundations, banks, or attorneys. The advantage of this type of reserve fund is that it permits the principal to remain intact and also allows the income to be shared among several organizations. The donor has the security of knowing that should one of the organizations go out of business, an alternate could be selected.

Board-designated funds are unrestricted by the donor in regard to both the principal and the earned income. The donor places no limitations on the use of the gift, thus providing trustees complete flexibility in determining how to use both the principal and the income. Because the principal can be used by the board for unusual situations, this is technically not established as an endowment fund. Many organizations, however, treat open-ended gifts as "quasi-endowments." That is, they use the interest income from the gift and avoid drawing on the principal in the same way they would treat true endowments. This requires self-discipline not to expend the principal, even if this might include delaying or forgoing desired expenditures, such as increasing salaries or avoiding layoffs. By being disciplined, the organization ensures long-term use of funds.

Some organizations go so far as to withdraw only part of the investment for operating purposes and then return a portion of the investment income into the principal, which helps it keep pace with inflation. For example, suppose the principal based on a portfolio of stocks and bonds increases at the rate of 9% a year, and the organization determines it will use 6% for operating purposes. The remaining 3% is reinvested so that the principal becomes greater the following year. A $2,000,000 endowment becomes $2,030,000 the following year and is added to each year thereafter.

By compiling board-designated funds, agencies seeking funds from other sources such as the United Way may have to deal with the criticism that all or portions of board-designated funds should be used before tapping their outside sources. If this issue surfaces, it is imperative that the organization educate the outside funder that board-designated funds are not considered a part of the operating reserves but are quasi-endowment funds—that is, only the income is used. In the previous example, the $30,000 added to the board-designated funds will not be used for operating purposes. Increasingly, this position is being accepted because of the recognition that an aggressive PGP in the long term benefits the organization, which becomes less dependent on outside community funders.

Be mindful that some donors, although not specifically prohibiting organizations from invading principal, may prefer the organization not do so, and this must be respected. In fact, some donors may strongly desire that their undesignated gift be kept in perpetuity. Others might not care about the principal being invaded. Indeed, knowing how much organizations change, they may find flexibility appealing. This point should be clarified at the time the gift is being considered and, when feasible, reviewed after it is received.

True (Permanent) Endowments

To provide funding for specific programs, donors may require that the income from the principal be restricted for specific purposes, or they may permit the organization's board to determine its use. Restricted, permanent endowments cannot invade the principal. Donors may prefer to make a permanent endowment gift because they want to keep the fund intact in perpetuity and assure the nonprofit organization of ongoing income.

Some organizations may assign planned giving a low priority because other approaches—annual giving, special events, and grant writing—can produce funding more quickly to meet the current needs of the organization. Tangible results from the efforts to expand the organization's income through planned giving may not begin to be seen for 15 to 20 years—and even then a $200,000 gift may translate only into an annual $6,000 amount. Planned giving, however, is a strategy for building long-term, continuous, and sustained financial support. Over a period of 15 years, an aggressive PGP could increase from $200,000 to $2 million.

CORPORATE CONTRIBUTIONS

Although general corporations contribute only a small percentage of the total funds raised by nonprofit organizations, at some point many organizations will seek corporate contributions.[41] These corporate contributions can take the following forms:

Company foundations are established by large corporations to respond to charitable requests. They can provide a continuous level of funding because they are not subject to the rise and fall of corporate profits.

Corporate giving funds are provided directly from the corporation's profits. Some companies match the gifts of their employees based on a predetermined ratio to designated charities.

Executive discretionary funds are available to the chief executives of a company for providing small grants to organizations with which they are actively involved.

Subsidiary funds are available to local organizations of a national corporation for distribution of funding in the local community.

Marketing budgets allow a company to compensate an organization based on perceived value in marketing the company's identity and promoting its products and services. These funds can also be used to promote the company at community events. Sometimes, this is known as cause-related marketing, which is discussed later.

Contacting Corporations

Because of the tremendous competition for corporate funding, many companies concentrate their giving on local United Way campaigns or prefer organizations in which they can make an identifiable impact. Giving has become more focused and tied to company objectives. They seek to be identified with organizations that will make them look good in the eyes of their customers. In addition, companies seek ways to leverage their support by using challenge grants. That is, they require the nonprofit to raise an equivalent amount from other sources before the company provides its own support. When approaching a corporation for a contribution, you must keep in mind several considerations.

First, the organization must provide a rationale for why a company should support the organization for a particular project. It is especially important to show a link between the contribution and the benefits to the company.

Second, the organization should conduct research on the companies most likely to contribute and then take time to understand what might motivate the companies to make a contribution. If your agency provides tutoring, you would identify a CEO who is interested in education. If your agency helps abused women, you would seek out a top corporate manager who has shown a commitment to women's issues.

Third, you should try to make an appointment to cultivate a relationship with the appropriate corporate executive in charge of philanthropy. These personal presolicitation calls provide helpful information in understanding the interest of the corporation. One of the most effective cultivation approaches is to involve the business's employees in the organization. In fact, some organizations request companies in their community to identify employees who can be involved on committees or as trustees. Some of these people eventually end up in the top management positions of the company and then are able to be helpful in the organization's solicitation requests.

Fourth, learn as much as possible about the company's giving guidelines and procedures. Company committees develop priorities for funding and have a timetable for decision making.

In summary, the best way to achieve success is to research, cultivate, and solicit those businesses that are most likely to be supportive of the organization's cause.

Cause-Related Marketing

Cause-related marketing (CRM) is defined as the public relationship of a for-profit company with a nonprofit organization intended to promote the company's products or services and also to raise money for the non-profit organization. CRM is different from corporate philanthropy because the money involved is not actually a gift but serves the marketing purposes of the company.[42] Corporations and nonprofit organizations can enter into the following kinds of marketing alliances:[43]

1. In transaction-based promotions, the corporation donates a specific amount of cash or equipment in direct proportion to sales revenue—often up to a set limit—to one or more nonprofits. For example, a local grocery chain would contribute a percentage of its sales from November 1 to December 31 to a hunger-prevention program.
2. In joint issue promotions, the company and a nonprofit agree to deal with a social problem through distributing products and promotional materials. For example, a clothing manufacturer distributes red ribbons as part of a promotion to prevent drug abuse.
3. In licensing the name or logo of a nonprofit to a corporation, the nonprofit receives a fee or a percentage of revenues. This is more likely to occur at a national level. For example, the Heart Association logo appears on many food products.
4. In a partnership arrangement, the company agrees to provide funds and even employees to volunteer at a public or nonprofit agency. As part of the arrangement, the company receives a considerable amount of good will publicity. For example, companies may join in an adopt-a-school program or a mentoring project.[44]
5. In an event sponsorship, the company agrees to provide funding in exchange for having its name prominently displayed as part of the event.

Although CRM is tempting for nonprofits because of the infusion of funding, several risks must be considered. Major funders may reduce donations if they think the nonprofit appears to be obtaining sufficient money from its corporate sponsor. The association of the nonprofit might also discourage potential contributors because they are unhappy with a particular corporation. A second problem is that the nonprofit will come to unduly rely on corporate funding and then be greatly disappointed when the corporation decides to spend its marketing budget in a different manner. Program discontinuation is an inherent risk that organizations assume when they become involved with CRM.[45] A third risk relates to having the nonprofit linked to a company that might harm its image in the community (e.g., a beer company).

Despite these risks, CRM can be a "win-win" situation for both partners. The corporation enhances its image and may even increase sales, whereas the nonprofit obtains crucial funding. Both parties also focus attention on social issues that might otherwise be neglected.

NOTES

1. H. A. Rosso, *Rosso on fund raising* (San Francisco: Jossey-Bass, 1996), pp. 17-18.

2. H. A. Rosso, *Achieving excellence in fund raising* (San Francisco: Jossey-Bass, 1991), pp. 289-293; W. E. Lindahl, *Strategic planning for fund raising* (San Francisco: Jossey-Bass, 1992), pp. 4-5.

3. K. A. Williams, *Donor focused strategies for annual giving* (Gaithersberg, MD: Aspen, 1997), pp. 47-50.

4. A. Kihlstedt & C. P. Schwartz, *Capital campaigns: Strategies that work* (Gaithersburg, MD: Aspen, 1997), pp. 31-42; K. A. Williams, pp. 103-118; H. A. Rosso, *Achieving excellence,* pp. 39-47.

5. W. C. Mengerink, *Hand in hand* (Rockville, MD: Fund Raising Institute, 1992), p. 8.

6. H. A. Rosso, *Achieving excellence,* pp. 51-64; K. A. Williams, pp. 33-43.

7. E. R. Tempel, Assessing organization strengths & vulnerabilities, in *Achieving excellence in fund raising* (H. A. Rosso, Ed.) (San Francisco: Jossey-Bass, 1991), pp. 23-27.

8. W. C. Mengerink, p. 18.

9. K. A. Williams, pp. 41-43.

10. K. A. Williams, pp. 83-88.

11. K. Grace, Leadership & team building, in *Achieving excellence in fund raising* (H. A. Rosso, Ed.) (San Francisco: Jossey-Bass, 1991), pp. 162-170.

12. A. Kihlstedt & C. P. Schwartz, pp. 76-78.

13. H. A. Rosso, *Rosso on fund raising,* pp. 10-15.

14. K. A. Williams, p. 40.

15. W. C. Mengerink, p. 32.

16. A. Kihlstedt & C. P. Schwartz, pp. 1-14.

17. H. A. Rosso, *Achieving excellence,* pp. 80-85.

18. W. C. Mengerink, p. 85.

19. A. Lauffer, *Grants, etc.* (2nd ed.) (Thousand Oaks, CA: Sage, 1997), p. 213.

20. A. Kihlstedt & C. P. Schwartz, pp. 98-108.

21. H. A. Rosso, *Rosso on fund raising,* pp. 12-15.

22. H. A. Rosso, *Achieving excellence,* pp. 28-35.

23. H. A. Rosso, *Achieving excellence,* p. 176.

24. C. F. Mai, *Secrets of major gift fund raising* (Washington, DC: Taft Group, 1987), pp. 21-22.

25. A. C. Frantzreb, Seeking the big gift, in *Achieving excellence in fund raising* (H. A. Rosso, Ed.) (San Francisco: Jossey-Bass, 1991); A. Lauffer, pp. 240-243.

26. W. C. Mengerink, p. 95.

27. A. C. Frantzreb, pp. 138-139; H. A. Rosso, *Rosso on fund raising,* pp. 41-54.

28. H. A. Rosso, *Rosso on fund raising,* pp. 41-45.

29. A. Lauffer, p. 221.

30. K. A. Williams, pp. 195-198.

31. H. A. Rosso, *Rosso on fund raising,* pp. 61-62.

32. K. A. Williams, pp. 149-181.

33. K. A. Williams, p. 158.

34. H. A. Rosso, *Rosso on fund raising,* p. 13.

35. C. Dolan & R. Brody, *Planned giving* (Cleveland, OH: Federation for Community Planning, 1991), pp. 2-3; R. D. Barrett & M. E. Ware, *Planned giving essentials* (Gaithersburg, MD: Aspen, 1997), pp. 35-50; H. A. Rosso, *Achieving excellence,* pp. 97-99; A. Lauffer, pp. 214-216.

36. C. Dolan & R. Brody, pp. 3-4.

37. C. Dolan & R. Brody, pp. 13-16.

38. W. C. Mengerink, p. 64.

39. C. Dolan & R. Brody, pp. 19-22.

40. C. Dolan & R. Brody, pp. 9-12.

41. K. S. Sheldon, Corporations as a gift market, in *Achieving excellence in fund raising* (H. A. Rosso, Ed.) (San Francisco: Jossey-Bass, 1991), pp. 229-242.

42. W. C. Mengerink, p. 59.

43. A. R. Andreasen, Profits for nonprofits: Find a corporate partner, *Harvard Business Review, 74* (1996, November/December), pp. 47-49.

44. J. D. Marx, Strategic philanthropy: An opportunity for partnership between corporations and health/human service agencies, *Administration in Social Work, 20*(3) (1996), pp. 57-73.

45. A. R. Andreasen, pp. 47-59; J. P. Shannon (Ed.), *The corporate contributions handbook* (San Francisco: Jossey-Bass, 1991), pp. 139-151.

Chapter 19

PREPARING EFFECTIVE PROPOSALS

PRELIMINARY CONSIDERATIONS

The process of obtaining funding for important projects or programs can be both enriching and overwhelming. Preparing proposals disciplines thinking and stimulates more purposeful fund-seeking endeavors. The process can also be awesome, however, because of the many details you have to focus on and the many decisions you have to make. The purpose of this chapter is to identify aspects of the proposal-preparing process that will make your grant-seeking activity more effective.

Conducting a Preliminary Assessment

Because you will be investing a considerable amount of time, energy, and organizational resources in a proposal, you should conduct a preliminary assessment. During this preproposal phase, you should review several fundamental questions.[1]

First, is the project idea desirable and feasible? Conduct a preliminary review of the literature, and contact persons who have undertaken similar projects. Judge whether the problem to be addressed is truly solvable. Clarify during this exploratory period whether the project idea is unique; if a similar project has been done elsewhere, are there compelling reasons to duplicate it? Assess the urgency of embarking on the target population at this time. Determine who might support the project. Make a preliminary assessment about the feasibility of the project, given anticipated difficulties in implementation.

Second, is your organization able to carry the project forward? Analyze the project in relation to the current mission and goals of the organization. Review whether there is sufficient organizational will and staff capability to take on a new endeavor. Consider your competitive position in relation to other potential applicants. Assess your ability to take on the demands of the project considering other pressing priorities. Will taking on a new project divert funds and staff time away from ongoing projects?

Third, are there funders who might be interested in the project idea? Determine through preliminary direct contacts or through descriptions of funding sources whether their priorities match your proposal idea[2] (see Chapter 20).

Fourth, what are the potential financial consequences of obtaining funding? Examine whether the likelihood of new funding will limit your autonomy and curb your decision making regarding people to be served or ways of functioning. Consider the impact of discontinued funding at the end of the grant period. Review whether the funding you are seeking is likely to be sufficient to carry out the program adequately.[3]

These issues contain cautions that must be weighed against the almost irresistible attraction of seeking funding for new projects. The clear message: Anticipate as much as possible before you formally begin writing your proposal. Do your homework!

Prior to Writing the Proposal

Because foundations will give grants only to organizations that are incorporated as nonprofit agencies, you will need to obtain this designation from the Internal Revenue Service (IRS). An attorney can help you obtain the designation 501(c)(3) status. To achieve this status, you will need to have a board of trustees. The secretary of state or the state's attorney general's office can provide you with the 501(c)(3) application. Once completed, your organization is eligible to receive tax-deductible gifts. While you are waiting for approval, it is possible for you to receive tax-deductible gifts if you have made arrangements with another organization to serve as your fiscal agent. This organization serves as a conduit of funds and may need to give assurances to the grantor that the budget will be monitored.[4]

Assuming that you have either 501(c)(3) status or a creditable fiscal agent, you should strive to assure the funder that you have an organization worthy of investment. In some instances, funders may be willing to take a chance on a new organization if they are excited about the idea and have confidence in the leadership. Your strategic plan should convey a sense of direction and an ability to implement programs.

You must be clear about your priorities. Because it is impossible for organizations to meet all the needs of their clients or the community, it is vital that the organization, through its trustees, staff, and volunteers, determine its priorities. Then the organization can be proactive in searching out funding for programs around which consensus exists. This approach is far better than selecting programs that fit priorities of funders but are not in keeping with the mission of your organization or the commitment of your constituencies.

When you are about to do the actual writing of the proposal, make sure that you have gathered all the information you need to document your case. You may need to assign several people to gather the necessary data. Make sure that you are prepared to discuss in clear terms your goals, objectives, implementation plan, timetable, and staffing requirements. Because you are only at the beginning of the process, details about the budget may have yet to be worked out. You should have a general idea of the expenses involved, however, so that you can decide whether you can realistically pursue funding or whether you have to reduce the magnitude of your projected program. Create a preliminary outline that will help you separate your main ideas from subordinate ones. To add human interest to your document, be prepared to discuss actual situations of need and how people could benefit. Real-life experiences and human-interest stories will enhance your proposal.

How Fundable Is Your Project?

If your idea is new, do not expect foundations to be immediately receptive. Although foundations are in the business of providing risk capital, they nevertheless generally like to feel that there has been some experience or track record that indicates the feasibility of the idea. If you can start your program on a small-scale pilot project before requesting funds, you can considerably increase your chance for funding. At the very least, identify programs similar to yours that have succeeded elsewhere. Searching for grants similar to yours could reveal successes elsewhere.

Generally, foundation and corporate funders prefer specific projects rather than general operating requests. This reality can be frustrating for organizations that require ongoing support. Your search process may identify those foundations that are amenable to general support. Generally, however, funders prefer to know exactly how their money will be used and the specific impact it could make.

To increase your chances of funding, you should demonstrate to potential funders that you have embarked on ways to raise your own resources. Funders are impressed to learn that 100% of your trustees contribute to your annual fund-raising campaign. Knowing that you are raising money in various ways gives them confidence that your organization's proposed projects can be sustained. Consider seeking funding for general operating purposes from nonfoundation sources, such as local United Ways, fund-raising events, or membership campaigns.

PREPARING PROPOSALS

Proposal formats and lengths may vary depending on the requirements of funders. Government proposals use a highly structured format. Proposals for foundations are not usually as structured, but generally all will want to know what you intend to accomplish and how you propose to accomplish these goals. The following format is offered as a guide, which can be modified if the funder requests a different outline:

Summary statement

Statement of need

Goals and objectives

Program components

Evaluation

Organizational capability

Program continuation

Budget

Appendixes

Summary Statements

Normally, a summary statement should appear first because readers need an overview to orient them to the project and to prepare them for the details that are to follow.[5] The summary should be less than 1 page and contain the following elements:

- What is the need

- What will be accomplished
- Who you are and why you are qualified
- What activities you will perform
- What it will cost
- How long it will take

The summary should be prepared after the full proposal is written because it should accurately reflect its major elements.

Statement of Need

The purpose of this section of the proposal is to define precisely what condition your organization wants to change. Focusing on local conditions would likely appeal to a local foundation. Dealing with a problem or issue that has implications beyond your own community may appeal to a large national foundation or a federal agency. Whether you approach a local or a national foundation, focus on the people who will be served, not on how funding will be used to benefit the organization.[6] Specify the target population, what specific problem will be addressed, where the problem is located, the problem's origin, and why it continues to exist. If the problem is multifaceted, then all the significant aspects need to be identified. For example, a problem statement about out-of-school, unemployed, adolescent ex-offenders living in poverty would need to describe their lifestyle, educational lags, and need for income.

Within the statement of need, distinguish between risk, target, and impact populations.[7] The risk population is the total group needing help or at risk. For example, there are 800 ex-offenders in the community. The target population is that subset toward whom the program is aimed; for example, 70 ex-offenders are to be served. The impact population is the subset likely to benefit from the program; for instance, 45 of those served will obtain jobs. If possible, the theoretical basis for the problem should also be discussed. You should review the literature on the target population's needs to develop a conceptual understanding of the factors causing the problem. Avoid circular reasoning. For example, it is not enough to say that the problem is the lack of the service you intend to provide.[8]

To demonstrate your grasp of the problem, provide prospective funders with data from a variety of sources: national studies and their local applications, testimony from congressional records, surveys, or quotes from authorities. Give special attention to provide local data on the issue. Use information that is most relevant to your project. Document as best you can through data obtained through local sources (e.g., United Way, department of human resources, and juvenile court). Be as specific as possible when describing the need.

Unless a funding group requests detailed information in the narrative, do not inundate it with pages of statistics; summarize the data and place detailed, statistical tables in an appendix. Because many problems are chronic, the statement of need should convey why there is a special urgency to seek funding now. What new crisis has arisen? For example, are the kinds of crimes being committed by adolescents more serious than in the past? Does new state legislation place a special burden on the local community to deal with delinquency? Are local institutions more prepared now than in the past to deal with delinquency? A description of special circumstance makes the importance of funding the project more compelling. The potential funders must view the problem as both timely and critical.

Where feasible, indicate how the community constituency or client group has been involved in defining the problem. Such involvement is obviously desirable if the proposal relates to community improvements because the clients are in the best position to comment on their special needs. Even those who normally do not participate, such as mentally retarded offenders or recently released mentally ill patients, can be consulted. Their participation in the problem-defining process conveys the message that you have a more profound depth of understanding.

Although the statement of need is presented before the section on goals and objectives of the proposal, it should be written with objectives clearly in mind. Because needs and objectives must be consistent with each other, it might even be desirable to write the latter section first. This is especially necessary if the prospective funder has specified what the proposal should accomplish, which is usually the case with federal grants.[9]

If your program is to be considered a model, show how your model can be replicated. If, however, your program is a replica of another project done elsewhere, document the success of that program and show how it can be of benefit to your community.[10]

Goals and Objectives

As discussed in Chapter 4, organizational or program goals represent broad statements of what the organization wants to accomplish. They provide a general direction for commitment to action. They are global descriptions of a long-term condition toward which the organization's efforts will be directed. Goals are idealistic, timeless, and rarely achieved. Goals should inspire all those associated with the organization to want to move toward a desired end point.[11] The following are examples of goal statements:

Reduce crime in the community

Upgrade housing

Improve interracial relations

Provide information to low-income clients

Prevent illegitimate births by teenagers

Eliminate child abuse and neglect

Although goal statements are inspiring, they are not amenable to clear definition and measurement. Objectives, in contrast, represent relevant, attainable, measurable, and time-limited ends to be achieved. They are relevant because they fit within the general mission and goals of the organization and because they relate to problems identified in the proposal. They are attainable because they are capable of being realized. They are measurable because achievements are based on tangible, concrete, and quantifiable results. They are time limited because the proposal specifies the time frame within which results can be achieved. Objectives provide the funder with clear-cut targets for organizational accountability. Be aware that although objectives are intended to be realistic and achievable, their accomplishment may not necessarily eliminate a problem described earlier in the proposal. Obtain- ing jobs for 45 ex-offenders will not solve the high rate of recidivism in the community.

Four kinds of objectives can be considered: operating, service, product, and impact objectives.[12] Operating objectives convey the intent to improve the general operation of the organization. Achieving them puts the organization in a better position to help its target population. Examples include the following:

- To sponsor four in-service training workshops in the next 3 months for 40 staff
- To increase the size of membership by 150 within the following year

Service objectives (sometimes called activity objectives) are based on the organization's quantifying units of service rendered. For example,

- To serve 300 clients in the program year
- To conduct 680 interviews
- To provide 17 neighborhood assemblies
- To refer 125 clients to agencies in a year

Product objectives relate to a tangible piece of work that will be delivered at the end of the funded period. For example,

- To prepare a resource directory
- To create a case management system
- To produce a videotape that will provide clients with information

Impact objectives specify outcomes to be achieved as a result of process activities. Whereas activity objectives reflect the amount of effort to be expended, impact objectives detail the return expected on the investment of time, personnel, and resources. Impact objectives focus on results. Examples include the following:

- To place 50% of the youth enrolled in the vocational training program in full-time jobs within 18 months
- To increase educational attainment of a school's 200 entering students, 80% of whom will complete at least 1 full year of school
- To obtain a commitment from the board and the youth commission to incorporate the program, by the end of the third year, into the regular school program

The advantage of these objectives is that they alert the funders to expect a clear-cut outcome from the project. Stating the objectives in measurable terms disciplines you to set realistic achievements, not ideal ones. Although considerable flexibility can be used to prepare impact objective statements, the following criteria are suggested:

1. Generally use a strong verb that describes an observable change in a condition. "To reduce," "to improve," "to strengthen," and "to enhance" are examples.

2. State only one aim with one specific result. An objective that states two aims may require two different implementations, and confusion could later occur regarding which of the two objectives was achieved. "To reduce the recidivism rate by 10% and obtain employment for 20 former delinquents" is an example of an objective with two aims.

3. Be certain that the objective is realistic. For example, do not promise to reduce significantly unwed teenage pregnancies through a program designed to work with 100 youngsters in a community that experiences 2,000 unwed births per year. Furthermore, although the format presented here separates goals and objectives from program components, they may be combined so that specific activities and tasks are listed under each objective.

Program Components: Activities and Tasks

This aspect of the proposal presents a work plan of how the organization intends to accomplish its objectives. To convey the logic and continuity of the project, the proposal should describe, in relation to each objective, what will be done, by whom, and by when. In planning the work that needs to be accomplished, undertake reverse-order and forward-sequence planning, as discussed in Chapter 5. For a project designed for ex-delinquents in which one of the objectives is to obtain jobs, a simplified work plan would be formatted as follows:

Objective: Place 50% of previously delinquent youth in the vocational training program in full-time jobs within 18 months.

Activity 1: Develop a pool of not less than 40 potential jobs.

Tasks:

~ 1. Have employers sign contractual agreements.
~ 2. Follow up letters with personnel contacts.
~ 3. Mail letters of inquiry.
~ 4. Devise contractual forms.
~ 5. Train job recruiters.
~ 6. Hire job recruiters.

Activity 2: Provide orientation for youth.

Tasks:

~ 1. Prepare training materials.
~ 2. Obtain facility.
~ 3. Train staff.
~ 4. Recruit staff.

In addition to a visual timeline chart (see Chapter 5), you should describe in detail how the program would actually function. When relevant, state in the narrative details such as how the proposed work has been successfully used elsewhere, how it will relate to existing programs in the community, and what current resources of the organization will be used. The determination of activities and tasks will typically involve a group process because knowledge is not usually concentrated in one person, and a consensus may need to emerge if organizational members are to be involved in implementing the proposal. The actual proposal writing, however, cannot be done by a committee; one or two people have to take primary responsibility. The group can react to a draft, and their suggestions can then be incorporated.

Evaluation

For most proposals, the essential worth of evaluation is to be able to compare intended results with actual outcomes. Objective statements should be written to foster subsequent evaluation by incorporating measurement indicators, as indicated by the following examples:

- To improve school performance (as indicated by teacher evaluation) of past offenders in 50% of the cases served in one program year
- To improve personal adjustment (as determined by specifically constructed psychological tests of ex-mental hospital patients) in 75% of those served during one program year
- To reduce the rate of recidivism of juvenile offenders (as measured by official police rearrest data) by 50% during the next program year
- To develop ongoing funding for the innovative delinquency prevention project (as indicated by letters of commitment from the Youth Commission and the United Way) by the end of the second year

In some instances, it is necessary to devise instruments, called performance indicators, to measure results. In the objective statements illustrated previously, these might be teacher assessment forms or psychological tests.

Each organization will have to determine whether it will create its own performance indicators or adopt existing ones. When the information has been collected, the organization can compare its planned performance with the actual outcome. Process evaluation (sometimes referred to as monitoring) examines the internal processes and structure of the program to determine whether it is functioning as planned. Is it achieving its objectives in a timely manner? Is it keeping an accurate record of who is being served and under what conditions? Are clients being processed as expected? What administrative problems are being encountered? The major value of process evaluation is that it helps the program staff review whether they are heading off course and allows them to take corrective action before the end of the funding period.[13] Process evaluation ensures funders that proper feedback is being built into the project.

To carry out process evaluation, a local advisory committee could be appointed to judge the effectiveness of the effort and report to the funder. Another possibility is to identify an expert in the field to visit the project periodically and furnish reports to the donor. A third possibility is for the project staff to monitor the project and to report the results, particularly when objectives are measurable. Regardless of the design model, the proposal should explain the questions to be answered and the details of the evaluation plan, including who will perform it, how evaluators are to be chosen, and what instruments are to be used.

Capability of the Organization

Funders want to know that the organization is capable of implementing the project.[14] Because they must be convinced of your competency to accomplish what you promise, you need to demonstrate your credibility for undertaking the project. Describe briefly how and why the organization was formed, past and current activities, the support you receive from other organizations, and your significant accomplishments. Especially if your organization is unknown to funders, provide evidence of your involvement and competency in the area in which you are requesting funds. Indicate what financial or other resources are available. Letters of endorsement are desirable, but letters committing actual resources (staff, equipment, and funding) are even more impressive. (You have the option of discussing the organization's capability as part of a general introduction or in a separate section after discussing program evaluation. Review the funder's guidelines for the specific format.)

Because the proposal must be concise, you may want to refer to the competency of the staff in the appendixes and provide a list of positions, titles, qualifications, salary levels, and specific responsibilities and an organization chart. If appropriate, describe the selection process for key personnel. Funders appreciate knowing that your board of trustees is actively involved in decision making and fully supports the proposal. List trustees and their identifying information in the appendixes. Testimony from key figures in the community is also useful if their endorsement letters are sincere and reflect genuine support. Indicate the role and names of an advisory committee, if appropriate. If requested, include in the appendixes an annual report, documentation of your organization's IRS nonprofit status, latest audit statement, and a copy of your agency's affirmative action policy.

Program Continuation

In this section of your proposal, indicate whether the organization will be able to continue the program beyond the grant period. Foundations that give time-limited funding want assurance that the project will be sustained. Among the options for continued revenue are the organization's operating budget, revenue from client fees, third-party payments such as insurance, special fund-raising drives, application for membership or special funding in a United Way or other federated fund-raising program, and an assumption of costs by a voluntary organization or government agency.

Although it may be difficult to anticipate sources of funding 2 or 3 years hence, funders find this point so crucial that you should make a concerted effort to explore other funding options as part of the proposal preparation process. If you intend to have a scaled-down version of your program absorbed by other community agencies, indicate how you plan to have your program incorporated into their programs.

The Budget

The budget is important, but unless it reveals major weaknesses or is overinflated, it will not be the primary reason for the rejection or acceptance of a proposal. If your idea is sound, the budget is generally negotiable. Your search process (see Chapter 20) should reveal whether your funding request is within the funder's contribution pattern or whether your budget requires you to seek funding from several sources. Consider several general guidelines in preparing the budget.[15]

Different funders require varying degrees of detail in the budget. Most governmental agencies require much detail and usually provide budget forms and instructions for their completion. Foundations and corporations are less structured in their requirements but will want a budget that is well thought out and complete. Some governmental agencies have regulations that provide special instructions for preparing the budget. These instructions are continually being revised. Use the most recent instructions available rather than delaying the preparation of your budget. Allow time to make necessary changes if you find that a new set of instructions is to be issued shortly before the final application is due. Grant application instructions generally include information regarding budget forms, examples of how to calculate specific budget items, agency formulas for determining the maximum allowance in major budgetary categories, and allowable rates for consulting fees, per diem expenses, and travel. Be prepared to document your needs when costs exceed the agency formula.

As an aid in developing the budget, prepare worksheets. They provide a structure for budget planning so that no type of expense is overlooked. Make detailed records of each budgeted item, and be prepared to discuss the potential impact of budget cuts during negotiations. The worksheets will provide a plan that can be used when the project is actually in operation. A good budget will relate directly to the project's objectives and activities. Each budget item should be justified on the basis of its potential contribution to the project.

The budget is an estimate of the program's revenues and expenses. In regard to projected revenues, foundations will want to understand both your committed and anticipated revenues for your particular project. Adapt Table 19.1 to your situation to provide information that you have obtained—or anticipate obtaining—funding from various sources inside and outside your organization. Completing this form will clarify for the foundation how their contribution relates to other possible funding sources.

Table 19.2 provides a format for indicating project expenses. Modify it based on your particular circumstances. Note that in Table 19.2 direct costs include items related to contract services, office space, equipment, supplies, and travel. In the narrative that accompanies the budget, be as specific as possible about costs. This is particularly necessary if the funder is not familiar with the nature of the project. Be able to document exact costs for each major item. If it is necessary to create new positions, survey other agencies with similar jobs to justify salary scales. If you include items in the budget that you cannot fully support, the integrity of your project may be questioned. Regarding salaries, provide a detailed breakdown of each position and the percent-

Table 19.1
Projected Revenues

	Committed	*Requested*	*Total*
Government sources (e.g., city, county, and state)			
Foundations (list)			
Income from the organization			
Events			
Fees			
Other			
Total projected income			
In-kind contributions (list)			

age of the given employee's time that would be allocated to the program. Fringe benefits include workers's compensation, state unemployment insurance, social security, and retirement.

Indirect costs are more difficult to determine than are direct costs, but they are important to the financial well-being of your organization. Indirect expenses may include estimated portions of time spent on the project by other staff members, such as the director, accountant, and maintenance personnel. Such costs can also encompass expenditures that are difficult to account for with precision, such as the depreciation of office equipment.

Some grantors will permit indirect costs to be included in the budget as a percentage of total direct costs of the grant.[16] This percentage is usually determined after an analysis of your overall financial operations by an experienced accountant. Many organizations that engage in extensive grant activity within federal agencies negotiate an acceptable percentage with one governmental agency and are then able to use the same rate in contracts with other governmental agencies. The federal government will allow indirect expenses determined either as a percentage of total salaries involved in the project or as a percentage (much lower) of the total direct costs of the grant. Some foundations are becoming more accepting about including indirect costs; depending on the policies of a particular foundation, however, you may have to absorb indirect costs in other parts of your budget. Check with your funder on its policies on indirect costs.

Generally, you will have a degree of flexibility in spending, as long as you do not exceed the total amount of the grant. Requests for budgetary changes should be made in writing to the funding source and, if approved, become formal budget modifications that change the conditions of your grant.

Table 19.2
Project Expenses

Expenses	*% on Project*	*Agency Contribution*	*Other Funding Sources*	*Foundation Request*	*Total*
Personnel costs					
Position A	_____	_____	_____	_____	_____
Position B	_____	_____	_____	_____	_____
Subtotal	_____	_____	_____	_____	_____
Fringe benefits	_____	_____	_____	_____	_____
Subtotal personnel	_____	_____	_____	_____	_____
Nonpersonnel costs					
Audit	_____	_____	_____	_____	_____
Consultants	_____	_____	_____	_____	_____
Rent	_____	_____	_____	_____	_____
Utility	_____	_____	_____	_____	_____
Furnishings	_____	_____	_____	_____	_____
Maintenance	_____	_____	_____	_____	_____
Insurance	_____	_____	_____	_____	_____
Office	_____	_____	_____	_____	_____
Office supplies	_____	_____	_____	_____	_____
Printing	_____	_____	_____	_____	_____
Postage	_____	_____	_____	_____	_____
Copier rental	_____	_____	_____	_____	_____
Telephone	_____	_____	_____	_____	_____
Computer supplies	_____	_____	_____	_____	_____
Out-of-town travel	_____	_____	_____	_____	_____
In-town travel	_____	_____	_____	_____	_____
Conference fees	_____	_____	_____	_____	_____
Indirect costs	_____	_____	_____	_____	_____
Other costs	_____	_____	_____	_____	_____
Subtotal nonpersonnel	_____	_____	_____	_____	_____
Total projected expenses	_____	_____	_____	_____	_____

Adequately planning your budget reduces the number of changes that may be required and also establishes a degree of credibility necessary to obtain permission for needed modifications. Usually, if the grant is to cover more than 1 year, funders want a breakdown of the year-by-year budget and a total amount. Be prepared to have your program reviewed each year for a multiyear funding request. Also, if more than one funder is being asked to contribute to the costs, indicate the expected income from each source. If the organization can make in-kind donations to the project, such as staff time and building space, then the budget should reflect these donations.

If you intend the program to serve a certain number of people, divide this number into the costs to determine if the cost of service per client is reasonable. Funders often calculate this figure; therefore, if you have not provided it in the proposal, be prepared to defend the program's per capita cost. Do not accept less money than is needed for a successful effort just to obtain the grant. You receive no credit for good intentions if they are not accomplished. It is irresponsible to accept the accountability for a project without having the essential resources to follow through with it. If you decide to accept fewer dollars, be sure you revise your anticipated achievements.

Any earned income (e.g., fees, special events, and use of endowment income) anticipated should be included in the budget. The funder will appreciate your acknowledgment of anticipated revenues that will offset anticipated expenses.[17]

Appendixes

The proposal appendixes provide information that is not essential to making the case but lends reliability and understanding to the organization and its request.[18] Include the following items: a list of your board of trustees, documentation of your agency's 501(c)(3) tax-exempt status from the IRS, audit, job descriptions, affirmative action policy, statistical charts, letters of support or agreement, evaluation instrument, and other items that bolster your proposal or that may be required by the funder.

APPROACHING FOUNDATIONS FOR FUNDING

After identifying foundations whose funding patterns appear to match your interests, the next step is to determine how to approach them. Before submitting a proposal to a foundation, determine exactly how the grant maker wants to be approached by accessing information supplied in a grant's directory (see Chapter 20), or call or write the foundation.

There is no universal rule of operation; each foundation has its own style. In general, small, private foundations require a brief (2- or 3-page) letter stating who you are, what your concern is, what you propose to do, and how much funding you seek. Letters to small, private foundations suffice because such organizations rarely have full-time staff and have limited funds and scope; staff can therefore readily determine whether the proposal is within their area of interest.[19]

This same procedure can be used when approaching corporate-sponsored foundations. After sending a letter, it is important to make a personal contact with the person responsible for the corporate foundation (sometimes the president of the company, a person in public relations, or a specially designated program officer). In considering corporate support, ask the following questions:

- Does the firm have significant business or employees in the community?
- Is the business related in any way to the type of project you are developing?
- Does your organization deal with issues that are of unique importance to the firm?
- Can the firm gain special benefit for being associated with the project, including publicity or visibility with key consumers?
- Does the firm sell substantial products or services to your primary constituents?

Positive answers to these questions will enhance your chances of securing funding.[20] In addition to providing grants, corporations can provide other valuable resources, including the expertise of their personnel, gifts from their inventory, company facilities, and released time of employees.

Community foundations in large urban areas typically have program officers who are inundated with many proposals each year. They must screen these and determine which ones will be submitted to their distribution committee for final approval. Some community foundations prefer that you first submit a proposal and then arrange to meet and discuss it. Others encourage you to discuss a proposal with the program officer before investing considerable time and energy in it. If you can manage to submit a proposal several weeks ahead of the deadline, you may have the opportunity to meet with the program officer far enough in advance to be able to make revisions. Meeting with staff is crucial because, although not everything they recommend to the board of the foundation passes, their opinions and recommendations are highly regarded.

A general rule of thumb proposed by the Foundation Center is that you should approach three funders for every grant that you need. Because competition for funding is great, be prepared to be turned down by several foundations before finally succeeding. If you send your proposal to more than one funder, indicate in the cover letter other sources from which you are requesting funds.[21]

Using the Internet to Apply for Funds

Expect that in the near future foundations will be accepting applications over the Internet. The first step in this process will be for foundations to accept grant applications as transferred files. Your proposal can be attached to your e-mail letter. Another possibility is for the foundation to provide a grant application on an on-line form, which the grantee fills out and submits on line, thus allowing for instant submission. Currently, the Kellogg Foundation provides an on-line application form (*www.WKKF.org*).

Using the Internet in the future could provide innovative ways for an agency to convey its range of activities to a potential funder. The grant application could involve a combination of text, graphics, and links to give the program officer an in-depth understanding of the organization. Video and audio clips could demonstrate agency activities and provide powerful testimonials. A community organization, for example, could demonstrate how it participates in community partnerships by linking with its partner organizations. These virtual documentations could also be employed to meet the funders' reporting requirements.[22]

THE PROPOSAL IS ONE PART OF THE PROCESS

Proposals by themselves—even well-written ones—do not necessarily ensure that funding will be forthcoming. To maximize the chance that a grant request will succeed, you must make a meaningful connection with a potential funder.

Those who give away money want to be inspired and believe that their funds are going to a good cause that will result in meaningful impact. Funders want their grants to be used by an organization that can implement a worthwhile program. Therefore, expect that your potential grantors will be greatly interested in your program if they anticipate a dynamic collaboration.[23]

Ideally, the proposer should strive to develop a partnership with the potential donor. Building the relationship is an essential part of the funding process. Although it is true that funders examine the track record and consider the reputation of the organization, fundamentally they are investing in people, not the organization as an abstract entity. The old adage, "people give to people," is certainly appropriate.

In keeping with the idea of developing a relationship with potential funders, it is generally a good idea to contact a foundation staff person (assuming there is one) to determine whether there is a good fit between your proposed ideas and the foundation's priorities. This contact provides an additional opportunity to obtain input from the funder about the criteria that will be considered. For example, you could determine the time period, the amount of the request, the need for evaluation, and the expectations of results.

Depending on the initial interest of the foundation and its style of operating, you will determine various ways of contacting the funder: phone calls, face-to-face meetings, and possibly foundation trustee contacts. (Note, however, that some foundation officers may be offended that you are "going over their heads" to influence voting trustees.) These efforts are designed to help the funder understand your organization and its programs. Even if you do not succeed in obtaining funds for your current project, you lay the groundwork for possibly succeeding with future proposals.

CRITERIA FOR EFFECTIVE PROPOSALS

Obviously, the criteria used by funders for judging a proposal will vary. As indicated previously, government agencies will have specific and unique criteria for each grant. Foundation funders will tend to be more flexible in using criteria to judge proposals. The following criteria should be considered when preparing your proposal:

Competency of the individuals involved

- ~ Are those who have prepared the proposal considered highly competent?
- ~ Are they dedicated to making their ideas a reality?
- ~ Do they have a successful track record?
- ~ Do they demonstrate a depth of knowledge about what is happening in their community and throughout the country?
- ~ Are they sufficiently aware of the complexity of the problem?

Participation of the organization's membership

- ~ Are board members familiar with the proposal? Have they approved it?

~ Is the board composed of the best possible combination of members of the community, client representatives, and others who can be effective resources for the organization?
~ Is the board willing to provide some of the organization's own resources?
~ If applicable, has provision been made for client or consumer participation in the design and implementation of the project?

Desirability of the project

~ Does the proposal make a strong case for the urgency of funding?
~ Is it clearly a high priority for the requesting organization and for the community?
~ If similar programs already exist, does the proposal acknowledge this and strongly convey why, nevertheless, one more program is necessary?
~ Is the project creative in proposing an innovative approach to dealing with a community problem?
~ If asking for renewal of a grant, has the project adequately demonstrated accomplishments?
~ If the project has fallen short of its goals, does the proposal adequately explain why and what the organization intends to do about it?
~ Is the proposal in keeping with the funder's own priorities?

Feasibility of the project

~ Does the proposal illustrate how it will adequately cope with the problem it has identified, and is it neither too limited in its objectives nor too grandiose in its claims?
~ If it proposes to meet a long-standing problem, does the proposal have a well-conceived rationale for how it expects to succeed?
~ Does the proposal demonstrate a depth of knowledge about what is happening in the community and throughout the country?
~ Does the proposal show sufficient awareness of the complexity of the problem?
~ On the basis of research of programs in other communities, does the proposal indicate why it can succeed in the same way as have others?
~ If others have failed, what modifications are proposed to ensure success?

Possibility of leveraging funds

- Will the project draw on other private or public funding?
- If the amount of the request for funding is large, has the organization explored combining this request with requests to other funding organizations?
- If several funders are involved, can each funder's contribution be separately identified?

Continuity of the project

- If funds are being requested for a start-up project, what are the assurances of the requesting organization or another group to continue it?
- If the proposal is a demonstration project, what is the likelihood it might be replicated if it proves successful?

Impact potential

- Are the results likely to be transferable to other programs and other communities?
- Will the results have a significant impact on the community?
- Does the organization have a record of being able to involve other organizations and outside individuals to work together to achieve objectives?
- If the proposal purports to make institutional changes, what assurances can it offer that it will be able to succeed?

Dedication

- If the proposal was previously rejected, has it been resubmitted with necessary modifications made?
- Does the organization demonstrate a willingness and ability to obtain resources from its own community or constituency?

Clarity of proposal

- Is the proposal written clearly with professional jargon used selectively?
- Are subheadings used to guide the reader?
- Is the proposal concise?

Fiscal soundness

- ~ Is the budget adequate to do the job but not wasteful?
- ~ Are there contingency plans if income or expenses are not as expected?
- ~ Does the operational budget of the organization appear sound?
- ~ Does the organization have a 501(c)(3) tax-exempt status with the IRS?

Record of results

- ~ Will there be accurate recording of results to demonstrate the project's success?
- ~ Has appropriate evaluation advice been considered?
- ~ Will the funder be kept informed through written or verbal reports?

Following these guidelines can both enhance your competitiveness and provide a basis for a well-thought-out plan that can be implemented effectively to achieve your objectives.

NOTES

1. R. Brody, *Guide for applying for federal funds for human services* (Cleveland, OH: Case Western Reserve University, School of Applied Social Sciences, 1974); R. Brody, *Problem solving: Concepts and methods for community organizations* (New York: Human Sciences Press, 1982), pp. 170-172; M. S. Hall, *Getting funded: A complete guide to proposal writing* (Portland, OR: Portland State University, 1988), pp. 15-20.

2. M. S. Hall, pp. 15-20.

3. R. Brody, *Problem solving,* pp. 170-172.

4. J. C. Geever & P. McNeill (Eds.), *The Foundation Center's guide to proposal writing* (Rev. ed.) (Washington, DC: Foundation Center, 1997), pp. 1-4.

5. L. F. Jacquette & B. I. Jacquette, *What makes a good proposal* (Washington, DC: Foundation Center, 1977), pp. 1-7.

6. J. Gooch, *Writing winning proposals* (Washington, DC: Council for the Advancement of Education, 1987).

7. R. Brody, *Problem solving,* pp. 41-42.

8. N. J. Kiritz, *Program planning & proposal writing* (Los Angeles: Grantsmanship Center, 1980), p. 15.

9. R. Brody, *Problem solving,* p. 179.

10. J. C. Geever & P. McNeill, *The Foundation Center's guide,* pp. 111-120.

11. A. Lauffer, *Grants, etc.* (2nd ed.) (Thousand Oaks, CA: Sage, 1997), pp. 272-275.

12. P. F. Drucker, What results should you expect? A users' guide to MBO, *Public Administration Review* (1976, January/February), pp. 12-39; R. Elkin & D. J. Vorvaller, Eval-

uating the effectiveness of social services, *Management Controls* (1972, May), pp. 104-111; A. P. Raia, *Managing by objectives* (Glenview, IL: Foresman, 1974), p. 24.

13. H. Rossi & H. E. Freeman, *Evaluation: A systematic approach* (Newbury Park, CA: Sage, 1989), p. 141.

14. R. Steiner, *Total proposal building* (Albany, NY: Trestletree, 1988), pp. 121-122.

15. R. Brody, *Problem solving,* pp. 185-187.

16. L. E. Decker & V. A. Decker, *Grantseeking: How to find a funder and write a winning proposal* (Charlottesville, VA: Community Collaborators, 1993), p. 71.

17. J. C. Geever & P. McNeill, *The Foundation Center's guide,* pp. 111-120.

18. M. E. Burns, *Proposal writer's guide* (Hartford, CT: Development & Technical Assistance Center, 1989), p. 18.

19. J. C. Geever & P. McNeill, *Guide to proposal writing* (New York: Foundation Center, 1997).

20. J. C. Geever & P. McNeill, *Guide to proposal writing,* p. 140.

21. M. Morth & S. Collins (Eds.), *The Foundation Center's user friendly guide: A grantseeker's guide to resources* (New York: Foundation Center, 1996).

22. M. Johnston, *The nonprofit guide to the Internet* (2nd ed.) (New York: John Wiley, 1999), pp. 129-130.

23. J. C. Geever & P. McNeill, *The Foundation Center's guide,* pp. 111-120.

Chapter 20

SEARCHING FOR FUNDS

MAJOR SOURCES OF FOUNDATION FUNDING

Because there are potentially thousands of funders, you must be highly selective in finding those few that are appropriate for your organization and your proposal. Initially, you may have to identify many funding sources and then undertake a process of elimination to determine which ones are right for you. To avoid a time-consuming and often futile approach, it is best to initially select a core of foundations that match your interests. The ease of word processing might tempt you to send out "boilerplate" proposals indiscriminately. This kind of diffused distribution, however, is generally ineffective. Through research, you can pinpoint those foundations whose patterns of giving during the past several years reflect an interest in your area.

The best way to learn about foundations is to write to the Foundation Center at 79 Fifth Avenue, New York, NY 10003. The center will send you a publication catalog that describes major sources of information about foundations. These sources, which include summary statements of each foundation's requirements, are available for purchase or through the facilities of the center in New York or its offices in Atlanta, Washington, D.C., Cleveland, or San Francisco. The center also has a network of Cooperating Collections (books, periodicals, fund-raising materials, and directories) in all 50 states and some foreign countries. For information, call 1-800-424-9836.

The names of the Cooperating Collections can also be found at the Foundation Center web site (*www.fdncenter.org*). At this site, you can find grant-maker information and funding trends, take a short course in proposal writing, or read summaries on recent newspaper articles about philanthropy. The Foundation Center's web site is updated and expanded on a daily basis and provides a wide range of philanthropic resource information. For weekly information on grant makers' new requests for proposals, use the web site *www.fdncenter.org/pnd/current/.*

Human service organizations are likely to request funds from three types of foundations: community foundations, independent foundations, and corporate foundations. *Community foundations* are publicly supported organizations that make grants for social, religious, educational, or other charitable purposes. They are supported by, and operated for the benefit of, a specific community or region. They receive their funds from a variety of donors, both living and those who have made bequests in their wills to establish endowments. Their endowments are frequently composed of many different trust funds, some of which bear their donors' names. Their grant-making activities are administered by a governing body or distribution committee representative of community interests. Investment funds are managed professionally, usually by trustee banks. You can find out about community foundations through their IRS 990 tax return, which is available to the public. Many publish guidelines or annual reports.[1]

A community foundation responds to such a broad range of community concerns that almost anything fits within that charge. Even community foundations develop priorities, however. You can determine what they are through their 990 tax returns, annual reports, foundation directories, or CD-ROM (discussed later). For best results, concentrate on the community foundation that serves your local area.

Private, independent foundations are established to provide funds for community, educational, religious, or other charitable purpose. They derive funds from individuals, families, or groups of individuals. They may be operated under the direction of the donor or members of the donor's family, a type often referred to as "family foundations," or they may have an independent board of trustees or directors that manages the foundation's program. Many people can be responsible for making decisions in these foundations: the donor, members of the donor's family, independent directors, or a trust official acting on the donor's behalf. Because independent foundations can be inundated with requests, many have specific guidelines and priorities. Frequently, they limit their giving to the local area; in many instances, they may not wish to have applications submitted to them.

Information about independent foundations can be found by contacting them directly. Only a small percentage issue separately printed annual reports. Annual information can be obtained from the IRS tax returns (990-PF) that must be made available to the public. These can be found at the Foundation Center offices. The following are good directory sources of information: the *Foundation Grants Index,* the *Foundation Directory,* the *Foundation Directory Part II,* and the *Guide to U.S. Foundations.* (Specific directories will be discussed later.) Also, use the Foundation Center's web site for 900 links to grant-maker web sites (*www.fdncenter.org/grantmaker/*). If you have the name of a foundation and all you need is its address, contact name, or basic fiscal information, the Foundation Center's Foundation Finder can provide this information (*www.Inp.fdncenter.org/finder.html/*).

Corporate foundations, also called company-sponsored foundations, are created and funded by business corporations for the purpose of making grants and performing other philanthropic activities, which they do as separate legal entities. Generally, they are managed by a separate board of directors composed of corporate officials, although the board may also include individuals with no corporate affiliation. (In some company-sponsored foundations, local plant managers and senior officials are also involved in grant making and policy decisions.) Their giving programs usually focus on communities in which the company has operations or other company interests. A corporate foundation makes it possible for a company to set aside funds for use in years when earnings may be reduced and the needs of charitable organizations may be greater. Some corporations maintain both a company-sponsored foundation and a direct-giving program, with the two often coordinated under a general giving policy.[2]

Company-sponsored foundations should not be confused with corporate contributions or direct-giving programs that are under the full control of the corporation, with funds drawn solely from the corporation's pretax earnings. In addition to monetary grants, direct-giving programs may also encompass noncash "in-kind" contributions, such as donations of equipment, office space, supplies, or the labor of volunteer employees. In contrast, a company-sponsored foundation, despite its close ties to the parent company, is legally an independent organization. It is classified as a "private foundation" under the Internal Revenue Code and is subject to the same regulations as any other private foundation. The foundation receives funds from the parent company's pretax earnings, which it then "passes on" to nonprofit organizations in the form of contributions. It may also maintain its own endowment, however small.

In some instances, a corporation may choose to make charitable contributions to the same nonprofit organization through both its foundation and its direct-giving program. In such situations, there may be little difference in the giving interests and procedures of the two vehicles, and they may even be administered by the same staff and board. There are significant differences, however, in the type and amount of information available to the public about these two funding vehicles.

By law, corporate foundations must report annually on their activities and grant programs to the IRS on Form 990-PF, which is used by all private foundations. Many corporate foundations also issue annual reports or informational brochures detailing their program interests and application procedures. Corporations are not required, however, to inform the public about contributions and grants made directly through the corporation. As a result, even with an increasing number of corporations choosing to publicize their giving interests, restrictions, and application procedures, it is generally much more difficult to research direct corporate giving programs.

Faced with justifying philanthropy, corporate decision makers are increasingly expecting grant receivers to provide measurable program results. Corporate contributions must be shown to result in direct and tangible benefits to strategic business objectives. Programs that can document success in improving community services and racial harmony, for example, are attractive to corporate donors because of their potential to benefit community relations.[3]

Government Funding

Tracking governmental funds can be a daunting challenge. The payoff can be great, but so are the restrictions. To be chosen over many competitors, you will have to conduct careful research and have tremendous perseverance. Despite a general decline in support, the federal government is still the largest resource for external funding. Government funding information can be obtained from a variety of major sources.[4]

The *Federal Register* is published each weekday. For those who are interested in a variety of grant possibilities and who are able to respond to short deadlines, the *Federal Register* should be read daily. The Highlights section in the front lists major topics. The Notices section describes grant availability. Announcements are made of rules governing programs so that, although money is not immediately available, you can gain an idea of which grants are likely to be funded later. The *Federal Register* is available at most major public or university libraries, or write to Superintendent of Documents, U.S. Government Printing Office, Washington, D.C. 20402 for subscription information. You can also write to the Office of the Federal Register, c/o National Archives and Records, 8th and Pennsylvania Avenue, NW, Washington, D.C. 29408. Use the Internet to access the *Federal Register* (*www.access.gpo.gov/su_docs/aces/aces140.html*).

The Commerce Business Daily lists all potential contracts. Unlike grants, which give grantees more latitude over the use of funds, contracts require activities that their funders specify in advance. The federal agency determines the type of program, format of activity, expected outcome, costs, and length of time. This is a good resource if you are interested in marketing your goods and services to the government. Write to the Superintendent of Documents.

The *Catalog of Federal Domestic Assistance,* published annually, is the most comprehensive source of government grant programs. It provides detailed information for each program on applications, procedures, condition of eligibility, and deadlines. The financial section describes monies available for the past and current year and indicates the pattern of grant giving. Descriptions of each program provide detailed information on the purpose of the program, eligibility requirements, and application procedures. Indexes by sponsoring agency, subject, functional program categories, and eligible applicant groups enable users to identify the most appropriate funding programs. Call the Government Printing Office (202-783-3238). It is not absolutely current, and changes may have occurred since it went to print. Check with the appropriate program officer for updated information, or you can write to the Superintendent of Documents. It is also on the General Services Administration web site (*http://www.gsa.gov/fdac*).

The Federal Assistance Program Retrieval System is a computerized question-answer system designed to give rapid access to information provided in the catalog. Contact the Federal Assistance Catalog, General Services Administration Reports Building, 3007 7th St., SW, Washington, D.C. 20407.

On the basis of readings and general contracts with officials, you should be able to determine what is being funded. Your next step is to make alterations in the framing of your original issue or problem area to fit government priorities. To obtain federal funding, you must conform to the federal requirements rather than expect that the federal government will make changes to meet your agency's particular needs. Federal agency priorities are published in the *Federal Register* and usually include the specific population to be served, the application deadline, and the type of proposal document to be submitted.

It is generally a good idea to communicate with the program officer responsible for the grant in either the regional office or in Washington, D.C.; the officer's name and number can be obtained from the *Federal Register.* The program officer will be able to provide you with selection criteria. These criteria are extremely important because they indicate the basis on which the proposal will be judged by impartial readers. Because proposal reviewers subtract points when a proposal does not fit selection criteria, your proposal should be as responsive to these as possible.

In addition to these regular sources, every federal agency will periodically announce funds available for specified projects. These announcements provide detailed guidelines. It is useful to contact the appropriate federal agency to get on its mailing list for an application packet. You will be sent a request for proposal kit that contains details of the grant, the average award amount, the possibility of renewal, eligibility requirements, required format, restrictions, and the role of local or state government. This information should serve as your guidelines for preparing the proposal.

The grants and awards site dealing with multiple or single government agencies is *www.access.gpo.gov/su-docs/dpositopicsigrants.html.* At this site, there are many government references related to health and human services. Click "Grants and Awards," and then click on a category in which you are interested. You will be taken to a grant's page that will provide you with a wealth of information on funding possibilities. The categories are

Federal Domestic Assistance Catalog

Department of Health and Human Services Grant Net, Department of Education

Department of Housing and Urban Development, National Institute on Aging

National Institute of Health

Economic Development Agency

Justice Department

DESCRIPTION OF FOUNDATION DIRECTORIES

Directories on community, corporate, and private foundations are available at the four Foundation Center offices in Cleveland, Atlanta, Washington, D.C., and San Francisco or at the Cooperating Collections, usually located in libraries serving urban communities.[5] For the location nearest you, check with the Foundation Center web site (*www.fdncenter.org*), or write to the Foundation Center for the latest catalog. Many directories are available.

The *National Directory of Corporate Giving* gives reliable and up-to-date entries for more than 2,700 foundations and direct giving programs. Corporate funders often make grants that reflect the priority interests of their parent companies. The *National Directory* provides detailed information for more than 1,800 corporate foundations and approximately 900 direct giving programs. It features the following essential information: application procedures, names of key personnel, types of support generally awarded, giving limitations, financial data, and purposes and activities statements. Many entries include descriptions of recently awarded grants and program analyses to further indicate the grant-maker's interests.

The *Foundation Grants Index* is the most current and accurate source of information on recent grant-maker awards. The *Grants Index* details the grant-making programs of more than 1,000 of the largest independent, corporate, and community foundations in the United States and features more than 73,000 grant descriptions of $10,000 or more. Designed for quick grants-based research, its descriptions are divided into 28 broad subject areas, such as health and social services. Within each of these broad areas, the grants are listed geographically by state and alphabetically by name. The subject index targets grant makers by thousands of key words so that you can identify programs similar to the one you are interested in having funded. The geographic index directs you to foundations that have made grants in various geographic areas. The recipient category index helps you find foundations that have supported your type of organization (community organizations, human services, etc.). The recipient name index allows you to determine the foundations that have funded specific nonprofits that share your goals.

The Foundation 1,000 provides the most comprehensive information available on the 1,000 wealthiest foundations in the United States. These foundations hold more than $168 billion in assets. They award approximately 200,000 grants worth $8 billion to nonprofit organizations each year. This directory describes which major foundations support projects similar to yours in your geographic area, what projects they have recently funded, how much of their budget they have earmarked for your interest area, and the names and affiliations of the foundations' key personnel. You can target potential funders by using subject areas preferred, types of support favored, and geographic areas typically funded.

The Foundation Directory features current data on more than 7,900 grant makers that have assets of at least $2 million or annually distribute $200,000 or more. The directory provides fund raisers with insight into foundation giving priorities by describing more than 38,000 recently awarded grants.

The Foundation Directory Part 2 is designed specifically for nonprofit organizations that want to broaden their base to include midsized foundations that hold assets between $1 million and $2 million or with annual grant programs from $50,000 to $200,000. It includes more than 20,000 grant descriptions.

The *Guide to U.S. Foundations* provides current information on more than 40,000 foundations. The comprehensive trustee, officer, and donor index will be useful to determine possible foundation affiliations of your board members, donors, and volunteers. This is a good guide to use for identifying smaller foundations. Arranged by state and total giving, it can assist in pinpointing where to concentrate your search for local grant dollars. Also, you can check the trustee, officer, and donor names to learn more about the giving choices of local families. The guide uses codes to indicate if another Foundation Center reference book includes more detailed information on the grant maker that you are researching. Using this guide, you can note the employer identification number that will help you locate the foundation's IRS information return (990-PF), which is the best source of information for foundations too small to be included in the Foundation Directory Part 2.

The *Grant Guides* provide current information on grants recently awarded in your field. Each guide gives descriptions of hundreds of foundation grants of $10,000 or more recently awarded in your subject area. The subject index lets you search for grant makers by hundreds of key words. The geographic index directs you to foundations that have funded projects in your state or county. The recipient index lets you track grants awarded to similar organizations in your field. The following guides are relevant to human services:

Aging

Alcohol & Drug Abuse

Children and Youth

Community/Economic Development, Housing, & Employment

Crime, Law Enforcement, & Abuse Prevention

Health Programs for Children & Youth

Homeless

Literacy, Reading, & Adult/Continuing Education

Mental Health, Addictions, & Crisis Services

Minorities

Physically & Mentally Disabled

Program Evaluation Grants

Social Services

Women & Girls

THE SEARCH PROCESS

For a more manageable process of searching for funds through one or more of the directories noted previously, consider conducting your search in several phases.

Phase I. Prior to beginning your search, you should formulate a description of what you want to accomplish, including the problem you want to deal with, your target population, and your specific outcomes. The more focused you are, the easier your grant-seeking search will be. Although at this point in the process you need not have developed a complete proposal, it is highly desirable to write your ideas on 2 or 3 pages. The discipline of writing will encourage you to think through who you want to reach and what you want to do. Your quest at this phase is to develop a focused, easily searchable idea.

Phase II. In Phase II, you want to develop a broad list of potential supporters. Think of the search process as an inverted pyramid. You want to identify as many possibilities as you can and then work toward refining the list to a few that are most appropriate. Initially, your thought may be too broad. Therefore, even in this initial phase, you may want to be focused. Your 2- or 3-page document should be helpful in providing you with this focus. For example, if your broad idea is social service counseling, you could potentially have hundreds of possible funders. By narrowing your idea to counseling teenagers who are involved in substance abuse, you can embark on a more productive and manageable search.

Be mindful, however, not to be too narrow in your initial selection of topics. The search process involves a truly creative exploration of different possibilities. The example of trying to find funds for counseling teenagers could include the following different subject categories:

Adolescents

Alcoholism

Mental health

Drugs

Suicide

Pregnancy prevention

By scanning the subject indexes in the *Foundation Directory* and the *Foundation Grants Index,* you will get some ideas of relevant subjects for your grant proposal. During this phase, it is important not to focus your search too narrowly because, on the one hand, it is possible that those funders who have previously funded projects identical to yours may not want to repeat their funding. On the other hand, you may be able to locate funders who have similar, although not identical, interests to yours. They may be looking for fresh ideas.

Phase III. In Phase III, you will begin to narrow down your broad list of possibilities to as many as 10 or 20 potential funders. Assuming you have access to various previously discussed directories, you would consider using one or more of the following:

1. If you are seeking a grant of more than $10,000, use the following sources:
   - *Indexes of Foundation Grants* provides information on actual grants of $10,000 or more by the largest foundations.
   - The *Grant Guides* identify foundations in other states that might fund organizations in your specific subject area and geographic location.

- ~ *The Foundation 1,000* gives detailed information on major foundations in your state or nationally.
- ~ *The Foundation Directory* is a major source for foundations that give sizable grants.

2. If your grant is likely to be less than $10,000, use the following sources:
   - ~ *The Foundation Directory* identifies smaller grants in addition to large ones.
   - ~ *The Foundation Directory Part 2* provides information on foundations that annually give between $50,000 and $200,000. Also check the subject index for foundations in your state.
3. If you are interested in applying for a corporate foundation grant, the *National Directory of Corporate Giving* is an essential resource.

Phase IV. In this phase, your interest is in narrowing the list of approximately 20 possible foundations to 3 to 5. You do this by identifying various criteria: the geographic focus, contact information, limitations, range of donations, trustees, and pertinent information contained in the 990 forms. You can find out most of this information from the directories or the *FC Search* CD-ROM (discussed later). You may wish to keep a worksheet of your findings, as shown in Figure 20.1.

Focus primarily on foundations that fund grants in your local area. Do not, however, limit your search only to those whose address is limited to the central city. You can probably scan foundations listed by your state to determine those that could fund programs in your local community. Most foundations restrict their giving to a specific community, state, or multistate region. If you are seeking a relatively small grant with a purely local impact, you need to identify foundations that fund primarily in your local area. Most corporations will provide resources to communities in which they have facilities. Review the location of these facilities for possible connections to your community.

If you are seeking corporate support, it is a good idea to obtain an annual report or printed guidelines that will contain the company's philosophy and its plans for the future. Determine whether you need to send a letter of inquiry or a full proposal. Some corporations have established separate foundation offices. Others may implement their giving programs through their marketing department, in which case their corporate giving is more closely tied to

Information source:

Name
Address

Contact person: **Phone number:**

Financial data:

Total assets
Grant ranges
Single year Multiyear

Subject focus priorities:

Target populations:

Special limitations:

Geographic
Funding restrictions

Types of support:

Program development
Ongoing support
Other

Trustees:

Application information:

Printed guidelines
Application forms

Initial approach (letter of inquiry, formal proposal, or phone call):

Deadlines:

Proposal submission dates
Trustee decision times

Follow-up notes:

Figure 20.1. Worksheet on Potential Funders[6]

marketing company products. Always call to determine where your letter of proposal should be sent.

Typically, foundation descriptions, located in the various directories, will indicate limitations. Read this section carefully to determine what the specific foundation will not fund. For example, some foundations will not provide funds for ongoing operations, new projects, capital campaigns, or certain subject categories. In addition, some foundations will not provide funds for equipment or conferences. Descriptions also indicate the highest, lowest, and average grants given in the past. You may conclude that your grant request may be inappropriate based on your funding needs.

Another method of determining prospective funders is to review the list of trustees connected to the foundation and to consider whether members of your board have a relationship with them. In the case of corporate foundations, access to trustees who are employed by a corporation that could fund your project might give you an advantage.

To find out more about specific foundations, you should check their publications, including annual reports, guidelines, and newsletters. Many community foundations produce these, and even large, private foundations will provide you with copies. If you have access to the Foundation Center or Cooperating Collections, you can obtain detailed information on private and corporate foundations by examining their IRS 990-PF forms. Contact your local IRS office or nearest Foundation Center library for the latest 990-PF forms, which include lists of all foundations' funding interests, restrictions, application procedures, and deadlines. Some libraries also keep a news clippings file on foundations.

In summary, the sequence of the foundation search process involves two major steps. First, using the *Foundation Directory, Grants Index,* and other specialized directories (including, in some instances, state foundation directories), identify foundations that make grants in subject areas similar to yours. Second, research the foundations you have identified by checking their sourcebook profiles, published annual reports, and tax returns. It is imperative that you try to ascertain their funding priorities.

Using the *FC Search* CD-ROM

Several CD-ROMs provide data on foundations. Their advantage compared to hard-copy directories described earlier is that they can save you a tremendous amount of searching time as you seek to pinpoint the proper match.

The most comprehensive CD-ROM is called *FC Search,* which provides information on more than 53,000 U.S. foundations and corporate givers. This disc also provides information on approximately 200,000 associated grants and identifies more than 183,000 trustees and donors.

FC Search includes data found in the following sources:

The Foundation Directory

The Foundation Directory Part 2

The Foundation Directory Supplement

The Guide to U.S. Foundations: Their Trustees, Officers, and Donors

The National Directory of Corporate Giving

The Foundation Grants Index

The Foundation Grants Index Quarterly

Because it costs $1,200 per year, the *FC Search* CD-ROM is too expensive for most organizations that only occasionally need to undertake a search. It is updated semiannually, which is important because foundations are constantly being added or eliminated. If your organization frequently searches for grants, this may be a good use of organizational funds. Otherwise, try to convince your local university or public library to purchase one. To locate the 200 Cooperating Collections that have the CD-ROM available, use the Foundation Center's web site (*www.fdncenter.org*). Click on "Cooperating Collections," and then note those nearest you that have the CD-ROM icon next to their names.

The CD-ROM provides information on both grant makers and grant files. By browsing through these two files, you can determine the kinds of grants awarded by different grant makers and then obtain more detailed information on the grants.

FC Search has a browse function that allows you to review lists of records in each database. You can browse the entire list or concentrate on specific states. By browsing the grant-maker file, you can quickly locate a specific grant maker and then search a list of grants previously made by that foundation. Browsing the grant file lets you scan a list of grants given to organizations, and then you can review the individual grants given to that organization.

The search function lets you pinpoint grant makers or grants meeting your specific criteria. Such criteria may include the following:

Geographic focus (nationally, state, or local)

Fields of interest (e.g., social services)

Types of support (capital, seed money, etc.)

Total assets

Total giving

Subjects

Annual dollar amount

Text search (based on specific words that you select that may be in the grant record)

In the Advanced Grants mode, you can conduct an in-depth search of grants, the grant makers that awarded them, and the specific organizations that received them. This is especially helpful if you want to determine which grant makers provide grants in a specific subject area, for a specific population group, and in a specific locality. One of the benefits of this search process is that it contains an index that is especially helpful in guiding your search. The following are among the general fields of interest that are appropriate for health and human service agencies:

Civil rights

Community development

Crime/law enforcement

Education

Employment

Environment

Health care

Health organization

Housing/shelter

Human services

Mental health/crises services

Mutual aid societies

Philanthropy/volunteerism

Recreation

Social sciences

Social services

Youth development

Within each field of interest is a listing of subject categories. Become familiar with these categories because your search can be matched more directly with key words from the index. For example, if you were interested in searching for fund programs for ex-offenders, you could search for this subject under the crime/law field of interest.[7]

The following items are illustrative of the searches you could undertake with *FC Search:*

- The address and telephone number of specific foundations
- An alphabetical listing of all nonprofit organizations in your state or community
- All the grant makers in your state that fund social services
- Foundations in your state that have given grants relating to aging and Alzheimer's disease
- Names of the trustees of a particular foundation
- Foundations that give more than $100,000 for capital grants
- Corporate foundations in your state that have given funds for specific purposes such as building equipment
- Foundations that provide basic operating funds in your local community
- Foundations that have given money for specific purposes, such as workshops or technical assistance
- Foundations that have given to organizations similar to yours (e.g., Boy Scouts, YMCAs, and the Red Cross)

Suggested Search Strategies Using the *FC Search*

The search strategies described earlier also apply to the *FC Search.* The obvious advantage in using the CD-ROM instead of the directories is the speed with which you can conduct your search. If you plan to use the CD-ROM, the following suggestions may prove useful:

1. Your primary objective is to locate foundations that will be amenable to funding your project based on past giving patterns. For example, you assume that a particular foundation that previously funded a foster care recruitment program will be receptive to your foster care recruitment proposal. This may or may not be the case; having funded a previous foster care program, the foundation may be searching for other kinds of programs to help vulnerable children. Through an inquiry letter or a phone call, you may be able to determine whether the proposal you have in mind is still a priority for the foundations you have identified.

2. Conversely, foundations that may not have previously funded a program similar to what you have in mind may now be open to considering an innovative foster care recruitment effort. Knowing that these foundations are interested in vulnerable children in general may be a good starting point for exploration.

3. The search process can thus be too broad or too narrow. Therefore, expect to use the *FC Search* as a tool for exploration. The search process can involve a certain amount of trial and error. For example, suppose you are interested in establishing drug-free zones in your community. Perhaps very few foundations have funded such an effort. That need not deter you from exploring foundations that have an interest in substance abuse, prevention, alcoholism, or neighborhood development. You can explore all these categories to determine your initial list of subjects. Be prepared to broaden your search if you identify too few "hits"; be prepared, however, to narrow your search if you identify too many hits.

4. You need to learn the specific techniques for using the *FC Search.* It is worth your time to take a workshop if one is offered by your Cooperating Collection or at least to study the manual that is available with the CD-ROM. You will learn specific techniques and vocabulary for expanding or narrowing your search.

5. Assume you have a particular topic in mind. In conducting a search, you can either scroll through a field of interest, and you will have available a preselected index, or use Text Search, which will search for words appearing anywhere within the grant-maker records. Using Text Search will require experimenting and time to understand the rules, but mastering it will allow you to explore vast amounts of data.

The manual will indicate how focused your query can be. For example, putting quotes around the first three letters of a local zip code would narrow the list to local foundations that fund grants in your community and nearby suburbs. Also, by typing "applications not accepted," you would eliminate from the search process those foundations that do not accept outside grant requests. There are many other techniques discussed in the manual that will greatly enhance your search process.

6. Check the "Types of Support Index" to limit your search to the types of support various grant makers provide. The following list can be useful in determining how foundations categorize their support:

Annual campaigns	Equipment
Building/renovation	General/operating support
Capital campaigns	In-kind gifts
Conferences/seminars	Internships
Consulting services	Loaned talent
Continuing support	Matching funds
Debt reduction	Program development
Donated equipment	Public relations services
Donated products	Publication
Emergency funds	Research
Employee volunteer services	Seed money
Endowment funds	Technical assistance

7. In considering foundations that might give funding to your community, focus not only on those foundations located in your community or your state but also those located elsewhere that have given grants in your area.
8. With *FC Search,* you can print or save the search results lists or grant-maker records you have specifically marked, and then you can examine them later.

SUMMARY

Searching for funds requires a considerable amount of creative ingenuity. The availability of directories and CD-ROMs makes it possible to explore a wide variety of possibilities in a fairly short time period. Expect a great deal of trial and error. Above all, be persistent in your quest.

NOTES

1. M. F. Nauffts (Ed.), *Foundation fundamentals: A guide for grantseekers* (5th ed.) (New York: Foundation Center, 1994).

2. M. F. Nauffts, p. 3.

3. J. D. Marx, Corporate strategic philanthropy: Implications for social work, *Social Work* (1988, January), pp. 35-41.

4. K. Borden, *Dear uncle: Please send money—A guide for proposal writers* (Pocatello, ID: Auger, 1978).

5. The Foundation Center, *Fundraising & nonprofit development resources catalog* (New York: Author, 1997, Fall).

6. The Foundation Center, Prospect worksheet, in *The Foundation Center's user-friendly guide* (Rev. ed.) (New York: Author, 1994).

7. The Foundation Center, *FC search manual* (New York: Author, 1997), p. 27.

Chapter 21

FUND-RAISING EVENTS
Strategies for Success

FACTORS TO CONSIDER IN PLANNING AN EVENT

Before undertaking a fund-raising event, two fundamental questions should be asked. First, how much money does the organization need to raise from a fund-raising event? The answer cannot simply be "All we can raise." Obviously, you want to raise as much money as possible, but for the purposes of exploring possibilities it is desirable to have a financial objective in mind. Prior to a discussion of any particular event, you should have determined a budget for the year, including how much you intend to raise from an event. If your budget calls for raising $4,000 from an event, this will suggest one kind of activity; if it calls for $40,000, you will need to consider a different kind of activity. You must therefore determine a money amount to be raised prior to considering the range of possibilities. Then, examine the financial returns from a variety of events. For example, if you need to raise $4,000, do not consider a bake sale. If one event will not be sufficient, then you may want to consider planning several events to achieve your financial objective.

Second, do you have the people resources to undertake a fund-raising event? One of the most essential elements of any event is people who are committed, hardworking, creative, talented, and experienced. Determine if you have the kind of people who are willing to invest in making an event a success and a sufficient number of people to carry it through. Also, look inward to your members and constituency groups for special talents and experiences. Examine your group's connections, such as theater owners, party hall proprietors, owners of mansions or townhouses, or hotel managers. Compile a list of resources within the organization and those to which your members have access.

Gathering Ideas for an Event

Most organizations will find it helpful to develop imaginative ideas and to think creatively to make their events special. You will want to promote creative thinking because you want people to view your event as being different from the usual. Developing a special niche for your event in the charitable marketplace is an important way to attract a following.

If you have been offering an event for several years, you know that people can become tired of repeating the same program in the same way. Volunteers become stale, and the audience becomes bored unless something new and distinctive is provided. This should not be surprising: Clothing styles, musical tastes, automobiles, and soap packages are constantly revised to appeal to the changing tastes of consumers. Consider change and innovation as a natural way to prevent your fund-raising event from winding down.

Another reason to be creative is competition. In the long run, whatever initial niche or special advantage you have for your event, there is a tendency for decline because, if you are successful, you can be certain others will try to copy your idea. You may enjoy the advantage of uniqueness for awhile, but expect this to be only temporary. You need to consider adding innovation to your program or undertaking different imaginative events to stay ahead of your competition.

To think creatively, you must first develop an attitude geared toward imaginative thinking. This will enable you to search for ideas and draw on your knowledge and experience. With this open approach, you can try various slants. Assume that nothing is fixed and that any fund-raising event that you or others have tried is open to change. Even though previous events may have been successful, different circumstances may be operating currently or there may be better and different ways to continue the event. You must be open to challenging familiar formats. Also, if necessary, you have to be willing to fall out of love with a cherished tradition or program.

You must be willing to take risks. Exploring new ideas means exposing your organization to the possibility of failure. Following the exploration of creative ideas, you should be critical to reduce risk of failure. Build on ideas. For example, suppose someone suggests a jog-a-thon, and you are well aware that the community is saturated with jog-a-thons. Someone else, however, might then suggest combining this with Halloween and having people wear costumes as part of the jog-a-thon; it could become a new, exciting event.

Throughout the creative process, remember that you are not seeking the unique for the sake of just being different. What matters most in this exploratory process is the willingness to search for worthwhile ideas. Before ideas are acted on, you must go through the critical phase of determining whether the new event, or the modification of an existing one, is feasible. Every fresh, imaginative proposal needs to be scrutinized from a variety of perspectives through a feasibility analysis.

Conducting a Feasibility Analysis

After you have generated many event possibilities, you need to ask whether each idea under consideration is worthwhile. Your goal is to narrow the list so that you can select one event that is right for you. Certainly, the possibility exists that an excellent idea will be dropped. An equal danger, however, is pursuing an event that should have been dropped but was not due to inadequate screening. It is better to abort early than to continue with an idea that could result in a dud. The screening process should eliminate all but the most desirable and feasible project ideas.

The following major questions should be considered in making a selection:

- Is the event appropriate for our organization and community?
- Will the event appeal to our members?
- Do we have the capacity to undertake the event?
- Will the event provide sufficient funds to warrant the effort?
- Can the event accomplish objectives beyond raising funds?
- Will the event appeal to our audience?
- Can the event compete successfully with those of other organizations?

The process of selecting an event is like an accordion. Initially, you will want to consider as many ideas as possible. Asking fundamental questions, brainstorming by using your imagination, and uncritically considering diverse suggestions will help expand the range of possibilities. Following this creative period, you will need to narrow the list of ideas through a series of feasibility questions into a few selected ones from which you can make your final decision. During this exploratory period, set a "go/no-go" date to discipline yourself to make a timely decision. Generally, you may want to allot approximately 2 months for the process of selecting an event.

SETTING OBJECTIVES

Every fund-raising event should have objectives that are relevant, attainable, and measurable. Objectives should pertain to the general mission and goals of the organization. Furthermore, objectives should be capable of being realized within a specified time period, such as 3 months to 1 year. Also, if possible, objectives should be based on tangible, concrete, and quantifiable results. For most events, financial objectives can be more easily measured than nonfinancial ones.

Financial Objectives

An event should establish income and expense objectives, as illustrated by the following examples:

Income objectives

- Sell a minimum of 350 tickets.
- Raise $15,000 total (gross) income.
- Obtain underwriting support of $2,000 from five corporations.
- Achieve a net income of $12,000.

Expense objectives

- Keep expenses under $3,000.
- Secure free floral decorations.
- Obtain free printing services.

Note that each of these is an action-oriented objective that conveys concrete results to be achieved.

In establishing financial objectives, be as realistic as possible. If you strive for net income objectives that are too high, volunteers will feel unduly pressured. Also, if the objective is not achieved, they will experience a sense of defeat—even if more money is raised than ever before. Setting too low a financial objective, however, might result in volunteers not working hard enough. Finding the right balance of encouraging people to extend themselves without causing undue frustration is indeed a challenge. A financial objective that is within reach, reasonable, and achievable, even though it involves tremendous work, gives everyone a sense of positive accomplishment.

Usually, net income objectives should be related to a specific cause or project. People generally like to feel that their donations will be applied to something concrete. Money raised at a special event should not be lost in the basic operating budget of the organization. Ideally, these funds should be segregated out from the base budget and earmarked for a specific purpose in which volunteers and donors can take pride. Examples include a scholarship program, improving day care facilities, or funding a special teen counseling program.

Nonfinancial Objectives

Establishing nonfinancial objectives for a particular event is an individualized matter. Each organization has to decide its specific nonfinancial objectives for the event. In the following examples, indicators of success are identified:

Objective: increase the quality and quantity of volunteer participation

- Indicators of success
  - ~ Number of volunteers participating (compared to last year)
  - ~ Percentage of new volunteers
  - ~ Leadership opportunities
  - ~ Committee involvement

Objective: increase membership in the organization

- Indicators of success
  - ~ Number of people who attend the event and become new members following the event
  - ~ Number of former members who become reinvolved following the event

Objective: increase visibility of the organization

- Indicators of success
  - ~ Number of times the event is mentioned in the media
  - ~ Percentage of people attending the event who are not affiliated with the organization

Objective: increase goodwill toward the organization from the community

- Indicators of success
  - ~ Number of residents participating as volunteers
  - ~ Number of neighborhood persons attending

Defining the nonfinancial objectives and indicators of success in advance can benefit the organization, independent of financial objectives. Also, establishing objectives sharpens your thinking about events and activities you do not want to undertake in addition to those that you do want to undertake. For example, if your primary objective is to improve goodwill within your community, you should obviously think twice about sponsoring a booth at another community's festival.

PLANNING AN EVENT

Paying attention to details can contribute to the success of a fund-raising event. In any event, there are many details to master, and the omission of one or several can make the difference between a smoothly run event and a failure. Comprehensive, detailed planning can prevent cost overruns, volunteer burnout, and other failures; it can greatly contribute to the success of an event. Two tools that will facilitate paying attention to details are an activities list and a timeline chart.

Preparing an Activities List

An activities list can be produced through reverse-order planning or forward-sequence planning. In reverse-order planning, the group begins with the final result to be accomplished and identifies the tasks that feed into the activities. This is achieved by asking the following questions: "What must we do just before reaching our final result? What needs to be done before that, and before that, and so forth?" In this way, the group eventually arrives at the beginning point. In forward-sequence planning, the group begins with what it considers to be the appropriate set of tasks and then asks "What should be done next, and what after that, and so forth?" until the actual event occurs.

In reality, no group would compile a complete activities list in its first round of discussions. Whether forward-sequence or reverse-order planning is used, a review of the list of tasks will reveal the need to omit some tasks because they are unnecessary, reschedule some tasks to prevent overload, and add some tasks initially omitted. Even when the activities list appears to be in final form, be prepared for additional refinements based on new knowledge and circumstances.

After you have prepared an activities list, you may want to display the tasks and activities on a timeline chart (see Chapter 4) to check your progress visually. The advantage of a timeline chart is that it is comprehensive and comprehensible, easy to prepare, and simple to revise. The lines related to each task graphically show beginning and ending points. By reading the chart from top to bottom, it is possible to determine which activities and tasks are expected to occur within a particular time period.

ANALYZING POTENTIAL CUSTOMERS

For many events, you will have to recruit people from outside your organization because most memberships are too small to support most events. Certainly, you want your own members to be involved, but their greater value lies in their ability to mobilize and encourage outsiders to participate. By reaching beyond your core membership, you avoid "going to the same well too often," and you spread the base of commitment. Analyzing your market of potential customers is a major component of the planning process because it can enable you to involve more people in a major component of the planning process.

Market Segmentation

As you implement your event, ask the following important question: "To whom is this event likely to appeal?" A major way of analyzing potential customers is to divide them into constituencies based on how they are related to the organization. These can include a core constituency consisting of persons closest to the organization, such as board members, volunteers, and clients. They could also involve a second circle of constituents (sometimes called an incidental constituency), including families, friends, vendors, and inactive members. A third constituency is composed of members of the general community. Although not directly involved with your organization, community members may choose to participate because they believe in your cause or find the event particularly appealing.

Target Marketing

It is usually helpful to target your event to particular persons or groups in the community. Although some organizations try to develop an event that appeals to everyone, you run the risk of attracting a limited response if only a few consider the event especially related to them. By pinpointing segments, you develop an event that directly appeals to a particular group or groups. If you identify a fairly homogeneous group that will naturally respond, or if competition is fairly intense in all but a few segments of the market, you may want to concentrate on a narrow segment.

The following are examples of concentrated marketing:

Suppose your organization is a free clinic offering services to older teenagers and young adults. To attract your clientele and their friends, you determine that a rock concert at a farm outside of the city would be appealing.

Suppose your health organization is planning to sponsor a golf tournament for businessmen. You would most likely try to obtain mailing lists from country clubs and public golf courses to increase attendance at the event.

Suppose your organization is a family planning association organizing a boutique that has special appeal to young, single adults. To reach this population, you would probably promote the event among singles clubs and young adult groups affiliated with religious and other organizations.

With differentiated marketing, you concentrate on several specific marketing segments, tailoring an effective activity for each. For instance, you may decide to hold an event consisting of several components that would appeal to different market segments. Also, in the course of a year, you could purposefully decide to hold several different events, each appealing to different market segments. By offering event variations, you can achieve higher attendance and income, although expenses may also increase.

MANAGING FINANCES

Budgeting for an Event

Budgeting is an ongoing process that requires estimating and tracking income and expenses. Often, you must deal with projections or "guesstimates" that need to be revised as you obtain more information. Consider dividing the budget process into four phases. First, prepare an initial budget to determine whether the event has the potential for sufficient profit. Be conservative by estimating expenses on the high side and income on the low side. Second, prepare a detailed budget after you have decided to proceed with the event. Third, monitor income and expenses, and compare actual with budgeted amounts. Finally, after the event, review income and expenses to determine whether to repeat the event.

Setting Fiscal Objectives

Prior to establishing fiscal objectives, you should become familiar with certain key terms. The financial terms and calculations discussed in this section should be understood.

Gross profit is the amount needed to cover all costs and net profit. To determine gross profit, add expected costs and the desired financial objective. For example,

Costs	$1,200
Financial objective	$3,000
Gross profit	$4,200

Net profit is the amount left over after all costs are deducted from income. For example,

Income	$4,200
Costs	$1,200
Net income	$3,000

Fixed costs are those that occur no matter how many people attend the event. For example, no matter whether 200 or 300 people attend a dinner dance, there will be fixed costs of the band, hall rental, and promotional materials.

Variable costs are related to per-person units. For instance, the cost of a luncheon will vary according to the number of people attending. Similarly, the cost of souvenirs for a swim-a-thon will vary with the number of entrants.

Break-even point is the amount of sales you have to make to meet your expenses. After this point, all sales are net profit. If your costs are primarily fixed, then you can simply divide the total cost of the event by the cost of each ticket to determine your break-even point. For example, if your costs are $2,200 and you charge $10 per ticket, you will need to sell 220 tickets to cover the costs and break even. Any ticket sales more than 220 are your profits.

If, in addition to fixed costs, you have to consider variable costs, then these must be subtracted from the projected per-ticket income before dividing by the cost per ticket. For example, assume that the fixed costs of a dinner dance (band, hall rental, and promotion) are $2,200 and that each meal has a variable cost of $15, and you believe $50 is an appropriate price for each ticket. To calculate the break-even point, use the following formula:

$$\frac{\text{fixed costs}}{\text{ticket price} - \text{variable costs}} = \text{break-even point}$$

$$\frac{\$2{,}200}{(\$50 - \$15) = \$35} = 63 \text{ tickets}$$

In this example, you would have to sell 63 tickets to break even.

Percentage of profit reflects an event's cost-effectiveness by relating the profits to the costs. Sometimes, this is referred to as the profit margin. Determine what percentage of your gross profit is net profit so that you can determine the efficiency of the event and can make comparisons of the event under consideration with other events you have conducted or plan to conduct. For example, assume that you expect a gross profit of $25,000 from your dinner dance, and your costs are $11,000 and net profit is $14,000. Calculate your percentage of profit as follows:

$$\frac{\text{net profit (gross profit} - \text{costs)}}{\text{Gross profit}} = \text{profit percentage}$$

$$\frac{\$14{,}000\ (\$25{,}000 - \$11{,}000)}{\$25{,}000} = 56\%$$

You can now compare the profit percentage of this event. For example, for an art auction from which you expect to raise $10,200 gross profit and have expenses of $2,000, your net profit will be $8,200. The net profit of $8,200 divided by $10,200 equals 80%. Clearly, the auction is more cost-effective than the dinner dance. Of course, you may want to override the cost-efficiency consideration if you determine that the net amount raised is your primary objective. You may decide to undertake the dinner dance because it is likely to produce a higher net profit, even though it is less cost-efficient than the auction.

Once you are familiar with key financial terms, you can prepare your budget. In setting up a budget, you should determine two fiscal objectives. First, as discussed previously, establish a net profit objective that is achievable. It is better to set a $1,500 goal for a raffle and raise $1,800 than to establish a $2,500 goal and raise only $1,800. If you do not reach your goal, you risk having your volunteers become discouraged and unwilling to repeat an event that is identified as a partial failure. You may hope to eventually achieve $2,500 for this annual event as your ultimate financial objective, but expect to raise less than your optimum goal the first year of the event. Consider it a "dry run" as you work to establish a structure, procedures, and training for your volunteers. In subsequent years, expect to exceed your first year's performance, but be mindful that events plateau and even decline. If you are uncertain about establishing a specific net profit objective, consider a range (e.g., $2,000-$2,500). Another reason for establishing a net profit objective is that later you will want to evaluate your event by asking the fol- lowing questions: "Did we achieve our profit goal? If not, why? Were expenses higher than expected?" Setting objectives forces you to ask important questions.

Second, determine your percentage of profit (or profit margin). In the previous example, the estimated profit margin of a dinner dance was 56%. Suppose you determine that this figure is too low. To increase your profit margin, strive to reduce expenses or increase income. As a general rule, any anticipated profit margin less than 65% to 75% should be seriously assessed. For profit margins less than 50%, you should ponder whether to hold the event. For example, if you expect to raise $120,000 through a concert with anticipated expenses of $80,000, for a profit margin of 33%, you may still consider the $40,000 net profit worth the effort, despite the extremely low profit margin. In other words, in special circumstances you may accept a low margin of profit if this is the price you have to pay to achieve your financial or nonfinancial objectives. This should be a purposeful decision, however.

MAXIMIZING PROFITS

It is important to be on the lookout for ways to maximize profits from fund-raising events, whether they are new, successful, at a plateau, or declining. To do so, you need to develop marketing strategies.

There are six major marketing strategies designed to enhance income: (a) market penetration, which involves increasing income through increased sales to your existing event; (b) market development, which involves attracting new customers to your current event; (c) event expansion or development, which involves expanding your current event or providing a new event for your existing customer base; (d) diversification, which involves both developing new events and seeking new customers; (e) promoting sales; and (f) using the Internet to raise funds.

Penetrate Existing Markets

Market penetration consists of enhancing income through the increased sale of your existing event. The event remains essentially the same, but you present it to your customers in more attractive ways or you promote your efforts more aggressively. You would use a market penetration approach to increase the number of people attending an event. For instance, for the dinner dance example, you would explore the following questions, which could be adapted to other events:

- Should we increase the frequency of the event by offering more than one dinner dance each year?
- Should we lower the price from $75 to $50 to make the event appealing to more of our members?
- Can we improve our promotion efforts through more publicity and advertising to attract more people?
- Can we make the dinner dance more attractive by altering the locale or the time? For example, should we change from a Friday night at a local gym to a Saturday night at a hotel?
- Can we make the event more accessible by arranging for transportation for people who are reluctant to drive?

- Can we heighten the attractiveness of the event by using a more exciting theme or decorations?
- Can we schedule preevents to build up excitement for the event and attract more people to the actual event (e.g., dance lessons before the event)?

The purpose of these questions is to examine ways to make the current event more attractive to your anticipated audience while still preserving the inherent character of the event.

Develop New Markets

Market development consists of seeking increased sales by attracting new market segments to the event. The following are the kinds of questions to be explored regarding the same dinner dance example:

- Can we expand to additional geographic markets by holding the dance on the north side of town instead of on the customary south side?
- Can we appeal to different market segments, such as younger and less affluent groups, by offering a "night owl" arrangement (e.g., dessert and dancing) at a reduced cost?
- Can we attract a special segment of the community by honoring a community leader who has many personal and business associates who will want to attend?
- Can we add to our current potential attendance by expanding our mailing list of invitations from 1,000 to 4,000?

These questions reflect a way of thinking about seeking changes in your customer base.

Expand or Develop Events

Event expansion or development consists of seeking increased attendance by significantly improving the event for current market segments. The following are the kinds of questions to be explored:

- Can we alter the program by adding, rearranging, or combining features? Examples include adding special entertainment, including additional money raisers (e.g., a raffle, a cash bar, or charging for photographs), shortening the length of the speeches, or combining two major events, such as a dinner dance and an auction.

- Can we change the basic character of the event? For example, you might make the dinner dance more formal (black-tie) or less formal (square dance).

Considering questions such as these encourages thinking about ways to improve the event.

Diversify to Different Events and Markets

Diversification consists of developing a new event for a new market. This strategy makes sense when the organization believes that its current event is waning or if other opportunities appear to offer a superior financial return. Of course, this means focusing on areas in which members have skills and interests. The following are questions that might be asked:

- Can we change the event from a dinner dance to an entirely different event such as a decorators' showcase tour, which in turn could attract a different market?
- Should we continue to hold a dinner dance but shift some of our energy and time to another event such as a rummage sale? The result may be a slight decline in dinner dance attendance, but the rummage sale should draw new people and more than enough money to offset the decline in the income from the dinner dance.

The previously discussed four strategies are valuable because they force you to think purposefully about current and potential events in relation to current and potential markets.

Promoting Sales

Selling is what you think about first. This is how most successful event chairpersons proceed. They know that to raise money for their events, they must wage a tremendous selling campaign.

A few events may be so popular that you need not undertake a major selling campaign. If the event is sufficiently popular, all that may be necessary is to send out invitations and wait for the reservations to be made. Either the event is inherently attractive or the cause is so appealing that the main task is not selling but taking reservations. For some events, publicity, invitations, and word-of-mouth may be sufficient. Generally, however, these approaches do not bring people to an event. You must build a sales force of people to reach out aggressively to convince others to attend.

Some organizations make selling tickets mandatory. Unsold tickets are in effect purchased by the members. This approach requires a high degree of loyalty and commitment. Many organizations do not require this sell or purchase approach but rely on the voluntary participation of their sales force. Consider forming a special ticket-selling committee consisting of people who can contact large numbers of friends. People sell to people!

Also, focus on group sales. For example, ask people to commit to selling two or three tables to an event or set a number such as 30 tickets. Encourage friends to attend the event as a group. Identify table hosts and hostesses who commit to selling tables and are listed on the invitation or in the program book. Prepare a selling kit for sellers that gives details of the event, who will be benefiting, and a description of the work of the organization. If possible, hold a kickoff party for ticket sellers to generate enthusiasm. Keep in continuous contact with your sales force, preferably in person or by telephone. You may want to consider offering premiums for those who sell the most tickets. In summary, convey to your sellers that personal contact and continuous follow-up sell tickets.

Using the Internet to Raise Funds

The Internet offers an exciting opportunity for even the smallest organizations to reach out to both their members and nonmembers for fund-raising activities. Many agencies have web sites that they use to attract people navigating the Internet to become interested in their organization. An appealing web site can provide excellent publicity for an agency. Such a site can also encourage people to use membership forms to enroll. New members can become part of the organization's e-mail database and receive material immediately. Agency web sites can also provide a donor solicitation page. Potential donors are offered the opportunity to give directly, call a toll-free number to donate, or even use their credit cards to make a donation. When using a credit card, the potential donor is ensured a secure method of payment through the use of encryption, which codes the transaction. In this kind of secured transmission, all data are encoded—that is, translated into an undecipherable jumble of data that can be unscrambled only by the intended recipient.[1]

Some organizations use the Internet to directly conduct special events. For example, the Internet can be used to conduct auctions; sell products, such as candy or recording disks; or seek corporate sponsors for events. Organizations also use the Internet to participate in cause-related marketing (see Chapter 18). Persons committed to a particular agency are more likely to buy a company's product if they know that a percentage of the profits will be returned to the agency.[2]

REDUCING EXPENSES

There are several ways to reduce expenses, which in turn can maximize profits. First, assign at least one volunteer the task of purchasing items for the event at the lowest possible price. This shopper or "scrounge" should seek out items in person and keep meticulous records. The shopper should ask for a donation or at least a discount on items. Second, where possible, buy large quantities so you can obtain a discount. Perhaps you could consider joint purchasing with another local organization. Third, consider bartering by exchanging your services with those of another organization or business. For example, if you were sponsoring a concert, you could give free admission tickets to the printing company that provides promotional materials. Fourth, ask your volunteers to absorb some of the cost of the event in return for their listing expenses as tax-deductible donations. Finally, whenever possible, try to obtain free gifts and services—for example, an accounting firm providing a free audit or a grocery chain contributing food items.

Companies will sponsor events when they think they will benefit from the visibility of their participation. Whereas typical company sponsorship of a golf outing will be allocated from the public relations budget, support for an agency's annual fund drive would be allocated from the civic affairs budget. For example, the latter is used to underwrite tables as part of the organization's charitable contribution.

Corporations become involved because (a) they believe in your organization and its cause, (b) they view the event as a means of providing benefits to their employees, (c) they become more visible to current and potential customers throughout the community, and (d) they want to respond positively to a request from a high official or special customer. In considering corporate underwriting or sponsorship, focus on companies that have a natural relationship with the organization. This relationship can include company employees on your board of trustees, an honoree who is a company employee, or a company that has a connection with the type of event you are offering. For example, if your event is a "chili cook-off," you might interest a company that produces spices.

If you are interested in a company underwriter or sponsor, contact the appropriate person that handles requests. Try to time the request in advance of the company's normal annual budgeting process so that the event can be included in its allocations. After transmitting your letter, it is extremely important to follow up with phone calls if you do not receive a response.

In seeking corporate underwriting and sponsorship, be forewarned about the following: (a) Do not expect support to continue indefinitely, and beware of becoming too dependent on any one source of funds; (b) do not let your expenses become so high that questions are raised about how much funding is actually available for direct services; and (c) be careful not to make excessive demands from the same company. For example, if you ask for a major underwriting gift, do not then ask for a direct corporate contribution a few months later.

EVALUATING THE RESULTS

Review the event as soon as possible. The longer you delay, the less vivid will be your memories and impressions. Review what happened in an objective, frank manner, but avoid individual accusations. Invite ideas on how problems can be dealt with the next time. Your primary approach is to elicit ideas for improvement and determine if mistakes or miscalculations are correctable. Ask for ideas for new activities. If the organization has previously laid the groundwork by setting objectives and determining action plans, activities, and tasks, evaluating results will be easier and can be done with greater sophistication. The evaluation process should consist of two parts: monitoring tasks and assessing the achievements of objectives.

Through a monitoring process, you can determine whether, and to what extent, tasks were carried out as planned. The following are questions to ask:

- Should the timetable have been altered to permit an earlier start and better sequencing of tasks?
- Were there sufficient funding resources and volunteers to do the job?
- Did the expected expenditures for tasks match the budget perceptions? If not, what are the explanations for the discrepancies?
- Was there a proper number of volunteers assigned to tasks? Can imbalances (e.g., too many tasks for some persons and too few for others) be identified?

These kinds of questions will help you review your ability to implement the activities and tasks that you had planned. If you detect deficiencies, you can determine the remedies you will take next year.

If your event does not achieve its financial objectives, the following questions should be asked:

- Was the financial objective unreasonably high? Perhaps this was a first-time event and you guesstimated incorrectly. Perhaps there were unforeseen and unique circumstances that were unpredictable.
- Were adequate resources available to accomplish the event? Was the number of ticket sellers and backup staff sufficient, and was there enough up-front money?
- Was the timetable appropriate? Would an earlier start-up time ensure better results? Could the tasks be scheduled better?

Although the financial objectives were not achieved, were other equally important, nonfinancial objectives accomplished? This is perhaps the most difficult assessment to make. Frequently, groups that do not achieve their financial objectives decide that benefits such as good public relations, esprit de corps of volunteers, identification of new members, or leadership development compensate for poor financial results. In fact, the achievement of these and other objectives may be sufficient to overcome the limited financial results. Only your organization can make that highly subjective assessment.

NOTES

1. M. Johnston, *The nonprofit guide to the Internet* (2nd ed.) (New York: John Wiley, 1999), pp. 101-107.
2. M. Johnston, pp. 120-124.

Part VI Review

ENHANCING AGENCY SURVIVABILITY

17. FINANCIAL MANAGEMENT

- Use budget preparation to achieve organizational objectives.
- Where feasible, divide the budget into categories (program budgeting) so you can relate income and expenses to specific programs.
- Determine that the greater proportion of expenses relate to programs rather than support services.
- Strive for positive cash flow. Establish reserves or working capital that would help prepare for the future.
- Understand the different kinds of income available to your agency and the restrictions that apply to their use.
- Determine how administrative overhead (indirect costs) can be used. Know what different funders require in relation to administrative overhead.
- Preparing an organizationwide budget entails setting objectives, establishing commonly followed policies and procedures, setting overall income and expense targets, and requiring each unit to draft budgets that are then reviewed by top management before being presented to the organization's governing body.
- Provide opportunities for staff at the lowest levels to have input into the budgeting process.
- Monitor a budget by systematically comparing projected income and expenses to actual financial reports. Pay particular attention to variances that exceed predetermined percentages or dollar amounts. Be prepared to take corrective action as soon as possible to keep the budget in balance.

- Consider a variety of cost-cutting measures (as outlined in Chapter 17), but be aware that some attempts to cut costs will have consequences that need to be addressed.
- Ensure that your programs are cost-effective as you weigh the financial costs against the achievement of objectives.

18. STRATEGIC FUND RAISING

- Fund raising must be an integral part of an agency's strategic plan. The purpose of raising money is to assist the organization in achieving its goals.
- The particular fund-raising approach will depend on the strengths of the organization.
- Different kinds of fund raising can build on and reinforce each other.
- Before beginning a fund-raising campaign, an organization should update its strategic plan, develop a good working relationship between board and staff, be able to demonstrate a track record of accomplishments, and prepare a case statement that articulates a compelling reason for funding.
- The annual campaign provides funding for agency operations, stimulates many people to give, builds the organization's constituency, and uses a gift chart to pinpoint from whom funds can be expected.
- The capital campaign is a special fund drive designed to request major gifts from funders for needed projects.
- In identifying major contributors, consider those who have a relationship with members of the organization, an ability to make donations from discretionary funds, and a commitment to the organization.
- Recruit volunteers to solicit major gifts who have made a substantial contribution and who are (or can be helped to be) comfortable in making a request for a specific amount.
- Continually keep in touch with major contributors, and communicate agency accomplishments to them.
- Encourage contributors to provide significant funding from their personal assets to a planned giving program.
- Tailor planned giving gifts to meet the needs of contributors and their families, depending on their income and tax requirements.
- Establish agency income from beneficial trusts, board-designated funds, and endowment funds.
- Raise corporate contributions by being selective, doing your research, and having a relationship with the company.

- Use the approach of cause-related marketing to raise money for your agency while simultaneously providing public relations for a company's products and services.

19. PREPARING EFFECTIVE PROPOSALS

- Before writing a proposal, conduct a preliminary analysis to determine whether the idea is desirable and feasible, whether the organization is capable of implementing it, whether potential funders exist, and whether your organization will likely have the capacity to continue the program after the conclusion of the grant.
- Qualify your organization to receive funding as a nonprofit, or secure the services of a fiscal agent.
- Identify a compelling need that will be met in a creative and resourceful manner.
- Indicate in the proposal clear and measurable objectives. State how the achievement of these objectives will be evaluated.
- Show that the proposal is in keeping with the funder's priorities.
- Provide a detailed listing of activities either in the narrative or in an appendix.
- The budget should be accompanied with a narrative that explains income and expenses.
- If possible, establish a relationship with the potential funder.
- Address the various funding criteria discussed in Chapter 19 regarding competency, board participation, leveraging funding, impact potential, dedication, fiscal soundness, and demonstrable track record.

20. SEARCHING FOR FUNDS

- In the private sector, community, independent, and corporate foundations are the major sources of funding for most nonprofits.
- For information on government funding, the *Federal Register,* the *Commerce Business Daily,* the *Catalog of Domestic Assistance,* and the Federal Assistance Retrieval System are good sources. Also, check with the Grants and Awards Internet site noted in Chapter 20.
- The Foundation Center and many cooperating libraries provide highly useful directories as well as special guides specifically related to health and human services.
- In conducting the general search process, develop a focus for your search, consider initially a broad list of candidates, and narrow the list to a few that are most likely to fund your project.

- To expedite your search process, use the *FC Search* CD-ROM, which contains information on thousands of grant makers. Learning the specific techniques for narrowing or expanding your search will greatly enhance your ability to find the right funding source.

21. FUND-RAISING EVENTS: STRATEGIES FOR SUCCESS

- Fit the fund-raising event within an overall strategic plan so that the event complements other fund-raising activities. Establish both financial and nonfinancial objectives.
- Think creatively and uncritically about a variety of event possibilities, and then conduct a feasibility analysis to narrow your choices.
- Use a market-oriented approach in selecting your event: Determine to what specific audiences or customers you are trying to appeal. Remember that your cause is important, especially to your supporters, but for most people it is a secondary reason for attending the event.
- Even successful events can lose their appeal over time; be prepared to modify. Put sizzle and zest in your event by giving old ideas a new twist, holding the event in a unique place, or selecting an appealing theme.
- Make clear to your contributors what portion of their donation can be considered a charitable gift and what portion is a nondeductible purchase of goods and services.
- Base pricing decisions on profit expectations, competition, and how customers perceive the value of what they will be receiving.
- Consider whether you should penetrate your existing market, attract new market segments, alter your event, or diversify through both new events and new markets. Consider ways to increase income from an event by establishing different price categories.
- Keep the following principle foremost: People sell to people.
- Be prepared to take corrective actions and allow enough time to exert extraordinary efforts when mistakes or unanticipated situations occur. Prepare a contingency plan in case something goes wrong.
- Evaluate your results to determine what modifications, if any, you would make next time.

REFERENCES

Albert, S. (1988). Eight steps to productive committees. *Nonprofit World, 4,* 24-25.

Alexander Hamilton Institute. (1991). *Conducting successful appraisal interviews.* Maywood, NJ: Author.

Alexander Hamilton Institute. (1991). *A manager's guide to creating a drug- and alcohol-free workplace.* Maywood, NJ: Author.

Alexander Hamilton Institute. (1997). *Lawsuit-free documentation: A manger's guide to fair and legal recordkeeping.* Ramsey, NJ: Author.

Alexander Hamilton Institute. (1997). *Making teams succeed at work.* Ramsey, NJ: Author.

Alexander Hamilton Institute. (1997). *A manager's guide to avoiding termination lawsuits.* Ramsey, NJ: Author.

Alexander Hamilton Institute. (1997). *A manager's guide to productive meetings.* Ramsey, NJ: Author.

Alexander Hamilton Institute. (1997). *What every manager must know to prevent sexual harassment.* Ramsey, NJ: Author.

Alexander Hamilton Institute. (1997). *What every manager should know about the Americans With Disabilities Act.* Ramsey, NJ: Author.

Alexander Hamilton Institute. (1998). *Coaching & counseling: Managers' secrets for improving employee performance.* Ramsey, NJ: Author.

Alexander Hamilton Institute. (1998). *Conducting successful appraisal interviews: The right way to discuss employee performance.* Ramsey, NJ: Author.

Alexander Hamilton Institute. (1998). *A manager's guide to the do's and don'ts of discipline.* Ramsey, NJ: Author.

Alexander Hamilton Institute. (1999). *A manager's guide to motivating without money.* Ramsey, NJ: Author.

Alexander Hamilton Institute. (1999). *Interviewing made easy: The right way to ask hiring questions.* Ramsey, NJ: Author.

Andreasen, A. R. (1996, November/December). Profits for nonprofits: Find a corporate partner. *Harvard Business Review, 74,* 47-59.

Argyris, C. (1994, July/August). Good communication that blocks learning. *Harvard Business Review,* 77-85.

Askenas, R. N., & Schaffer, R. H. (1982). Manager can avoid wasting time. *Harvard Business Review, 3,* 98-104.

Barrett, R. D., & Ware, M. E. (1997). *Planned giving essentials.* Gaithersburg, MD: Aspen.

Barrien, F. K. (1968). *General and social systems.* New Brunswick, NJ: Rutgers University Press.

Barry, B. W. (1986). *Strategic planning workbook for nonprofit organizations.* St. Paul, MN: Amherst H. Wilder Foundation.

Barton, G. M. (1990). Manage words effectively. *Personnel Journal, 1,* 32-33.

Beer, M., Eisenstat, R. A., & Spector, B. (1990). Why change programs don't produce change. *Harvard Business Review, 6,* 158-166.

Beer, M., Spector, B., Lawrence, P. R., Mills, D. Q., & Walton, R. E. (1984). *Managing human assets.* New York: Free Press.

Bennett, J. E. (1991-1992, Winter). Reflections on successful CEOs: The match is everything. *Cleveland Enterprise,* 18-20.

Bennis, W. (1989). *On becoming a leader.* Wilmington, MA: Addison-Wesley.

Bisno, H. (1988). *Managing conflict.* Newbury Park, CA: Sage.

Blanchard, K. J., Carlos, P., & Randolph, A. (1999). *The 3 keys to empowerment.* San Francisco: Berrett-Koehler.

Bliss, E. (1976). *Getting things done.* New York: Bantam.

Borden, K. (1978). *Dear uncle: Please send money—A guide for proposal writers.* Pocatello, ID: Auger Associates.

Bowen, W. (Ed.). (1977, November). Japanese managers tell how their system works. *Fortune,* 127-138.

Boyett, J. H., & Conn, H. P. (1988, Summer). Developing white-collar performance measurement. *National Productivity Review,* 209-218.

Boyett, J. H., & Conn, H. P. (1988). *Maximum performance management.* Macomb, IL: Glenbridge.

Bramnall, M., & Ezell, S. (1981). How burned are you? *Public Welfare, 1,* 23-27.

Brinckerhoff, P. C. (1996). *Financial empowerment.* Dillon, CO: Alpine Guild.

Brody, R. (1974). *Guide for applying for federal funds for human services.* Cleveland, OH: Case Western Reserve University, School of Applied Social Sciences.

Brody, R. (1982). *Problem solving: Concepts and methods for community organizations.* New York: Human Sciences Press.

Brody, R., Goodman, M., & Ferrante, J. (1985). *The legislative process: An action handbook for Ohio Citizens' Group* (3rd ed.). Cleveland, OH: Federation for Community Planning.

Brody, R., & Nair, M. D. (2000). *Macro practice: A generalist approach* (5th ed.). Wheaton, IL: Gregory.

Browman, M., Baanante, J., Dichter, T., Londner, S., & Reiling, P. (1993). Measuring our impact: Determining cost-effectiveness of non-governmental organization development projects. In G. L. Schmaedick (Ed.), *Cost-effectiveness in the nonprofit sector.* Westport, CT: Quorum.

Brown, R. (1979). *The practical manager's guide to excellence in management.* New York: AMACOM.

Bruce, S. D. (1989). *Face to face: Every manager's guide to better appraisal and discipline interviewing.* Madison, CT: Business and Legal Reports.

Bureau of Business Practice. (1989). *Front line supervisor's standard manual.* Waterford, CT: Author.

Bureau of Business Practice. (1990). Building loyalty. *Front Line Supervisor's Bulletin, 146,* 1-3.

Bureau of Business Practice. (1990). The performance appraisal: Yours. *Front Line Supervisor's Bulletin, 151,* 1-3.

Bureau of Business Practice. (1991). Get the best from your employees. *Front Line Supervisor's Bulletin, 157,* 1-2.

Burns, M. E. (1989). *Proposal writer's guide.* Hartford, CT: Development & Technical Assistance Center.

Butler, J. K., Jr. (1995, December). Behaviors, trust, & goal achievement in a win-win negotiating role play. *Group & Organizational Management, 20*(4), 486-501.

Campbell, A., & Alexander, M. (1997, November/December). What's wrong with strategy? *Harvard Business Review, 75,* 42-51.

Campbell, R. B. (1982, May). *The process.* Speech given at Higbee's annual meeting, Cleveland, OH.

Cangemi, J. P., & Claypool, J. C. (1978). Complimentary interviews: A system for rewarding outstanding employees. *Personnel Journal, 2,* 87-90.

Caplow, T. (1976). *How to run any organization.* Hinsdale, IL: Dryden.

Carew, J. (1987). *You'll never get no for an answer.* New York: Simon & Schuster.

Carl, J., & Stokes, G. (1991). Seven keys to an excellent organization: Fostering innovation and respect. *Nonprofit World, 5,* 18-22.

Cassedy, E., & Nussbaum, K. (1983). *9 to 5: The working woman's guide to office survival.* New York: Penguin.

Chandler, A., Jr. (1966). *Strategy and structure.* Garden City, NY: Doubleday.

Cherrington, D. (1987). *Personnel management: The management of human resources* (2nd ed.). Dubuque, IA: William C. Brown.

Cohen, S. (1988). *The effective public manager: Achieving success in government.* San Francisco: Jossey-Bass.

Conger, J. A. (1998, May/June). The necessary art of persuasion. *Harvard Business Review, 76,* 84-95.

Connellan, T. K. (1980). *How to grow people into self-starters.* Ann Arbor, MI: Achievement Institute.

Conner, D. R., & Gold, B. (1993, May). Hospital corporate culture and its impact on strategic change. *Dimensions in Health Care, Peat Marwick,* 3.

Copeland, L. (1988, May). Learning to manage a multicultural work force. *Training,* 1-5.

Coulton, C. (1990). *Developing quality assurance programs: Managerial considerations and strategies.* Unpublished manuscript.

Coulton, C. J., Keller, S., & Boone, C. R. (1985). Predicting social workers' expenditures of time with hospital patients. *Health and Social Work, 1,* 35-39.

Crow, R. T., & Odewahn, C. A. (1987). *Management for the human services.* Englewood Cliffs, NJ: Prentice Hall.

Croxton, T. A. (1999). Liability & risk management. In J. E. Tropman & E. J. Tropman (Eds.), *Nonprofit boards.* Washington, DC: CWLA Press.

Cyert, R. M. (1990). Defining leadership and explicating the process. *Nonprofit Management and Leadership, 1,* 29-37.

Dabel, G. J. (1998). *Saving money in nonprofit organizations.* San Francisco: Jossey-Bass.

Deal, T. E., & Kennedy, A. A. (1982). *Corporate cultures.* Reading, MA: Addison-Wesley.

de Bono, E. (1973). *Lateral thinking.* New York: Harper Colophon.

Decker, L. E., & Decker, V. A. (1993). *Grantseeking: How to find a funder and write a winning proposal.* Charlottesville, VA: Community Collaborators.

Delbecq, A. L., Van de Ven, A., & Gustafson, D. H. (1976). *Group techniques for program planning.* Glenview, IL: Foresman.

Design for peak performance. (1991). *Nonprofit Management Strategies, 4,* 1-4.

Dishy, V. (1989). *Inner fitness.* New York: Doubleday.

Dolan, C., & Brody, R. (1991). *Planned giving.* Cleveland, OH: Federation for Community Planning.

Doyle, M., & Straus, D. (1976). *How to make meetings work.* New York: Berkley.

Dropkin, M., & LaTouche, B. (1998). *The budget-building book for nonprofits.* San Francisco: Jossey-Bass.

Drucker, P. (1976, January/February). What results should you expect? A users' guide to MBO. *Public Administration Review,* 12-39.

Drucker, P. (1985). *The effective executive.* New York: Harper & Row.

Drucker, P. (1989). What business can learn from nonprofits. *Harvard Business Review, 4,* 89-93.

Drucker, P. (1990). *Managing the nonprofit organization.* New York: HarperCollins.

Drucker, P. (1998, October). Management's new paradigms. *Forbes,* 152-176.

Drucker, P. (1999). *Management challenges for the 21st century.* New York: HarperBusiness.

Eadie, D. C. (1997). *Changing by design.* San Francisco: Jossey-Bass.

Eadie, D. C. (1998). Planning and managing strategically. In R. L. Edwards, J. A. Yankey, & M. Altpeter (Eds.), *Skills for effective management of nonprofit organizations* (pp. 453-468). Washington, DC: NASW Press.

Eisenhardt, K. M., Kahwajy, J. L., & Bourgeois, L. J., III. (1997, July/August). How management teams can have a good fight. *Harvard Business Review,* 77-85.

Elkin, R., & Vorvaller, D. J. (1972, May). Evaluating the effectiveness of social services. *Management Controls,* 104-111.

Ellis, R. J. (1992, Spring). Centel Corporation: Using human resources programs to support cultural change. *Wyatt Communicator,* 4-9.

Employment involvement: What it's about. (1989). *Commitment Plus, 9,* 1-4.

Espy, S. N. (1988). Planning for success: Strategic planning in nonprofits. *Nonprofit World, 5,* 23-24.

Espy, S. N. (1988). Where are you, and where do you think you're going? *Nonprofit World, 6,* 19-20.

Espy, S. N. (1989). Putting your plan into action. *Nonprofit World, 1,* 27-28.

Etzioni, A. (1968). *The active society: A theory of society and political processes.* New York: Free Press.

Evans, D. S., & Oh, M. Y. (1996, June). A tailored approach to diversity planning. *Harvard Business Review, 41*(6), 127-134.

Feit, M. D., & Li, P. (1998). *Financial management in human services.* New York: Haworth.

Flannery, R. B. (1989, February). The stress resistant person. *HMS Health Letter,* 6.

Ford, S. (1983). *The ABC's of managing with employee teams.* Campbell, CA: Sondra Ford & Associates.

Foundation Center. (1994). Prospect worksheet. In *The Foundation Center's user-friendly guide* (Rev. ed.). New York: Author.

Foundation Center. (1997). *FC search manual.* New York: Author.

Foundation Center. (1997, Fall). *Fundraising & nonprofit development resources catalog.* New York: Author.

Frantzreb, A. C. (1991). Seeking the big gift. In H. A. Rosso (Ed.), *Achieving excellence in fund raising.* San Francisco: Jossey-Bass.

Friedman, S. D., Christensen, P., & DeGroot, J. (1998, November/December). Work & life: The end of the zero sum game. *Harvard Business Review, 76,* 119-129.

Garner, L. H., Jr. (1989). *Leadership in human services: How to articulate a vision to achieve results.* San Francisco: Jossey-Bass.

Gaylin, D. H. (1990, Summer). Break down barriers by communicating your company's strategy. *The Human Resources Professional,* 20-21.

Geber, B. (1990, July). Managing diversity. *Training,* 23-30.

Geever, J. C., & McNeill, P. (Eds.). (1997). *The Foundation Center's guide to proposal writing* (Rev. ed.). Washington, DC: Foundation Center.

Geever, J. C., & McNeill, P. (1997). *Guide to proposal writing.* New York: Foundation Center.

Gibelman, M., Gelman, S. R., & Pollack, D. (1997). The credibility of nonprofit boards: A view from the 1990s and beyond. *Administration in Social Work, 21*(2), 21-40.

Goering, S. A. (1990, August 21). Steps can protect company from ex-employee lawsuits. *The Plain Dealer,* p. F2.

Goleman, D. (1998, November/December). What makes a leader? *Harvard Business Review,* 93-102.

Gooch, J. (1987). *Writing winning proposals.* Washington, DC: Council for the Advancement of Education.

Gordon, T. (1977). *Leader effectiveness training.* New York: Bantam.

Grace, K. (1991). Leadership & team building. In H. A. Rosso (Ed.), *Achieving excellence in fund raising.* San Francisco: Jossey-Bass.

Gubkin, J. (1985). *Persuasive communication.* Cleveland, OH: Jack Gubkin & Associates.

Gummer, B. (1995). Go team go! The growing importance of teamwork in organizational life. *Administration in Social Work, 19*(4), 93-94.

Haas, R. N. (1994). *The power to persuade.* New York: Houghton Mifflin.

Hall, M. S. (1988). *Getting funded: A complete guide to proposal writing.* Portland, OR: Portland State University.

Haller, M. C. (1989, July/August). The new balancing act: Variable but equitable pay. *Human Resources Professional,* 31.

Hammer, M. (1990). Reengineering work: Don't automate, obliterate. *Harvard Business Review, 4,* 104-112.

Hammond, J. S., Keeney, R. L., & Raiffa, H. (1998, September/October). The hidden troups in decision making. *Harvard Business Review,* 47-58.

Havassy, H. M. (1990). Effective second-story bureaucrats: Mastering the paradox of diversity. *Social Work, 2,* 103-109.

Heifetz, R. A., & Laurie, D. L. (1997, January/February). The work of leadership. *Harvard Business Review,* 124-134.

Hemphill, B. (1999, June). Organize your increasingly complex work life. *Bottom Line Personal,* 9-10.

Henderson, R. I. (1989). *Compensation management: Rewarding performance.* Englewood Cliffs, NJ: Prentice Hall.

Herman, R. D., & Heimovics, R. D. (1990, Winter). The effective nonprofit executive: Leader of the board. *Nonprofit Management & Leadership, 1*(2), 167-180.

Herman, R. E. (1990). *Keeping good people: Strategies for solving the dilemma of the decade.* Cleveland, OH: Oakhill.

Herzberg, F., Mausner, B., & Synderman, B. (1959). *The motivation to work.* New York: John Wiley.

Herzlinger, R. (1994, July/August). Effective oversight: A guide for nonprofit directors. *Harvard Business Review,* 52-60.

Hildebrand, K. (1996, August). Use leadership training to increase diversity. *Harvard Business Review, 41*(8), 53-60.

Hogan, R., Raskin, R., & Fazzini, D. (1990). How charisma cloaks incompetence. *Personnel Journal, 5,* 73-76.

Hollingsworth, A. T. (1989). Creativity in nonprofit organizations: Preparing for the future. *Nonprofit World, 3,* 21-22.

Hout, T. M. (1999, March/April). Are managers obsolete? *Harvard Business Review, 77*(2), 161-168.

Howard, R. (1990). Values make the company: An interview with Robert Hass. *Harvard Business Review, 5,* 133-143.

Improving customer satisfaction. (1988). *Commitment Plus, 1,* 1.

Ingram, R. T. (1995). *Ten basic responsibilities of nonprofit boards* [Governance series booklet]. Washington, DC: National Center for Nonprofit Boards.

Jacquette, L. F., & Jacquette, B. I. (1977, August). *What makes a good proposal.* Washington, DC: Foundation Center.

Janis, I. L. (1971, November). Groupthink. *Psychology Today,* 43-46, 74-76.

Johnston, M. (1999). *The nonprofit guide to the Internet* (2nd ed.). New York: John Wiley.

Joinson, C. (1999, May). Getting the best results from teams requires work on the teams themselves. *Human Resource Management, 44*(5), 30-36.

Jordan, P. C. (1986). Effects of an extrinsic reward on intrinsic motivation: A field experiment. *Academy of Management Journal, 29*(2), 405-412.

Jorgenson, J. D., Scheier, I. H., & Fautsko, T. F. (1981). *Solving problems in meetings.* Chicago: Nelson-Hall.

Joseph, B. (1986). Writer's block: Is there a cure? *Nonprofit World, 3,* 27-28.

Joseph, W. R. (1998). Trustee liability: A practical view. *Weston Hurd Fallon Paisley & Howley L.L.P.,* 1-4.

Joyaux, S. P. (1997). *Strategic fund development.* Gaithersberg, MD: Aspen.

Kadushin, A. (1985). *Supervision in social work* (2nd ed.). New York: Columbia University Press.

Kahn, S. C., Berish Brown, B., Lanzarone, M., & Zepke, B. E. (1994). *Legal guide to human resources* (3rd ed.). Boston: Warren, Gorham, & Lamont.

Kaplan, M. L. (1990). Labor of love: The joys and stresses of nonprofit management. *Nonprofit World, 3,* 26-28.

Katzenbach, J. R., & Smith, D. K. (1993). *The wisdom of teams.* New York: HarperCollins.

Kepner, C. H., & Tregoe, B. B. (1974). *The rational manager.* New York: Berkley.

Kettner, P. M., Moroney, R. M., & Martin, L. L. (1990). *Designing and managing programs.* Newbury Park, CA: Sage.

Kihlstedt, A., & Schwartz, C. P. (1997). *Capital campaigns: Strategies that work.* Gaithersberg, MD: Aspen.

Kirby, T. (1989). *The can-do manager.* New York: AMACOM.

Kiritz, N. J. (1980). *Program planning & proposal writing.* Los Angeles: Grantsmanship Center.

Kirkpatrick, S. A., & Locke, E. A. (1995). Do traits matter? In J. T. Wren (Ed.), *The leader's companion.* New York: Free Press.

Kotter, J. (1990). What leaders really do. *Harvard Business Review, 3,* 103-111.

Kotter, J. P. (1999, March/April). What effective general managers really do. *Harvard Business Review, 77*(2), 145-159.

Lakein, A. (1973). *How to get control of your time and your life.* New York: New American Library.

Lauffer, A. (1982). *Assessment tools for practitioners, managers, and trainers.* Beverly Hills, CA: Sage.

Lauffer, A. (1984). *Grantsmanship and fund raising.* Beverly Hills, CA: Sage.

Lauffer, A. (1985). *Careers, colleagues, and conflicts: Understanding gender, race, and ethnicity in the workplace.* Beverly Hills, CA: Sage.

Lauffer, A. (1987). *Working in social work.* Newbury Park, CA: Sage.

Lauffer, A. (1997). *Grants, etc.* (2nd ed.). Thousand Oaks, CA: Sage.

Lawler, E. E. (1986). *High involvement management.* San Francisco: Jossey-Bass.

Lawler, E. E., III. (1989). Pay for performance: A strategic analysis. In L. Gomez-Mejia (Ed.), *Compensation and benefits.* Washington, DC: Bureau of National Affairs.

Leadership at work. (1980). *The Royal Bank Letter, 7,* 3.

Lindahl, W. E. (1992). *Strategic planning for fund raising.* San Francisco: Jossey-Bass.

Lloyd, K. L. (1991). *Sexual harassment: How to keep your company out of court.* New York: Panel.

Maclean, B. P. (1990). Value added pay beats traditional merit programs. *Personnel Journal, 9,* 46-52.

Mai, C. F. (1987). *Secrets of major gift fund raising.* Washington, DC: Taft Group.

Marash, S. (1989). Blueprint for quality improvement. *Personnel Journal, 3,* 120-123.

Martin, D. C. (1989). Performance appraisal, 2: Improving the rater's effectiveness. In M. Sashkin (Ed.), *Performance appraisal.* New York: American Management Association. (Reprinted from *Personnel,* August 1986)

Marx, J. D. (1988, January). Corporate strategic philanthropy: Implications for social work. *Social Work,* 35-41.

Marx, J. D. (1996). Strategic philanthropy: An opportunity for partnership between corporations and health/human service agencies. *Administration in Social Work, 20*(3), 57-73.

Maslow, A. H. (1954). *Motivation and personality.* New York: Harper & Row.

Mattessich, P. W., & Monsey, B. R. (1993). *Collaboration: What makes it work.* Saint Paul, MN: Wilder Research.

McAfee, R. B., & Deadrick, D. L. (1996, February). Teach employees to just say "no!" *Human Resource Management, 41*(2), 86-89.

McClelland, D. C., & Burnham, D. (1976). Power is the great motivator. *Harvard Business Review, 2,* 100-111.

McConkey, D. D. (1975). *MBO for nonprofit organizations.* New York: AMACOM.

McCormack, M. (1997, November 25). Giving instructions that make things happen. *The Plain Dealer,* p. 3C.

McCormack, M. (1998). *On communicating.* Los Angeles: Dove.

McCormack, M. (1999, March 9). A fine line separates dumping & delegating tasks. *The Plain Dealer,* p. 5C.

McCormack, M. (1999, August 3). Reliance on e-mail may erode the quality of communication. *The Plain Dealer,* p. 8C.

McCormack, M. H. (1996). *Mark H. McCormack on managing.* West Hollywood, CA: Dove.

McCreight, R. E. (1983). A five role system for motivating improved performance. *Personnel Journal, 1,* 22-26.

McFarland, L. J., Senn, L. E., & Childress, J. R. (1995). Refining leadership in the next century. In J. T. Wren (Ed.), *The leader's companion.* New York: Free Press.

McGregor, D. (1960). *The human side of enterprise.* New York: McGraw-Hill.

Mengerink, W. C. (1992). *Hand in hand.* Rockville, MD: Fund Raising Institute.

Middleman, R. R., & Rhodes, G. B. (1985). *Competent supervision: Making imaginative judgments.* Englewood Cliffs, NJ: Prentice Hall.

Mihal, W. L. (1983, October). More research is needed; Goals may motivate better. *Personnel Administrator,* 63-68.

Milkovich, G. T., & Boudreau, J. W. (1988). *Personnel/human resource management* (5th ed.). Plano, TX: Business Publications.

Mills, C., & Ivery, C. (1991). A strategy for workload management in child protective practice. *Child Welfare, 1,* 35-43.

Mintzberg, H. (1990). The manager's job: Folklore and fact. *Harvard Business Review, 2,* 163-176.

Moon, F. (1990, November). The annual operating plan: Converting long-term strategies to achievable tasks. *Management Issues, KPMG Peat Marwick,* 1-4.

Moon, F. (1990, October). Building a strategic plan: The second step toward an action blueprint for the future. *Management Issues, KPMG Peat Marwick,* 1-3.

Moon, F. (1990, August). Decade of transition: The strategic plan as action blueprint for the 1990s. *Management Issues, KPMG Peat Marwick,* 1-2.

Moon, F. (1990, September). Step one of strategic planning: Discover your organization, inventory your resources, and identify issues. *Management Issues, KPMG Peat Marwick,* 1-3.

Moore, C. M. (1987). *Group techniques for idea building.* Newbury Park, CA: Sage.

Morth, M., & Collins, S. (Eds.). (1996). *The Foundation Center's user friendly guide: A grantseeker's guide to resources.* New York: Foundation Center.

Moss, L. (1981). *Management stress.* Reading, MA: Addison-Wesley.

Murdock, R. G., & Ross, J. E. (1975). *Information systems for modern management.* Englewood Cliffs, NJ: Prentice Hall.

National Assembly of National Voluntary Health and Social Welfare Organizations. (1985). *A study in excellence: Management in the nonprofit human services.* Washington, DC: Author.

National Institute of Business Management. (1991). *Fire at will: Terminating your employees legally.* New York: Author.

National Leadership Coalition on AIDS. (1991). *Small business and AIDS: How AIDS can affect your business.* Washington DC: Author.

Nauffts, M. F. (Ed.). (1994). *Foundation fundamentals: A guide for grantseekers* (5th ed.). New York: Foundation Center.

Nelson, W. C. (1991). Incentive based management for nonprofit organizations. *Nonprofit Management and Leadership, 1,* 59-69.

Newman, J. M. (1989). Compensation programs for special employee groups. In L. Gomez-Mejia (Ed.), *Compensation and benefits.* Washington, DC: Bureau of National Affairs.

9 to 5. (1990). *Sexual harassment* [Brochure]. Cleveland, OH: Author.

Nord, W., & McAdams, J. L. (1989, May/June). Performance-based reward systems: Which will work best for you? *Human Resources Professional,* 27-32.

Parmadale Children's Village. (1991). *Value statement.* Parma, OH: Author.

Peck, M. S. (1978). *The road less traveled.* New York: Touchstone/Simon & Schuster.

Pecora, P. J., & Austin, M. J. (1987). *Managing human services personnel.* Newbury Park, CA: Sage.

Peters, T. J., & Waterman, R. H. (1982). *In search of excellence: Lessons from America's best run companies.* New York: Harper & Row.

Petrock, F. (1991). Corporate culture and productivity. *Nonprofit Management Strategies, 7,* 13-14.

Pileggi, A., & Hickey, D. T. (1991). Incentive pay plans. *Nonprofit Management Strategies, 6,* 1-3.

Poulin, J. E. (1995). Job satisfaction of social work supervisors and administrators. *Administration in Social Work, 19*(4), 35-49.

PricewaterhouseCoopers. (1999, July/August). Building high-performing strategic alliances. *Growing Your Business,* 3.

Pryor, F. (1985, March). Manage your meetings effectively. *The Nonprofit Executive,* 7.

Public Children Services Association of Ohio. (1988). *PCSAO caseload study.* Columbus, OH: Author.

Quinn, J. B. (1978, Fall). Strategic change: Logical incrementalism. *Sloan Management Review,* 3-16.

Raia, A. P. (1974). *Managing by objectives.* Glenview, IL: Foresman.

Renauer, A. M. (1990, April). A trained facilitator can be instrumental in successful strategic planning. *Management Issues, KPMG Peat Maurwick,* 2-3.

Reynolds, H., & Tramel, M. E. (1979). *Executive time management.* Englewood Cliffs, NJ: Prentice Hall.

Rollins, T. (1989). Pay for performance: Is it worth the trouble? In *Performance and rewards: Linking pay to performance* [HR magazine series]. Alexandria, VA: Society for Human Resource Management.

Rossi, H., & Freeman, H. E. (1989). *Evaluation: A systematic approach.* Newbury Park, CA: Sage.

Rosso, H. A. (1991). *Achieving excellence in fund raising.* San Francisco: Jossey-Bass.

Rosso, H. A. (1996). *Rosso on fund raising.* San Francisco: Jossey-Bass.

Rothman, J., Erlich, J. L., & Teresa, J. G. (1976). *Promoting innovation and change in organizations and communities.* New York: Macmillan.

Sametz, L., & Hamparian, D. (1990). *Innovating programs in Cuyahoga County Juvenile Court: Intensive probation supervision and probation classification.* Cleveland, OH: Federation for Community Planning.

Sandroff, R. (1992, June). Sexual harassment: The inside story. *Working Woman,* 47-51.

Sanzotta, D. (1977). *Motivational theories and applications for managers.* New York: AMACOM.

Sathe, V. (1983, Autumn). Implications of corporate culture: A manager's guide to action. *Organizational Dynamics,* 5-23.

Schaef, A. W., & Fassel, D. (1990). *The addictive organization.* San Francisco: Harper & Row.

Schaefer, M. (1987). *Implementing change in service programs.* Newbury Park, CA: Sage.

Schaffer, R. H. (1981, August). Productivity improvement strategy: Make success the building block. *Management Review,* 46-52.

Schaffer, R. H. (1989). *The breakthrough strategy.* Cambridge, MA: Ballinger.

Schaffer, R. H. (1989, September). Quality now! *Journal for Quality and Participation,* 22-27.

Schaffer, R. H. (1991). Demand better results and get them. *Harvard Business Review, 2,* 145-149.

Schaffer, R. H., & Michaelson, K. E. (1989). The incremental strategy for consulting success. *Journal of Management Consulting, 2,* 1-5.

Schein, E. H. (1970). *Organizational psychology.* New York: Prentice Hall.

Schein, E. H. (1986). *Organizational culture and leadership.* San Francisco: Jossey-Bass.

Schein, E. H. (1987). Coming to a new awareness of organizational culture. In L. E. Boone & D. D. Bowen (Eds.), *The great writings in management and organizational behavior.* New York: Random House.

Schmaedick, G. L. (Ed.). (1933). *Cost-effectiveness in the nonprofit sector.* Westport, CT: Quorum.

Schuler, R. S. (1987). *Personnel and human resource management* (3rd ed.). St. Paul, MN: West.

Schultz, W. N. (1984). What makes a good nonprofit manager? *Nonprofit World,* 3-32.

Schwartz, A. E. (1989). When good ideas are needed fast. *Nonprofit World, 6,* 22-23.

Seers, A., Petty, M. M., & Cashman, J. F. (1995, March). Team-member exchange under team & traditional management. *Group & Organizational Management, 20,* 18-38.

Senge, P. M. (1990). *The fifth discipline.* New York: Doubleday/Currency.

Senge, P., Kliener, A., Roberts, C., Ross, R. B., & Smith, B. J. (1994). *The fifth discipline fieldbook.* New York: Currency.

Shannon, J. P. (Ed.). (1991). *The corporate contributions handbook.* San Francisco: Jossey-Bass.

Sheldon, K. S. (1991). Corporations as a gift market. In H. A. Rosso (Ed.), *Achieving excellence in fund raising.* San Francisco: Jossey-Bass.

Shepherd, J. S. (1990). Manage the 5 C's of stress. *Personal Journal, 4,* 64-69.

Skidmore, R. (1995). The nature of dynamic teamship. In *Social work administration.* Boston: Allyn & Bacon.

Slater, P., & Bennis, W. (1990). Democracy is inevitable. *Harvard Business Review, 5,* 167-176.

Smith, H. (1999, March). Hyrum Smith's simple steps to much better time management. *Bottom Line Personal,* 11-12.

Solomon, C. M. (1990). Careers under glass. *Personnel Journal, 4,* 96-105.

Stanton, E. S. (1983). A critical reevaluation of motivation, management, and productivity. *Personnel Journal, 3,* 5-6.

Stayer, R. (1990). How I learned to let my workers lead. *Harvard Business Review, 6,* 66-83.

Steinberg, R. (1990). Profits and incentive compensation in nonprofit firms. *Nonprofit Management and Leadership, 2,* 137-149.

Steiner, R. (1988). *Total proposal building.* Albany, NY: Trestletree.

Swain, R. L. (1989, September/October). 66 ways to avoid trouble when terminating the long-termer. *The Human Resources Professional,* 28-31.

Swanson, A. (1986, July/August). Who's in charge here? *Nonprofit World, 4*(4), 14-18.

Tambor, M. (1995). Employment-at-will or just cause: The right choice. *Administration in Social Work, 19*(3), 45-57.

Tannenbaum, R., & Schmidt, W. (1973). How to choose a leadership pattern. *Harvard Business Review, 3,* 162-180.

Tarkenton Productivity Group. (1977). *Motivational theories and applications for managers.* New York: AMACON.

Taylor, B. E., Chait, R. P., & Holland, T. P. (1996, September/October). The new work of the nonprofit board. *Harvard Business Review, 74,* 36-42.

Taylor, W. C. (1999, June). The leader of the future. *Fast Company,* 132-138.

Teal, T. (1996, November/December). The human side of management. *Harvard Business Review, 74,* 35-44.

Tempel, E. R. (1991). Assessing organization strengths & vulnerabilities. In H. A. Rosso (Ed.), *Achieving excellence in fund raising.* San Francisco: Jossey-Bass.

Terpstra, D. E. (1979). Theories of motivation: Borrowing the best. *Personnel Journal, 6,* 15-18.

Thomas, D. A., & Ely, R. J. (1996, September/October). Making differences matter: A new paradigm for managing diversity. *Harvard Business Review, 74,* 79-90.

Thomas, R. R. (1990). From affirmative action to affirming diversity. *Harvard Business Review, 2,* 107-117.

Thomas, R. R. (1991). *Beyond race and gender: Unleashing the power of your total workforce by managing diversity.* New York: AMACOM.

Tjosvold, D. (1991). *The conflict-positive organization.* Reading, MA: Addison-Wesley.

Total quality management. (1990). *Commitment Plus, 4,* 1.

Townsend, R. (1984). *Further up the organization.* New York: Knopf.

Tropman, J. E. (1980). *Effective meetings: Improving group decision-making.* Beverly Hills, CA: Sage.

Tzu, L. (1944). *The way of life according to Lao Tzu* (W. Bynner, Trans.). New York: Capricorn.

Uris, A. (1986). *101 of the greatest ideas in management.* New York: John Wiley.

von Oech, R. (1983). *A whack on the side of the head.* New York: Warner.

von Oech, R. (1986). *A kick in the seat of the pants.* New York: Harper & Row.

Vroom, V. H. (1973). *Choosing a leadership style: Applying the Vroom & Yetton Model.* New York: AMACOM.

Wadia, M. (1980). Participative management: Three common problems. *Personnel Journal, 11,* 27-28.

Wageman, R., & Mannix, E. A. (1998). Uses and misuses of power in task performing teams. In R. M. Kramer & M. A. Neale (Eds.), *Power & influence in organizations.* Thousand Oaks, CA: Sage.

Waldroop, J., & Butler, T. (1996, November/December). The executive as coach. *Harvard Business Review,* 111-117.

Wallack, L., Dorfman, L., Jernigan, D., & Themba, M. (1993). *Media advocacy and public health.* Newbury Park, CA: Sage.

Weber, W., Laws, B., & Weber, S. (1987). Real world planning: Fresh approaches to old problems. *Nonprofit World, 2,* 25-27.

What is culture? (1985). *Commitment Plus, 3,* 1.

Wiebush, R. G., & Hamparian, D. (1986). *Probation classification: Design and development of the Cuyahoga County Juvenile Court Model.* Cleveland OH: Federation for Community Planning.

Williams, K. A. (1997). *Donor focused strategies for annual giving.* Gaithersburg, MD: Aspen.

Winer, M., & Roy, K. (1997). *Collaboration handbook.* Saint Paul, MN: Amherst H. Wilder Foundation.

Wolf, T. (1984). *The nonprofit organization: An operating manual.* Englewood Cliffs, NJ: Prentice Hall.

Work in America Institute. (1983). *Productivity through work innovations.* New York: Pergamon.

Zaremba, A. (1989). Communication: The upward network. *Personnel Journal, 3,* 34-39.

INDEX

ABOUT THE AUTHOR

Ralph Brody, PhD, currently teaches courses on administration and social policy at Cleveland State University and service delivery models at Case Western Reserve University. He was previously executive director of the Federation for Community Planning, which is an organization that provides research, planning, and advocacy on health and human services. His other managerial positions include director of a job training program, director of five multiservice centers, and associate director of a college urban institute. He has provided consultation or training to more than 30 community agencies; the Ohio Bureau of Employment Services; the Ford Foundation; the United Way Services; the Ohio Department of Human Services; the YMCA of Kenya; the Ministry of Civil Affairs, People's Republic of China; the School of Social Welfare in Barcelona, Spain; and to agency directors in Kerala, India. He conducts professional workshops on supervision, time management, leadership development, strategic planning, and grant writing. He has written articles and manuals or given presentations on welfare and work, human service systems, supervision of the disadvantaged, organizing a community drug strategy, proposal writing, and planned giving. He is author of books on case management, the state legislative process, fund-raising events, tax levy campaigns, and community problem solving, service learning, and macro practice.